1999

ETHICS

THE ENEMY IN THE WORKPLACE

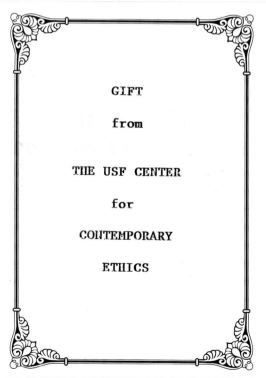

GIFT

from

THE USF CENTER

for

CONTEMPORARY

ETHICS

W9-AEB-974

An International Thomson Publishing Company

Acquisitions Editor: Randy G. Haubner
Production Editor: Christine O. Sofranko
Production House: Bookmark
Cover Design: Craig LaGesse Ramsdell
Internal Design: Russell Schneck Design
Marketing Manager: Stephen E. Momper

GW62AA
Copyright © 1995
by South-Western College Publishing
Cincinnati, Ohio

1 2 3 4 5 6 7 MA 0 9 8 7 6 5 4

Printed in the United States of America

Library of Congress Cataloging-in-Publication Data

Barton, Laurence, 1956–
    Ethics: the enemy in the workplace / Laurence Barton.
      p. cm.
    Includes bibliographical references and index.
    ISBN 0-538-83873-6
    1. Business ethics.   I. Title.
  HF6387.B36   1994   94-31478
  174'.4--dc20   CIP

I(T)P

International Thomson Publishing Company

South-Western College Publishing is an ITP Company.
The ITP trademark is used under license.

For Judy, my endless love

About the Author

Laurence Barton is Associate Professor of Management and Organization at the Pennsylvania State University at Great Valley. He is in demand as a speaker on organizational ethics and crisis management for corporate and academic audiences around the world.

He previously taught crisis management and management communication at Harvard Business School, the University of Nevada, Tufts University, and Boston College.

A native of Arlington, Massachusetts, Dr. Barton received an A.B., magna cum laude, from Boston College in speech and communication, the M.A.L.D. from The Fletcher School of Law and Diplomacy at Tufts University, and a Ph.D. in international public policy from Boston University.

The author of nearly 40 articles in leading academic journals such as *Long Range Planning* and *Industrial Management*, Dr. Barton serves on the editorial boards of *The Journal of Management Communication, Journal of Business and Economic Perspectives, Management Decision*, and *The Journal of Contingencies and Crisis Management*. His first book, *Crisis in Organizations* (also from South-Western), has been adopted by major universities and Fortune 500 companies.

As a leading consultant to corporations worldwide on crisis management and strategic issues, Dr. Barton's clients have included British Petroleum, Motorola, Ford Motor Company, and Arthur D. Little, as well as government agencies such as the Japanese Ministry of Justice, the U.S. Internal Revenue Service, and the U.S. Department of Energy. He has lectured throughout Japan, Korea, Hong Kong, France, and elsewhere on many of the issues in this book.

Dr. Barton has been named Ascendant Scholar of the Year by the Western Academy of Management and was selected as a 1994 Fulbright Senior Scholar, researching crisis management and ethical conduct by managers in Japan. He has been interviewed by *The Wall Street Journal, Los Angeles Times*, and the four major television networks.

Dr. Barton and his wife Judy live in Exton, Pennsylvania. They are the parents of two sons, Matthew and Mark.

Preface

When I first "floated" several titles of this book among colleagues and friends, the one option that seemed to intrigue them most was the one on the cover.

"Okay, so just who *is* the enemy in the workplace?" many would inevitably ask. And my response usually played out something like this:

The enemy in the workplace is truth. You see, for many managers and employees, any acknowledgment that they fudged on their résumés, accepted or offered bribes, used insider information to land contracts, harassed fellow employees, or read someone else's E-mail inappropriately—well, that kind of truth just plain hurts.

So we tend to conceal or manipulate truth. Many times, the process of deception is rather trivial (a receptionist informs an incoming caller that you are not in the office when you are), but deception can also reach enormous heights (medical institutions denying for 40 years that unknowing patients were injected with plutonium). Where does acceptable behavior begin and end? Who can effectively police ethics in the workplace? And, as the courts and the news media become more aggressive in investigating inappropriate acts, many are forced to wonder, why work at all?

Today, all 37 states and the federal government have whistle-blower statutes that financially reward employees for exposing coworker fraud. Most large employers enforce stringent codes of ethics that govern how we manage and even how we communicate in the workplace, and most people know at least one individual who has been accused of one kind of wrongdoing or another in their organization.

If the enemy is the truth, then the enemy is also deceit. After researching nearly 640 cases of ethical abuse for this book, I am convinced that most people truly *want* to do the right thing in their daily professional endeavors. Yet the desire to be ethically "clean" is often muddied by sentiments that seem perfectly natural: wanting to keep one's job, wanting to please one's boss, and wanting to secure a healthy salary increase during the next performance review. Thus, employees sometimes acquiesce to inappropriate requests of supervisors or coworkers. Worse yet, many on the fringe of ethical misconduct just look the other way. Some would argue that in such cases, the bystander who does nothing about unethical acts should assume as much of the blame as the perpetrator.

What all of this boils down to is the individual perception of truth and deceit. And although countless philosophers, theologians and scholars have theorized about the validity of their own perceptions through the ages, consensus continues to elude us. Some explain our current ethical dilemma in terms of a battle. These individuals, such as former Secretary of Education William Bennett, believe that we are in the midst of an unprecedented struggle between those who value traditional Western values of moral truths (as articulated by the Bible, for instance) and secular humanists, who reject traditional definitions of good and evil and who believe that everyone should basically design their own moral code.

Before writing this book, I thought that the notion of secular humanism was hollow, a mere cop-out for those who simply dislike organized religion and its political influence. It also seemed to me that some of the more conservative traditionalists, who use religion as an explanation for every social evil (such as AIDS is a punishment from God—a frightening statement offered by the Reverend Billy Graham in 1993), had equally stumbled.

To my way of thinking, organized religion provides an enormously important role in any society such as ours: churches and synagogues inspire the depressed, feed and clothe the destitute, and articulate messages about ethical behavior in a seemingly unethical world. In fact, organized religion remains the most successful, permanent social force in which ethics is taught, studied, and emulated. Yes, colleges offer courses on the subject, but even academics openly debate when, where, and even *if* ethics should be taught. At many institutions, ethics programs can be found in departments of philosophy, theology, business, communication, public administration, fine arts, and even engineering. As a result of any agreement on the best "home" for teaching this subject, students, I believe, are shortchanged. They miss an invaluable opportunity to examine the interdisciplinary connectors of ethics from their personal to professional lives. In that sense, this book is intended to serve as a thread, analyzing a number of those links for reader reflection.

The challenge for each of us is to ask questions about the role of truth and deceit in our society and how we relate to ethical propositions. The agenda is expansive, considering that:

■ Worldwide, losses from various scams involving credit cards totaled $1.18 billion in 1992; in the United States alone, thieves stole goods worth $720 million of this total via credit card fraud. (Chan, 1D)

■ Since 1960, there has been an estimated 600 percent increase in violent crime in the United States. (Bulger, A1)

■ Bank employees steal 11 times more money than bank robbers each year. (Barton, 6)

■ Distrust about business ethics is at a low ebb: a 1971 Harris poll showed that 27 percent of respondents had "a great deal of confidence in the people running major companies," yet 20 years later a repeat study by Harris indicated that the number had sunk to 15 percent. (Piper, 2)

■ According to KPMG Peat Marwick, more than three-quarters of large companies experience fraud by accountants and others each year, with an *average* loss per incident of about $200,000. At more than 23 percent of companies surveyed, however, the numbers become staggering: the cost of fraud exceeds $1 million per year. (Calabro, 12)

■ Individual cases abound. To wit: In August 1993, the acting secretary of the army, John Shannon, resigned his post after admitting that he stole two items of women's clothing from the Fort Myer military base store in Arlington, Virginia. His antics were videotaped by store surveillance cameras, which led to his arrest three days later.

And consider for a moment this cornucopia of ethics cases that has filled our headlines in recent years:

Race Discrimination In 1993, a black warehouseman for Lucky Supermarkets was awarded $314,000 after a jury concluded that he had been denied a promotion because of his race. Lucky's has been anything but lucky: one year earlier a federal judge concluded that the California-based chain practiced widespread sex discrimination in its Northern California stores over a 10-year period. A U.S. district judge has approved a formula that will provide $90 million in back pay to 10,000 former and current female employees.

Fraud President Clinton's secretary of commerce, Ron Brown, faced intense Congressional questioning amid allegations that in return for a $700,000 payment made to an off-shore bank that he would agree to provide insider clout to Vietnamese business interests eager to resume trade with the United States. After adamantly saying he couldn't remember ever meeting Vietnamese businessman Nguyen Van Hao, Brown changed his tune.

One national political columnist argued, "It was only after the *Miami Herald* revealed there were three meetings, including one while he was in the cabinet, that the commerce secretary admitted anything." (Hunt, A17)

Conspiracy National Medical Enterprises (NME), Inc., has been called "Public Enemy No. 1 in Washington's crackdown on health care fraud" by *Newsweek,* and allegations of "false medical claims, conspiracy, kickbacks and fraud against Medicare, Medicaid and the Pentagon's insurance plan" have already led to some settlements by the company. Well-paid psychiatrists reportedly kept perfectly healthy patients in NME facilities until their health care coverage had expired. One young man featured in *Newsweek* was supposed to spend two weeks in a Sonoma, California, NME facility due to depression regarding his parent's divorce. A year later, when his insurance expired, he was released. NME had taken in $127,300 in hospital fees and $41,400 in doctor bills. (Yang, 70)

Sexual Harassment Female navy officers attending the 1992 Tailhook convention at the Las Vegas Hilton found themselves fondled, sexually assaulted, and repeatedly harassed while senior Pentagon officials stood nearby. The result: 30 top commanders had received reprimands by October, 1993, including the navy's top ranking officer, Frank B. Kelso, for their failure to stop or report harassment.

Finance Twelve former top executives of the now defunct Bank of Credit and Commerce International (BCCI) were convicted of fraud and mismanagement on June 14, 1994; several of the guilty received jail sentences of up to 12 years. Although ordered to pay $9.13 million in restitution to governments and investors who had been swindled, it is unlikely any of the 257,000 depositors and creditors will receive but a few cents on the dollar. (Machado, 37)

Cheating Ten months after the Tailhook incident, the civilian panel overseeing the U.S. Naval Academy at Annapolis agreed it would investigate a cheating scandal on an electrical engineering exam involving as many as 125 midshipmen. Charges of cheating are especially injurious to an institution that has prided itself on the honor concept which dictates that naval officers do not "lie, cheat or steal." ("Annapolis' Civilian Panel." *Boston Globe*, 14). Of course, cheating is pervasive at all levels of society and the military only reflects a larger syndrome of dishonesty: 80 percent of nearly 2,000 U.S. high school students surveyed in late 1993 reported that they had cheated on an exam or copied someone else's homework. (Associated Press, 5A)

Deceptive Advertising The Federal Trade Commission recently sued Jenny Craig, Inc., for false and deceptive claims following a two-year investigation into weight-loss programs that promised customers the chance "to lose all the weight you want." According to *Advertising Age*, "The company is also accused of falsely representing that the advertised prices were the only costs associated with the programs and that the company failed to adequately disclose additional mandatory expenses." (Levine, 44)

Bribery In New York, Orange & Rockland Utilities, Inc., was rocked by a major scandal involving bribery and illegal campaign contributions made by the utility. In October 1993 Linda Winikow, former vice president of communications, pleaded guilty to grand larceny, receiving bribes, and illegal contributions. She and three former employees had been named in a civil racketeering suit. One week later company chairman, James F. Smith, was ousted by the company's board of directors amid the controversy. ("Orange & Rocklands," *Wall Street Journal*, B10)

Largesse In an era of corporate restructuring and downsizing in which hundreds of thousands of Americans lost their jobs in the early 1990s, some were far more fortunate. To wit: the retiring chairman of Blue Cross-Blue

Shield of Massachusetts, John Larkin Thompson, received a grand send-off with a $3.8 million retirement package in 1993. *The Boston Globe* noted that Blue Cross experienced a $57.7 million *loss* in 1988, and that this same company "was well known in the business community for blowing $100 million on an inferior computer system." The paper calculated that Thompson's retirement package would pay for 760,000 child immunizations at a cost of $5 each or health care coverage for one year in 11,275 households. (Jackson, 15) Just as Thompson retired, a new book by former Harvard president Derek Bok called *The Cost of Talent* proposed steep, progressive income taxes to deter outrageous income. A case in point: Toys 'R Us president Charles Lazarus earns about $3,400 an hour in an era when the minimum wage in the United States is $4.50. (Solomon, 58)

Résumé Fraud A major research survey conducted in 1993 determined that as much as 75 percent of all résumés contain some false information. (Wieder and Addas, 23)

Money Laundering The chief fund-raiser for Paul Tsongas, who sought the Democratic presidential nomination in 1992, admitted a year later that he had engaged in mail fraud, money laundering, and campaign finance violations. Nicholas A. Rizzo was sentenced to four years in prison and ordered to pay restitution after the U.S. attorney proved that Rizzo had stolen and diverted for personal use at least $1 million that had been raised for Tsongas. Rizzo was a former fund-raiser for President Jimmy Carter and Vice-President Walter Mondale. (Associated Press, 4A)

Undue Influence In a state where teachers pay upwards of $600 in union dues annually, the California Teachers Association (CTA) was accused of "strong arming" the Governor and other political leaders in late 1993 when it sought to defeat a ballot proposition on tuition vouchers for private schooling. *Forbes* accused the organization of "legal callousness" in the manner it handles excess fees and noted that "during the last school budget battle, Governor Pete Wilson's office was deluged with letters from grade-schoolers—some worded identically and apparently copied from the blackboard" regarding budget issues. (*Forbes*, 90)

Predatory Practices In October, an Arkansas court found a unit of Wal-Mart, the nation's largest retailer, guilty of illegally practicing predatory (below cost) pricing of items—a strategy commonly used to undermine competition. Judge David Reynolds concluded that Wal-Mart engaged in "injuring competitors and destroying competition," a charge that Wal-Mart faces in some 22 other states where lawsuits are pending or planned. (Ortega, A3)

Deceptive Tactics Widespread, documented cases of deceptive sales practices by Metropolitan Life Insurance salespeople, the nation's second largest insurer, led to a 1994 settlement in which MetLife paid a $95 million fee to settle claims. The company received so much negative publicity that "an exodus of agents" to other companies has taken place. (Roland, C1)

Theft Abroad Communism may be dead, but the living flee with cash. When managers in a large number of Russian, state-owned businesses realized by early 1991 that communism was doomed and that their workplaces would soon become privatized, they fled the country with cash, gold, and equipment with an estimated value of between $6 billion to $8 billion. (Davis, 17)

Professional Standards Two-thirds of psychiatrists responding to a national survey report that they have treated patients who had been sexually involved with other therapists, leading researchers to conclude that a substantial abuse of professional standards in psychiatry is occurring. (Micelli and Near, 93)

Clearly, the diversity of these cases underscores the complexity of this topic. While this book is hardly a panacea, the discussion in the following pages is intended to generate thought-provoking reflection and discussion. My intention is not to pass judgments on any of the individuals mentioned in this book or be sanctimonious. Yet this material should be the genesis for spirited debates on appropriate behavior in the workplace.

Organization

Ethics: The Enemy in the Workplace is divided into nine chapters.

Chapter 1 introduces the subject of business ethics by discussing the role of various stakeholders in the workplace. The discussion includes the phases of ethical behavior that are typically experienced by most professionals, followed by a foundation on ethics philosophy as rooted in scholarly and religious principles on the subject.

Chapter 2 discusses the notion that in the past few decades, employers have assumed more and more legal and moral responsibility for the acts of their employees. The relationship of the employer and employee is fundamental in any meaningful discussion on business ethics, and this chapter will prompt you to consider some basic questions of appropriate versus inappropriate behavior.

Chapter 3 poses a provocative question: "Do Corporations Institutionalize Dishonesty?" Some managers believe that illegal or immoral acts are always committed by people, not corporations per se. This chapter examines the validity of that argument and explores the sources of information at work, followed by a discussion on why employees sometimes steal from their employers.

Chapter 4 continues the journey launched in chapter 3 and focuses on the topic, "When Employees Are the Enemy." This chapter offers ample evidence that employers must be more vigilant in protecting themselves from the unethical acts of others. This analysis raises a broad spectrum of situations in which

alleged ethical misconduct, ranging from computer hacking to sexual harassment, triggered widespread discussion.

Chapter 5 explores financial impropriety, since cases in this arena have received substantial attention in the courts and news media in recent years. Specifically, the practice of auditing is analyzed, primarily because the traditional relationship between the client and the external auditor has been dramatically re-examined and changed in organizations nationwide as a result of the prominent case highlighted in the chapter.

Chapter 6 analyzes one of the most significant, emerging areas of the managerial sciences today—whistle-blowing. What is the effect on society when any individual can make a public allegation about a coworker (either a legitimate or an unfounded one) and receive instantaneous publicity as a result? How can society protect the rights of the unfairly accused while ensuring a fair hearing for the accuser? This chapter offers insight to the moral and practical applications of whistle-blowing in many work environments. It concludes with a powerful profile of one whistle-blower who was fired, only to be vindicated by the president of the company.

Chapter 7 asks the reader to consider the implications of how we perceive "right" and "wrong" work behavior in an international context where morals, values, and practices widely vary from culture to culture. This chapter includes a model for consideration, followed by an intensive roundtable discussion by several prominent business executives on the subject.

Chapter 8 raises significant questions about the complex area of new technologies and ethics. Questions about the systematic theft of intellectual property such as software are raised; the reader will see that the practice of copying software varies greatly from continent to continent. The chapter ends with a superb investigative report compiled by the editors of *Macworld* on this subject.

Chapter 9 examines another industry where charges of inappropriate behavior have spawned national debate: health care. Should pharmaceutical companies promote their products to physicians who will later prescribe company products via all-expenses-paid vacations and other marketing tools? This chapter explores ways to balance the effective business needs and morality.

Throughout the text, case discussions offer insights on ethics in our society. Professor Linda Loehr of Northeastern University in Boston questions public response to a state official arrested for drunk driving. Professor Frank Marra of Ithaca College in New York examines the candor of Syracuse University officials in the aftermath of basketball star Len Bias' death. Professor Lamar Reinsch of Georgetown University explores how university professors are caught in an ethical quagmire over teaching methodology.

Francis Taylor of the University of Nevada at Las Vegas questions the ethics of tactics used by animal rights activists to promote their message. Lynda Roth of Colorado, one of two million American women who now face complicated treatments as a result of silicone breast implants, tells her moving story about medical ethics and alleged fraud by implant manufacturers. Finally, Professor Chuck Williams of Texas Christian University details the embarrassing investigation by ABC and other news media outlets of the ethical standards in place at one of the largest supermarket chains in the United States, Food Lion, in the aftermath of several embarrassing charges of managerial misconduct.

Unique Features of This Book

This book has several features that you should find helpful.

- In Appendix A, you will find the "Best of the Best" ethical policies from corporate America ranging from Teledyne to AT&T. This collection of ethical policies is intended to provide the reader with unprecedented insight into how managers and employees at these organizations—which collectively employ millions of Americans—are expected to act on a daily basis. I am especially grateful to these employers for their enthusiastic support of this book.

- Throughout the book you will find "Ethics Briefs." These mini-cases and profiles examine practical dimensions to ethics and can be used both in training programs and for discussion purposes in the classroom.

- Several stimulating articles and reprints can be found in the book. These articles are intended to personalize ethics so that you can hear from workers who have confronted such ethical dilemmas as invasion of privacy and sexual harassment.

Acknowledgments

This work follows on the heels of my first book, *Crisis in Organizations: Managing and Communicating in the Heat of Chaos* (South-Western, 1993). After that work was published, a number of executives, scholars, and students wrote to me, offering additional stories and insights about cases that had become, or nearly became, ethical disasters at their organizations. The depth of that communication prompted me to develop a different kind of ethics book, one that reflected on the traditional, theoretical foundation of this field, but that also captured the contemporary dimensions of actual cases of ethics abuse in the workplace.

To accomplish this goal, a number of wonderful people contributed their time and effort. I am especially grateful to Jeanne Busemeyer, who signed this project, and to Randy Haubner of South-Western College Publishing, who skillfully directed the work through to fruition.

Five talented researchers assisted with the process of research, and I am most appreciative for their spirited efforts: Chad Jahn, Mary Smith, Michael Hayek, James West, and Nikki Shields. Kris Davidson, my assistant, carefully kept this project on track.

A faculty development leave from the University of Nevada at Las Vegas was instrumental in starting this project. To Dr. Robert Maxson, Provost John Unrue, and Professor Emeritus Ed Goodin: I am grateful for your friendship and support of this project.

For their enthusiasm and encouragement as I completed the work, my thanks are also extended to Lawrence C. Cote, campus executive officer, Professor Roger Vergin, and Dr. Lynda Phillips-Madson, all of Pennsylvania State University. I am delighted to be a part of the Penn State team.

Finally, I am blessed to have the continued support of my wife Judy and our two sons, Matthew and Mark.

Laurence Barton
Pennsylvania State University
P. O. Box 818
Frazer, PA 19355

Note: The author welcomes any suggestions on cases for future editions of this work. They may be sent to the address above or you may call or fax the author at (610) 594-7639.

References

Associated Press. "Student Cheating Prevalent." *Las Vegas Review-Journal*, October 20, 1993, A5.

Associated Press. "Tsongas Fund-Raiser Sentenced." *Las Vegas Review-Journal*, October 14, 1993, 4A.

Barton, Laurence. "Financial Improprieties by Bank Employees." Presentation to 1993 New Avenues in Risk and Crisis Management Conference, University of Nevada.

"Annapolis' Civilian Panel to Review Cheating Scandal." *The Boston Globe*, September 28, 1993.

Bulger, William M. "The New Civil War." *The Boston Globe*, October 3, 1993.

Calabro, Lori. "The Incidents and Costs Mount." *CFO Magazine*, November 1993, 12.

Chan, Sau. "Credit Card Fraud Takes Many Forms." Associated Press story in the *Las Vegas Review-Journal*, October 11, 1993, 1D.

Davis, L. J. "International Gumshoe." *The New York Times Magazine*, August 30, 1992.

Forbes. "Apple a Day." October 19, 1993, 90.

Hunt, Albert R. "Ron Brown, His Own Worst Enemy." *The Wall Street Journal*, October 14, 1993.

Jackson, Derrick Z. "A Healthy Package." *The Boston Globe*, September 22, 1993.

Levine, Daniel S. "FTC Sues Jenny Craig over Ad Claims." *Advertising Age*, October 4, 1993.

Machado, Lawrence. "12 Ex-BCCI Executives Convicted." *The Philadephia Inquirer*, June 15, 1992, 37.

Miceli, Marcia, and Near, Janet. *Blowing the Whistle.* New York: Lexington Books, 1992.

"Orange & Rockland Ousts Its Top Officer Amid Controversy." *The Wall Street Journal*, October 11, 1993.

Ortega, Bob. "Wal-Mart Loses a Case on Pricing." *The Wall Street Journal*, October 13, 1993.

Piper, Thomas R. "Can Ethics Be Taught?" Boston: Harvard Business School, 1993.

Roland, Neil. "An Exodus of Agents from MetLIfe." *The Philadelphia Inquirer*, June 17, 1994, C1.

Solomon, Jolie. "How Much Should We Be Paid?" *Newsweek*, November 8, 1993.

Weider, Howard L., and Addas, William D. "Justices Likely to Address Resume Fraud." *The National Law Journal*, October 25, 1993.

Yang, Catherine. "Put the Head in the Bed and Keep It There." *Business Week*, October 18, 1993.

Photo Credits:

CONTENTS

An Introduction to Decision Making and Business Ethics

In a recent survey by Korn/Ferry and Columbia University Graduate School of Business, over 1500 executives from twenty countries rated personal ethics as the number one characteristic needed by the ideal CEO in the year 2000.

Laura L. Nash
Good Intentions Aside
(1990), p. 7

If it is true that business ethics "comprises moral principles and standards that guide behavior in the world of business," (Fraedrich, 5), we must recognize that these principles and standards vary from person to person, company to company, religion to religion, and society to society. There is no single common standard of business ethics in an increasingly interdependent world, presenting an incredible challenge for any manager seeking to succeed in the twenty-first century.

Ethics in business is somewhat like politics; it is rare that you will ever encounter another individual whose opinions on a whole series of policies or events exactly parallel your own. Indeed, what makes business ethics so interesting is that even within most organizations no common set of principles exists on what constitutes appropriate behavior toward coworkers, customers, and even the competition.

Decision making has both an objective and subjective element. Dr. Albert Schweitzer, the highly regarded theologian, humanitarian, and Nobel Peace Prize recipient, argued that when making decisions we ideally consider both our own good, which we understand well through subjectivity, and the needs of others, which can be often attained only through searching for and achieving objectivity. But the ideal is difficult to obtain and few people have the capability or time to ponder the ethical ramifications of their actions. This does not justify serious mistakes that compromise the well being of an entire organization, however.

Assume that you are a senior manager of a company that is about to hire an assistant vice-president of sales. The objective element of your subconscious tells you that your company needs a bright, energetic individual with a relevant college degree and maybe six years of industry experience. Then your subjective side may kick in: Wouldn't it be nice if the person selected just happened to be good-looking, hailed from the same region of the country as yourself, and was willing to "bend the rules" on giving gifts to clients whenever you asked? The ultimate team player—that's the kind of person you *really* want!

The mixed signals in this scenario are unfortunately quite common, and this simple example underscores reality in many organizations. Your preferences and prejudices may not always correspond to the best interests of your employer. Let's look further at the objective and subjective side of managerial decision making before we examine how managers often lose sight of their primary goal—success—by failing to balance objectivity and subjectivity.

OBJECTIVITY

In order to be objective, one must be open-minded and willing to set aside one's own biases in order to achieve a common goal benefiting the entire organization. Objectivity in journalism is often seen as an opinion-free story; a reporter is expected to convey pertinent facts and balance the content of the story with at least two distinct sides, if they exist. The reader can expect that the personal opinion of the reporter and the publication will be reserved for the editorial page where it belongs.

Similarly, objectivity in finance takes place when an auditor informs a client in an updated, detailed financial statement of the assets and liabilities accumulated during the past fiscal quarter. Ideally, this report is objective and straightforward; the authors' recommendations, insights, and warnings about the potential shortcomings of certain projects or departments is reserved for either an accompanying report, an appendix, or a personal meeting.

In our society, we expect managers to be objective in the execution of their daily duties. For example, we expect decisions will be based on a reasonably objective set of standards such as the strength and durability of a proposed product. However, to accomplish successful decision making, managers must rely on the opinions and reactions of a variety of actors—subordinates, colleagues, and other parties—in order to achieve their goals. Each day we try to gauge the quality of the information these and other individuals share with us. Among the questions we may ask ourselves include the following:

- Is the information at my disposal complete?

- Is all pertinent information available for my review, or only selected information that my colleagues think I want to hear?

- Do I have a clear sense of the timeliness of this issue?

- Have the consequences of acting, or *not* acting, on this issue been fully assessed?

- What are the costs, both human and financial, inherent in this decision?

- Are my actions likely to help or hurt this organization? Will my actions help or hurt the broader public, such as our customers and stockholders?

In reality, it is considerably easier to make some objective decisions than others. Deciding to close a business because of a snow storm that jeopardizes the well-being of employees requires little ethical insight: Both common sense and thoughtfulness are inherent in the decision. Closing that same office because you do not care to pay your hourly workers when you know you will have no customers (and thus no income) does present a series of ethical choices. What are your real intentions? What are you telling your employees versus the real truth?

Appearances and Reality

Let's look at another case. The manager at a radio station repeatedly gives exposure to a local rock band. The issue seems to have no ethical relevance; the manager must simply execute a decision (based on market demographics) of what is likely to attract listeners and, subsequently, increase ratings and sales revenue. In another simple example, the manager of a retail store decides to keep the business open later on Christmas Eve, believing that customers are likely to purchase in larger quantities just hours before the Christmas holiday.

How does ethics apply in these two cases? When the managers at the radio station and retail store execute their decisions based on some of the criteria raised in the questions listed previously, an objective assessment will contribute to success. Objectivity and subjectivity collide, however, when management decisions are *unduly* influenced by personal choices.

When the radio station manager selects a particular band because he is dating the group's manager, chances are that he is more interested in pleasing his friend than in satisfying listener tastes. Yes, providing a local group with an audience can be justified on the grounds that it exposes listeners to a new sound, but what is more likely happening is that the manager's motivations are suspect. Similarly, the manager who asks salespeople to work several hours overtime on Christmas Eve can justify that decision on the grounds that it underscores an organizational commitment to customer service. The question of ethics emerges, however, when that same manager later refuses to pay overtime, arguing that sales during those extra hours simply did not amount to his or her expectations and the capital necessary to support the overtime never materialized.

Stakeholders and Pressure Points: The Case of Orange Computer

Before we discuss how to weigh the impact of ethics in business, let's take a quick look at a hypothetical organization to ascertain the difficult environments that most corporations face.

Most organizations have at least three levels of stakeholders. These groups can influence the success of the corporation. Orange Computer is a mid-sized but rapidly growing manufacturer and distributor of personal computers. The levels of stakeholders at Orange Computer are illustrated in Exhibit 1-1. At the core of the stakeholder model, Orange Computer must be concerned with *internal*

EXHIBIT 1-1   Stakeholders of Orange Computer

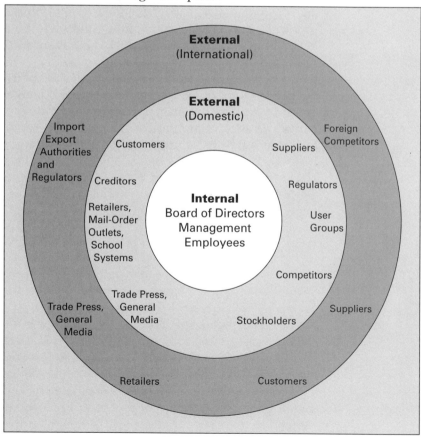

audiences such as its board of directors, who establish or approve goals and objectives; management, which executes those policies; and employees, whose productivity ensures that the company meets its goals.

The next group of stakeholders are those *external* groups that exist in Orange Computer's domestic environment. This group includes company stockholders, who seek maximum return on their investment and who will exert pressure at the company's annual meetings if their expectations are not met; company customers, who expect that the company will remain true to promises of exceptional customer service; the computer trade press, which will report positive product launches (and any rumors of mismanagement or botched products); and numerous other groups.

The outer ring of the stakeholder model is composed of groups *external* to Orange Computer *internationally*. This group includes foreign customers who expect qualified local technicians to service their problems, and foreign competitors, who will be eager to match or better Orange Computer's product, reputation, and pricing appeal.

A number of ethical "pressure points" can emerge in any company operating in such a complex, multitiered environment. Exhibit 1-2 presents six quick examples of ethical dilemmas that could be raised by different managers working at all three levels of the company. If Orange Computer has an articulated set of policies addressing these issues, its solution may be expedient and not embarrassing. However, in the absence of training and ethical standards, any serious error in judgment could lead to devastating results.

In the sections that follow, you will read how society has assessed the important balance of right and wrong in how we conduct business affairs.

SUBJECTIVITY

Many decisions are shaded by personal preference. Workplace psychologists assert that most managers tend to make decisions based on what they know, or *think* they know, about their boss, colleagues, customers, and even industry regulators.

This type of cognitive bias is enormously important in understanding the methodology of this book because understanding how we tend to go astray of objectivity will explain many of the serious

EXHIBIT 1-2   The Hypothetical Ethical Pressure Points
for Stakeholders of Orange Computer

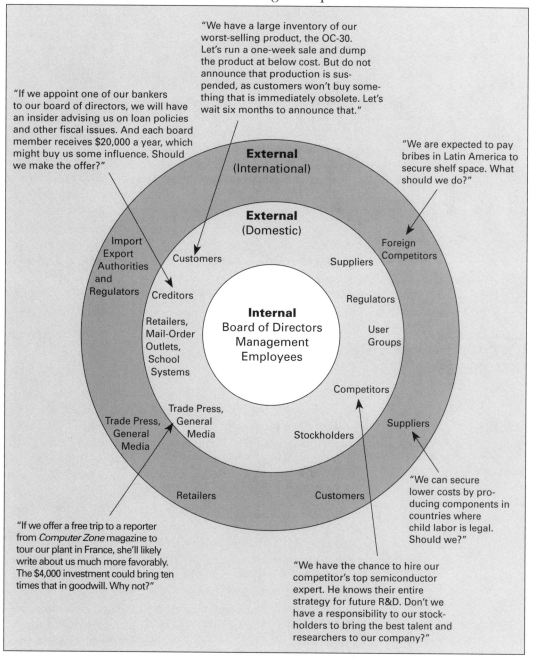

"We have a large inventory of our worst-selling product, the OC-30. Let's run a one-week sale and dump the product at below cost. But do not announce that production is suspended, as customers won't buy something that is immediately obsolete. Let's wait six months to announce that."

"If we appoint one of our bankers to our board of directors, we will have an insider advising us on loan policies and other fiscal issues. And each board member receives $20,000 a year, which might buy us some influence. Should we make the offer?"

"We are expected to pay bribes in Latin America to secure shelf space. What should we do?"

External
(International)

External
(Domestic)

Import Export Authorities and Regulators

Customers

Creditors

Retailers, Mail-Order Outlets, School Systems

Suppliers

Foreign Competitors

Regulators

Internal
Board of Directors
Management
Employees

User Groups

Competitors

Trade Press, General Media

Trade Press, General Media

Suppliers

Stockholders

Retailers

Customers

"We can secure lower costs by producing components in countries where child labor is legal. Should we?"

"If we offer a free trip to a reporter from *Computer Zone* magazine to tour our plant in France, she'll likely write about us much more favorably. The $4,000 investment could bring ten times that in goodwill. Why not?"

"We have the chance to hire our competitor's top semiconductor expert. He knows their entire strategy for future R&D. Don't we have a responsibility to our stockholders to bring the best talent and researchers to our company?"

errors in judgment enumerated in these pages. Major studies conducted in the past five years (Dunnette and Hough, 870) confirm the notion of cognitive bias, from which several observations can be made:

- Managers prefer to interact on a daily basis only with those colleagues who provide them with positive feedback.

- When dominant individuals in the workplace receive negative feedback from colleagues, they actually increase their dominant behavior in order to "channel the reaction of others" toward the desired behavior they get.

- In general, "people attend selectively to data that confirm their expectations and make judgments that preserve their existing beliefs."

An undeniable relationship exists between cognitive bias and the notion that managers often employ a variety of influence tactics to achieve their goals. The definitions of various influence tactics are presented in Exhibit 1-3.

HOW WE BALANCE OBJECTIVITY AND SUBJECTIVITY

Thus far it has been suggested that managers use objectivity and subjectivity in weighing the ethical components of decisions. But they also integrate *assumptions* into the process. For example, Richard Nixon's 30-year knowledge of Washington, cradled in the House of Representatives, the Senate, the vice-presidency and ultimately the presidency, was based on assumptions. He *assumed* that Congress would never subpoena his personal recordings of White House conversations with close advisors as the Watergate investigation intensified. That miscalculation, coupled with the mammoth, incorrect assumption that the Supreme Court would protect his presidential privilege to keep secret those taped conversations, further contributed to the disintegration of his presidency.

In a more recent case, senior managers of the Bank of Commerce and Credit International (BCCI) designed an incredibly elaborate organizational scheme to deceive creditors and bank regulators in a dozen countries, assuming that as long as the bank did not default on

EXHIBIT 1-3   Definitions of Influence Tactics

Legitimating tactics	The person seeks to establish the legitimacy of a request by claiming the authority or right to make it, or by verifying that it is consistent with organizational policies, rules, practices, or traditions.
Rational persuasion	The person uses logical arguments and factual evidence to persuade you that a proposal or request is practical and likely to result in the attainment of task objectives.
Inspirational appeals	The person makes a request or proposal that arouses enthusiasm by appealing to your values, ideas, and aspirations, or by increasing your confidence that you can do it.
Consultation	The person seeks your participation in planning a strategy, activity, or change for which your support is desired or is willing to modify a proposal to deal with your concerns and suggestions.
Exchange	The person offers an exchange of favors, indicates willingness to reciprocate at a later time, or promises you a share of the benefits if you help accomplish a task.
Pressure	The person uses demands, threats, frequent checking, or persistent reminders to influence you to do what he or she wants.
Ingratiation	The person seeks to get you in a good mood or to think favorably of him or her asking you to do something.
Personal appeals	The person appeals to your feelings of loyalty and friendship toward him or her when asking you to do something.
Coalition tactics	The person seeks the aid of others to persuade you to do something or uses the support of others as a reason for you to agree.
Upwards appeals	The person gets assistance from higher management to influence you to do something.

Challenge: Consider several of your friends or coworkers and the manner in which they influence you when you are jointly trying to accomplish something. Which influence tactics do they exhibit? Which ones would they select to characterize you?

any loan, it would escape scrutiny and prosecution. In the end, subjectivity overpowered objectivity, and bank depositors lost billions of dollars in one of the largest tales of business deception in history.

We cross the line of objectivity into subjectivity every day, and rarely if ever do our .actions have consequences similar to those of Richard Nixon or the management team at BCCI. But societal expectations about the ethical behavior of managers are increasing in the aftermath the many scandals and miscalculations we will read about in this book and elsewhere. We can learn from these mistakes, both small and large, and apply the faulty judgments used by managers in politics, business and the arts to our advantage. If, as Plato asserted, knowledge is power, then the learning curve ahead of us about objectivity and subjectivity is overwhelmingly powerful.

Subjectivity is an intensely personal, unverifiable set of beliefs that leads to subsequent decisions. It is this state of mind that often contributes to failure in managerial decision making. For instance, most people have different perceptions of what constitutes the full meaning of the topics listed below:

■ Success	■ Discrimination	■ Humor
■ Loyalty	■ Honor	■ Decency
■ Faith	■ Integrity	■ Pragmatism
■ Honesty	■ Ingenuity	■ Achievement

Because we differ on our personal approach to these themes, we also often differ on the rules that govern them in the workplace. Among the issues that managers should ask about their level of subjectivity in making workplace decisions are these:

■ Am I making decisions based on past successes that may or may not be *relevant* to this set of circumstances? Put another way, am I relying on a comfortability factor, rather than facts and objective research?

■ Will my decision provide *unfair advantage* to friends or family members?

■ Have my *personal opinions* and prejudices about people—influenced by their gender, age, race, national origin or other factors, somehow clouded what I say or do?

■ Have my *fears* about others, including their possible rejection of me or my decision, unduly influenced whether I should act?

ETHICS BRIEF

Even the Supreme Court?

The nine justices of the U.S. Supreme Court are sworn to uphold the Constitution of the United States, but that doesn't necessarily mean that they don't bend the rules when it is to their benefit.

According to an investigation of the Associated Press, justices have used the court's security force "to provide taxi service for visiting relatives, work overtime at wedding receptions and push supermarket carts." When the daughter of Justice Anthony M. Kennedy was married in December 1993 at the Supreme Court Building—free of charge, of course—a dozen Supreme Court police officers were on hand to assist with a variety of duties.

But no one beats retired Chief Justice Warren E. Burger. Although he may have been a brilliant constitutional historian, that did not prevent him from forgetting that he was a steward of public trust. The Associated Press recalled that during his tenure as a member of the nation's highest tribunal, court police officers routinely drove his wife "to the supermarket and pushed her cart through the store's aisles."

Source: "High Court Use of Guards Questioned", *The Boston Globe*, December 23, 1993, p. 26.

In making decisions about right and wrong behavior in the workplace, we must recognize that an amalgam of forces contribute to our perception of business ethics. As Exhibit 1-4 shows, there are four general phases that influence the set of principles we eventually integrate into our work habits.

THE PHASES OF ETHICAL BEHAVIOR

The Formative Phase

During our childhood and teenage years, our ethical behavior is based largely on observation and education. In this *formative phase*, the morals and values that are shared by our parents and family members, the influence of religious teachings, and what we learn about reward and punishment by observing others at home and in school all build a foundation for learning about ethics. It can be argued that one of the principal reasons for the success of books such as *All I Really Wanted to Know I Learned in Kindergarten* and *The Book of Virtues* is that they remind us, with simplicity and grace, of ethical

EXHIBIT 1-4   Forces That Influence the Ethics of Managers

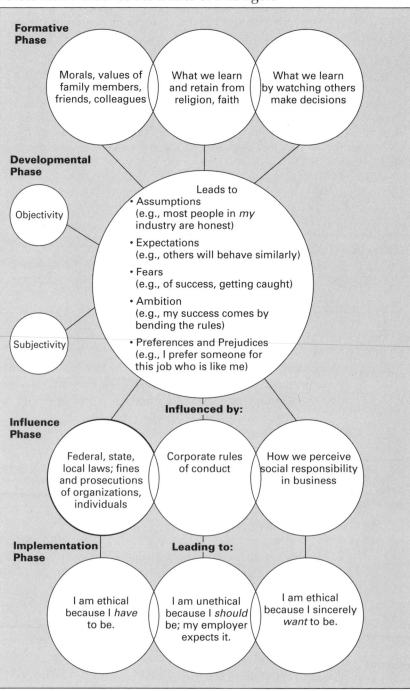

and moral messages we learned—and somehow lost contact with—during our formative phase.

The Developmental Phase

The time early in our careers when we are first forced to test the limits of acceptable and unacceptable behavior often parallels the onset of the *developmental phase*. We may make assumptions about ourselves and others, create expectations for what we personally believe will constitute success, and think about issues such as fear, ambition, preferences, and prejudices. It is often during this period that we are first forced to deal with that important balance of objectivity and subjectivity, where reality and what we want reality to look like become clouded.

The Influence Phase

The *influence phase* often occurs concurrently with the developmental phase. As managers we are often told that we must conform to a series of organizational norms, rules, and regulations, including those addressing harassment, disabilities, sleeping on the job, paying bribes, and political contributions.

Some of these influences are profound in that they are shared by society as a whole (for instance, federal, state, and local laws forbid any illegal activity such as theft of company property). Other influences are less profound because no societal force (such as police) is in place to enforce them (for example, the problem of sleeping on the job). Instead, we rely on corporate codes of conduct and the vigilance of management to articulate what activities will and will not be tolerated by our employer. On the broader scale, the influence phase generally entails a whole series of issues related to social responsibility, including the concept that it is ethical for our employer to be philanthropic to local charities, to interact with other companies in a chamber of commerce, and to meet societal expectations on issues such as affirmative action.

The Implementation Phase

The *implementation phase* theoretically starts as a child at the moment we make our first conscious decision to engage in a right or wrong choice. For our purpose, however, this phase is initiated when a manager has been empowered by the employer to make decisions affecting capital, products, or organizational policies. It is here that our judgments are based on the variety of messages from the first three phases, as well as intuitive reactions to situations.

As managers, we may not feel that we are "implementing" ethics on an everyday basis, but in reality, that is precisely what happens whenever a manager ignores a call from a complaining customer, cheats an employer on a travel reimbursement request, or places his or her name on an impressive business proposal that was actually written by a junior colleague.

What is fascinating about the sociological and psychological studies conducted over the years about managers is the general conclusion that individuals rarely practice one consistent set of ethics standards. Indeed, we tend to shape our perceptions of right and wrong based on the personalities and *perceived power* of the persons involved in the decision and on the desired outcome and the degree of importance we attach to the issue. In some cases we make decisions because we *have to* (the law is explicit), we *should* (I'm afraid of getting caught) or we *sincerely want to* (it seems like the right thing to do given what is expected of me).

HOW EGO AND PERCEPTIONS INFLUENCE OUR DECISIONS

Professor of management Linda Trevino of Penn State University (*Academy of Management Review*, 603) has designed an excellent model of ethical decision making called interactionist. She argues that a manager's perception of an ethical situation is influenced by his or her cognitive moral development. She believes that three principal factors contribute to how managers resolve ethical issues:

- Perceived ego strength (your personal convictions)
- Field dependence (how much you tend to rely on mentors or company standards in following directions)
- Locus of control (your perception of how much independence you have in making a decision)

The interventionist approach concludes that a manager with high ego strength, moderate field dependence, and a high locus of control may try to defend a bad decision even when the manager knows in his or her heart that the decision is wrong. In that example, subjectivity can cripple effectiveness. When we are "blind" to the impact of our decisions on others—especially poor decisions—many people may suffer as a result.

STAKEHOLDERS AND SUBJECTIVITY AT TAMBRANDS, INC.

Let's look at an actual example where the role of stakeholders and the interventionist approach at a major corporation were publicly questioned.

In 1993, *The Wall Street Journal* investigated the ouster of Martin F. Emmett, chairman and chief executive officer of Tambrands, Inc., a large New York City-based company that sells personal hygiene products (August 23, 1993, 1). On the surface, it appeared that Emmett was ousted because the market share of the company's Tampax tampons and other products was decreasing, and Tambrands' Board of Directors sought new direction for the beleaguered company. In reality, however, the *Journal* suggested that objectivity and subjectivity had collided in a hemorrhage of mistrust and bad judgment. The newspaper reported that Emmett enjoyed a close relationship with the two owners of Personnel Corporation of America (PCA), a Norwalk, Connecticut, consulting firm that actually "had a role in Mr. Emmett's landing his job." The two consultants reportedly received both an annual retainer *and* a yearly personal contract estimated at $250,000, more than many senior executives working full time at Tambrands. Emmett's relationship with PCA and its two owners then escalated over the next four years:

> He steered contracts worth an estimated $2 million annually to PCA on a variety of projects including compensation, pension administration and out placement. . . . At a time when Tambrands was cutting its work force by a third, the consultants' studies, surveys and recommendations were instrumental in persuading the Tambrands board to vote itself a pay increase and to award Mr. Emmett stock options and benefits more appropriate for a company twice Tambrands' size. . . . When a chief executive hires an outside compensation consultant who in turn advises the board on the CEO's remuneration, "it is, or can be, an incestuous relationship" says Judith Fisher, publisher of the newsletter, *Executive Compensation Reports.*

In this case, the *Journal* was openly questioning the degree of objectivity and subjectivity practiced by a CEO. The paper concurrently questioned the quality of ethical judgment exercised by, and the oversight role of, Tambrands' outside board of directors.

Tambrands' board of directors is composed of 13 current and former executives of such respected companies as Time Magazine Group and Sara Lee. If both the CEO and the board of an organization have a fiduciary responsibility to protect stockholder interest by minimizing conflicts of interest, something was seriously wrong at Tambrands. Both the market share and stock price of Tambrands had fallen by the time the board intervened and Emmett was let go. To underscore the unusually close relationship between Emmett and PCA, the *Journal* reported that when Emmett was finally ousted by Tambrands' board, his new office and secretary would be found not in a downtown office park, but (not surprisingly) at PCA's headquarters.

Subjectivity is driven by self-interest. We develop an accumulated sense of what actions will benefit us, our department, our compensation, and, as Professor Trevino points out, our ego. Subjectivity can certainly have a *positive* influence on our work when our choices increase sales, enhance productivity, and contribute to high organizational reputation and public goodwill. But few companies and few managers always make the right call. Therein lies the dilemma of working between the two extremes of objectivity and subjectivity.

For the moment, let's assume that the Trevino model is valid and the Emmett case is a good example of a situation where egos, field dependence, and locus of control—the interventionist theory—contributed to a matrix of decision making that went astray. It could be argued that some of Tambrands' managers lost sight of the *raison d'être* for their position of authority and the best interests of the organization. As we will see in later cases, this is a common failing for managers, supervisors, and workers regardless of the industry.

Unfortunately, there is every reason to believe that this quagmire is becoming more commonplace. If that is true, American society must quickly intervene. The public trust does matter, the customer does matter, the bottom line does matter. But so, too, does right and wrong.

UNDERSTANDING AN ORGANIZATION'S ENVIRONMENT

Business and society share an mutually dependent relationship; they need one another in order to effect the delivery of goods and services. Society provides the human talent and access to raw materials needed to produce the food, housing, and products that constitute the sustenance of life. Business provides an incentive for people to *want* to produce these goods by offering income and benefits in return for skills, labor, and productivity.

Both sides theoretically benefit from the contributions of the other, because societies advance to higher standards of living when individual productivity and incomes are high. This occurs when consumers are receptive to products and services; eventually, their spending generates the very capital that permits expansion and more profit for owners.

For the relationship of business and society to succeed, however, there must be rules. Government often serves both as the originator of those rules and as its arbitrator when charges of foul play are made by clients, customers, stockholders, and others. Thus, we have a tripartite system of government: The legislative branch writes the laws, the executive branch executes and proposes new ones, and the judicial branch ensures that justice is not unevenly distributed in the process.

Business and society co-exist in an environment where ethics is synonymous with breathing: We just sort of *expect* it to happen. In reality, however, we know that this analogy is a poor one—human beings bend and break rules routinely, sometimes out of ignorance, sometimes intentionally. The fear of punishment by one's boss, by a board of directors, or by a jury of one's peers is often enough of a motivator to prevent serious miscalculations in business. Yet many managers fail to understand the societal and industrial environment around them, and their subsequent misreading of that environment can prove costly. It is this misreading of what society considers to be fair play that has led to major embarrassments at Exxon, Lockheed, Honda, Hitachi, General Motors, and thousands of other organizations in recent years. Managers at each organization knew how to raise capital and expand market share, but some of them forgot to instill a sense of right and wrong into their corporate culture.

Exhibit 1-5 explains the various forces at work in our perception of right and wrong in societal interactions. As you read the exhibit, ask yourself, which of the forces listed were especially helpful in shaping how you perceive ethics? Which ones played a lesser role, and why?

THE ROLE OF STAKEHOLDERS: NESTLÉ AND FOOD LION

Organizations, whether profit or nonprofit, share a common desire to satisfy the needs of various *stakeholders*. A multinational corporation

EXHIBIT 1-5 Societal Forces Shaping Our Perceptions of Right and Wrong

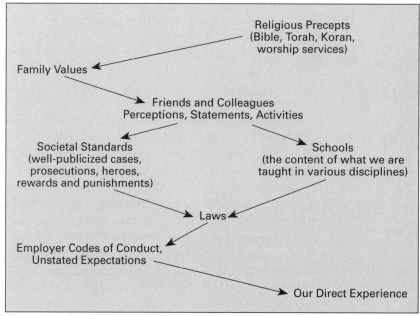

such as Nestlé must consider the complex role of government regulators, customers, stockholders, and employees in every jurisdiction where it produces and sells its products. A neighborhood supermarket such as Food Lion must be concerned with competition, suppliers, creditors, and customers, to name but a few.

Although most organizations work diligently to ensure that their managers conduct themselves in a highly ethical manner, Nestlé and Food Lion are fairly typical of companies where faulty decision making led to serious charges of ethical misconduct.

Nestlé Makes the Very Best . . . Boycott

Swiss-owned Nestlé, with an estimated 40 percent share of the worldwide infant formula market in the early 1980s, was the target of a global seven-year boycott by some consumers. Nestlé was blamed "by many social and civic organizations throughout the world for the deaths of infants in the Third World countries." (Rue and Byars, 143) Specifically, health officials and parents argued that Nestlé was encouraging mothers to substitute infant formula for breast milk, dis-

Are boycotts ethical? Cesar Chavez championed the cause of migrant farmworkers who were mistreated and underpaid; his leadership led to the creation of the United Farm Workers (UFW). He organized a successful boycott of table grapes in 1968. Corporations responded that union workers were merely engaging in extortion and that a boycott forced workers to lose their only income, leading to misery for some of the poorest American families.

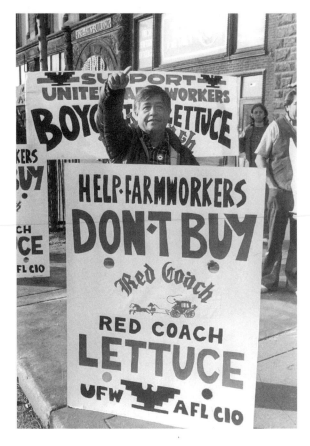

tributed free products to entice customers, and failed to provide adequate printed labeling information (many potential customers, it was argued, were illiterate and did not realized that they must mix the formula with water, which is often contaminated in the Third World.) When Nestlé was asked to change these practices, it initially refused, leading to citizen activism that to some degree impaired other Nestlé products, such as its chocolate products.

One expert examined Nestlé's attitude toward ethics and social responsibility as well as its response to consumers and health officials during the boycott and concluded that the company's arrogance backfired, triggering "the most successful boycott in the history of the international consumer movement." (Salmon, 47)

A variety of stakeholders entered the picture, including Swiss-based consumer groups, a U.S.-based activist group named INFACT,

E T H I C S   B R I E F

Profit and Children

Formula controversies continue. Canned infant formula, as opposed to the dry formula offered by Nestlé, is essentially made of milk and vitamins. *Consumer Reports* recently chastised the three largest manufacturers of the product—Abbott Laboratories, Bristol-Myers Squibb, and American Home Products—for a variety of questionable practices. The three companies have been accused of "rigging bids to supply formula for state Women, Infants and Children programs that provide nutrition counseling and basic foodstuffs to more than a million low-income parents."

And *Consumer Reports* didn't mince words over profit: "From 1979 to 1989, the price of formula shot up 155 percent while the price of milk increased only 36 percent." So far the three companies have paid more than $230 million toward settling federal antitrust suits, but the manufacturers continue to deny wrongdoing.

What are some of the ethical issues generated by a case of this nature?

Source: *Consumer Reports*, October 1993, p. 626.

and dozens of churches who collectively accused Nestlé of unethical corporate behavior. By 1984, both Nestlé and the leading activist groups eventually reached a settlement and the activist groups urged members to resume purchasing Nestlé products. But, as one of the world's leading experts in brand name equity has asserted, Nestlé may have won the battle but "lost the war despite an aggressive public relations campaign to convince people that they were doing good and not harm." (Aaker, 180). The perception of right and wrong at Nestlé was the centerpiece of the controversy.

Food Lion Faces Charges of Child Labor

The public perception that Food Lion's management had lost sight of ethical business practices first emerged in a 1992 ABC news report regarding alleged poor sanitation methods used in the storage and distribution of beef products. These allegations are discussed in a case later in the book. A second round of nationwide scrutiny emerged when Food Lion agreed in August 1993 to pay a $16.2 million settlement after acknowledging that it had violated child labor laws and failed to pay thousands of workers required overtime.

The U.S. Labor Department said that its eight-month investigation had revealed "widespread and extensive" violations of child labor and overtime rules by Food Lion. (Associated Press, August 30,

1993) Once again, a company was forced to pay a major financial fine because it had broken the public trust. In the case of Food Lion, the same stakeholders who were already familiar with allegations regarding beef sanitation received a further infusion of ethical scrutiny when the company admitted it had violated child labor and overtime laws on multiple occasions.

These issues lead to a series of questions: Where was the oversight? Who was serving as corporate conscience? Could any of these charges been avoided if proper ethical mandates were known throughout all levels of the organization? Is there any way that organizations such as Food Lion can avoid errors in judgment? Is education and training the answer? What about management by example? Should whistle blowing policies openly encourage employees to report wrongdoing by colleagues *before* the entire organization is embarrassed, or fined?

With both the Nestlé and Food Lion cases, organizations led by talented and experienced managers somehow lost sight of the incredibly powerful role of societal stakeholders. There are no simple solutions, but the search for an ethical standard to define right and wrong is a pivotal journey in an era when consumer activism, government prosecutions and media scrutiny place new burdens on both industry and nonprofit organizations.

A FRAMEWORK FOR RIGHT AND WRONG

Just as individuals struggle to determine right from wrong, so too do their employers. Later in the book you will read a variety of corporate ethics standards from such leading institutions as Mercedes-Benz, Harvard University, AT&T, and Teledyne. One of the reasons that major employers increasingly articulate these rules on paper is their assumption that if rules did not exist in organizations, employees would create their own, thereby manipulating situations to fit their personal needs. Given human nature and the variables discussed earlier, that is probably a very good assumption.

Corporations need a framework from which to examine ethical and unethical behavior, and a brief review of three of the major ethical decision making theories used by modern societies will build a foundation for your understanding of the cases that appear later in the book. The three theories we will discuss are the utilitarian theory, the theory of justice, and the theory of rights.

E T H I C S   B R I E F

Who Defines Right and Wrong?
The Role of Religion in Business Ethics

Two-thirds of the armed conflicts in the past hundred years have been invoked in the name of religion. Associated Press, September 1, 1993

The incredible impact of the above statement upon the transaction of business across national borders, let alone upon individual and family lives, is almost incomprehensible.

A number of factors contribute to our understanding of business ethics, including our personal morals, family values and any set of ethical expectations articulated for us by our employer, among others. Yet religion remains one of the most powerful, lasting influences on both our society and other cultures. A brief overview of several of the world's major religions and how they shape the lives of their followers can assist in understanding the complexities of international business and differing perceptions of how those devoted to certain religions may view proper business behavior.

The Differing Perceptions of Faith

In the beginning, there were rules. The Bible provides civilization with an astounding number of profound messages related to stealing, lying, honor and truth. Many of the most commonly cited passages in both the Old and New Testaments relate to commercial exchanges of how we are expected to honor our customers and colleagues.

As various individuals and societies debate what God or a supreme being intends for us to do in both our personal and professional lives, literally hundreds of cultures have emerged, each incorporating certain principles of theology and philosophy. Yet the Bible remains the most cited general reference for what constitutes right and wrong in Western society. The power of these messages is integrated into our Constitution, into state laws, regulations and even corporate codes of conduct. In other parts of the world, however, these same messages are either ignored or are completely different, posing a Herculean challenge for executives of multinational corporations seeking to adjust to different customs and religions abroad.

A summary of some of the classical interpretations of contemporary religions with the largest constituencies in the world appears below. This list provides only a cursory introduction for understanding various moral and social attitudes.

Hinduism

Louis Renou (*The Spirit of Hinduism*, 18) explains that Hinduism views life and work as a complicated rite; "there is no absolute dividing line between the sacred and the profane . . . There are no approaches to the spiritual life; and there is *dharma*, or maintenance, which is at once norm or law, virtue or meritorious action, the order of things transformed into moral obligation—a principle which governs all manifestations of Indian life."

He argues that Hinduism is not an intellectual game, but rather, a spiritual experience that guides its followers in how to conduct their personal and business lives. Many Western business people who operate in parts of the world where Hinduism is practiced, find it very difficult for to understand what is expected of them because of the complexities of the religion.

Catholicism

George Brantl (*The Meaning of Catholicism*, 17) explains that the Ten Commandments and the life of Jesus form the foundation of a 2,000-year-old faith that is the single largest denomination in the United States. Catholicism, he says, provides a timeless message: "Prepare the spirit for sincere search, kindle human desire for meaning, and God is everywhere, answering every fundamental need of man in every area of his life and inspiring a response." Through the ages, church leaders such as the Pope have resolutely argued that societal opinions and morals may come and go, but the fundamental message of Jesus—to love others as thyself—remains. An 1871 encyclical asserts that "there is one only true and living God . . . all powerful, eternal, immense, incomprehensible, infinite in intelligence, in will and in every perfection."

Because it is such a visible force in American life, the Catholic Church often comments on social issues such as abortion and the need for increased benefits for lower-wage earners. In doing so, it galvanizes opinions on all sides of major issues. Church officials believe they have a moral obligation to lead public debate whenever spirituality is concerned.

Buddhism

In more than 30 Asian countries, as Richard A. Gard explains, (*The Way of Buddhism*, 13), Buddhism is a "historical expression of a universal human ideal. It offers any individual or society a voluntary way of thought and conduct. . . . The Buddhist principle of tolerance for everyone is experientially based and expressed in the belief and practice that all beings can attain freedom in perfect existence." It integrates religion and philosophy to define Buddha as "the Enlightened One." Adherents seek to attain a state of being where nature and purpose are one.

Islam

John Williams (*The Tradition and Contemporary Orientation of Islam*, 85) writes that for Muslims, there is only one God, Allah, who has spoken through the Qur'an. His powerful message is revealed in Arabic and constitutes the word of God. Mohammed revealed messages in the seventh century from the valley of Mecca, and he is the ideal model and guide for Muslims in their personal life and in conducting transactions.

In the modern business world, the impact of Muslims is often linked to terrorism inspired by individuals such as Sheik Omar Abdel-Rahman, who was arrested for alleged involvement in the 1993 bombing of the New York World Trade Center. According to *The Wall Street Journal* (September 1, 1993, 1): "Unbowed by the rule of law or state persecution, he has preached *jihad*, or Muslim holy war, in Egypt, Saudi Arabia, Pakistan, Europe and the U.S. His message to followers is simple: the path to paradise is found through martyrdom. They must be ready to suffer as the Prophet Mohammed did." Yet many Islamics have been unfairly painted as violent and the majority of adherents detest violence.

Judaism

Arthur Hertzberg (*The Unity of the Jewish Spirit throughout the Ages*, 13) writes that God's covenant is revealed through the Torah, the law that Jews are to obey, "as the particular burden of the Jews and as the sign of their unique destiny in the world." As a chosen people, Hertzberg writes, Jews believe that "their task is to achieve redemption for themselves and to lead mankind to the day when, in the words of the liturgy, 'the Lord will be One and His name One.' Judaism is history, and the Torah is commandment in every sense." Geoffrey Parrinder, in his extraordinary work *World Religions* (181), notes the "great influence of the Bible" on

Judaism. He points out that the summary statement in *Ethics of the Fathers* focuses on the Bible (v:25): "Turn it, and turn it, for everything is in it; contemplate it, and grow old and gray over it, and do not stir from it. You can follow no better course than this."

Protestantism

J. Leslie Dunstan *(The Spirit of Protestantism,* 35) notes that Protestant Christianity began with the work of Martin Luther and John Calvin and today embraces an amalgam of religions articulated by many other spiritual leaders through the centuries. Dunstan writes that Protestantism developed after a lengthy contest between the Catholic Church and emerging religions over which institution should have ultimate political and moral authority. Various reformers through the years sought a model religion where authority came from God and less from the *institutions* of God. He writes that "The Protestant faith is also the product of a tremendous creative act: a bringing into being of a formal expression of the Christian gospel in which man stands as a free, autonomous person before his God." Protestantism is unique in that it serves as an 'umbrella' for a wide variety of faiths, including Methodists and Baptists, and others denominations such as Lutherans, who are increasingly seeking formal linkages with the Roman Catholic Church.

The Influence of Modern Religions on Business

Business people today in the United States and abroad are increasingly challenged to understand the influence of religion on business practices. In many middle eastern countries, no business is conducted on the day of the Sabbath; in other societies, business activities flourish on the Sabbath. In many societies, the impact of religion upon ethical beliefs is profound, particularly in Islamic and Christian nations. In others, especially throughout Asia, the role of

Buddhism is seen as more of a personal philosophy, and its impact on daily business activities is barely discernible.

An emerging issue as we approach the twenty-first century is the justification of religion for personal or politically related activities aimed at industry. In multicultural societies such as the United States, this poses an especially difficult challenge for the courts and a public that supports freedom of religion and freedom of expression.

For instance, a very small but visible percentage of Roman Catholics, Protestant Fundamentalists and others have targeted abortion clinics and birth control centers, with violence against doctors or owners the result. Those arrested believe that the Bible provides a justification for their opposition to what they believe to be the murder of the unborn. Those injured believe that religion has been misinterpreted and misapplied. In another example, Islamic fundamentalists were ordered by their leaders to murder author Salmon Rushdie, whose book *The Satanic Verses* greatly offended church leaders for what were perceived as inflammatory and false statements.

Terrorism on a worldwide scale has been orchestrated by Christians (such as the repeated bombings in England and Ireland by the Irish Republic Army and other factions) as well as Islamics and many other religious groups. Increasingly, worldwide police and security forces such as Interpol and the Federal Bureau of Investigation have found it necessary to infiltrate certain religious groups in order to ascertain future targets in industry and government.

Fortunately, the overwhelming influence of religion on business is a positive one. Many senior managers and employees actively contribute to community projects sponsored by various denominations, and a number of partnerships between industry and religious groups have contributed to such causes as higher literacy in inner cities, AIDS education programs, summer camps, and overseas missions. Religion provides a frame of reference and a foundation for

Parliament of the World's Religions

ideology that often compliments the messages of ethics that can be found in corporate mission statements.

In examining the relationship of religion and business in the United States a few years ago, *Fortune* (September 25, 1989, 116) asserted:

> Religion in America is big business. The U.S. has more clergy than Ford and Chrysler have employees. If American religion were a company, it would be number five on the Fortune 500 list with $50 billion in revenue. . . . Each week 40% of U.S. adults attend a church or synagogue, a percentage unchanged since 1970. . . . In successful churches, boardroom directors today talk about market share, customer satisfaction and asset management. Meeting client needs is important. Successful churches today provide pastoral counseling, child care, entertainment, occasional low-cost meals, transportation services, support groups and even financial assistance. Customer orientation and service are the keys to success.

As we saw earlier in the chapter, government responds to societal needs for justice in business by creating legislation based on the theory of justice. Similarly, world religions are beginning to follow this model. On August 31, 1993, after several years of meetings, conferences, and draft documents, the Parliament of World Religions, representing 20 of the world's largest religions, signed the Declaration of a Global Ethic in Chicago. This document is the first attempt by different faiths to seek a common ethic for global agreement on what is acceptable in our personal and business lives. The ethic represents the first common agreement on sins among adherents to Christianity, Judaism, Buddhism, Islam, and Hinduism, and the topics it covers include such issues as environmental abuse and sexual discrimination in the workplace.

After 100 years of debate, representatives of 20 of the world's largest religions signed the Declaration of a Global Ethic in Chicago in 1993. The document outlines agreements or moral behavior in business and personal endeavors.

Although the authors of the Global Ethic acknowledge that their work will not change the world immediately, they stated that their desire is to raise public awareness about the moral responsibility of individuals to reduce conflict by respecting the fact that most religions do share common beliefs. "Time and again we see leaders and members of religions incite aggression, fanaticism, hate and xenophobia–and even inspire and legitimize violent and bloody conflicts. . . . We are filled with disgust," their statement said.

Interestingly enough, the Parliament of World Religions was the first gathering of the world's major religions in exactly 100 years. A global interfaith movement leading to a global agreement on ethics in personal and professional lives may not shake Wall Street, but it nevertheless reminds us of the influence that religion can and should have in conveying powerful messages of right and wrong.

Utilitarian Theory

This approach toward decision making is best analogized with the notion of the "greatest good for the greatest number," a practical model in which we ask how our actions will impact those individuals who are eventually or possibly may be affected.

To make sound judgments, we must weigh the costs and benefits of our decisions, recognizing that the benefits that come to some individuals may trigger costs to others. For instance, raising the wholesale price of a 16-ounce package of Oreos® by 20 cents could eventually trigger cost increases to consumers of as much as 45 cents, but the increased profits would ultimately benefit producer Nabisco and its stockholders.

The utilitarian theory is necessary in a free enterprise environment. Nothing is inherently wrong with a price change if Nabisco believes it will increase its fiscal performance. If consumers reject the price increase by reducing their purchases, Nabisco can offer a bonus-size package to compensate for the higher price. Or the company may find that it must rescind its price increase altogether if competitors such as Keebler seize the moment with a corresponding price *decrease* to lure away Nabisco customers. Eventually the marketplace adjusts and even triggers the notion of the greatest good for the greatest number.

What the public tends to find repugnant are unilateral, unjustifiable price increases or other actions that appear unreasonable. Thus, President John F. Kennedy vowed to prosecute U.S. Steel and other steel manufacturers on April 11, 1962, when they raised prices by $6 a ton just days after signing two-year contracts with employees that kept wages and benefits uniform. In a nationally televised news conference, President Kennedy took off the gloves and told U.S. Steel and their contemporaries that he would not tolerate price gauging at the expense of workers:

> The American people will find it hard, as I do, to accept a situation in which a tiny handful of steel executives whose pursuit of private power and profit exceeds their sense of public responsibility and show utter contempt for the interests of 185 million Americans. . . . At a time when they could be exploring how more efficiency and better prices could be obtained, reducing prices in this industry in recognition of lower costs, their unusually good labor contract, their foreign competition and their increase in production and profits which are coming this year, a few gigantic corporations have decided to increase prices in ruthless disregard of their public responsibilities.[9] (Nevins, 196)

Twenty years later, President Ronald Reagan followed suit and summarily dismissed hundreds of air traffic controllers who threatened to cripple the nation's airlines in a job action. His public opinion ratings skyrocketed when he argued that the controllers failed to understand that their actions could weaken the entire economy and lead to significant loss of income for millions of American workers dependent upon civilian air traffic.

The utilitarian theory of justice is driven by the thirst for satisfaction: Both corporations and not-for-profit organizations succeed *only* if they satisfy decision makers (boards of directors, stockholders, senior management), regulators, the news media, and, ultimately, the public. To be effective in fulfilling the mandate of the "greatest good for the greatest number," organizations must continually work to ensure that they are financially healthy and price competitive, that they deliver a product that meets customer needs, and that they are staffed by talented and honest individuals.

Of course the utilitarian theory is just that, a theory. It is a model that is very difficult to implement fully because of the variabilities and pressures in different industries and, indeed, in human personalities. Ultimately, some managers do miscalculate, some do overstep their bounds, some do discriminate. Unfortunately, these and related actions often culminate in a breach of the public trust.

Theory of Justice

Although not incompatible with the utilitarian theory, the theory of justice takes a somewhat different approach to ethics in that it emphasizes equity and fairness rather than cost and benefits.

The justice theory is often cited in the legislative process whenever society has recognized the need to create new laws governing business activities. Because companies can sometimes become too myopic, focusing only on costs and benefits (thus leading to monopolies or price fixing, for instance), society responds with the justice theory. Exhibit 1-6 lists of just a few of the significant legislative landmarks where the justice theory has been manifest into law.

Theory of Rights

Also called the moral rights approach, the theory of rights argues that in our society, we must work doubly hard to ensure that minority interests are protected. An illustration occurs when a utility

EXHIBIT 1-6   Selected Major Legislative Acts Derived from the Theory of Justice

The United States Congress.

Sherman Act of 1890	Any contract or activity that is intentionally designed to restrain the trade of others is illegal. As a result, monopolies and conspiracies that border on a monopolistic situation will be prosecuted. Over the years, oil companies, banks, and retail chains have been prosecuted for such unfair practices.
Federal Trade Commission Act of 1914	Deceptive trade practices are unfair to consumers and to the competition if it suffers from these practices. This law creates the Federal Trade Commission (FTC) to pursue and punish violators. Each year the FTC pursues several hundred major cases against manufacturers, mail order firms, and telemarketers who allegedly defraud consumers.
Hart-Scott-Rodino Antitrust Improvement Act of 1976	A decade before mergers and acquisitions (M&As) would become household words, this act required organizations to publicly disclose deals before their completion. As seen later in the book, this law was widely disobeyed, leading to multiple prosecutions.
Civil Rights Act of 1964	Equal opportunity in employment, housing, and other situations is guaranteed to all citizens regardless of race and national origin. Subsequent enhancements to the original legislation extend this act to discrimination based on age, gender, and related issues.
American Disability Act of 1990	This act provides justice for any individual who has been discriminated against, or who *perceives* he or she has been discriminated against, based on physical or mental health disability. The ADA has resulted in sweeping changes in the workplace, from the interview and promotion process to physical access provided employees and customers.
False Claims Act of 1992	This legislation assures justice and financial rewards to those who can prove that the government has been the victim of fraud by individuals or corporations. This is the first federal legislation of its kind to legitimize and reward whistle blowing in the workplace in over 100 years.

ETHICS BRIEF

Excommunicating a Dissenter

David P. Wright served as assistant professor of Judaic and Near Eastern studies at Brandeis University, a leading university in Waltham, Mass. As a scholar, he was noted as an accomplished author and lecturer in his area of specialization. Dr. Wright was also a member of the church of Jesus Christ of Latter-Day Saints, also known as the Mormons. In fact, his Mormon roots reach back to the founding of the church in Utah a century ago.

In May 1994, Dr. Wright says he was excommunicated because his research concludes that the Book of Mormon, the church's principal scripture, was not ancient but rather had been written by the founder of the church, Joseph Smith. He also argued that the Book of Mormon was not infallible.

"If I'm guilty of anything, I'm guilty of trying to find a way to believe and to assess Mormon tradition positively," he argued. Despite an inquisition by the 12-member Council of the Church, he was excommunicated and told that he would have to renounce his views. His reply: "You can't *unknow* what you know."

Similar cases of scholars whose research places them in conflict with their religion have been documented in the past decade.

At the heart of these cases are questions of freedom of speech that conflict with theology and devotion. How can these conflicts be resolved, if at all?

(For more information, see "Biblical Scholar at Brandeis Is Excommunicated," *The Chronicle of Higher Education*, May 18, 1994, p. A18.

---

guarantees that a small group of stockholders who wish to see their company change management direction is guaranteed freedom of expression at the company's annual meeting. In hospitals, where smoking is almost universally banned, the theory of rights argues that individuals who wish to smoke should be accommodated in a separate facility as long as their smoking does not impair the welfare of other workers.

The Integration of Theory into Law   An excellent example of a case in which the theory of rights was enacted into law is the U.S. False Claims Act of 1992. This sweeping legislation provides a mechanism for U.S. workers who believe that the federal government has been victimized by fraud to report that wrongdoing. For instance, a former vice-president of United Technologies, Inc., Douglas Keith, received $22.5 million from the federal government in 1994 after proving that his former employer had cheated the Defense Department by engaging in "accounting irregularities." United Technologies also had to

When consumers boycotted Exxon gas stations after the catastrophic Valdez oil spill in Alaska, the company paid for full-page newspapers ads in large cities. The message reminds the public that local, independent operators were being unfairly punished for a corporate dilemma. As noted in the chapter, boycotts can be devastating to the bottom line (e.g., Nestlé) or can have a minimal effect. Exxon is the single largest company in the world and was only marginally impaired financially by the massive spill.

Most Exxon stations are privately-owned small businesses.

The oil spill in Alaska was not their fault.

There's been talk lately about boycotting Exxon stations.

Obviously, that's not going to help clean up the Alaskan oil spill.

But it is going to hurt a lot of small businessmen in your community—and their families and employees.

They have nothing to do with the accident in Alaska, but they're taking the brunt of the anger. And they stand to lose income at the same time.

Truth is, it's not their fault at all. We at Exxon Corporation recognize our responsibility, and we are doing everything in our power to clean up the spill.

So please, don't blame your Exxon dealers. They've worked hard for your business for many years. They don't deserve to lose it over something which is not their fault.

pay the government a $150 million fine. (*Philadelpha Inquirer*, February 16, 1994, p. D2)

The False Claims Act is rooted in the theory of rights: It guarantees the complaining worker and her supervisor the right to a fair hearing. It further ensures that the worker will not be censured or fired because of an accusation. It also provides a financial incentive to the whistle blower by giving the petitioner up to 25 percent of any moneys recovered. (As seen with the case above, some employees have already received millions of dollars as a result of a single claim against their employer.) Later in the book you will read about the significant impact that whistle blowing and the False Claims Act have had upon a wide variety of organizations just since 1992.

As the case for this book is built chapter by chapter, we see that society is incrementally institutionalizing perceived notions of right and wrong through formal channels. Whether we like it or not, legislative restrictions and fines are increasingly used as tools of punishment. The combined influence of the news media, stockholder

E T H I C S   B R I E F

Selected Contemporary Ethics Cases

Although charges of ethical abuse are as old as history itself, the following is a sampling of cases over the past quarter century that have shaped public discussion on the issue.

1970

Ford Motor Company introduces the Pinto after a record-breaking 25-month period from initial concept design to product launch. In his research study, former Ford manager Dennis Gioia concludes that company managers were required to produce the car within "limits of 2,000"—meaning no more than $2,000 in cost and 2,000 pounds in weight. Within months of delivery to consumers, reports of rear-end accidents that cause fire, passenger injuries, and some deaths reach the National Highway Traffic Safety Association and several public interest groups. Numerous judgments against Ford would be issued by juries in subsequent years, including a landmark 1978 case in which a burn victim was awarded $6.6 million, upheld on appeal.

1971

Ralph Nader and colleagues sponsor the first Conference on Professional Responsibility where abuses in the atomic energy field are exposed, including collusion between some employees of the Atomic Energy Commission and private contractors.

1971

Psychiatrist Daniel Ellsberg releases The Pentagon Paper to *The New York Times*, a series of internal policy papers, including some classified "top secret," detailing the history of U.S. military involvement in Vietnam. The reports were first commissioned by Secretary of Defense Robert McNamara in 1967, and Ellsberg was one of its anonymous authors whose former pro-military sentiments radically changed as the war in Vietnam escalated. The Justice Department prosecuted Ellsberg and received an injunction against *The Times* which lasted for 15 days until the Supreme Court overruled the injunction by a vote of 6 to 3. In writing with the majority of the Court, Justice Hugo Black concluded that "In revealing the workings of government that led to the Vietnam war, the newspapers nobly did precisely what the founders hoped and trusted they would do."

1972

An anonymous source named "Deep Throat" approaches *Washington Post* reporters Bob Woodward and Carl Bernstein following the bungled burglary of the Democratic National Headquarters in the Watergate Hotel in Washington, D.C. Revelations by the source result in an investigative series by the two reporters that leads to impeachment proceedings against President Richard M. Nixon and his eventual resignation in August 1974.

1972

The Bank of Credit and Commerce International (BCCI) is incorporated in Luxembourg, launching what *Newsweek* would later term "the Muslim world's first banking powerhouse." With ties to criminal organizations and intelligence operations worldwide, and with more than 400 branches and subsidiaries, BCCI largely escapes regulation—and public scrutiny—in nearly 70 countries. Deposits are used to subsidize drug cartels, arms smuggling, and other assorted crimes. In 1989, New York

District Attorney Robert Morgenthau begins an investigation into BCCI operations that eventually leads to a declaration of global insolvency in 1991. Former U.S. presidential advisor Clark Clifford, chairman of First American Bankshares, and his law partner Robertt Altman, would later be implicated but never directly found to have engaged in bank fraud and accepting $40 million in bribes to keep BCCI's control of the institution hidden. *Newsweek*'s penetrating article "The Dirtiest Bank of All" (January 29, 1991) concludes that "Never has a single scandal involved so much money, so many nations or so many prominent people."

1974

In September, Karen Silkwood, a technician at the Kerr-McGee plant in Oklahoma, testifies to the Atomic Energy Commission regarding safety violations and the possibility of worker exposure to plutonium. On November 13, she is found dead in a suspicious car accident while traveling to be interviewed by the *New York Times* reporter David Burnham. She had privately and publicly questioned safety standards in place at the facility.

1983

Environmental Protection Agency managers in Chicago testify before the House Subcommittee on Oversight and Investigation. They argue that Dow Chemical had routinely discharged dioxin and other poisonous wastes into the Tittabawassee River and other sites near Dow's Midland, Michigan, plant. This case of whistle blowing by government officials is rare and captures international media attention, leading Dow to curtail its practices. The company later institutes sweeping environmental reform.

1986

In Washington state, Rockwell Corporation quality control manager Casey Ruud recommends to his superiors that the Hanford Nuclear Reservation be closed due to the absence of safety controls at the facility where plutonium is processed. *Seattle Times* reporter Eric Nalder launches an investigative series into the possibility that workers and residents could be exposed to the lethal substance, leading to Congressional and U.S. Department of Energy investigations. Within two years, Hanford's two plutonium plants are closed.

1986

The NASA Shuttle *Challenger* explodes, killing all seven astronauts aboard and triggering a comprehensive review of how government contractors were pressured by the procurement process to approve a launch, even in the midst of poor weather conditions that could weaken a critical O-ring device. Morton Thiokol scientist Roger Bojoly becomes a prominent whistle blower, telling Congress and a presidential review panel that he and others advised against a *Challenger* launch but were pressured against their own recommendations by a corruptive process of decision making.

1990

On September 24, *The Wall Street Journal* publishes an extensive investigation that documents an orchestrated campaign by a senior manager at American Express to discredit international banker Edmond Safra. The paper reported that Harry L. Freeman, an aide to AMEX chairman James Robinson, "supervised and approved the hiring of the two American Express operatives who carried out the Safra campaign." This effort "spread rumors and news articles containing patently bogus information about (Safra). . . . For American Express, a company that enjoyed a virtually unrivaled reputation for integrity, the Safra affair reveals a willingness to engage in unseemly corporate revenge when confronting a rival, and, at the very least a jarring lack of oversight on the part of top company officials."

1991

Dozens of women, including naval officers, report that they were pawed and subjected to sexual harassment by navy and marine corp fliers at a three-day Tailhook aviators' convention at the Las Vegas Hilton. Among other charges, the women asserted X-rated movies were shown openly and that officers displayed their testicles in the hotel corridor. The embarrassing fiasco led to the resignation of a half-dozen high-ranking Pentagon officials including a secretary of the navy. A subsequent 1993 Pentagon report recommended that 140 individuals be tried in military court for possible disciplinary action.

1992

Dow Corning finally acknowledges that silicone breast implants may pose serious health threats to female patients after years of generally denying that any threat existed beyond those identified in product packaging. With several thousand lawsuits pending by women who claimed they suffered serious side effects from the product, the company acknowledges on January 17, 1994, that its total liability was at least $1.24 billion.

1993

In a stinging May 17 report, *Newsweek* analyzes the business practices of financial consultant and author Charles J. Givens and concludes that part of his empire was based on "useful, defective and self-serving advice." The article chronicles "truth" from "legend" and reviews lawsuits from dissatisfied purchasers of Givens tapes and books and investigations against the Givens' organizations by various state officials. Yet in a full-page advertisement in May 27 *USA Today,* the Givens' organization responded that the *Newsweek* piece, authored by another financial consultant, Jane Bryant

Quinn, may have been spawned by professional jealousy, as Quinn also authors books and columns offering financial advice. "We have heard," the ad read in part, "your articles are carried in slightly over 200 papers and you actually and shamelessly accept money without divulging your money-making scheme to your readers—something similar to what you criticized Charles J. Givens for doing."

1994

The federal government acknowledges that several hundred adults and children were not warned of risks of radiation to their bodies when they underwent injections of plutonium and other carcinogens under the auspices of the Atomic Energy Commission in the 1940s and 1950s. At the Fernald School in Waltham, Massachusetts, retarded boys were fed radioactive milk; in Albuquerque, New Mexico, several newborn boys (all black) were injected with a radioactive iron to study the function of the thyroid glands. Researcher Constantine Maletskos, formerly with MIT, defended the radiation tests, telling *The Christian Science Monitor* (December 31, 1993, 2) that the research produced valuable medical information. Although medical consent as we now know it did not exist 50 years ago, Dr. Jack Geiger, former president of Physicians for Social Responsibility, argued that anyone involved in such experimentation nevertheless violated a credo in existence for about a millennium: "Do no harm."

1994

In the aftermath of several scandals regarding executive compensation at companies that were losing money, public television managers nationwide expressed concern regarding reports of investigations into their finances given their non-profit status. In a front page story in *The Wall Street Journal* (January 17, 1994), the paper reported that four top executives of WQED in Pittsburgh received salaries ranging from $205,000 to $325,000 plus allowances—more than ten times the income of the average American worker. This outraged corporate and individual donors to WQED. The *Journal* noted: "Its finances are in shambles, local subscribers are furious, board members are embarrassed and the station management is on the defensive. . . . As recently as last year, the station ran myriad telethons exhorting viewers to send in money while its chief executives collected handsome salaries and benefit packages. Meanwhile, WQED had racked up a $4.5 million deficit."

1994

Two major restaurant chains came under scrutiny for different types of ethical quagmires. Denny's Restaurants, which admitted that it had received over 4,300 complaints of racial bias where minority customers were poorly served or encouraged to leave the restaurant, paid a $46 million fine to the Justice Department. The case received national prominence when six black Secret Service agents assigned to protect President Clinton were not served for almost an hour while 15 agents who accompanied them were served in minutes and enjoyed seconds. A second chain, Dunkin' Donuts, installed about 500 electronic devices in stores in the Northeast so that the conversations of those in the restaurant could be monitored. The discovery of the concealed recorders led many customers to stop patronizing the popular chain. One New Hampshire customer was quoted in *The Philadelphia Inquirer* as saying: "It's like spying. It sounds like Nazism or the KGB. It's not American." (May 30, 1994, D1).

activism, government prosecutions, organized boycotts and whistle blowing are profoundly changing how we make decisions. Whether or not any of these tools actually contribute to a more ethical society is very much open to conjecture. The two following case studies are aimed at eliciting your response to the difficult question: "What would you do?"

CASE STUDY:
DRINKING, DRIVING, AND INFLUENCE

In the following case study, the arrest of a state official for drunken driving sparks a heated debate. Various members of the public must consider issues surrounding the incident and examine questions of credibility, shared ethical and moral responsibility, and public and private trust. On trial is the tacit contract between citizens and the officials they entrust to promote the general welfare and uphold the laws.

Source: This case was written by Linda Loehr, assistant professor of English at Northeastern University in Boston.

Early in the morning of April, 17, 1993, police in Norwood, Massachusetts, stopped a driver whose car had apparently drifted out of its lane on a street in Norwood Center. Norwood Police Lt. Brian Murphy, quoted the following day in *The Boston Globe*, noted, "It was a routine stop and the officers did a field sobriety test." The driver in question, Daniel J. Harrington, a career law enforcement officer and recent appointee to the Massachusetts Alcoholic Beverage Control Commission (ABCC), reportedly failed that roadside test and was subsequently charged with drunken driving. But the real testing of Daniel Harrington and related others had just begun.

The Globe account indicated that Dan Harrington would take a paid temporary leave of absence from the ABCC, pending the court disposition of the case. A capsule summary of Harrington's career noted that he served for more than 30 years as a member of the Boston police force, provided volunteer personal-security services to William Weld during Weld's successful 1990 campaign for governor, was appointed chief of the Capitol Police in 1991, and finally, was recently appointed as associate commissioner of the ABCC. The ABCC controls the sale and distribution of alcohol in the state.

Harrington's ABCC position involved working with another associate and the full-time ABCC chairman, Stuart Krusell. Together they comprised the commission responsible for conducting hearings of state liquor law violations (such as serving alcohol to drunk patrons or minors.) Krusell described Harrington as "very pleasant," noting that "it's been trying to learn about the agency and how things operate." Others quoted in press reports after the drunk driving arrest were more specific and less forgiving.

Gloria Larson, Weld's secretary of consumer affairs called the incident "a big disappointment." McGrory, reporting in this account, moved the indictment to a higher level, hailing Harrington's arrest as "another in a string of political and person embarrassments for (Governor) Weld who has taken considerable pride in his law-and-order rhetoric and repeated proposals for harsher drunk driving penalties." Later in the day, Dan Harrington resigned his position with ABCC.

Media coverage exacted quick and public penalties of Harrington: accounts of Harrington's long and distinguished career, headlined by the charge of driving drunk; references to patronage (Harrington's daughter also worked with the state police); and, notably, Ray Howell's statement as the governor's spokesperson, "that no matter what the final outcome of the case would be, [Harrington] would be forever tainted as a member of the ABCC."

Radio talk shows blazed with expressions of outrage. Harrington supporters rushed to his defense, decrying the administration's quick abandonment of a loyal friend. Others used the issue of personal connection as a point of departure, an additional ethical issue, citing lax standards for the very people who should be held to the highest ones. For many others, the questions came down to a combination of ethics and personal safety standards: How much is too much alcohol for anyone entrusted with a drivers license?

Amid heated commentary and growing speculation that Harrington had been pressured to resign, Governor Weld and Lt. Governor Paul Cellucci issued a joint statement, noting that "Dan Harrington has done the right thing, and we wish him well." As Harrington left his position and prepared for his hearing, controversy continued.

At the political level, many expressed outrage that a Weld appointee and member of the ABCC could commit such an offense. Press accounts of the Harrington case revived public outcry over an earlier incident, the March 31 arrest of Ron Kaufman, a former aide to President George Bush, also for drunken driving.

Kaufman acknowledged that his car was swerving just before he was stopped, an hour and 15 minutes after leaving a poker game held at Governor Weld's Cambridge residence. Kaufman's alcohol testing at the scene of that arrest included the same kind of breath-analysis test that Harrington allegedly had refused when officers stopped him. Although others who were guests at the poker party indicated that Kaufman did not seem drunk when he left Weld's home, Kaufman reportedly registered a 0.10 blood-alcohol level at the time of testing, the level at which a driver in Massachusetts is considered legally drunk.

According to Kaufman, his erratic driving on the night in question was due not to intoxication, but rather to fatigue and a chocolate bar that had dropped on his pants. Kaufman explained that he had stopped on the way home from the party to ask directions after becoming confused when leaving Weld's neighborhood. He insisted that he had purchased the candy, not the bottle of beer found nearly empty in his car at the time of his arrest. Kaufman's wife supported her husband's story, arguing that her husband was not a heavy drinker and describing his public penalty as nothing less than character annihilation.

After the Kaufman arrest, Governor Weld experienced credibility damage and the danger of political fallout on several fronts. One local columnist enjoyed a veritable field day with Kaufman's "chocolate defense" and Governor Weld's reference to seeing Kaufman "nursing" an "amber" colored drink during the poker game. Other voices focused on the deep contrast between Governor Weld, the host with mounting personal- and political-liability problems, and Governor Weld, the tough leader champion of the victims of drunk driving.

The ABCC's record did little to offset Governor Weld's tenuous position. At the time Dan Harrington was appointed to the ABCC, critics described the agency as a lax enforcer of liquor laws, particularly those prohibiting the sale of alcohol to minors.

Gloria Larson, whose duties as state consumer affairs secretary include the oversight of the ABCC, acknowledged enforcement deficiencies. Larson attributed those deficiencies to staff reductions (45 ABCC investigators were assigned to police in the 1970s; 21 in the 1980s; about 10 reduced to 5 during the Weld administration). Additionally, retailer citations were down from 450 in 1990, the year before Weld was elected, to 170 in 1992.

Despite the ABCC's dwindling head and body counts, Governor Weld promoted an image of a tough law-and-order administrator and continued to exert pressure to require harsher penalties for drunken driving. Earlier in March, on the occasion of filing such legislation, Governor Weld described his bill as

> [sparing] no one who is foolish and negligent enough to get behind the wheel of a car while intoxicated. We regard this kind of behavior as criminal, and we are going to treat drunken driving as a crime that deserves strong punishment.

Supporters on the scene included the Secretary of Public Safety, representatives of Mothers Against Drunk Driving, Alcoholics Anonymous, and members of various police departments. The legislation filed would lower to 0.08 the blood-alcohol level constituting legal intoxication for drivers 21 and older; blood-alcohol levels of 0.02 or higher would cause drivers under the age of 21 to lose their licenses for a year.

Some observers speculated that the Harrington and Kaufman arrests might damage the new bill's chances of success. Some supporters of the bill insisted that these incidents, although embarrassing, affected the legitimacy of the people involved, not that of the bill itself.

Others noted that practice and preaching must correspond. Phillip's and Lehigh's *Boston Globe* account of the Kaufman incident noted the innocent verdict obtained earlier for former state Senator Theodore Alixo, who was also charged with drunken driving after driving the wrong way on the Southeast Expressway, a major highway.

Governor Weld, quoted in the same article, noted the "political ramifications" of the Kaufman incident and referred to possible con-

sequences as an unknown "on the Richter scale." One related calcula-
tion, however, is known and officially on record: 147 deaths in alcohol-related traffic accidents in Massachusetts in 1992 alone.

The Harrington and Kaufman citations for drunken driving
resulted in serious damage to the personal and professional reputa-
tions of not just the two men charged, but to varying extents to their
families and colleagues as well. Fortunately, these two cases involved
no property damage or bodily harm.

But there was one unexpected benefit: The incidents sparked an
extended public debate on the issues of personal and shared responsibility and apparently some ethical soul-searching as well. In May,
Sally Jacobs of *The Boston Globe* offered a follow-up piece on drinking
and driving, with a report this time featuring only a brief mention of
Harrington and Kaufman. For the piece, Jacobs interviewed public
and private officials concerned with the issue and some citizens who
regularly drink and drive.

Dennis McCarty, director of substance abuse services for the State
Department of Health, noted changing attitudes about drinking and
driving in the 1990s:

> Among casual drinkers it is no longer accepted. The folks who continue
> to drink and drive have a serious problem with alcohol.

Jacobs offered statistics indicating that drunken driving is in
decline, a result of public-awareness initiatives to some extent, but
also to declining levels of enforcement. Increasing numbers of repeat
offenders, however, indicate that hardcore rather than casual drinkers
are breaking the law.

One of Jacob's most disturbing statistics, however, involves the
delay in apprehending habitual offenders: Alcohol specialists estimate that people arrested for drunken driving have probably driven
while under the influence 150 to 200 times before their first arrest.
Louis Sullivan, quoted in 1992 as secretary of Health and Human
Services, advised

> If we want to bring down escalating health care costs, one thing we
> should do is look at the role of alcohol consumption in injuries . . . half of
> all injuries could be avoided by not drinking when you are driving,
> boating, operating machinery, feeling angry, or using a firearm.

Offering a similar warning, the National Center for Statistics and
Analysis for the National Highway Traffic Safety Administration estimates that "about 2 in every 5 Americans will be involved in an alcohol-related crash at some time in their lives."

The economic costs of alcohol-related traffic-crash injuries, estimated in a fact sheet distributed by the National Clearinghouse for Alcohol and Drug Information, placed 1985 costs at about $15 billion. At the 1992 Secretary's National Conference on Alcohol-Related Injuries, Lewis Eigen calculated that the economic costs of injuries and deaths encompassed in that 1985 figure—not including property damage—represented about $73 for each man, woman, and child in the U.S. population that year.

Statistics also show that traffic fatalities usually claim people younger than those who die from diseases. Each alcohol-related, crash fatality costs the nation an average of 37 years of a person's life or, in single year, more than 900,000 life years, a staggering cost to the nation that is preventable.

Dr. Ralph Hingson of Boston University's School of Public Health is well known for his research on alcohol abuse. He has argued for lowering the standard of intoxication to 0.05, basing his case on studies showing that each increase of 0.02 in the blood-alcohol level doubles a driver's chances of being in a single-car, fatal crash.

In late May, a *Boston Globe* account of Governor Weld's continuing woes again placed Dan Harrington's name in boldface type, one citation in a listing of "the governor's missteps." This time the mention of Harrington referenced his work as a bodyguard and driver for Weld during the 1990 campaign, not his distinguished career as a law enforcement officer. Republican consultant Ron Mills cited Weld's biggest problem as seeming "unengaged, not paying attention, . . . allowing things to drift." The issue came down to one of damage control, and ethics. When do you fire a friend who could cause you political harm? How do you encourage themto resign? When is public perception paramount over personal loyalty?

Epilogue

On Wednesday, September 15, 1993, a jury acquitted Daniel J. Harrington on the charge of drunken driving. *Boston Globe* staffer Peter J. Howe reported that the Weld administration expressed happiness over the acquittal and acknowledged the possibility of again appointing Harrington to the Weld administration, but not to his former position with the ABCC. Howe also offered capsule summaries of the opposing positions, reiterating the testimony of police officers who were at the scene and Harrington's defense. Harrington testified that he failed field sobriety tests because the flashing police lights had made him nervous.

Discussion Questions

1. What factors distinguish alcohol *use* from alcohol *abuse*?

2. To what degree do we share ethical and moral responsibility for the actions of those with whom we work?

3. Why are many people reluctant to intervene when a coworker, particularly one who is away from the workplace, seems to have had too much to drink?

4. What do avoidance strategies such as denial, delay (waiting for a problem to reach crisis stage), or abandonment (such as firing someone) accomplish?

5. How can we communicate expectations about ethical role performance on and off the job?

6. How can we channel concerns about questionable behavior without violating people's privacy or endangering their jobs?

7. Can policy be the answer?

References for Case Study

Barnicle, M. "Weld Guest Just Hungry." *The Boston Globe*, April 6, 1993, p. 21.

Eigen, L. D. "The Cost of Alcohol-Related Traffic Crash Injuries." Washington, D.C.: National Clearinghouse for Alcohol and Drug Abuse, March 26, 1992.

Gorov, L. "Hosts Actions Key Issue in Injury Suit, Lawyers Say." *The Boston Globe*, April 3, 1993, p. 18.

Hohler, B. "ABCC Official Resigns Position; Faces Charge of Driving Drunk." *The Boston Globe*, April 19, 1993, p. 17.

Howe, P. J. "Harrington Exonerated, But Won't Get Job Back." *The Boston Globe*, September 17, 1993, p. 29.

Jacobs, S. "Mass. Roads Still Plagued by Some Veteran Drinkers." *The Boston Globe*, May 6, 1993, p. 1.

Lehigh, S. "Weld Stepping Softly Amid Controversies." *The Boston Globe*, May 26, 1993, p. 1.

McGrory, B. "Alcohol Official Charged with DWI; Weld Appointee Takes Paid Leave of Absence." *The Boston Globe*, April 18, 1993, p. 29.

Phillips, F. and Lehigh, S. "Ex-Bush Aide Was Drinking at Weld's House Before Arrest, Governor Says Kaufman Did Not Seem Intoxicated Then." *The Boston Globe*, April 2, 1993, p. 1.

Phillips, F., and Lehigh, S. "Wife Gives Kauman's Account; Says He Got Lost, Stopped, Bought Candy after Poker." *The Boston Globe*, April 3, 1993, p. 13.

"Poker Game Postmortem." *The Boston Globe*, April 8, 1993, p. 18.

U.S. Department of Health and Human Services. "Alcohol-Related Injuries: The Hurt and the Harm." Washington, DC: U.S. Government Printing Office, 1992.

U.S. Department of Transportation. "1991 Alcohol Fatal Crash Facts" (RP 0805). Washington, DC: U.S. Government Printing Office, 1992.

CASE STUDY:
THE NEW YORK AFRICAN BURIAL GROUND:
THE ETHICS OF PLACE

We are familiar with the ethical dilemmas embedded in workplace practices. The actual *placement* of worksites can also become entangled in similar conflicts over politics, the bottom line, and ethics of public responsibility. This was the case in 1991, when the federal government began construction on a multimillion dollar federal office tower on a New York City site.

This site was acquired in 1988 through an agreement with the city government and is located on prime real estate in lower Manhattan. Before this land was incorporated into the city, it had served as a burial ground for African-Americans during most of the 18th century—under British rule and a slave-labor economy, throughout the American Revolution, and during the nation's founding when the national capital was New York. The African Burial Ground closed in 1792, and was assumed to have been destroyed decades ago by urban development. Since the city now requires archeological testing prior to any construction, the General Services Administration (GSA), the federal government's real estate developer, sponsored an excavation to explore the soil's historical resources. To their surprise, they found that within the building lot, hundreds of burials were largely intact within the outlines of decayed coffins, and that as many as 20,000 burials probably lay beneath the site and nearby buildings.

Archeologists immediately began to exhume the burials and cultural remnants buried with them, such as beads, buttons, and cowry

Source: Written by Susan Pearce, Gettysburg College, PA.

shells. The GSA proceeded hastily with the excavation, arguing than any construction delays or a new building design for an alternate site would result in escalating costs to the agency (and taxpayer). No longer a residential area, there was no continuously existing neighborhood to advocate for their rights to protect the cemetery. And due to the absence of records, it is unknown to which families these burial remains rightfully belong. New York City, however, has the largest African-American presence in the country; once the discovery was publicized and a construction accident damaged the burials, community activists began to argue for protection, memorialization, respect for the remains, and African-American involvement in decision-making. For some activists and religious leaders, the Burial Ground was considered sacred; for many, it was also a place where their own ancestors may be buried; for historians and other academics, it offered an unprecedented opportunity to learn the details of life and death for early Africans that were never properly recorded. This is the country's largest excavated skeletal population and the oldest African-American excavation.

There were several complications that made decisions over this site difficult to resolve: David Dinkins, the first African-American mayor of New York, had recently been elected. He saw both an obligation to the African-American community to protect the burials and the fact that, in a deep economic recession, the construction project promised employment for that same community. A second complication was that some activists fought to suspend the construction and leave the Burial Ground untouched; other activists supported excavation to learn more about their community's history. New York had never granted landmark protection to cemeteries with no aboveground markers. And compounding the complications was the skepticism over the federal government's actual need for office space when many Manhattan offices were empty, and over the GSA's interest in caring for and interpreting the burials with proper sensitivity.

Despite these difficulties, an impassioned and political intervention led to changes. Although burials were removed from the office tower site and construction continued, the GSA suspended the excavation for, and construction of, a pavilion annex. The contract for the physical anthropology of the remains was transferred to African-American directorship at Howard University in Washington, DC. In addition, a federal advisory committee with strong activist membership has overseen plans for the future, including memorials, a museum, reinterment of the remains, and broad public education. Federal and city landmark designations now protect the entire African Burial Ground.

Discussion Question

Question: What would you do, given the legitimate concerns of the African-American community as well as the government's desire to proceed with a necessary facility for its federal agencies?

REFERENCES FOR CHAPTER 1

Aaker, David A. *Managing Brand Equity*. New York: The Free Press, 1991.

Brantl, George. *Catholicism: The Meaning of Catholicism*. New York: George Braziller, Inc., 1961.

Dunnette, Marvin D., and Hough, Leaetta M. *Handbook of Industrial and Organizational Psychology*. 2nd ed., vol. 3. Palo Alto: Consulting Psychologists Press, Inc., 1992.

Dunstan, J. Leslie. *Protestantism: The Spirit of Protestantism*. New York: George Braziller, Inc., 1961.

Fraedrich, John, and Ferrell, O. C. *Business Ethics*. Boston: Houghton Mifflin, 1991.

Gard, Richard A. *Buddhism: The Way of Buddhism*. New York: George Braziller Inc., 1961.

Hertzberg, Arthur. *Judaism: The Unity of the Jewish Spirit throughout the Ages*. New York: George Braziller, Inc., 1961.

Nash, Laura L. *Good Intentions Aside: A Manager's Guide to Resolving Ethical Problems*. Boston: Harvard Business School Press, 1990.

Nevins, Allan. *President John F. Kennedy: The Burden and the Glory*. New York: Harper & Row, 1964.

Parrinder, Geoffrey. *World Religions from Ancient History to the Present*. London: Hamlyn Publishing Group, 1983.

Renou, Louis. *Hinduism: The Spirit of Hinduism*. New York: George Braziller, Inc., 1961.

Rue, Leslie W., and Byars, Lloyd L. *Management: Skills and Application*, 6th ed. Boston: Irwin, 1992, 144.

Salmon, Carol-Linnea. "Milking Deadly Dollars from the Third World," *Business and Society Review*, Winter, 1989.

Trevino, Linda. "Ethical Decision Making in Organizations: A Person-Situation Interactionist Model," *Academy of Management Review* 11 (July 1986).

Williams, John Alden. *Islam: The Tradition and Contemporary Orientation of Islam*. New York: George Braziller, Inc., 1961.

CHAPTER 2

The Changing Dynamics of Ethics at Work

Last summer, International Paper, headquartered in Purchase, N.Y., implemented the Compliance Line. This confidential 800-number hotline was described in a company announcement as a "simple way for employees to report activities that may involve criminal conduct or corporate policy violations." In other words, International Paper wants it's staff to snitch.

"It's a frightening concept," says a 16-year veteran of the company. "If someone doesn't like you, he can call the number. Even if there's nothing to back it up, they're still going to do some kind of investigation. It's a big brother thing. You're encouraged to report on your neighbors and friends."

"The Curse of Whistleblowing,"
The Wall Street Journal,
March 14, 1994, p. B6

In the first quarter of the twentieth century, several industries (notably railroads, banks, and meat-packing concerns) overshadowed commerce in the United States; the greatest innovations and capital, however, emanated in small businesses. The "mom and pop" shops that dominated small town America had little to worry about in terms of affirmative action, employee lawsuits, and sexual harassment. The courts, and certainly public opinion, favored the notion that "the buck stops here" whenever an entrepreneur, especially a successful one, spoke or acted.

AN ERA OF INCREASING RESPONSIBILITIES FOR EMPLOYERS

That trend disappeared with the advent of World War II. By 1944, the incredible resources necessary to exert the U.S. position of military strength in three theaters of fighting (Europe, the South Pacific, and Africa) helped Ford Motor Company, Boeing, General Electric, and hundreds of other companies all prosper. Such organizations that had previously produced civilian goods and products now found themselves earning a disproportionately high share of income from military research as well as product manufacturing.

By the end of 1945, rapid industrialization and the emergence of new technologies allowed U.S. companies to grow beyond their wildest dreams. The race to attract and retain quality employees had begun in earnest. Corporations found that offering a decent salary was simply not good enough: Now employers raced to offer retirement packages, stock options, and annual bonuses in order to remain competitive. Training opportunities, such as the GI Bill of Rights, were offered to returning veterans to enhance or build their skill development. Millions of women who produced vital goods on the assembly line during the war returned home to raise families.

By the 1950s, the United States formally recognized that the "melting pot" foundation it boasted of in literature and song was not mere fantasy: A major transformation in racial and ethnic equality was underway. Various court rulings and civil rights protests led to slow but certain gains for minorities in terms of hiring and, to a lesser degree, promotional opportunities.

With the passage of the Civil Rights Act of 1964, employers who had chosen to ignore these events were motivated to change under threat of Federal penalties. The news media played an enormously influential role in identifying abuses that had been committed against blacks, women, the disabled, and other discriminated publics.

At the same time, special interest groups launched unprecedented activism: Student protests of U.S. presence in Vietnam, race riots and protests, and events promoting environmental responsibility are just a few of many examples.

Let's fast forward two decades to the mid-1980s. By this time, more than half of all new entrants (54 percent) in the workplace were women, and their educational credentials and skills could no longer be dismissed by corporate America as merely second class. With organizations such as 9-to-5 and the National Organization of Women galvanizing women who had been historically subjected to salary and promotional discrimination as well as sexual harassment, public perceptions about access to better jobs and salaries began to change, albeit slowly. Managers were forced to ask themselves about the legal, ethical, and moral choices that were inherent in the dozens of decisions they made regarding each candidate seeking employment or upward mobility.

Whereas widespread employee litigation was virtually unheard of at the turn of the century, today our society faces a major change: Lawsuits by employees now constitute the *single largest class of suits in our civil courts*. We have gone from an era of employee subservience to one where employers must consider the actions and reactions of employees in almost every decision they make; the multitude of employee-rights statutes has mandated a major shift in how managers balance operational with human resource needs. Has the pendulum swung too far or not far enough?

CREATING AN ETHICAL ENVIRONMENT

We use three primary vehicles in the workplace to communicate our commitment toward ethics: statements and communications (written, verbal, or facial), decisions and actions (formal and informal), and the access we provide to others (access to learning by subordinates as well as access to key information by the community, courts, and special interests). These approaches to ethics are presented in Table 2-1. While many other criteria exist, these three visible vehicles shape how others perceive whether or not we are ethical in our careers.

TABLE 2-1   How We Share Our Approach to Ethics

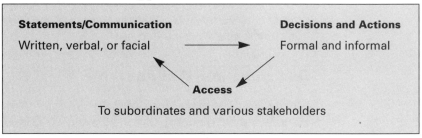

| **Statements/Communication** | | **Decisions and Actions** |
| Written, verbal, or facial | | Formal and informal |

Access

To subordinates and various stakeholders

Statements and Communication

Our statements are an explicit expression of how we view ethics. For example, managers may tell their staff members that they favor "an open work environment" but then proceed to cut off debate in staff meetings when an opinion other than their own is about to achieve momentum. Other managers legitimately support an open-door policy, where complaints and concerns can be aired without formality and, usually, without an appointment. But some managers who profess to believe in an open-door policy provide little or no meaningful feedback to an employee with a grievance.

For example, in 1993, Florida regulators accused Metropolitan Life Insurance Company, the largest seller of life insurance in the United States, of having agents in its Tampa, Florida, office substitute the word *deposit* for *premium* in several hundred sales contracts—the agents allegedly sold life insurance to registered nurses who thought they were buying retirement accounts. In 1992 alone, state regulators say that Met Life agents in the Tampa area earned $4 million in commissions in the scheme. According to *The Wall Street Journal:*

> It began by sending promotional materials to registered nurses across the country whose names came from lists filed with state licensing agencies . . . Agents in the office generally had no prior insurance experience. Their in-house training consisted of having to memorize, word-for-word, a detailed sales pitch typed on an 11-page, single spaced memo. (Steinmetz, B1)

The Met Life example is a case in the extreme. Many managers act and sound ethical because they genuinely believe that honesty and candor is the foundation for success. The ethical manager communicates to the staff that harassment will not be tolerated, that inappropriate sales tactics will lead to censure or termination, that fraud will not be tolerated—this individual can help create an ethical environment where the rules of work are grounded in morality. As you will see in the discussion that follows, managers in human resources have numerous opportunities to apply their ethical convictions when making such decisions.

Decisions and Actions

When managers make decisions, they usually take into account information at their disposal and their intuitive knowledge after looking at one or more alternatives. Many decisions in management are routine and have no apparent ethical value (such as approving a purchase order or travel request), but many others do have implications on moral reasoning.

When President Ronald Reagan fired hundreds of air traffic controllers in the first year of his administration, he reasoned that expected job actions of these federally regulated workers threatened the safety of the traveling public, the income of millions of people dependent upon the airline industry, and the overall effectiveness of public transportation.

President Reagan believed that a walk-out would virtually hold the public hostage. His decision, though a controversial one, was rooted in the "greatest good for the greatest number" principle. In the end, the federal courts agreed not only that the president could legally fire those who did not remain on the job (he did), but also that he was fundamentally correct in his assertion that certain classes of employees agree as a condition of their employment not to strike because they could cripple public services. Yet the courts were careful in their written decisions not to address whether the president should fire the controllers because they apparently did not want to pass judgment on whether it was *morally right* to fire employees; they only indicated that it was *legal.*

Although the controllers argued that they were poorly compensated, the ethical implications of their threat was tantamount to extortion: give in, or we will halt every commercial aircraft in this country. President Reagan was viewed by the public as decisive and reasonable. The controllers were viewed as bullies.

Sears, Roebuck and Company provides another case where decisions were shaped by ethics that can be best termed as mediocre by anyone's standard. In September 1992, the retailer settled claims with 42 states that it had engaged in a scheme in which it recommended tens of thousands of auto repairs that were unnecessary. Sears admitted to California officials that service center managers were told to meet sales quotas; company service advisors were actually paid according to the amount of car repair services they sold. After an embarrassing national scandal, Sears agreed to pay a $15 million fine and refund another $50 million to customers. The California Department of Consumer Affairs "said a yearlong investigation found Sears oversold auto repair work 90 percent of the time, with unneeded repairs averaging $223 per car." (Driscoll, 12E)

The decisions of most managers are far less dramatic and rarely as deceiving as those that were systematically practiced at Sears. Decisions that are more common, but which certainly have ethical and moral ingredients, include choices about hiring, firing, and promotion; the allocation of resources among staff members; pricing products or services below cost to impair or even eliminate the competition; and numerous others.

Access

Is providing or denying access to a particular employee ethical? Does the manager have the prerogative to share information with whomever he or she wishes even if other individuals do not have the opportunity to present their sides of the story for a more balanced representation of ideas? One of the most common complaints of workers is that access to their superior is selective, reserved for only a few choice favorites.

Full and complete access to every level of the organization is not only unreasonable, it is a prelude to anarchy and financial ruin. Managers are paid to manage, not hold town meetings in which every decision is scrutinized and debated. But employee complaints that meaningful access is reserved for only a few individuals or groups often holds some credibility.

For instance, union representatives often argue that senior managers will "cozy" up to shop stewards and grievance panel members in the months just prior to renegotiation of a new labor contract; access that was previously difficult to procure is now suddenly available. The message for those managers is clear: You will be perceived as a more ethical, reasonable individual if you are consistent in the manner in which you provide access to those who seek your attention. You can still cap the amount of time for dissent, you can still ignore the messages given you, and you can still make the decisions you are paid to make but realize that your credibility is enhanced when access is equal to all of those publics that command your attention.

In the next model you are reminded of the distinct relationship between human resources and ethics. Table 2-2 reminds us that the employer has the opportunity to promote ethical behavior at least

TABLE 2-2   Ethics in Human Resources

Hiring	Who am I hiring? Those who look and sound like me, or those best equipped for the position as documented by their talent, skills, and expertise?
Wage Determination	At what level will this candidate be compensated? Is my judgment based on figures from industry/trade sources, the marketplace, or other factors? Are those of different genders and race who are performing the same functions being compensated differently?
Task Responsibilities	Have I ensured that this candidate will have equal access to tasks that, if performed successfully, will make the candidate eligible for future promotional opportunities? Or is it possible that I have limited the range of this employee's tasks and projects, thus "locking in" his or her future growth?
Promotional Opportunities	When two candidates of equal talent and rank are being considered for an advancement opportunity, what criteria will I use to ensure fairness and equity? Will underrepresented groups receive additional consideration? What if the leading candidate is simply not the best person for this job?
Policies That Are Enforced	Has this organization articulated policies to equitably adjudicate any disputes or concerns involving ethical or moral questions that may emerge during the employment of the candidate?

five times during the employment of every individual, from the warehouse clerk to the chief executive officer:

Hiring. Employers use a set of judgments to weigh their decisions when hiring: Does this candidate possess the right skills? The right background? Proven expertise? These questions can be evaluated in a rather objective, quantifiable method. The less objective value judgments that are considered offer far more speculative possibilities: Is this person likely to get along with colleagues? Will he or she fit in? Is this candidate likely to be a trouble maker?

Although several major pieces of legislation such as the 1964 Civil Rights Act and Americans with Disabilities Act of 1990 can help the employer maintain an obligation to minorities, the disabled, and others, the law does not pick the right candidate for the job: people do. Our beliefs, judgments, and prejudices all factor into the equation. How ethical or moral we are in matching the best candidate with the needs of the organization is always open to scruntiny.

When President Lyndon B. Johnson signed the Civil Rights Act of 1964, the full force of federal prosecution prompted many employers to engage in fair hiring practices. Many claimed they already did hire and promote minorities, but the evidence was completely contradictory.

In business ethics, we are faced with a series of complicated issues in hiring. One of the most difficult issues is nepotism, where a manager or business owner decides to hire a family member rather than someone who is unknown and whose skills have not been tested.

The courts have been generally unwilling to intercede when an entrepreneur hires a daughter, son, or other close relative, as this is seen as the prerogative of the hiring manager. However, in larger companies where there are established human resource policies and where minimum skills for the job have been articulated in a public advertisement (for example, eight to ten years of overseas sales experience required), the employer may be forced through litigation to prove that the selection of a relative had merit and was not merely for the sake of convenience.

Wage Determination. Several national consultants such as Hay Consulting Group of Washington, DC, publish wage comparison studies that can help an employer determine if the salary and benefits it offers fall within a reasonable range given the company's geographical location, pool of available talent, and other factors.

In some organizations (such as the military, school systems, and federal, state, and local governments), salary levels are fixed by established criteria. In the private sector, however, managers have considerable room to adjust wage rates based on what they think an employee will accept or simply by what the employer thinks is reasonable. The discrepancies that emerge in this arena can be enormous, leading to jealousy, lower morale, and conflict among coworkers. For example, charges of inappropriate wage determination are likely in an organization where two individuals of equal rank, tenure, and near equal expertise have a 30 percent differential in pay.

Task Responsibilities. Although each of us brings a unique set of experiences and talents to any new position, it is an employee's job performance that ultimately determines future upward mobility. We demonstrate our capabilities by performing both those tasks assigned to us as well as expressing interest in—and successfully executing—new projects and responsibilities.

The ethical and moral dilemma that human resource professionals face in this arena is complex: Who ensures that Jane Doe receives the direction necessary to tackle these new projects? What if she is being set up for failure by a superior? What if Jane's boss decides that she would rather be a mentor to Denise, who is a personal friend? If

Jane complains that Denise is getting all of the plum assignments, who is to adjudicate these charges?

There is an embarrassing gap in the management literature regarding task responsibilities. While it is true that the vast majority of managers work hard to ensure that tasks are assigned with fairness and an eye toward nurturing new talent, this is not always the case. As human beings, we may have biases that cannot be readily identified, such as who we trust versus who we find untrustworthy. Human resource professionals have an enormous window of opportunity to guarantee that their workplace practices equity by monitoring task responsibilities.

Promotional Opportunities. Most people want to be promoted—it is intrinsic in most individuals to desire a higher salary that is commensurate with greater responsibilities. But the desire to be promoted presents myriad challenges to organizations: Who decides who will be promoted? Is this an individual or a group function? When is promotion-from-within healthy versus the employer's prerogative to infuse its team with talent and skills that can only be realized from hiring from another company?

The moral choices inherent in offering promotional opportunities are also complex. For instance, a common complaint of many workers who have failed to achieve a promotion is that the job description was written in such a way that only one candidate commanded the skills and expertise necessary to achieve. "It's a bag job" is a frequently heard comment.

Another common complaint that has found its way into litigation is that affirmative action results in the promotion of nonqualified minorities. Quotas continue to be hotly debated in both the public and private sectors, and for good reason: No one seems to win. The qualified minority employee who receives a managerial position or promotion is often subject to suspicion and "hush" talk about how he or she received the job; the person denied the opportunity may believe that the employer is two-faced, encouraging upward mobility on the one hand and "babying" protected classes on the other.

Employers often argue that it is ethical and socially responsible to employ even a quasi-qualified minority candidate so as to balance the workforce composition with a fair number of minorities. Nonminorities argue that talent, not race, should always be the most important selection criteria.

One solution to encouraging an ethical promotional environment is a group-think process where a committee of employees provides

initial screening and several recommendations to senior management. By removing the decision maker from the first layer of evalua-
tion but also presenting a series of credible alternatives, workers feel
that promotional opportunities are not locked up before they even
apply. Empowerment to such teams is ethical but not always achievable given the unwillingness of some senior managers to share
decision-making powers.

Policies That Are Enforced. Have you ever worked for a company
that had a policy about paying overtime and then found out when
you submitted a time slip that your supervisor chastised you for
"kicking the budget"? Millions have. The problem, of course, is that
many organizations have dozens of policies that are never (or selectively) enforced. An ethical and moral workplace can be achieved
when organizations articulate norms about issues such as work standards, safety, tardiness and absenteeism, overtime, harassment, theft
of company property, promotability, and related issues. These standards, if they are to hold any credibility, should be printed, periodically updated, discussed in training sessions, and consistently and
equitably enforced. Serious infractions (such as embezzlement)
should be well publicized as part of an ongoing managerial message
that emphatically states: We believe in employee *and* employer
rights.

THE RELATIONSHIP BETWEEN
ETHICS AND WORKER RIGHTS

How do ethics and morality impact individual workers every day?
The following discussion provides background on several of the most
controversial arenas involving human resource topics.

Employee Rights

An amalgam of state and federal laws specifically protect employees
from behavior that is illegal and/or inappropriate. Let's look at some
of the more important rights that are often at the heart of controversies and legal cases where ethics and morality are questioned.

Employment at Will. Although the European Community and more
than 70 other nations provide specific legal protection to workers

who are subject to wrongful termination, the United States adheres to the notion of employment at will—most individuals are hired without a stated term of employment and thus are subject to discharge without cause. The justification for employment at will is that since employees are free to leave an organization at any time, the employer should retain the right to hire, promote, censure, or terminate an employee at will.

Today, our courts are filled with cases in which employees argue that they were inappropriately fired. Some charge (and are often able to substantiate) they were fired because of their age, ethnicity, or gender, because of false accusations regarding their competency to complete tasks, or because of false allegations of illegal behavior on the job. Employers respond that laws protecting employees are so numerous that companies can barely function. Although the organizations can require drug testing, psychological profiles (sometimes) and pre-employment screening methods before hiring, once a company hires a worker, it may believe it is essentially stuck with that person, even when the person underperforms or when financial hardship on the employer requires a reduction in force.

Employment at will has some limitations: Employees cannot be terminated because of military or jury service, for instance. At least 27 states now also enact legislation that prevents an employer from dismissing a worker who is a whistle-blower—someone who has exposed organizational wrongdoing by the employer. (Whistle-blowing is discussed in Chapter 6) Some employers are seeking to strengthen their position on this issue by mandating that all new hires sign a statement affirming that they are an employee at will and that they will not pursue any remedy if they are later discharged; several state courts have discussed such clauses. This kind of pressure tactic has obvious ethical implications.

One of the primary reasons why employers feel the compulsion to act in such a manner is the cost of litigating wrongful termination suits—to defend just one of these cases now averages an astounding $80,000. In addition, employees have achieved a 70 percent success rate in California alone, where awards against former employers range from $300,000 to $500,000. (Aalberts, 338)

Some professionals such as university professors face different employment circumstances, even with at-will statutes. Generally, professors cannot be terminated unless the employer can prove professional incompetence, negligence in the execution of duties, or a compelling financial hardship that requires the elimination of an entire academic program.

Universities periodically review the performance of a professor in her or his first six years in terms of teaching, research, and service to the profession, but by granting tenure in the professor's seventh year, the university makes an institutional commitment to that professor. One of the primary reasons why professors seek such guarantees is to ensure that they will have the academic freedom to lecture and write without fear of retribution by their department colleagues or the university itself. In positions of responsibility where freedom of expression is pivotal, such as in teaching, the employer must be especially careful not to infringe on employee freedoms.

Employee Privacy. In most jurisdictions, employees have the right to inspect their personnel file at least twice a year. Doing so does not jeopardize or impair the employer's perception of the employee, at least on paper. An employee may also engage an agent to review his or her file (typically, but not always, the employee's attorney).

The ethical dimensions to employee privacy are currently being debated in the courts and in the forum of public opinion. If a company psychologist determines that employee James Smith is prone to violence (thus potentially jeopardizing colleagues), should this information be placed in his personnel file so that future managers may consider this evidence in reviewing James for promotional opportunities? If James is even suspected of having psychological problems, shouldn't that information be brought to light before an incident occurs? What is the employer's responsibility to James, his family and his coworkers? What if the psychologist is *wrong?*

One of the reasons that employee privacy is at the center of studies into business ethics is that both the employer and employee can offer reasons to support their contentions. *Fortune* created a bit of paranoia in the workplace in a major 1993 story and drew this conclusion:

> Business is increasingly vulnerable to corporate espionage. The employee who uses a cellular telephone is operating a mobile radio station that may inadvertently be broadcasting confidential information to anyone within radio-wave earshot. (Smith, 89)

Privacy regarding company secrets is one thing, but privacy regarding employee health matters and sexual preference is another. For example, although companies cannot dismiss an HIV-positive employee as long as that person is able to perform her or his job, several hundred layoffs targeting young gay men are now being heard by the courts, such as those dramatized in the motion picture *Philadelphia*.

Employers who fear that the health care costs of all their workers will skyrocket because of one or more treatment-intensive cases in its midst will sometimes try to exclude certain conditions. New York City construction worker Terrence Donaghey provides a good example. Donaghey found that the U.S. Equal Opportunity Commission was willing to join him as a plaintiff in his suit against Mason Tenders Local 23 after the union quietly eliminated reimbursement for AIDS treatments in 1992. (Smith, 91)

Employee privacy, then, has several dimensions: It includes the right to privacy in conversations (although employers may listen in if the employee is aware of a policy that allows eavesdropping to monitor employee effectiveness), privacy in not releasing the results of random drug testing (although a physician or attorney can request results on the employee's behalf), and privacy in not having to reveal whether or not an employee has ever been arrested or convicted (although failure to do so could embarrass the employee years later if an incident were to become public).

Although most people are aware that employers may not inquire about an employee's religion or marital status, less clear are strange policies that appear in dozens of corporate manuals around the country. For instance, two employees of an Albany, New York, Wal-Mart claimed in 1992 that they were dismissed "after their supervisor learned they violated a company policy that forbids married employees to date." The state attorney general agreed with the couple that Wal-Mart's policy was ridiculous and filed a suit forcing the retailer to reconsider. Wal-Mart was imposing a moral code on its employees, one that seemed particularly stringent since one of the employees was single, the other separated.

"The manager said it wasn't morally right. Who is she to make a moral judgment on me?" said Laural Allen, one of the plaintiffs. "I didn't think I was doing anything wrong." (Associated Press, 10D)

Although we can debate the appropriateness of such policies, one thing is clear: the law. Consider this list of pre-employment questions—developed with the assistance of University of Nevada, Las Vegas, professor of finance Robert Aalberts—that could be considered discriminatory under a host of federal and state laws. Attorney Aalberts says that organizations must be especially careful to instruct their hiring managers to avoid any discussion of issues in Table 2-3 during interviews, or they risk a lawsuit based on potential discrimination.

TABLE 2-3   Potential Discriminatory Issues to Avoid in Hiring

- Date of birth or graduation from high school (potential age discrimination)

- A job candidate's birth place, or that of the candidate's parents (may reveal national origin)

- Gender, marital status, number of children, religion, citizenship (all potential candidates for discrimination)

- Languages spoken by the candidate (may be evidence of nationality)

- Arrest and conviction record (may prejudice employer out of concern for future crimes)

- Physical limitations (Americans with Disabilities Act protects disabled workers)

Source: Robert Aalberts, University of Nevada at Las Vegas.

Discrimination Laws. Many large and small employers have learned a painful lesson over the past 20 years—discrimination lawsuits can be costly in terms of financial settlements and negative public relations. Dozens of corporations ranging from General Motors to Denny's Restaurants have been charged with discriminating against employees, customers, or other publics. Employment discrimination litigation increased an incredible 2,000 percent from 1970 to 1990, leading one expert to assert that "business people must make themselves aware of the antidiscrimination laws. Nondiscrimination is the law, and employees—and the plaintiffs bar—know it." (Aalberts, 1067)

For more than 20 years, U.S. society debated the ethical and moral underpinnings of a series of statutes which now mandate that we act equitably in considering candidates for hire or promotion. As shown earlier, these include the Civil Rights Act of 1964 (which prohibits discrimination based on race), Title VII (which prohibits discrimination based on gender), Pregnancy Discrimination Act of 1979 (which prohibits discrimination based on pregnancy or having given birth), and American with Disabilities Act of 1990 (which prohibits discrimination based on mental or physical impairments).

Truth in Hiring. Today, one of the most interesting ethical issues emerging in the workplace relates to the job candidate who is promised that her or his job will include one set of tasks and assignments, only to discover that the daily agenda on the job is radically different. "The theory behind these cases is that employees give up other opportunities in order to take a particular job," explains one analyst. "If they don't get the opportunities they were promised or if the firm goes out of business, the employees argue that they are entitled to damages because they could have gone to work elsewhere." (Moses, B1)

One of the nation's leading experts in this field, attorney Milton Bordwin, advises companies to avoid truth-in-hiring lawsuits by eliminating discussion of probationary periods, never indicating that the job is a permanent one, and in avoiding all references to salary or annual compensation. Bordwin argues that pre-employment letters can help both parties understand their legal and moral obligations in advance. He favors letters that say, "Your terms of employment are spelled out in this letter, and if they're not in this letter, they don't exist." (Mello, 17)

Nationwide, corporations are racing to ensure that their workforce understands conditions of employment. Serious ethical debates surface in organizations when there is misunderstanding, or no understanding, about employer expectations on a host of issues. For that reason, companies have an unprecedented opportunity when first hiring an employee to clearly and ethically outline all conditions of employment.

When employers later change the rules of employment, articulate new policies that contradict earlier ones, or respond to one incident in the company with an unfair policy that impacts many, questions of unethical management surface. Such charges undermine organizational morale and productivity and can backfire on the employer.

Competitive Concerns. A final area of examination that merits some consideration are clauses in employment contracts that are aimed at preventing a "brain drain" should a manager leave the company to start his or her own company or to work for a competitor. Although it is common for talented executives to want to tap outstanding colleagues when they leave so as to build upon successful team relationships, many employers find the practice repugnant, and some are fighting back.

For instance, Compaq Computer's chief executive officer and four of his senior executives would lose "millions in benefits and a special pension fund if they recruit just one Compaq employee when they leave the personal-computer maker," says *The Wall Street Journal.*

ETHICS BRIEF

Moonlighting or Sabotage?

This hypothetical situation is based on actual circumstances. How would you respond if you were a senior manager at Dwyer Advertising?

Mike Sullivan has worked as director of personnel for Dwyer Advertising, a full-service advertising and public relations firm, for 11 years. He reports directly to the company president and is one of the most liked and respected professionals in the organization. When Mike joined Dwyer as a sales associate, the company consisted of just seven people and had no written employee manual or even job descriptions! Now Dwyer employs over 80 persons.

Two months ago, a neighbor who owns a flourishing marketing company named Monan Marketing asked Mike if he would be interested in moonlighting on nights and weekends to develop an employee manual and training program. Mike and his wife are expecting a new baby, and the $7,000 consulting contract could not have come at a more opportune moment. Mike signed an agreement and has been working on his own time to help his neighbor.

This morning, Mike was called into the office of the president of Dwyer Advertising who learned at a chamber of commerce meeting of Mike's moonlighting. "Are you

crazy?" the president asked. "Monan Marketing is on our heels. They want to expand into advertising and public relations, and I understand you're helping them accomplish that very nicely!"

Mike is astounded. He tells his boss that he has developed nothing other than personnel policies and outlines of training courses that would help Monan Marketing, that Dwyer Advertising never told him that moonlighting was unacceptable, and that he would never do anything to undermine his years of service to the company.

"Look," Mike says. "I know what kind of work I've done for Monan, and it's so generic that anyone in human resources could have pulled off this job. I haven't given them a shred of our confidential information and wouldn't do that, ever. Every phone call and piece of work I have done for them has been on my own time. Lots of people here type reports, or build houses, or sell Avon on the side, and I don't hear you complaining about them. What's really eating at you?"

Identify the issues that favor the arguments of both the president of Dwyer Advertising and Mike Sullivan. How do you think the case is best resolved?

(Lopez, B1) Similarly, American Express often requires senior managers to sign noncompete and nonsolicitation agreements as a condition of employment, and a surprising number of smaller entrepreneurial ventures are following this model.

A more recent case involves John Sculley, who joined Spectrum International Technologies as chief executive officer in October 1993 after a celebrated tenure as chief of Apple Computer. Spectrum's stock was a healthy $11 a share when he joined the company; it plummeted to a meager $2.50 after his unexpected departure. In the three months that he was at the company, questions surfaced regarding what kind of competitive edge, if any, Spectrum enjoyed in the wireless communications market; Sculley suggested to the press that the company dazzled him with promises of new products that appeared less than promising. In any case, Sculley's departure hastened suspicion about his knowledge of the competitive position of Spectrum and whether he sold stock while still assuring reporters: "I am committed to Spectrum." That led *U.S. News & World Report* to question: "What did John Sculley know, and when did he know it?" ("John Sculley, a Man for Our Times," *U.S. News & World Report*, February 21, 1994, p. 76) The company lost more than $25 million during the last year.

Truth in Firing. A whole new series of ethical and moral quagmires emerge when an employee is fired. Here, too, the rules are cloudy, and state and federal legislation is just emerging on the issue.

In April 1993, a Texas jury awarded $15.6 million to Don Hagler, a 41-year (yes, 41-year!) employee of Procter & Gamble who was fired for having stolen a telephone worth $35. Hagler contended that the phone was his and that P&G embarrassed him by posting notices on 11 bulletin boards that read, in part:

> It has been determined that the telephone in question is Procter & Gamble's property and that Don had therefore violated Work Rule #12 . . . concerning theft of company property. (Stern, B1)

Hagler contended that a flood had damaged his office phone and that he purchased the new phone with personal funds and never sought reimbursement. A coworker who went with Hagler to a local mall to purchase the phone corroborated his story, and the jury decided in Hagler's favor. Hagler's argument was that P&G had defamed his character by posting the notice, costing him his reputation, and crippling future employment opportunities. He testified that after his firing he was turned down more than 100 times when seeking employment elsewhere "when prospective employers learned why he had been fired by P&G." (Stern, B7)

What would lead P&G executives to act in such a manner? What kind of ethical and moral message do they send with such activities? Finally, why must it take such a massive lawsuit for a change in corporate culture to occur?

E THICS B RIEF

How Can We Audit the Behavior of Others?

Between God and lawyers there is a new caste of secular priests—known as ethicists—who are helping Corporate America strive toward a higher moral plane. The goal: to get business leaders and their employees to operate on a level of conduct so ethical that they avoid ensnaring their companies in legal trouble and, possibly, experience greater spiritual satisfaction in their work.

"The crass truth about it is the more ethical you are, the better it is for business," says Harvey L. Pitt, a senior partner at New York's Fried, Frank, Harris, Shriver & Jacobson, who is a past Securities and Exchange Commission general counsel and the former attorney for the infamous insider trader Ivan Boesky.

These business ethicists are sometimes trained as lawyers, sometimes as philosophers, sometimes even as theologians. Sometimes they begin as management consultants or as businesspeople, occasionally in human resources departments. Increasingly, though, they are an identifiable group of outside consultants and in-house officers who offer an evolving set of services to U.S. corporations.

Right now, for example, outside consultants such as Gary Edwards of Ethics Resource Inc. and Michael Josephson of the Josephson Institute—two of the most prominent, who also happen to be lawyers—are performing "ethics audits," helping formulate corporate credos, running ethics training sessions and establishing ethics plans and committees to promote ethical thinking and conduct company-wide. They also set up confidential hotlines for whistleblowers.

Business is booming—although many say that the real takeoff is yet to occur. "Our market has just exploded," says Timothy C.

Mazur, a veteran consultant who started 10 years ago by working for Mr. Edwards after studying business ethics and corporate responsibility for an MBA from George Washington University. "All of a sudden huge companies need ethics training fast," says Mr. Mazur, pointing to Union Pacific Railroad (which launched its program in 1993); Dunn and Bradstreet; (whose program began about 1992); Donnelly Corporation (1992); NYNEX (1991); Levi Strauss (1991); and the redesigned ethics programs at Honeywell (1992), Northrop (1991), Hughes Aircraft (1992), and Harris Corp (1991).

Increasing Numbers

As a result, the number of in-house ethics officers is catapulting, and a substantial percentage of them are the companies' general counsel. This anointing of attorneys as the company priests is occurring despite a fierce debate about whether lawyers make good ethics officers, or can even properly grasp the difference between ethics and compliance. Ethics, explains Mr. Josephson, asks the hard question "What does virtue require of us?" while compliance asks instead "Will we get sued?" Those who call themselves ethicists rather than compliance experts argue that corporate needs go far beyond mere legalities.

"The line between unlawful and unethical is constantly changing, so you can't say that what we think is lawful today won't be the subject of a prosecution the following year," explains Jeffrey M. Kaplan of New York's Arkin Schaffer & Supino and one of the co-editors and authors of a comprehensive book on the subject, *Compliance Programs and the Corporate Sentencing Guidelines: Preventing Criminal and Civil*

Liability. (Clark Boardman Callaghan, New York, 1993).

Since 1990, says Mr. Mazur, there have been about 100 substantial contracts for outside ethics consultants each year; with about five major companies spending more than $1 million, about 25 to 30 spending more than $50,000, and all of them affecting thousands of employees.

The two-year-old Ethics Officers Association, headquartered in the Center for Business Ethics at Bentley College in Waltham, Mass., did a survey of Fortune 1000 companies and found that nearly half of its 205 respondents had ethics officers as of 1992. Nearly all of these officers had been appointed in the previous five years. More than one-third were the company's general counsel at the vice-presidential level or higher.

Whistleblower hotlines now ring on the desks of the likes of attorney George E. Lane, director of business conduct at the Harris Corp., a defense contractor.

Mr. Lane is responsible for company-wide ethics programming and says: "We tell people that good ethical decisions are good business decisions." He also acts as the liaison between Harris' management ethics committee and the 30 ethics officers the company now has based in comptroller or human resource departments throughout its division.

Those who are selected to be ethics officers at Harris usually are not in the legal departments because, Mr. Lane says in voicing a widespread concern, "We don't want people to feel that the person they go to is going to be the one who comes around to do an investigation" to sniff out wrong-doing.

Joseph E. Murphy, senior attorney at Bell Atlantic Network Services in Philadelphia, notes, however, some companies choose to make their lawyers ethics officers because the attorney-client privilege might later prove a shield in litigation.

Sentencing Guidelines

The biggest stream feeding into the business ethics movement flows from the federal corporate sentencing guidelines. But experts also identify as tributaries constituency statutes that broaden corporate responsibility, the downsizing of corporations and, some also say, a general, emotional need for more revival.

The federal sentencing guidelines, which went into effect Nov. 1, 1991, outlined seven elements for company programs. (For example: The company should have standards and procedures that are reasonably capable of reducing the risks of crime; and high-level personnel should be assigned responsibility.) In response, many lawyers are telling corporate clients that ethics programs can be new barriers to serious legal trouble: They'll help stop some employees from engaging in illegal conduct, catch others before too much damage is done and then possibly help convince prosecutors to enter agreements rather than file charges.

Among the most frequently noted signs that prosecutors really might go easier on companies that demonstrate a desire to reform are statements in 1992 by Otto G. Obermaier, then-U.S. attorney for the Southern Districts of New York. His decision not to seek criminal penalties from Salomon Inc. for the 1991 Treasury auction scandal, he said, was partially based on Salomon's having taken steps to prevent future misconduct.

But should a company with a strong ethics program in place actually be convicted for an employee's wrongdoing, the sentencing guidelines suggest that the heavy fines it could be exposed to might be substantially reduced.

The case that definitively shows all companies the legal necessity for comprehensive ethics programs has yet to occur, says Mr. Kaplan, and he predicts that the government eventually will come down hard on some company that blithely did without a viable ethics program. When that happens, says Mr. Mazur, the rest of corporate America will wake up, and he and his fellow ethics consultants "will be driving BMW's instead of Honda Preludes."

Corporate Responsibility

While federal sentencing guidelines prod companies toward the ethical high ground, constituency statutes are helping to clear the path. Some 39 states now have statutes that permit boards of directors to make decisions based on criteria other than maximizing shareholder returns. Now, with these statutes legitimate decisions also can take into account the needs of such "stakeholders" in the company as employees, the surrounding community, vendors and customers.

The challenge, according to Marjorie H. Kelly, founder and publisher of the Minneapolis, Minn.-based *Business Ethics* magazine, is "How do you balance those different interests?" And the greater ethical question, she says, has become, "Can I gear my whole company from its core vision outward toward having a positive impact on society?"

The drive toward ethics also is being fueled by the downsizing of U.S. corporations, according to Frank J. Navran, one of the best-known ethics consultants, who operates Navran & Associates in Atlanta and whose background is in business and management consultancy.

Companies that have streamlined management are finding that decisions are made lower in the organization, so it is imperative that every employee understand the values upon which the corporations want decisions based. Rather than say, "Follow the rules and do as you are told," says Mr. Navran, company leaders are realizing they must share rationales with employees, saying: "Here is the spirit and here is the intent."

But it's not enough for a corporate code simply to say, "Thou shalt not accept a gift," notes Thomas Donaldson, a professor at Georgetown School of Business Administration, an ethics consultant who holds a doctorate in philosophy. "The Japanese have not relied upon legalistic codes of conduct as Americans, who often suffocate with thousands of rules and regulations, often do."

Rather, Japanese corporations—and such companies as AT&T—make "broad declarations of values that try to bake into the heart of the corporation certain attitudes that are uplifting and motivational." AT&T's credo tells its employees that it believes in the individual and integrity, dedication to the customer, innovation and teamwork, notes Professor Donaldson.

Ethics Audits

Companies that want to translate their corporate morality into concrete action can hire outside consultants to perform ethics audits, for a charge that can range from $25,000 to $150,000, Mr. Josephson says. There also are a variety of ethics training programs. Ethics consultants, says W. Michael Hoffman, one of the best known, generally charge the same as all other consultants, which is to say about $1,500 per day to three times that.

Mr. Edwards of Ethics Resource Center says most employees who did wrong knew they were violating their company's stated policy, knew they were violating the law, yet believed they were benefiting the company. They substitute inferior materials, fail to inspect a product they ship, drag the accounting of sales into the next tax year and "revisit" accounting records.

"Ordinary people under pressure can delude themselves that it is all right to do improper things as long as they are doing it for the company and not lining their own pockets," says Mr. Edwards. And no amount of telling them the rules and the law, that is to say strict compliance training, "is going to have an impact on that kind of behavior, except at the margins." Instead, what's needed, says Mr. Edwards, is a clear, undiluted message about the corporation's values that is supported by both incentives and disciplinary structure.

An ethics audit, according to Mr. Edwards, involves a "risk assessment." Through interviews with focus groups and then a questionnaire, ethicists collect data about employees' knowledge of company standards of conduct, business law, attitudes toward ethics, ability to recognize ethical issues wrapped in fact patterns peculiar to the company and experience within the organization. The object is to localize potential problems and address them head on.

Ethics training is the next step, and all the experts stress it must consist of more than a lawyer getting in front of a group of employees and boring them with a lecture on the intricacies of regulations regarding, for example, the Foreign Corrupt Practices Act.

Not all motivation behind the business ethics movement is negative and involuntary. There also is, says Mr. Kaplan, echoing many observers of the phenomenon, "a yearning among businesspeople and among Americans generally, for a moral renewal."

The public now demands and employees also expect such moves as McDonald's drastically cutting its solid waste and the Monsanto Pledge to reduce the company's air pollution.

Says Mr. Pitt, "This is a fascinating area because the standards are changing. The things we consider today to be ethically inappropriate behavior, 30 and 40 years ago, may have been considered more defensible."

Mr. Hoffman, who also is director of Bentley College's business ethics center and executive director of the Ethics Officers Association, says, "A collective philosophy is being developed that does not just take into account individual integrity, but very much focuses on institutional integrity." Corporate ethics is no less, says Mr. Hoffman, than the revolution of the '90s.

Source: "Ethicists: Gurus of the 90s," reprinted with the permission of *The National Law Journal*, January 24, 1994, p. 1.

CONCLUSION

If we are to understand the major principles of workplace ethics, we need to recognize that employer-employee relations is at the core of our analysis. Rules, policies, and training programs are important in educating both management and the rank and file as to the expectations of the public and of company stakeholders. Common sense also plays an important role. But as you will see in the chapters that follow, there is considerable disagreement over what constitutes ethically and morally responsible activities in the workplace, and the absence of consensus on these points is leading to chaos and embarrassment for many respectable organizations.

CASE STUDY:
ETHICS, PROFIT . . . AND BEANS?

Marketing Specialists, Inc. (MSI), of Memphis, Tennessee, is a food processor whose line of organically grown products has increased from $3.4 million in annual sales in 1989 to a projected $12 million by the end of this year. Among the products produced by MSI are Harry's All-Natural Granola Surprise Bars and Grandma's All-Natural Apple Dumpling Mix. The company has 136 nonunion employees, including five executives and a dozen operational managers and division heads.

Late last year, MSI approached *The Organic Journal*, a yearly magazine that prints calendars, old-time stories, and weather forecasts, after reading about a special 80-year old recipe for a 20-Bean Soup Mix that has received wide acclaim from *The Journal* readers for many decades. The recipe is the most famous item ever printed in the long history of the publication but is difficult for consumers to produce at home because of the more than 20 *different* beans and spices required. MSI president Alan Gold flew to Hampton, New Hampshire, to meet Mary McGuire, president of *The Journal*, about the possibility of having his company add the soup mix to MSI's product line, using *The Journal's* famous logo and name on the product.

The meeting went exceptionally well: MSI would license the recipe and logo from *The Journal*, and the publication would receive a royalty of 3 percent of net sales in return. McGuire felt that the product, if successful, could generate substantial, supplementary income for her company. *The Journal* sells more than 2 million copies worldwide each year and is mostly read by environmentally conscious readers who prefer organically grown as opposed to processed foods.

Let's fast forward the case. The soup mix product has been on the market for just about one year, and MSI's sales projections were actually modest: Revenue to *The Journal* exceeded $465,000 in the first year of actual sales, and the lucrative winter season (best for soup sales) is still approaching! In today's mail, McGuire received an envelope marked "Personal and Confidential," and she was startled at its contents:

This case is completely fictional. Any relationship to persons, companies, or situations is contrived and unintentional.

Southern Fundamentalist Fellowship

"We Walk with Him" • 3847 Messenger Way • Atlanta, Georgia 98876

October 31, 199X

Ms. Mary McGuire
The Organic Journal
Hampton, New Hampshire

Dear Ms. McGuire:

It has come to the attention of our Church that *The Farmer Journal*'s 20-Bean Soup Mix is not actually produced by you, but only licensed by your company. That is the genesis for this letter. We have been unable to elicit a response from MSI of Memphis, Tennessee, and seek your immediate response and assistance.

After two-years of research by our Fellowship, we have developed a list of products produced by religious cults and licensed under well-known, well-respected brand names. Such is the case with 20-Bean Soup Mix. MSI is a company owned by members of Tomorrow Now, a cult of religious fanatics who seek to undermine high school and college students and recruit them to work in "God-inspired" manufacturing facilities. Their leader is the Reverend Alan Gold, who claims in the cult newsletter that "more than 60 million Americans have become acquainted with our products." His goal is to reach Americans through food products and to eventually use income from such ventures to finance a worldwide organization that will use profits to create a society that worships him and his cult. This man is dangerous.

As you may know, Southern Fundamentalist Fellowship is one of the largest organizations in the nation with more than one million members. One of our goals is to identify false prophets and slick businesspeople such as Mr. Gold. We are puzzled, amazed, and angry that a distinguished publication such as *The Organic Journal* would engage in a business relationship (shall we call it a conspiracy?) with this group.

We request the following:
a) A full and complete written letter detailing your relationship with MSI and your intentions now that this information is known to you, to be received by us no later than November 4. Nonresponsiveness will result in a national alert to our members and a letter to all of your advertisers.
b) A meeting to be held within two weeks at which time we will want a complete explanation as to the facts surrounding this case. We will also ask your company to join us in destroying MSI, which seeks to kill our children's minds through clever business relationships.
c) That you publicly denounce MSI at a news conference.
We await your reply.

Sincerely,

Reverend Ken McMaster

Reverend Ken McMaster

Assume that you are McGuire. Keep in mind the variety of considerations inherent in this crisis, for *The Organic Journal,* for MSI, for the two religious groups involved, and for consumers of both *The Organic Journal* and the soup mix. On paper, develop a decision tree that will help you decide how to best solve this case in which ethics, profit, religion, and public relations play a prominent role.

Remember that in designing your decision tree that your audience includes, but is not limited to the following:

- Consumers of both *The Organic Journal* and bean mix
- Alan Gold of MSI
- Rev. Ken McMaster of Southern Fellowship
- The sales and marketing staff of MSI
- The sales and marketing staff of *The Journal*
- The Associated Press Reporter (who was anonymously sent a copy of the letter from Fellowship to *The Journal*)
- The public relations staff at Kellogg's, the biggest advertiser in *The Journal* (who was also anonymously sent a copy of the Fellowship letter. Kellogg's deadline for advertising copy in the next issue of *The Journal* is in two weeks)

REFERENCES FOR CHAPTER 2

Aalberts, Robert, et al. *Law and Business.* New York: McGraw-Hill, 1994.

Associated Press, "N.Y. Sues Wal-Mart Over Dating Policy," *Las Vegas Review Journal,* September 9, 1993, 10D.

Driscoll, Paul A. "Sears to Settle Auto-Repair Charges." *Las Vegas Review Journal,* September 3, 1992, 12E.

Knight-Ridder Newspapers. "Employers Use Misdeeds to Fight Discrimination Suits." *Las Vegas Review Journal,* May 14, 1993.

Lopez, Julie Amparano. "Firms Use Contracts and Cash to Prevent Talent Raids by Departing Executives." *The Wall Street Journal,* July 9, 1993.

Mello, John P. "Beware Broken Hiring Promises." *CFO Magazine,* September 1993.

Moses, Jonathan. "Employers Face New Liability: Truth in Hiring." *The Wall Street Journal,* July 9, 1993.

Smith, Lee. "What the Boss Knows about You." *Fortune*, August 9, 1993.

Steinmetz, Greg. "Former Agents Draw a Picture of Met Life's Sales Practices." *The Wall Street Journal*, October 8, 1993.

Stern, Gabriella. "Companies Discover That Some Firings Backfire into Costly Defamation Suits." *The Wall Street Journal*, May 5, 1993.

CHAPTER 3

Do Corporations Institutionalize Dishonesty?

Amitai Etzioni, professor of sociology at George Washington University, recently concluded that in the last ten years, roughly two-thirds of America's 500 largest corporations have been involved, in varying degrees, in some form of illegal behavior.

Saul Gellerman,
Why 'Good' Managers Make Bad Ethical Choices,
p. 85

Nine Texas A&M University employees were charged last week with misdemeanors. Five were indicted by a grand jury. The others were charged by a district attorney.

Robert Smith, former vice-president for finance and administration, was accused of soliciting free trips to New York for his wife from a bookstore chain. The chain later won a $23 million contract with the university.

Wally Groff, director of athletics, was among those accused of records tampering. He said he had not broken any laws. The others accused of records tampering refused to comment. They are the vice-president for student affairs, the associate athletic director, the chemistry department's business manager, an assistant to the president, a business administrator and two senior professors.

Chronicle of Higher Education,
July 6, 1994, p. A4

In Chapter 1, you read about the basic framework for ethics in business. You were exposed to a theoretical foundation for this inquiry along with several examples in which faulty decisions by senior managers led to organizational embarrassment. In Chapter 2 you read about how employers and employees respond to ethical dilemmas with variations of success.

In this chapter, we will look deeper at the looming enemy within corporations, namely dishonesty. Along the way, we will continue to explore the fundamental causes of dishonesty as well as actual examples that underscore its increasing presence in our society. By the end of this chapter, you should have a clearer vision of the problem and the ways that some organizations are responding to this menace.

DOES HONESTY PAY?

In 1990, the *Harvard Business Review* published an article on business ethics with the compelling title "Why Be Honest If Honesty Doesn't Pay?" After an extensive set of interviews with senior executives in several industries, the two authors drew this conclusion:

> To our surprise, our pet theories failed to stand up. Treachery, we found, can pay. There is no compelling economic reason to tell the truth or keep one's word—punishment for the treacherous in the real word is neither swift nor sure. Honesty is, in fact, primarily a moral choice. Businesspeople do tell themselves that, in the long run, they will do well by doing good. But there is little factual or logical basis for this conviction. Without values, without a basic preference for right over wrong, trust based on such self-delusion would crumble in the face of temptation. (Bhide and Stevenson, 122)

What an illuminating moment when two professors at Harvard Business School conclude what many of us have known for years— treachery *does* pay!

Of course, Harvard Business School itself is not immune to criticism. In 1979 one of its own business professors was criticized by *The Wall Street Journal* for reportedly training students to intentionally misrepresent their positions in business negotiations. One analysis concluded that in the Harvard course, "students found that hiding certain facts, bluffing and even outright lying got them a better deal and, in part, a better grade. The course was designed to teach budding businessmen to negotiate in the 'real world' in which 'lying'—or 'strategic misrepresentation'—is resorted to in some cases." (Clinard and Yeager, 513). The fact is, of course, that 'strategic misrepresentation' can sometimes pay tangible dividends.

For many years, real estate brokers routinely emphasized the positive aspects of a particular property while failing to mention known or suspected flaws. Today many states require that both the broker and homeowner complete a disclosure statement that identifies any known or suspected flaws in the property such a leaky roof, known evidence of asbestos or radon, or similar problem. Yet it took scores of prominent lawsuits against shady salespeople and homeowners for the real estate industry to support such measures, which are still often voluntary.

Think about the reported dishonesty that was widespread in residential home sales just 20 years ago. In the aftermath of thousands of reports of questionable deals about poor construction abounding in the 1970s, a new industry sprouted. As a result, buyers carefully listened to the presentations of sellers and agents, but they protected themselves by engaging independent home inspectors to police the validity of the assurances they had received.

Sociologists, business analysts, and criminologists have concluded in a number of independent studies over the past five decades that the genesis of dishonesty is the organization itself, not individual employees. Indeed, it can be argued that we often learn about dishonesty, its incredibly complex design and execution, by colleagues and by on-the-job exposure on how to bend the rules effectively to enhance our careers. We learn from the trainer who initially informs us of the "unwritten rules" in our department, and from the boss who instructs us on how to "undermine" the competition in sales presentations, and so forth.

German sociologist Max Weber argued that in order to be successful, organizations must institutionalize a hierarchy that emphasizes rules and procedures over individual member relationships. He favored a bureaucratic management style where people knew exactly what was expected of them and to whom they reported so that they could satisfy organizational needs. This seems quite reasonable.

Another of Weber's arguments, which also has some merit, is that bureaucracy exists in order to make individuals *dispensable*. Indeed, what has developed in many organizations is that corporate culture, once celebrated as a uniform set of standards and expectations centered around quality and excellence, could actually backfire if it dilutes individual creativity and the open scrutiny of goals.

A Case in Point: Price Fixing

Over the past 30 years, in companies from Lockheed to General Electric, government prosecutions have focused on the question of organizational versus individual culpability in illegal activity. Of course, there is no black and white in this examination, but rather a mass of gray; the employer certainly has a role in institutionalizing dishonesty, but it is often an obscure one. Individual managers tend to learn more about "the rules behind the rules" from daily interaction with their colleagues.

In 1966, long before the term *corporate culture* entered our popular vocabulary, Cook completed an exhaustive study of price fixing in the electrical industry and formed this conclusion:

> They were men who surrendered their own individualities to the corporate gods they served. Though they knew that their acts were illegal, not to say unethical, though the shady maneuvering at times affronted their sense of decency, not one found it possible to pronounce an unequivocal 'no.' (Cook, 67)

Ten years later we learned that such abuse was widespread. In 1976, 23 carton manufacturers and their executives, including International Paper Company and Weyerhaeuser, were indicted for price fixing under the Sherman Antitrust Act. These companies were charged with conspiracy by agreeing not to submit a competitive bid or to supply no bid at all and agreeing to fixed prices to discourage competition. In presenting its case, the government argued:

> Price fixing was their way of doing business. The participants demonstrated a knowing, blatant disregard for antitrust laws. One grand jury witness testified that during a six-year period he personally engaged in thousands of price-fixing transactions with competitors that were illegal. The thousands upon thousands of exchanges of prices with competitors, the dozens upon dozens of meetings with competitors were done with a single purpose and design– to eliminate price competition in this industry. (*United States* v. *Alton Box Board Company*, Criminal Action No. 76 CR 199 [May 7, 1976], 11).

All but one of these corporate executives charged with price fixing pled guilty. Just read the testimony of one of the accused who was being questioned by federal authorities:

> **Q.** Mr. DeFazia, how were you informed that discussing prices was part of your job?

A. *I don't think I was ever really told it was part of my job. I think it was just something I sort of worked right into. That was Mr. Cox's responsibility back in those years. I was young. I was still a green kid, I just picked it right up from working along with him.*

Q. Mr. Cox provided guidance to you? Kind of discussed?

A. *No. We worked in the same office. I guess you just pick it up. I don't know how you would want to say it, just like learning your ABC's, you hear it repeated so often that it's just part of your daily activity.* (Clinard and Yeager, 511)

In many organizations where either price fixing or another type of criminal behavior has been exposed, prosecutors have success-fully painted a picture in which the enemy in the workplace is not always the individual employee, but, at least in part, the process of socialization in which employees learn about the process of work by observation and interaction with others. For instance, Kidder Peabody admitted in 1994 that at least seven managers were involved in a scheme in which it reported $350 million in fictititous profits. Although the company called the incident "reprehensible" most observers argued that the company was no innocent bystander. *The Economist* (April 23, 1994, p. 75) said it best: "At least part of the blame for the fiasco may lie with Kidder's own corporate culture. At an internal Kidder conference held in Florida, Mr. Jett [the trader who allegedly organized the scheme] told 130 of the firm's executives: "You do anything to win. You make money at all costs.'"

How do we learn about these rules, both written and unwritten? What happens when the company's board of directors is aware of dishonesty at lower levels but instead of taking corrective action chooses to ignore warning signs of trouble? Is loyalty so blind that managers select the most expedient route to success, even if that means that they must engage in illegal activity?

Manville Corporation and Deception

Managing is not easy. Indeed, the pressures of the workplace—to attract new customers, reduce costs, maximize profit, and so on—are enormous. Often, the responsibility for executing difficult decisions rests on the shoulders of junior-level managers with little or no expo-sure to the formal consequences of their actions.

Yes, these employees must understand the basic principles of business law and the fundamental philosophy of right and wrong to succeed. However, it may also be true, as has been suggested, that some organizations take advantage of the naiveté of new hires in indoctrinating them to questionable business practices.

For instance, Manville Corporation successfully sold asbestos and related insulation products for several decades. For nearly 35 years, the company knew that inhaling its product could cause asbestosis, a disease that cripples lungs and can cause mesothelioma. Yet Manville systematically concealed pertinent information from its employees and continually denied claims from consumers, employees, and family members that a link existed between the product and disease. A startling disclosure by one of Manville's lawyers came when he was asked under oath, "Do you mean to tell me you would let them work until they dropped dead?" His reply was "Yes, we save a lot of money that way." (Gellerman, 85)

Just what is going on in our society, and where is this madness coming from? In his analysis of the Manville case, Saul Gellerman says that "the managers at Manville may have believed that they were acting in the company's best interests, or that what they were doing would never be found out, or even that it wasn't really wrong. In the end, these were only rationalizations for conduct that brought the company down." (Gellerman, 86)

Once the largest manufacturer of asbestos in the world, Manville appropriately paid the price for dishonesty: The company was in bankruptcy from 1982 to 1988 because of nearly 20,000 lawsuits from former employees and their families that sought over $2 billion in claims. Now based in Denver, the Manville Corporation is slowly seeking to rebuild itself by now selling paperboard and building products.

Manville is hardly alone. Hitachi was prosecuted in the mid-1980s for stealing trade secrets from IBM. Senior managers at Beach-Nut were prosecuted for fraudulent marketing of mostly sweetened water that they advertised as fruit juice, and several of those executives were appropriately sentenced to jail sentences. Two executives of A.H. Robins were given prison sentences for their role in covering up abundant evidence that the Dalkon Shield caused cancer in women using the intrauterine device. Despite these and many other misdeeds, managers have rarely independently stepped forward to publicly claim responsibility for serious misdeeds in their organizations. Employers often insist that it is the individual managers whose judgment is faulty; individual managers claim that they were *forced* to commit illegal activity because either the pressure or motivation was enormous.

It appears that most companies accused of ethical misconduct fail because the enemy within—dishonesty—transcends both the employer and the individual. Each requires the other in order to flourish, and the guardrails to ensure that the other is behaving properly tend to be strong at some companies, bent and frayed at others, and completely nonexistent at still others.

SELECTIVE INFORMATION

Who is at fault in these cases? Are corporations nothing more than deceptive entities that intentionally scheme and lie so as to injure their customers and prostitute their employees? Hardly. Most corporations want to do the right thing. When a mistake occurs, the vast majority will acknowledge it and set the record straight before such activity leads to disarray.

So what about the employees? Are they merely automatons who follow instructions from leaders and are thus innocent pawns in the game of profit, or are they the actual architects of dishonesty? Again, although it may be impossible to find an individual who has not lied, stolen, or cheated at some point in their life, the vast majority of managers are generally honest. They earn their salary not through deception, but rather by diligently completing their duties in a creative, effective, and efficient manner.

Despite widespread honesty, however, serious lapses seem to be occurring with increasing, damaging speed. In this regard, the responsibility for dishonesty must be shared between the employer and the employees. The responsibility for *preventing* dishonesty must be shared, and the responsibility for taking *corrective action* whenever dishonesty is suspected or discovered must be shared.

At the very core of dishonesty is the question of information. In the famous testimony of John Dean, President Nixon's chief legal counsel, during the Watergate hearings in 1974, one fundamental question troubled the otherwise composed attorney. When asked, "What did the president know, and when did he know it?" Dean's response was that the president possessed early knowledge of the Watergate break in. That information effectively ended any question in the public's mind about the president's involvement in conspiracy and a cover-up of the truth.

In order to examine the genesis of dishonesty, let's look at the process of selective information to determine how this factor can contribute to a crisis of confidence in organizations. Sometimes the enormity of crime is so great, so incredibly complex, that it is almost impossible to ascertain how information about dishonesty is eventually conveyed to the rank and file. In other cases, we can identify the process through a virtual audit trail of how information is conveyed.

Selective information has another dimension: American Airlines is pursuing litigation against rival Northwest Airlines, alleging that several former American employess who went to work for Northwest took more with them than just the best wishes of colleagues. The Wall Street Journal reports: "American charges that within 20 months, Northwest hired 17 American managers and technical experts, all from American's finance and fare-setting departments . . . American says Northwest got a slew of other confidential documents that the employees brought with them. Northwest's aim, American alleges, was to steal American's computerized planning systems, including fare-setting techniques called a 'yield management system' . . . Amid today's fare wars, analysts say, such systems make the difference between millions of dollars of profits or losses." (July 7, 1994, 1) Better yet, Northwest lured the managers with impressive salaries. A good example: Ben Baldanza, a manager in American's yield department who made $60,000 until he jumped to Northwest starting at $115,000 a year. Was he hired for his knowledge of the industry, or his knowledge of American?

Information Sources of Right and Wrong

We learn about managing from a variety of sources, as indicated in the Exhibit 3-1. These sources are both formal and informal.
From these sources, we learn much about the corporate culture of the organization for whom we work. Ultimately, a series of attributes can help us judge whether or not some of these sources have more validity than others. These attributes include the following:

- *The real and perceived power of the message source.* Does the sender have a position of authority in the organization? Can they reward or punish me?

- *The clarity and personal appeal of the message.* Do I understand what is expected of me? Is my role clear, or is this just another one of the hundreds of memos or meeting agenda items that I will receive to this year?

- *The involvement of my immediate work group.* Will this issue be discussed within my immediate department in the near future? If the burden is on me to listen and interact with comments and recommendations, my interest is likely to be higher.

EXHIBIT 3-1   Information Sources in the Workplace

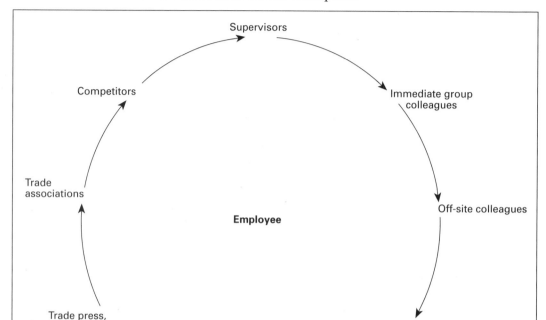

ORIENTATION . . . AND THEN SOME

Most employees tend to proceed through a three-step process of learning about the organization where are employed. Let's call these the *formal, informal* and the *situational* stages of our orientation to business ethics (see Exhibit 3-2).

Formal Orientation

Our initial, *formal* orientation as a new hire in an organization usually occurs within the first few weeks and is considered a rather mundane exercise grounded in paperwork. We are told about direct deposit,

EXHIBIT 3-2   The Three Phases of Orientation

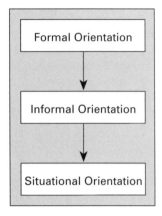

the availability of retirement benefits and stock options, and hopefully, codes of conduct regarding conflict of interest and the payment of bribes. The typical objective of a formal orientation is to convey information to new hires and to do so in no more than a few hours.

Informal Orientation

The *informal* orientation process tends to be far more provocative: We intently listen to colleagues about formal and informal networks, decide who to lunch with so as to access information pertinent to our careers, and observe how colleagues interact at staff meetings and presentations. We are looking for signals about acceptable and unacceptable behavior, about standards at our workplace or the absence of them.

During informal orientation, we gather information, however subconsciously, about how our colleagues address issues as those listed here:

- Ethnic humor
- Sexual harassment
- Bribes
- Forging signatures
- Spreading rumors
- "Problem" workers
- Drinking on/off the job
- Religious prejudices
- Circumventing authority

The informal orientation process can take weeks, months, or even years. It is a process of fact finding that is largely based on observation and interpretation. It is a journey about process, not facts. It is an inquisition that is selective, not objective. The motivation is often

ETHICS BRIEF

Soaking the Poor . . . Or Serving Them?

How we learn about corporate culture can be enlightening in more ways than one, and sometimes the temptation to take advantage of customer needs can be overwhelming. For example, a London-based conglomerate named Thorn EMI PLC, is known as a giant in the music industry. But its most profitable enterprise is Rent-A-Center, a subsidiary that controls 25 percent of the $2.8 billion center U.S. market where consumers rent everything from VCRs to refrigerators to diamond rings. In a stinging article called "How Thorn EMI Profits by Renting to the Poor," *The Wall Street Journal* reported that with high sales targets, Rent-A-Center salespeople routinely encourage unsophisticated customers to rent more products than they can afford. Top salespeople earn automobiles and sizable cash bonuses.

"Customers who manage to make every installment," *The Journal* reported, "may end up paying several times the item's retail value—at an effective annual interest rate, if the transaction is viewed as a credit sale, that can top 200%." As an example, a Sanyo VCR that would cost $289.98 generates $1003.56 over 18 months of rental, "for an effective annual interest rate of a breathtaking 231%." Former employees report that when repossessions are necessary, the company would on occasion "bring along members of a feared motorcycle gang or vandalize customers' homes, extract sexual favors from strapped customers and even, in one instance, force a late payer to do involuntary labor."

Rent-A-Center pursues hard-core sales practices. Door-to-door sales in low-income areas are strategically timed. Gerald Defiore, fired as a Rent-A-Center manager in Spartanburg, South Carolina, said, "You would brochure the projects one week before the welfare checks came out so you already had the seed planted in their mind. . . . Then the day the checks came out, you'd go back and knock on doors and fill out the forms there. Corporate was in on it, the stores were in on it. These people didn't stand a chance."

If you were hired by Rent-A-Center as a strategic consultant in the aftermath of this investigation, what would you recommend in terms of ethical and organizational changes?

Source: "How Thorn EMI Profits by Renting to the Poor," *The Wall Street Journal*, September 22, 1993, p. 1.

financial or status oriented. We have a natural desire to want to move ahead; to accomplish this, we need information and access to knowledgeable people. The kind of information we need is simply not printed in corporate brochures.

Nothing is inherently wrong with the process of informal orientation. It is human nature to want to know about the limits of acceptable and unacceptable behavior, and the single best source to learn about these limits is usually from those working in our department or division.

Consider this simple example. Over lunch with two other colleagues in a similar position, you learn that they typically "low ball" a potential client so as to encourage the client to sign a contract for a vending machine. They then describe how, after a client buys the machine, they wait one month and announce that the price of the brand name sodas required for the machine will cost substantially more than they originally quoted their new client.

"Do you think that's fair?" you ask.

"Are you serious? Fair! That's the only way you survive in this market," they tell you. And that's just about all you *need* to know. The rules seem pretty well established.

Consider a second example, in which a junior professor is learning about academic standards and dishonesty. A senior, tenured professor asks his junior colleague to help him out by coteaching a course for an entire semester because the senior professor is busy consulting for a client.

"Look, if you can help me with this, I'll list you as co-author on an article I have coming out in the *American Business Journal*." Since published articles are important to the junior colleague's career, and because the request comes from a superior who will later vote on his tenure, the request must be seriously considered.

The vending machine salesperson may choose not to pursue the bait-and-switch tactics used by colleagues and will hopefully succeed because he or she is inherently honest. In rejecting this approach, however, the salesperson runs the risk of alienating colleagues. His or her interest in 'playing ball' or 'teamwork' could be questioned. Similarly, the junior professor who declines the coteaching opportunity is informing his contemporary that he will not take credit for work he has not authored. But he may pay a professional price for his decision not to participate in such games.

In the end, there are no definitive answers, but the questions posed by the informal process of orientation are *real*. During the informal orientation process, we are listening and learning. Rarely will decisions during this process threaten the organizational reputation, but in some cases, especially those where a pattern of dishonesty seems institutionalized, this could occur.

Situational Orientation

By the third stage, the *situational* orientation phase, we have learned about the different work ethics of our colleagues. Over a process that can range in length from several months to several years, we typically ascertain quite a bit about those who are above reproach, those who bend the rules to fit their personal needs, those who are ethical team players and those who are, well, rats!

We can reasonably conclude that there are very few individuals who are not involved in the lifelong process of situational orientation. As your career assumes new and more important duties, you adjust to changing situations; new demands about promotion, staff selection, accepting assignments and other duties all challenge your skills about people, finance, and process.

As an executive enters the arena of senior authority, the content of his contemporaries' character influences his or her situational orientation. Rather than entering a meeting of subordinates, the executive is now surrounded by corporate legal counsel, a marketing vice-president, the chief financial officer, and possibly the chief executive officer. The very nature of new or challenging responsibilities includes questions about proprietary information, safeguarding company secrets, profitability statements, and competitive intelligence—all issues that the executive may have received only peripheral exposure to *before* assuming more important duties.

In situational orientation, there is no continuity. New situations and challenges will emerge to test our ability to pursue ethical choices. When we were new to the organization, for example, we may have condoned ethnic humor because we found it to be genuinely funny; now, as a senior executive, we do not want to give the appearance that we enjoy humor at the expense of others. Conversely, in a junior position where our travel reimbursements were more closely scrutinized by auditors, we may not take any opportunity to fudge an expense account. Now that the auditors report to *us*, however, we may include receipts for meals or expenses that were never actually incurred. Sometimes we *adjust* to situations, and they respond to us.

Situational Orientation Usually Involves Groups

Situational orientation is certainly the arena of the greatest interest for our purposes, because the vast majority of cases where ethical abuse occurs relate to situational processes. In most cases analyzed for this book, dishonesty was not an individual characteristic *per se*; rather, several or more individuals looked around, were enticed by an opportunity, and took actions that led to abuse.

Conspiracy to commit a crime is obviously a punishable offense, but a number of sociologists argue that white-collar offenses rarely result in jail sentences, a fact that is all too well known by managers. (Clinard and Yeager, 505) Indeed, the generally light penalties given to executives and managers (usually a financial fine and/or a requirement for community service) may actually motivate some managers to take the risks associated with dishonesty. Although Michael Milken and Charles Keating were both sentenced to jail for their abuse of the public trust, they are the exceptions, not the rule.

As you will see from various cases presented later in this book, situational orientation involving several employees all working the same scheme is a significant factor in cases of fraud or other crime. While in some cases it is quite easy for investigators to dissect a case and determine who was primarily responsible for orchestrating a crime, this is not always the case.

Charles Keating, president of the failed Lincoln Savings and Loan, was notorious in his ability to pressure federal regulators into changing regulations that would benefit he and family members on the Lincoln payroll. Keating used S&L funds to buy or subsidize vacation homes, jet airplanes, and works of art and is now in jail for his antics. Keating also hired three of his son-in-laws to executive positions that paid as much as $1.2 million a year. He was the subject of a brilliant PBS documentary, "Other People's Money."

ETHICS BRIEF

When Employees Steal

Employee theft is draining billions of dollars from American businesses.

Where huge amounts of cash circulate, the problem is even greater, local experts on crime in the workplace say.

The only plus is that preventing employees from stealing and defrauding companies is turning into a growth industry for private security companies.

The cost of employee theft to business may be as high as $60 billion a year, said Ray Chambers, executive director of the International Association of Security Consultants of Largo, Fla.

Knight-Ridder Newspapers reports the cost of employee theft "has soared from hardly anything to $114 billion in 1990 and will amount to an estimated $200 billion by the end of the decade."

Employee theft includes everything from notebooks to computers. employees steal produce from supermarkets, cash from registers, information from high-technology companies, cigarette packs from convenience stores and even time by taking bogus sick days.

Economic hard times, layoffs, and declining worker loyalty are major factors, national experts say.

"People just aren't making the money they used to, so they take what they want," said Jason Shaw, chief investigator for National Loss Prevention Association, in a *Los Angeles Times* story. The association is a Southern California security company that specializes in undercover work to catch employee thieves.

However, other experts say greed is the main reason for theft.

The amount of reported theft also is increasing because companies are keeping closer track of missing equipment and inventory, crime analysts say.

Las Vegas has weathered the economic downturn, but its rapid business and gaming growth make it vulnerable to employee theft, said Jim Erbeck, a lawyer who specializes in whit-collar crime with the local firm, Woodburn & Wedge.

The city has more cash transactions than the average community, and cash is harder to trace, he said. "In Las Vegas, employee theft is more of an issue because of our 24-hour lifestyle," said Craig McCall, a human resources consultant for the accounting firm McGladrey Pullen's local office.

"A lot of employee theft is related to substance abuse problems or gaming problems and the need to support those habits."

"You have to have a lot of folks coming here [to live] who are aspiring to make fortunes," said Greg Lousig-Nont, president of Lousig-Nont & Associates of Las Vegas that develops tests to screen job applicants. "They are seeking the pot of gold at the end of the rainbow. Many of them get into financial trouble."

Average employee thefts are seven times more costly than shoplifting incidents, according to the national consulting firm of Jack L. Hayes International. Its study of more than 3,600 stores shows a shoplifter steals an average of $53.32 in merchandise, while the average employee theft costs a company $387.06.

There are no businesses immune from employee theft, McCall said.

"Employee theft comes in many forms," he said. "Different industries have different types of theft. In the retail industry, it might be somebody stealing merchandise or vendors dropping things at a business and picking up things they shouldn't be picking up.

"In casinos, it might be people in collusion to steal money. There are thousands of ways employees can rip off an employer."

Retailers are particularly vulnerable during the Christmas holidays because they have to beef up staffs quickly, Lousig-Nont said. They have little time to check backgrounds of employees.

Ironically, it is often a trusted, longtime employee who is responsible for the theft, McCall said.

Longtime employees "know your systems and how to get around them," McCall said.

Businesses that deal in money, such as casinos, use the latest in technology to monitor employees, he said. This cuts down on employee theft, experts say.

Businesses are using closed-circuit cameras, door alarms and sophisticated methods to monitor sales receipts and cash drawers. some businesses even use undercover guards.

But it is often the mood created by the workplace—the way companies treat employees—that has the most effect on honesty, experts say. Employees who feel they are not getting a fair deal or proper recognition are more likely to steal.

"Sometimes an employee will use theft as a way to get back at an employer," McCall said. One way to prevent theft is to carefully screen job applicants and check backgrounds, he said.

More companies are using drug tests and written personality profile tests to determine the character and ethics of applicants. "The jury is still out on these (personality) tests," McCall said. The written tests can give employers an edge in determining which employees might be at risk, said Lousig-Nont, whose company has developed tests that are now used by 3,200 employers.

The tests are valuable because federal and state laws prevent companies from using polygraph testing to screen employees, he said. Companies can use lie detectors to test employees when there is "reasonable cause" to suspect theft, he added.

Because of polygraph restrictions and other civil rights issues, businesses have difficulties investigating theft internally, he said.

Businesses experiencing serious theft problems often turn to law enforcement agencies, who have more latitude in investigating crime. Many formerly preferred conducting their own investigations, and would simply fire guilty employees after making sure losses were made up, he said.

"This makes it even more critical to make sure employers are hiring dependable people," Lousig-Nont said.

His tests are designed to find out if employees have strong convictions about right and wrong, he said. The tests can show if an applicant is suitable to be hired, but should not be used in situations that require handling large amounts of money or other valuables.

People who have strong values because of their upbringing are less likely to steal, Lousig-Nont said. Good interviewing techniques are also available, McCall said.

In addition to screening applicants, companies should have ethical policies that explain the standards employees are required to live up to, said James Dallas, president of Dallas Security of Glenside, Pa.

One prevalent type of fraud involves contractors who turn in phony invoices with inflated amounts for construction materials. Developers pay the inflated price and contractors pocket the difference.

Another scam involves companies that truck in or remove dirt from construction sites. They can reap extra profits by falsifying figures, he said.

Erbeck estimates only 10 percent of construction frauds are detected. Developers often turn to civil courts rather than pressing criminal charges when they find they have been defrauded, he said.

Source: Tom Dye, "Dishonest Workers Stealing Billions," *Las Vegas Review Journal*, May 2, 1993, p. A36. Reprinted with the permission of the Las Vegas Review-Journal.

For instance, when several state attorney generals charged that Sears, Roebuck and Company pursued widespread fraud in automotive repairs in late 1991, they acknowledged that it was unclear if the policy of deceiving customers emanated at corporate headquarters in Chicago, at regional offices of the company, or if questionable practices had been orchestrated by individual store managers. In any case, it was clear that the pattern of abuse was similar throughout dozens and dozens of Sears stores; questions regarding the complicity of corporate management naturally followed.

As children we are asked, "Just because someone else jumps off a bridge, are you going to do the same?" Today, the question might be rephrased: "Just because someone else is profiting by bending the rules, are you going to do the same?" In the case of the bridge, the ultimate penalty—injury or death—led us to a logical response. Given the large number of cases of misdeeds in corporate America, it is clear that bending the rules may actually be beneficial, or at least that is the *perception* of many managers.

Although one would suspect that dishonesty occurs more often when an organization is financially at risk, the evidence is quite contrary; wrongdoing occurs more frequently when a company is financially healthy, indicating that greed is a motivator when an employee feels that his or her employer will not be impaired because of dishonest activities. (Baucus and Near, 36.) If you dispute that statement, here's a dose of reality: Miceli and Near (20) reported that in one recent year alone, federal statistics indicate that bank employees stole nine times more money than did bank robbers.

Much has been written about the process of "group think," a theory suggesting that corporate culture, socialization, and pressure from influential colleagues can contribute to a sense of group standards and an agenda for action. Group think can have excellent results such as when department colleagues collaborate on the design of a new product, for instance. But the process can also backfire. The pressure by colleagues to conform, or the enticement of scams and get-rich schemes all around us, can also suggest that such unethical activity is perfectly acceptable.

"SEE NO EVIL" DURING THE S&L DEBACLE

Three researchers traced one of the most spellbinding examples of situational orientation, the $450 billion savings and loan fiasco of the late 1980s. In their book, *Inside Job,* they uncovered traces of criminal activity in community S&Ls in almost every state. More importantly, they became deeply disturbed at a "see no evil" approach that permeated the regulators, institutional boards of directors, consulting companies, commercial banks, and Congress:

> Of course, the mob and swindlers didn't suck all the billions out of the thrift industry, although they certainly got their share. People who had never committed a crime in their lives fell prey to deregulation's promise of easy money. Thrift officers watched as the professional swindlers worked their scams and never got caught and decided, why not? Buttoned-down appraisers, plugging along in boring jobs making $200–600 per appraisal, learned that by simply raising their opinion of a property's value to match a borrower's needs or desires, they could raise their own standard of living as well. . . . Contractors, attorneys, title company executives and auditors all found their own ways to get a seat on the gravy train by perverting their particular business function for the cause. (Pizzo, Fricker, and Muolo, 463)

As you will see later in the book, the role of whistle blowing played a particularly important role in the S&L scandals, and many believe that this was the genesis for the widespread encouragement of whistle blowing that has since transpired in other industries.

In some cases, whistle blowers who provided testimony and documents to the federal government investigators in the S&L cases did so to secure immunity from prosecution themselves; some had criminal involvement that was far more than peripheral in nature. In other cases, employees of various institutions who witnessed fraud orchestrated by their S&L bosses stepped forward with testimony, sometimes jeopardizing their own careers to see justice prevail.

Although the S&L scandal is discussed in greater detail later in the book, one additional issue should be mentioned at this point, and that is the issue of fairness. Many of those who suffered because of the greed of Charles Keating's failed Lincoln Savings and Loan, the most infamous example of a corrupt financial institution in the past 50 years, believe that neither Keating nor his family paid sufficiently in terms of their limited jail terms and financial penalties. Others would make a compelling case that Keating merely bent deregulation rules to his personal advantage and injured no one to the degree of murderers, rapists, and saboteurs, whose acts cause widespread physical pain and injury.

Although we may want to believe that fairness will prevail in the case of the failed S&Ls, this simply did not materialize.

Comparatively few of the senior managers who orchestrated massive fraud went to jail; most pled guilty or *nolo contendere* and paid fines. If that were not bad enough, as late as fall of 1993, a full three years after failed institutions were first identified, seven states passed legislation to protect influential citizens living in their borders from prosecution.

These states—Louisiana, Nebraska, Oklahoma, South Dakota, Texas, Kansas, and Utah— enacted *retroactive* laws that shield bank directors and officers from lawsuits except those where "gross negligence" is evident. Most legal experts assert that "gross negligence" is virtually impossible to prosecute in court because defendants employ a wide variety of tactics to counter the charge. In learning about the action of the states, Senator Howard Metzenbaum of Ohio responded, "It's absolutely shocking, the total crass indifference of the legislatures to placing the blame where it belongs, succumbing to the entreaties of special interest lobbyists, representing the insurance companies and some of the officers and directors." (Lavelle, 34)

In the years to come, the *National Law Journal* predicts that these parochial laws, which also prevent the Federal Deposit Insurance Corporation (FDIC) and Resolution Trust Company (RTC) from prosecuting residents in these states, will be tested in the federal courts due to the classical impact of the federal-state conflict inherent in these cases.

In this chapter it was suggested that corporations have an obligation to set the tone, throughout the phases of orientation, for ethical expectations. Most are meeting this challenge with new ethics policies and programs, including several that are profiled at the end of the book. There is another side to the story. Sometimes an organization can be highly ethical and efficient and be victimized by employees intent on committing a crime, thus jeopardizing the market position and reputation of their employer. That is the focus of the next chapter.

CASE STUDY:
WHEN TRUTH AND TECHNOLOGY COLLIDE

Leahy Manufacturing Company (LMC) is a San Francisco-based manufacturer of sensitive technology utilized in the forecasting of earthquakes. Some of its advanced equipment was shown during a recent NOVA documentary on the Public Broadcasting Service. The company has 209 employees and has grown from $11 million in annual sales in 1970 to more than $97 million last year. Leahy's primary clients include state and national governments, university and research laboratories, and multinational organizations such as the United Nations and the International Red Cross.

Steve Leahy, the company's 58-year-old president, began the company in 1968. He was a hands-on manager until last year when he began to delegate an increasing number of duties to his son, Arthur. Although the senior Leahy is still active and visible, the son has become the centerpiece of day-to-day operations.

Leahy's newest product is the LM 5000, a highly sensitive instrument that not only measures the magnitude of earthquakes, but actually *predicts* their size and potency at least six hours in advance. The product was field tested for two years under the direction of Leahy's son and was kept secret until patents were secured last year.

For several months, LMC has been offering private simulations of the LM 5000, and the product has received outstanding response. More than a dozen machines, selling for $2.3 million each, are now in place—all without any significant advertising or marketing. The state agencies now using the LM 5000 consider it a breakthrough, their first and best way to be prepared in case of an earthquake. Because Leahy has such a reliable, respected name in engineering and earthquake preparedness, clients expected that this additional resource would be a wise investment that would ultimately save lives and assets. The magic Leahy used to persuade clients included the following:

- An hour long videotape dramatizing how the LM 5000 works

- Detailed reports and technical memos regarding more than 170 tests of the LM 5000 conducted by Leahy and its engineers

- Letters of enthusiastic support from several leading geologists and earthquake specialists, all consultants who were hired by Arthur Leahy and asked to evaluate the product

Today, the senior Leahy received the shock of his life. He found a telephone message on his desk when he returned from lunch, and the information in it could lead to a clear and compelling organizational quagmire. The memo has him depressed, angry, and determined to rebound.

WHILE YOU WERE OUT

To: Mr. Steve Leahy
From: Janice Hoy, Chief, California
           Earthquake Office
Re: Problem!!!

The state has just received test results of
LM 5000 from an independent consultant. The
product does not work in six major tests
conducted at Sandia National Lab in New
Mexico. The lab suspects that fraud may
have taken place—some letters of support in
our package were not written by actual scientists, according to the labs, and the
results reportedly were "doctored." Call
back *immediately.*

1. Identify the possible breaches of ethical and moral judgment (as you perceive them) for all of the actors in this case.

2. Write a point-by-point series of actions, statements, recommendations, and so on that must now emanate from Steve Leahy if he is to recapture his credibility and that of his company.

3. Write a code of ethics that Leahy may want to issue to his staff so that he can convince current and future clients that this kind of dilemma will not occur in the future.

Note: This case is completely fictional. Any relationship to persons or companies is purely coincidental.

REFERENCES FOR CHAPTER 3

Baucus, M. S., and Near, J. P. "Can Illegal Corporate Behavior Be Predicted? An Event History Analysis." *Academy of Management Journal* 34, 1991.

Bhide, Amar, and Stevenson, Howard H. "Why Be Honest If Honesty Doesn't Pay?" *Harvard Business Review*, September–October 1990.

Clinard, Marshall B., and Yeager, Peter C. "Corporate Organization and Criminal Behavior." *Deviant Behavior: A Text-Reader in the Sociology of Deviance.* New York: St. Martin's Press, 1989.

Cook, Fred J. *The Corrupted Land: The Social Morality of Modern America.* New York: Macmillan, 1989.

Gellerman, Saul W. "Why 'Good' Managers Make Bad Ethical Choices." *Harvard Business Review,* July–August 1986.

Lavelle, Marianne. "States Try Shielding S&L Execs." *The National Law Journal,* September 13, 1993.

Miceli, Marcia P., and Near, Janet P. *Blowing the Whistle: The Organizational and Legal Implications for Companies and Employees.* New York: Lexington Books, 1993.

Pizzo, Stephen, Fricker, Mary, and Muolo, Paul. *Inside Job: The Looting of America's Savings and Loans.* New York: HarperCollins, 1991.

Weber, Max. *The Theory of Social and Economic Organization*, translated. New York: The Free Press, 1947.

CHAPTER 4

When Employees Are the Enemy

"The cost of employee theft has soared from hardly anything in 1968 to $114 billion in 1990 and will amount to an estimated $200 billion by the end of the decade."

Las Vegas Review Journal,
May 2, 1993, p. 4

"Sexual harassment cases are landing on employers like sleet in February: so far this year [1993] the Equal Employment Opportunity Commission has received 24% more sexual harassment claims nationwide than in the equivalent period of 1992."

Forbes,
October 11, 1993

In this chapter, you will read about the internal enemy of the company, namely its employees. Although corporations often face trouble because of intentional, organized criminal activity, that is not always the case. Indeed, individuals acting independent of the corporate culture can cause considerable havoc for their employers.

In the beginning of this chapter, you will read about the internal abuses that impact a variety of industries. The chapter concludes with a different kind of internal abuse, sexual harassment.

DISHONESTY AND THE LIFE OF AN ORGANIZATION

In seeking to explain the game rules of competition, business instructors have employed a simple model for decades, commonly referred to as the life expectancy model or marketing paradigm. This four-stage concept, which has been modified over the years by various analysts, asserts that every company and industry progresses from one state to another, as shown in Exhibit 4-1.

This model features four phases: *introduction* (the company is embryonic and struggling to grow), *growth* (after surviving initial struggles, the emerging enterprise increases sales and market share), *maturation and saturation* (the developed company continues to grow and mature), and *decline* (having peaked in terms of sales and growth, the company loses market share and profitability).

EXHIBIT 4-1   The Life Expectancy Model I

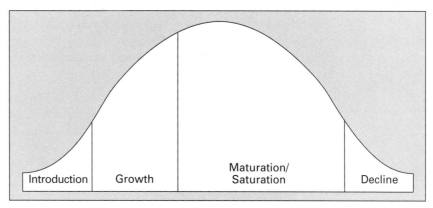

| Introduction | Growth | Maturation/Saturation | Decline |

Other analysts have modified this classical model to further explain that corporations today exist in an ecosystem, or a new ecology of competition. One leading strategy specialist has modified the life expectancy model and redefined these categories as *birth, expansion, leadership,* and *self-renewal.* His argument is that sustainable advantage can only be realized when the company prevents its decline by moving forward and energizing itself with new products and marketing strategies to attract customers. (Moore, 77)

When Do Problems Occur?

The author conducted a comparative analysis of 160 cases of criminal or reported unethical behavior by employees of American corporations (where the employee acted independently, without complicity by management) between 1990 and 1993. The goal was to determine if there were any patterns between *when* these cases occurred and the life expectancy or ecosystem of the corporation affected. The dates of events as reported by police or criminal investigators in the 37 states where these cases occurred were integrated into the life expectancy model using a subjective baseline. That baseline was designed to factor in the age of the company (1 to 5 years, 6 to 10, 11 to 20, and more than 20 years), competitiveness (diversity of products, domestic versus international presence), and profitability (using fiscal profiles from Morningstar, a mutual fund ratings company, and *Hoover's Handbook of Business*). The results were rather startling.

Only nonviolent incidents were studied for this segment of the study, such as extortion, embezzlement, insider trading, and computer sabotage. The major finding was that the vast majority of cases of unethical or illegal behavior (57percent) occurred in the maturation phase of organizational life, when the company was between 11 and 20 years old. The percentage breakdown of the cases studied appears in Exhibit 4-2.

Based on this research, we can form several hypotheses:

1. Often an organization in its infancy lacks the sophisticated knowledge and internal checks and balances to detect crime or unethical behavior. An entrepreneurial venture or other emerging business often focuses on issues related to market share, technology enhancement, and customer service. Such as company may lack the financial resources necessary to launch internal auditing procedures or departments.

EXHIBIT 4-2   The Life Expectancy Model II

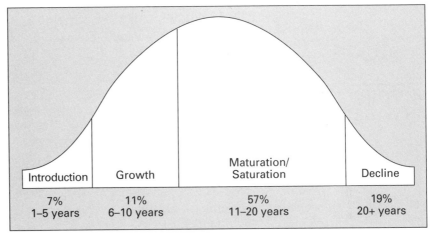

2. In many cases, employees are less motivated to commit a crime against an organization in its infancy, the company simply may not have much *worth* stealing or damaging.

3. When an organization is comparatively new, managers may not have had enough time to establish the patterns of behavior that may later irritate employees and serve as a contributing factor to retribution or intentional crime aimed at the employer.

4. As the organization progresses in age, various checks and balances emerge, sometimes preventing or reducing the attraction for wrongdoing. However, as shown with cases that follow, such barriers sometimes backfire if the offending employee has a personality that enjoys challenging systems and procedures.

    Although sometimes employees who commit criminal acts in-house are testing the limits of acceptable behavior, more often than not they are intentionally seeking to test security or surveillance systems or other established procedures. Criminologists find such deviant behavior to be commonplace in established organizations, especially when employees are unhappy with other facets of their professional or personal lives.

5. The second highest percentage of cases emerged in the final phase of the life expectancy model. When an organization is

declining, the appeal of inappropriate behavior may be enhanced an employee's belief that "even if I get caught, they won't prosecute me" or "nobody will notice, since they're spending all of their time with the balance sheet."

UNETHICAL AND CRIMINAL BEHAVIOR: UNMASKING THE ENEMY

For nearly 200 years, physicians, and later sociologists, have tried to determine if there are any detectable patterns in deviant behavior. Scientists and psychologists have joined in the search as well, all seeking to determine if criminals share any biological or behavioral commonalties. In 1989, the research resulted in a not-so-surprising landmark analysis that bridges these interdisciplinary pursuits:

> After decades of research, no biological characteristic which distinguishes criminals has been discovered, and this generalization applies even to particular types of criminals (e.g., murderers, bigamists, etc.). Consequently few theorists now even toy with the notion that all criminals are atavistic, mentally defective, constitutionally inferior. (Gibbs, 16)

This conclusion is hardly comforting to human resource professionals, security analysts, and other corporate officers who today find themselves constantly in search of ways to protect their organization from fraud and related crimes. If there is no commonalty or pattern to dishonesty in the workplace, where can one find insight? Two sources seem feasible: first, the warning signs of potentially dishonest employees, and second, case studies.

In terms of warning signs, the best research to date is from the mortgage banking industry, where widespread abuse in the 1980s led that industry to seek guidelines that managers could use to predict and prevent acts of dishonesty. Craig Wolfe, vice-president of Weyerhaeuser Mortgage Company in Los Angeles, researched numerous cases and identified traits that are common in cases of fraud: psychological or physiological disorders, drug/alcohol addiction, indifferent attitude toward white-collar crime, gambling debts, personal financial hardship, and numerous speculative investments. (Wolfe, 49)

The second and more colorful guide emanates from case studies, for it is here that we can begin to understand that the motivations for dishonesty in the workplace vary. They range from the psychopath

---

ETHICS BRIEF

Dear Abby, Attorney At Law . . .

The legal community is in disarray over the promise and risk associated with cyberspace technology. *The National Law Journal* (September 27, 1993, 1) reports that nationwide a large number of attorneys will use their personal computers and modems to answer questions about the law and computer technologies on Internet, CompuServe, and Prodigy, to name but a few popular services. Some attorneys use this free exposure as a marketing tool; others genuinely want to help users who cannot afford face-to-face counsel.

In its article, *The National Law Journal* asked: "Does a New York lawyer who responds to a question posed by a bulletin board member in Florida violate Florida's unlicensed-practice rules if he hasn't passed the Florida bar? Does a lawyer who advises a bulletin board member about a family law

matter risk creating an attorney-client relationship and, thereby, expose herself to a malpractice claim if the advice turns out to be wrong?" Each week more than 1,500 members of CompuServe ask such questions on LAWSIG, a regular feature of the program that now has over 50,000 members.

Adding to the puzzle is the increasing popularity of Internet, the informal communications network that has more than 10 million users in 50 countries, where attorneys in one country can respond to questions that may be posed by Internet users living in a different country—with different legal sanctions. Although most attorneys post disclaimers at the end of their advice, the availability and speed of computer networking is posing a galaxy of ethical questions never envisioned just a decade ago.

---

who is having "fun" by stalking a coworker to the computer hacker who seeks to undermine an entire telephone company's operations. In the cases that follow, you will learn about behavioral patterns as well as emerging issues such as employee privacy, sabotage, and embezzlement. Each case underscores the argument that while some organizational cultures may encourage unethical behavior, this is hardly true for all companies.

The Porsche and the Pentagon

People outside the company can become internal threats when given access. Consider the case of Kevin Lee Poulsen, a 24-year-old high school dropout whose brilliance as a computer hacker is so well established that as of this writing he has remained in jail for two years awaiting trial. The federal government, the state of California, and several large corporations have all argued that this young man poses such an immense threat to society that releasing him is simply out of the question. According to writer Jonathan Littman, Poulsen

- Succeeded in subverting the Pacific Bell phone system throughout southern California. In just one of his many exploits, Poulsen was the successful 102nd caller on radio station KIIS-FM during its $50,000 Porsche promotion. But he had reportedly manipulated telecommunication systems and was also the first through 101st caller, thus ensuring himself top prize.

- Tapped into the telecommunication system of the Pentagon and various military branches of the government, as well as unpublished telecommunication systems of the Rand Corporation (a military contractor), the Naval Research Laboratory in Washington, D.C., Strategic Air Command, and even the telecommunication systems of other governments, including the Soviet consulate in San Francisco

- Listened to an undetermined number of phone conversations of potentially thousands of U.S. citizens over a period of years, including at least one "Hollywood starlet."

Poulsen initially avoided prosecution by working with police and one of his targets, the highly-regarded security consultant firm SRI International of Menlo Park, California. His project was to teach SRI and the government how he and other "cyberpunks" succeed in undermining corporate and government telecommunication systems. He succeeded, but only to a degree. Poulsen acknowledged to police that he would search for code words and other computer secrets through Pacific Bell's trash bins and then destroy files, records, and entire projects, by changing the codes to make them inoperative. Once a part of SRI, he continued his alleged crime, but now enjoyed access to even better equipment and technology.

After avoiding the second arrest by escaping police, he became the target of a national search. When NBC's "Unsolved Mysteries" profiled Poulsen on October 10, 1990, and broadcast a telephone number asking for leads on his whereabouts, the network's phone lines went dead. To this day, according to the *Los Angeles Times*, it is unclear if Poulsen was responsible.

To date, police are uncertain why Poulsen targeted Pacific Bell and other companies in California; it is clear that he is but one of thousands of alleged hackers who can cause havoc to business and industry. In his excellent analysis, Littman indicates that what

E T H I C S   B R I E F

A Poker Game on Company Time

A 1993 survey of hundreds of U.S. office workers suggests that employees do more than steal paper clips and pens; they often mask the fact that they are typing by playing computer games such as Solitaire, which are widely packaged with products such as Microsoft Windows. Some 90 percent of respondents have access to games on their computers; of this number, 78% play several times a day or several times a week. Aren't computer games just a stress reliever in an otherwise hectic workday? That argument doesn't cut it, according to Rock Blanco, director of information at Garber Travel Service in New England. According to *Business Week*, Blanco pulled all games off the personal computers of some 500 employees after he "discovered several of them wasting away the day."

Source: "Computer Games", *Business Week*, October 11, 1993, p. 40.

appeared to trigger Poulsen was more than ambition: "Compulsion led him to computer secrets and the bar of justice." He continues:

> Abandoned by fellow hackers, friends and the family he never had, he seems bound to be the first of his kind to face the full brunt of the law. Today no one has any use for him, not the U.S. military complex, which once exploited his boyhood obsession as a national security advantage, not the cyberspace community, which once saw him as a symbol of freedom in the information age. (Littman, 65)

The ramifications of hacking are clear: The financial damage to corporate targets can be astronomical, requiring that the organization give attention not only to the sabotage that has been committed, but also to the costly and elaborate security measures that must be taken to prevent damage in the future.

Cases such as the Poulsen example are, fortunately, infrequent. However, *Personnel* magazine has advised human resource managers to alert their senior managers that such cases are proliferating to a frightening degree: "Computer sabotage is so easy to perform and can be perpetrated with such seeming innocence that all HR managers should know how to implement safeguards against it." (Crino and Leap, 32).

This warning makes sense: More than 30 million personal computers are now in use in the West, 60 percent of them are interconnected by local area networks (LANs).

ETHICS BRIEF

The Best to Work for and the Most Admired

Which U.S. companies offer the best benefits to their employees and continue to do so even during difficult economic periods? *Money* magazine surveyed the largest U.S. employers and graded them on medical and dental insurance, life and disability protection, vacation and pension benefits, as well as stock-purchase plans. Their most recent rankings are as follows:

Best Employers
1. IBM
2. Proctor & Gamble
3. Johnson & Johnson
4. Xerox
5. Eastman Kodak
6. Citicorp
7. Hewlett-Packard
8. AT&T
9. Merck
10. Quaker Oats

It is interesting to note that only one of the companies listed as "America's Best Employers" is considered to be among the most admired companies in the United States, as based on the exhaustive annual survey conducted by *Fortune* magazine. The latest rankings are as follows:

Most Admired Companies
1. Rubbermaid
2. Home Depot
3. Coca-Cola
4. Microsoft
5. 3M
6. Walt Disney
7. Motorola
8. J.P. Morgan
9. Procter & Gamble
10. United Parcel Service

Sources: "The Best Benefits," *Money Magazine,* May 1993, 130; "America's Most Admired Corporations," *Fortune,* February 7, 1994, 51.

While some threats emanate from covert sources, such as competitors who will pay a LAN expert to infiltrate, steal, or destroy files, the more common intruder is an insider who, according to one expert, is usually "disinterested, dishonest, disgruntled and disaffected." (Nickell, 26) Those who fear detection often bury a "logic bomb" in their networks that can completely destroy the entire computer system unless the employer deactivates the program with a predesignated code word.

One partial solution is increased vigilance. At Pittsburgh's Carnegie Mellon University, the Defense Department supports the Computer Emergency Response Team (CERT), a research center that pursues security breaches and notifies various computer networks of emerging threats. In 1992 alone, CERT responded to almost 800 reported cases of security infringement—a stunning 90 percent increase over the previous year. (Watson, 10)

The Ultimate Insider

Havoc can, unfortunately, be caused with relative ease for many organizations. Given their size and complexity, can corporations design the research protocol necessary to identify in advance employees who may be prone to dishonesty or ethical abuse? The task is a formidable one. As noted earlier, there are no common traits that distinguish dishonest employees, and in many cases our assumptions about unethical colleagues may be faulty. Let's look at a number of brief cases that illustrate the diversity of such challenges:

- In September 1993, 30-year-old Louis Pacich, a former project coordinator for AT&T in New Jersey, pleaded guilty to an elaborate plan in which he conspired to extort $1 million from his employer earlier in the year. Federal prosecutors say that Pacich admitted he stole nearly 4,000 customer account records and threatened to sell them to competing telecommunication companies unless AT&T paid him $1 million. When he arrived to pick up his first $500,000 installment, he was arrested. *(The Wall Street Journal*, September 13, 1993, A6).

- Even in the aftermath of well-publicized prosecutions of prominent insider trading cases involving such notables as Michael Milken and Ivan Boesky, stock abuses continue. The Securities and Exchange Commission (SEC) reports that most inside traders seek to profit from a "once in a lifetime" opportunity to take advantage of either positive or negative confidential news about publicly traded companies whose stock prices are likely to change when the information is announced. However, because most insider traders receive relatively light sentences and imprisonment is rare, the motivation to engage in the crime is high, given the potentially lucrative benefits.

- As a case in point, Edward Downe, Jr., a former board member of Bear Stearns Companies and founder of Downe Communications, Inc., was charged by the SEC of having gained more than an $8 million profit by trading insider information with associates and neighbors. In September 1993, Downe was sentenced to a three-year probation and 3,000 hours of community service. After expressing sorrow for his criminal acts, he was hugged in the courtroom by several supporters, including U.S. Senator Christopher Dodd. (Woo, B10)

- Both employees and competitors are increasingly utilizing voice mail to undermine their colleagues or competitors. Identifying the password of another worker has become a pastime at some organizations, and in sales environments in particular the pressure to score high on a monthly tally can encourage people to extreme acts. Kevin Hanley, AT&T's telecommunication security expert, says, "People lock their file cabinets at night. You have to treat information in a voice-processing system as securely as you would if it were on a piece of paper." (Bulkeley, B9)

- In 1993, Charles Schwab & Company accused several employees at its San Francisco headquarters of using masked messages on company computers to buy and sell cocaine; comments on the computer screen indicating that employees sought to buy basketball "tickets" actually referred to half-gram quantities of the drug which sold for about $40.

- Theft occurs whenever an employee calls in sick but is actually playing hooky. One researcher estimates that U.S. employers incur more than $2 billion in lost productivity every year when workers and managers lie by calling in sick when they are perfectly well. (Yoodin, 1993)

    In one case two supervisors who had called in sick at the East Bay Municipal Utility District in Oakland, California, were playing golf in October 1993 when they found a new partner—a subordinate who had also called in sick, enjoying a round of play at the same golf course. The supervisors turned in the worker. All three were subsequently "counseled about the inappropriateness" of their behavior. (Associated Press, 14)

- Across the Atlantic, three employees of AT&T's British headquarters reportedly rigged a phone system that would generate thousands of calls to a 900 number, allowing the employees to profit without AT&T being able to trace the 900-number company back to its own workers. (Carley, 1) In this reported scheme, AT&T was to pay for calls made by a computer to a company owned by its own employees.

- Employee sabotage is on the rise worldwide. The loss of nearly 3,000 lives at the Union Carbide plant in Bhophal, India, in December 1984, the catastrophic 1989 Pacific Southwest Airline crash in Cerritos, California, and the 1986 DuPont Plaza Hotel fire in Puerto Rico that left 95 persons dead "were allegedly initiated by disgruntled employees with a score to settle . . .

Employees who commit sabotage are not always the chronic malcontents who openly oppose company policies, rules and workplace procedures. Saboteurs may be smiling, compliant, but furtive individuals who quietly go about their business at work, rarely revealing their malicious intent." (Crino and Leap, 32)

- The financial services industry has historically been a prime target for insider abuses; four out of five crimes targeting banks involve some kind of fraud, most of it by employees or directors. The cost of internal abuse alone exceeds $2.1 billion *annually* in the United States. (Brown, 31)

Although banks had been targeted for years, it wasn't until 1972 that the revised Bank Protection Act required financial institutions to designate a security officer. Yet loss prevention continues in unprecedented numbers, largely because of check fraud, automatic teller machine fraud, and falsification of customer records. *USA Today* reports that in 1992 alone, 76 percent of 330 businesses surveyed by KPMG Peat Marwick were victimized by fraud. (September 13, 1993, D1)

Now that we have a better idea of the variety of cases where insiders can raise serious questions about dishonesty and ethics in the workplace, let's look at two other cases where actions internal to the company were clouded by those on the outside.

AMERICAN EXPRESS: DON'T LEAVE HOME IF YOU'RE CONSIDERED COMPETITION

In July 1989, the chairman and chief executive officer of American Express (Amex), James D. Robinson III, issued a formal apology to international banker Edmond Safra and agreed to pay $8 million, half to Safra and the remaining half to charities that Safra would designate. The reason for this unusual apology underscores one of the most bizarre cases related to ethical abuse in recent history.

According to *The Wall Street Journal*, Robinson's top aide, Harry L. Freeman, supervised the hiring of two individuals who launched a multiyear campaign to discredit Safra. These individuals, the paper said, "engaged in a covert campaign to ruin Mr. Safra's reputation by spreading rumors and articles in the international press." The Amex operatives, according to a lengthy investigation by reporter Bryan Burrough, spread rumors and news articles containing patently bogus information about him [Safra]. The articles linked Mr. Safra to drug trafficking, money laundering and murder, and to criminal elements ranging from Columbia's Medellin drug cartel to the late Mafia figure Meyer Lansky. . . . For American Express, a company that has enjoyed a virtually unrivaled reputation for integrity, the Safra affair reveals a willingness to engage in unseemly corporate revenge when confronting a rival, and, at the very least, a jarring lack of oversight on the part of top company officials. (Burrough, A1)

The paper found no concrete evidence that Robinson knew of the campaign, but its report raised serious questions about the motivations of corporate officers. After Amex bought a Swiss bank owned by Safra in 1983, Robinson and Safra failed to achieve the interpersonal synergy necessary for a multinational banking operation, according to the paper. Within two years, Safra resigned, followed by heated severance negotiations. Amex suspected that Safra was interested in opening a new, competing Swiss bank and would "reclaim" former employees and customers.

Although details of the *Journal* investigation are too lengthy to recount here, it is obvious that a company well regarded for its diversified financial services broke the public trust in the Safra case. Although the aggregate picture of American Express is one of a profitable, charitable, well-managed and ethical company, the Safra affair was a painful hemorrhage of credibility, where candor and ethics seemed overshadowed by revenge. Those inside the company had a responsibility for actions that could compromise the reputation of a fine organization. Such oversight appeared lacking surgery at American Express.

BANK OF BOSTON:
"BANKING BY THE PAPER BAG"

In 1985, the reputation of the 100-year-old Bank of Boston was tarnished amidst disclosures by the *Boston Globe* that the bank had violated U.S. currency reporting laws in actions that in many cases involved funds provided by organized crime.

Federal law requires institutions to report cash transactions of $10,000 or more that involve overseas banks, a requirement imposed to curb the money flow from organized crime and drug trafficking. The government charged that Bank of Boston had engaged in hundreds of such transactions with Swiss banks, failing to report a total of $1.2 *billion* in such transactions. (*Newsweek*, February 25, 1985, 16)

The story worsened. In 1983, the bank was warned by federal examiners that it was not in compliance with the law. (Palmer, 1) Yet in 1985 the bank continued to insist that it was unaware of the law, prompting Assistant Secretary of the U.S. Treasury John M. Walker to reply: "I have not been aware of any major bank not aware of this requirement." When bank chairman William Brown faced the press at a February 11, 1985, news conference to acknowledge that his institution had been fined $500,000 by the federal government, the *Globe* reported that "He admitted error but he was not contrite." (Stein, 1)

The story was further complicated by the bank's acknowledgment that it had frequent financial dealings with members of the Anguilo family, "named by federal authorities as the boss of organized crime in the Boston area." The Anguilos "regularly purchased enormous quantities of cashier's checks at a Bank of Boston branch in the city's North End, paying for the checks with cash." *Newsweek* also reported "loan sharking and racketeering by the Anguilo family" and that Anguilo family members "bought $1.7 million worth of cashier's checks in 1982 alone from Bank of Boston branches." (*Newsweek*, 16) *Newsweek's* headline was superb: "Banking by the Paper Bag."

In the aftermath of the Bank of Boston controversy, at least a dozen other major banks across the United States, including Wells Fargo, Chemical Bank, and Manufacturer's Hanover Trust Company, all acknowledged that they too had failed to report sizable cash transactions as required by federal law.

The cleansing process that comes from well-publicized cases of legal or ethical wrongdoing is healthy for society. On the other hand, we have to wonder: How many cases such as those at the Bank of Boston go *unreported* and *undiscovered*?

WHEN EMPLOYEE ACTIONS COMPROMISE THE ORGANIZATION

The Amex and Bank of Boston examples underscore the notion that while senior management cannot be aware of the actions of subordinates in all cases, they have a moral and ethical obligation to *try* to prevent such embarrassments. There is no evidence that the chief executive officers at either organization were aware of wrongdoing by others. Yet someone must be responsible beyond those immediately guilty of any alleged wrongdoing. This raises the need for corporate policies and training programs aimed at corrective action, which will be discussed later in the book.

ETHICS BRIEF

Who's Minding the Truck?

Although banks have their share of ethical controversies, they are hardly alone. Sometimes banks are the *victims* of questionable and illegal practices. The abrupt closure of New York-based Revere Armored, Inc., a company that transported and stored cash, came amidst charges from leading banks that millions of its dollars were missing. One bank client alone, National Westminster Bank PLC, found $6 million missing after a single audit.

Multiple signals existed for at least a year before Revere closed its doors in February 1993 that something was seriously wrong: For instance, Lloyd's of London canceled Revere's insurance upon learning of bank lawsuits and missing funds. *Business Week* reported that officials at Marine Midland Bank were aware of alleged thefts but continued to work with the company nevertheless.

In its investigation of Revere, *Business Week* identified three red flags that prudent managers should consistently monitor when working with outside vendors. First, Revere's unusually low bids should have signaled to clients that something was wrong; second, Revere filed financial statements with state regulators that claimed unusually large growth rates that would have been virtually impossible given such low bids; third, bank clients only rarely audited the vaults of Revere to determine that money that had been taken away from their institution was being securely held by the company. In the case of Revere, the enemy within was the absence of oversight.

Source: *Business Week*, October 4, 1993, p. 100.

For now, let's recognize that the threat of internal abuse poses financial, reputational, and legal costs. It is almost impossible to quantify the financial losses to an organization that faces charges of dishonesty. But we can and should ask the following questions:

- Do we measure lost future income, and if so, by what formula?

- How can we estimate the legal costs of defending such actions, when multiple lawsuits may be filed for several more years?

- How can we predict the lost business opportunities caused by internal abuse, including the organizational ability to attract strong candidates for future positions, retain existing top talent, and attract future clients?

Employees compromise the well-being of their employer in a number of situations. Although financial impropriety often heads the list, we need to broaden our discussion of internal abuse and focus on one of the most prevalent, namely sexual harassment.

SEXUAL HARASSMENT: "PEOPLE ARE KEEPING DIARIES AT WORK"

Sexual harassment is not a gender issue. It is a management issue. Women and men have both reported an alarming number of cases of harassment at work in recent years, although a disproportionately larger percentage of cases involves women who are harassed by colleagues, subordinates, superiors, and vendors.

When Professor Anita Hill charged in 1991 that then U.S. Supreme Court nominee (now Justice) Clarence Thomas had routinely harassed her a decade earlier, her accusations helped to refocus the nation's attention on one of the most complicated issues affecting workplace morale and productivity. Two other cases, described briefly here, illustrate the kind of activity that is all too common in organizations:

- Two vice-presidents of Aetna Life & Casualty Company resigned and two other employees were demoted in 1993 following a company investigation into charges that one of the employees "threw a dildo around" during a party following a company golf outing.

- Just months before a $3.8 billion real estate project called Lake Las Vegas was about to commence sales in Nevada, the former vice-president for the developer claimed that his president had engaged in activity that *The Las Vegas Sun* reported included "sexually harassing women in the office, trying to involve executives in real estate and kickback schemes and making racial and ethnic slurs in public." The newspaper interviewed a worker who alleged that company president Alton Jones "made crude sexual jokes, talked about her breasts and encouraged her to wear tight outfits and meet him after work." (German, 1D)

Background

For many years, the premiere case used in harassment cases was *Meritor Savings Bank* v. *Vinston* (106 S.Ct. 2399 [1986]). In that case, a bank employee charged that her supervisor asked for sexual favors shortly after she began working at the bank; she testified that she eventually consented in fear of losing her job. The employee reported that the stress of the relationship that was forced upon her required extensive sick leave, which resulted in her being terminated. Officials

The distinction between consensual sex and sexual harassment is sometimes obscure. In Japan, organized crime, also called the Yakuza, controls the prostitution market that openly flourishes in most business districts. Here, a sign in the Ikebukuro section of Tokyo advertises a half hour with a young woman for about 35 U.S. dollars. Although illegal, hundreds of such operations exist, even in the midst of opposition from women's groups and human rights activists.

of Meritor Savings Bank argued that they were unaware of the activities of the supervisor and of Ms. Vinson, but the U.S. Supreme Court ruled that the employer was nevertheless liable.

Until 1991, federal sex discrimination cases such as the *Meritor* case were decided by judges. With the implementation of the 1991 Civil Rights Act, the rules changed and costs became considerably higher. Today, jury trials are used to hear charges against employees (and against the employer, where complicity is alleged). Many litigators praised this change in federal law because jury trials often produce more sizable awards for those seeking damages. The 1991 law is explicit: Business owners are liable for sexual harassment that is caused by supervisors, clients, and even suppliers, including cases where owners are completely unaware that harassment was taking place. The term "contributory negligence" is often used, meaning that the company *should have known* or *could have known* about this activity.

So much publicity has surrounded sexual harassment allegations that a number of law firms have begun to specialize in representing plaintiffs who are suing coworkers or an employer. In many cases, documentation or witnesses can help a case but neither is necessary for a successful lawsuit. As a result, according to New York attorney Robert Heiferman who is a leading expert in harassment cases, "People are keeping diaries at work." (Jacobs, 34)

In addition to the embarrassment caused by these cases, employees often cite mental anguish and suffering when filing lawsuits. In small companies with between 14 and 101 employees, compensatory and punitive damages are limited by the courts to $50,000, but in larger corporations, damages can and have reached into millions of dollars. The employee charging harassment does not have to have suffered any financial loss in order to win compensation.

Another ethical quagmire emerges when sexual harassment by a third party occurs. For example, what is the company's obligation when one of its workers is harassed by a customer or supplier? Ask Catherine Holmes. As an account supervisor for New York's Avrett, Free & Ginsberg advertising agency, she claims to have been repeatedly harassed by one of the company's clients. "When I was dismissed, the agency told me, in so many words, that it was either me or the account," she says. She is currently in litigation against her former employer and the accused, a senior vice-president of Trans World Airlines (Winokur, B1)

In the past two years, federal courts have viewed the ethical and legal implications of third party harassment and held that employers may be liable if one of their employees is harassed by someone *outside* the company. A May 1992 ruling in Nevada involved a suit by a blackjack dealer at the Las Vegas Hilton who charged that despite repeated complaints to supervisors that she was being harassed by gamblers while she was working, she was suspended and terminated, allegedly for being rude to customers.

Three primary requisites must be met for a claim of sexual harassment to be successful: The action must be sexual in nature, take place in a hostile environment, and be "unwelcome." The victim's clothing style, age, and position are irrelevant; any statement, suggestion, or conduct (including physical, verbal, or visual activities) could be subject to a claim, including activities that one party considers to be merely playful, but others consider degrading.

Employers can also get into serious trouble when their policies and procedures (or absence of them) fail to address sexual harassment. In one of the most notorious cases, *Robinson* v. *Jacksonville Shipyards, Inc.*, 136 L.R.R.M. (BNA) 2920 (N.D. Fla. 1991), the management team was found to be negligent in seriously addressing this

ETHICS BRIEF

Harassment is a Serious Matter

Under Federal law, sexual harassment includes such activities as posting pornographic posters, cartoons, and drawings at work, requesting sexual favors, lewd remarks, unwanted hugs, touches and kisses, and retaliating against anyone who complains about sexual harassment.

Several resources are available to employees and employers who wish more information on sexual harassment policies.

They include the following:

- National Organization of Working Women, 614 Superior Ave. NW, Cleveland, OH 44113.
- Human Resources Center, 5431 Baldwin Ave., Temple City, CA 38340
- U.S. Equal Employment Opportunity Commission, 1801 L. St. NW, Washington, DC 20507.

issue. Although a 1980 policy informed employees that any indiscretions should be reported "immediately to the Equal Employment Opportunity coordinator at this facility," the EEO officer was not named and the policy was not widely circulated. Female employees charged that sexually oriented pictures posted on company walls and crude statements made to female workers constituted harassment, but the company failed to document their charges and generally ignored their claims.

One legal expert has asserted that the *Robinson* v. *Jacksonville Shipyards* case is important because the court was explicit—one page memos about sexual harassment are simply not enough to shield an employer from liability. (Connell, 191) An ethical solution is for every employer to articulate a strong harassment policy that is detailed, explaining who will adjudicate cases and what penalties are likely if an employee is found guilty of harassment. In the case of *Robinson* v. *Jacksonville Shipyards*, the court was so appalled at the attitude of management that it authorized the National Organization of Women Legal Defense and Education Fund to monitor employer compliance. A copy of the court-imposed Jacksonville Shipyards policy appears in the appendix of this book. It is one of the most far-reaching documents of its kind.

Of course, harassment is more than a sexual, financial, and legal issue—it is a moral one. Attitudes and behaviors change slowly through education and through prominent cases such as that involving Anita Hill and Judge Clarence Thomas. But some corporate policies are so bizarre that one can wonder if current legislation goes far enough. For example, the Equal Employment Opportunity Commission agreed with a Texas-based saleswoman for Ortho Pharmaceutical, Inc., that she was fired in 1985 because she was pregnant. A company manual indicated that the proper profile for a female hire was as follows:

> She's not pretty, she's not sexy. . . . She should have the look of someone who might clean her bathroom or kitchen on her hands and knees. . . . God was a He. No religion has a female leader or a role model except for saints: they all suffered greatly and died prematurely. It's the kind of thing that could give you (women) an inferiority complex. (Associated Press)

Small Businesses Are Not Immune

Although the most publicized claims of sexual harassment occur in large, well-known organizations, small businesses are especially vulnerable to charges of sexual harassment because they may lack the sophistication to educate workers in their responsibility to prevent such conduct.

In the fall of 1992, the author and Professor Donald Hardigree of the University of Nevada, Las Vegas, surveyed 80 small businesses with less than $1 million in annual sales in six southwestern states. The results, shown in Exhibit 4-3, indicate that small businesses lack policies on sexual harassment to an alarming degree, placing themselves in jeopardy should a documented charge of harassment be filed against them. (Barton and Hardigree, 17) Even fewer small businesses (only 11 percent) have sponsored educational seminars on the subject, probably because of the perceived costs of capital and lost time of key personnel who must be diverted from critical duties for such a program. Of course this is a faulty but understandable argument for some small businesses. Equally interesting is the fact that 42 percent of small businesses acknowledge that the issue is a looming problem for their enterprise.

Harassment is an enemy within. It can impair worker morale, injure organizational reputation, and, more importantly, violate a host of federal and state laws. Although those charged with sexual harassment would probably not consider their actions to be on the same level of ethical abuse as others whose actions are profiled in this book, such sentiment fails the test of logic: Harassers place their employer in a compromising position every time they engage in such activity.

The Other Side of the Coin

Employees should certainly pursue internal and external remedies whenever they believe that discrimination has been inflicted upon them. Increasingly, however, documentation of harassment or other wrongdoing is the key. Given the phenomenal increase in employee rights litigation, employers are increasingly fighting back by producing evidence that the employee's past misconduct should preclude the case from proceeding. A 1993 study by Knight-Ridder Newspapers drew this conclusion:

> The strategy is working. In several cases, employers convinced judges to throw out discrimination suits by producing evidence that a worker lied in a resume or job interview, falsified records, inflated claims for expenses or removed a confidential file. This defense tactic—known to lawyers as the doctrine of after-acquired evidence—has blossomed into a major, unresolved controversy that divides the federal courts. (Knight-Ridder, 2F)

SOLUTIONS TO INTERNAL THREATS

When employee activities undermine the normal operating functions of an organization, swift action must be taken to ensure that the employee is reprimanded or punished fairly but publicly. Many managers interviewed by the author reported regret that their organization pursued a quiet resolution to past incidents, largely because the lessons learned and injury inflicted on the company was never publicized to other employees.

In this sense, it seems odd that companies routinely publicize the positive contributions of their staff members, such as with Employee of the Month and Year recognitions, but fail to publicize the infrequent criminal in its midst. Yes, there is embarrassment associated with negative publicity, but a company that aggressively weeds out unacceptable behavior and knows that it is right in doing so is not only discouraging future acts, it is reassuring its stockholders, customers, and other audiences that it is an ethical but tough competitor who will aggressively pursue violations of its trust.

Employee infractions must be managed fairly; the presumption of innocence is as important in the internal adjudication of cases as it is

E T H I C S   B R I E F

Does Proctor and Gamble Spy on Employees?

Large corporations often face the greatest exposure to threats from its own staff because the theft of corporate funds, research secrets, or other assets is alluring to some employees.

A new book by *Wall Street Journal* reporter Alecia Swasy, *Soap Opera: The Inside Story of Procter & Gamble* (Random House, 1993) is a dazzling account of how she claims Cincinnati-based Procter & Gamble (P&G) coped with the menace of internal threats over its 157-year history.

The company has called her findings inaccurate, but Swasy's sources included a number of former P&G executives and consultants; she interviewed over 300 P&G insiders. She charges that P&G

- Closely monitors the activities of employees, vendors and advertising agencies with whom it works; some employees refer to the company as "the Kremlin"
- Has employed former FBI and CIA officers to monitor the phone calls and personal activities of some individuals
- Monitored the phone calls of employees at work when calling home and followed employees on business trips to ascertain the nature of their activities

- Supervises "seizing and scrutinizing personal medical records to pry into an employee's personal life," and
- Controls personnel changes at the various advertising agencies P&G engages to create promotional materials to ensure that its strategies are not compromised.

In writing her book, Swasy found that Cincinnati Bell supoenaed records to find anyone who had phoned or faxed her home and office, information that could have helped P&G in its attempt to identify her sources. The chief executive offices of P&G, Ed Artzt, was quoted in *The Washington Post* as telling his public relations staff, "Tell Swasy she's lucky if I piss on the best part of her." (*Washington Post National Weekly*, November 29, 1993, p. 36).

A former P&G executive interviewed by Swasy says that these and other activities at the company, such as harassment of environmental activists, amounts to "organizational fascism," a far cry from the carefully nurtured image of a company whose hallmark product, Ivory Soap, is "99 44/100 percent pure."

in our broader society. When an employee is charged with an ethical or criminal misdeed, she or he has the right to a fair hearing, to defend herself or himself, and to present evidence supporting such claims. Employees also have the right to have counsel represent them in such matters. To make charges and claims against a worker in this litigious society without documentation and a thorough, unbiased fact-finding procedure is to encourage a lawsuit that the company will probably lose.

The Procter & Gamble approach discussed in the Ethics Brief represents another kind of managerial solution that, while seemingly sinister at first glance, may unfortunately become common in years to come. Vigilance and open communication with employees about organization concerns appear to be two key routes to success in dealing with the unpleasant matters discussed thus far.

In terms of sexual harassment, a problem-free workplace begins when an organization defines and distributes its policies to workers, establishes policies to hear grievances, works to protect the confidentiality of the accuser and the position of the accused until an investigation is complete, and takes remedial action. The following case challenges you to solve a sexual harassment case involving a sales representative.

CASE STUDY: SEXUAL HARASSMENT

Let's take a look at a hypothetical (but all too real) example of how a company grapples with charges of sexual harassment. At the end of the case, you will be challenged to design a plan of action.

Selling More Than Furniture?

When Calvin Yorsborough, owner of Yorsborough Furniture Manufacturing, Inc., gave his daughter a summer job at the factory, he anticipated receiving unsolicited advice. Now that Sarah had finished her junior year in the business department at the University of Florida, she had plenty of insights to share with her father about the 30 employee, $4.6 million business.

But he never dreamed that she would present him with a major problem that he wouldn't know how to deal with. According to Sarah, the company's top sales rep was guilty of sexual harassment.

Calvin already knew that Jack Johnson—who brought in 50 percent of the company's sales—told dumb blond jokes and that he called all females "girls." Over the years, Calvin had heard Jack say

Source: Reprinted with permission of Small Business Forum, 432 N. Lake St., Madison, WI 53706-1498. Copyright © 1993 by the Board of Regents of the University of Wisconsin System.

ETHICS BRIEF

Philanthrophy as an Ethical Initiative

Although much of the discussion in this book focuses on the emergence of ethical misconduct as a negative force in industry, all is not lost. Many organizations are taking concrete steps to heighten their role as a positive force in society. This Ethics Brief will illustrate several prominent examples of positive ethics at work.

Social Responsibility as a Corporate Priority

In the past few years, a widely held notion has emerged that corporations must be socially responsible if they are to serve the broader environment in which they operate effectively. In board rooms and staff meetings, employees are raising fundamental questions about the need for employers to engage in ethical behavior by serving as role models. Social responsibility can be accomplished by donating a percentage of profits to charity or volunteering services to nonprofit organizations. A few examples are listed below:

- At Textileather in Toledo, Ohio, a committee of four employees (no upper management) meets quarterly and allocates a percentage of profits to local charities that the employees have designated.
- After Pacific Bell repairman Dave Goodenough was diagnosed with AIDS in 1986, company managers galvanized to raise awareness about the myths and realities of the disease. The company's monthly *Business Digest* prints regular features about how company employees donate time, services, and capital to local AIDS charities.
- Smoot Corporation, a large construction company in Columbus, Ohio, assists struggling minority contractors with a mentorship program where 30 percent of profits on designated projects are guaranteed to reach the minority enterprise. *Inc.* magazine (May 1993, 117) said that: "The catch to being a Smoot apprentice is that you are required to return the favor to another needy company." To date, over a dozen minority businesses have learned from their mentor and assisted comparable organizations after they completed their scope of work.
- At Stride-Rite's corporate headquarters in Cambridge, Massachusetts, a major initiative to offer child care and elder care to employees has been studied by governments and companies worldwide. Employees can drop off their children on one floor of the facility and their elderly parents who need modest care on another. The employees know that both will be well cared for at minimal cost (the company pays for approximately 70 percent of the costs of services). The program has led to a significant reduction in turnover at the company.

While the number of such initiatives is expanding in the mid-1990s, the social responsibilities of major employers equally expands. Increasingly, employers are recognizing that loyalty and productivity is enhanced, absenteeism is reduced, and worker satisfaction is increased when the company offers a broad array of philanthropic and outreach programs. This is especially true in the industrialized nations where a shrinking and changing labor force is demanding a greater array of benefits.

A recent study notes, for example, that in Europe and the United States, the under-

Dr. Edwin H. Land, founder of Polaroid, holds 535 patents. No one knew when this test photo was taken using a Polaroid camera in 1947 that Land and Polaroid would succeed. The company has an extensive community relations and philanthropy program that supports engineering education, emerging technologies, and scholarships for children of employees.

age-65 work force will grow about 10 percent between now and the year 2000; for the same period the growth rate of those 65 to 84 years of age will increase more than 22 percent. *(Select Committee on Aging,* 99*).*

The social implications of these statistics must be evaluated in terms of who will care for the parents of workers, what will be the meaningful nature of that care given, and how workers can balance the demands of their own families with those of their parents. This issue takes on complex significance when one considers that for many technical and advanced jobs in the industrialized world, employers expect—and many demand—that workers constantly pursue additional courses and degrees in order to remain competitive and skilled in their jobs. The ethical questions raised about the expectations of both the employer and employee remain vague at best.

Innovation in Social Responsibility: RJR Nabisco

Some companies have launched ethical programs aimed at assisting the diverse needs of their employees. Consider, for example, multinational RJR Nabisco's announcement in March 1992 that it would institute a new program supporting the educational needs of worker dependents. Highlights of Nabisco's program include the following:

- For each of four years that an employee contributes from pretax salary into an interest-bearing account, the company matches the employee contribution up to $1,000.

ARCO's Social Responsibility Program includes grants from the ARCO Foundation to various preschool programs, minority student retention efforts, and direct grants to public, parochial, and private schools. This graphic from the Foundation's annual report depicts the company's goal: "The return on investment in education is one of the easiest to measure. Every dollar spent on preschool education, for instance, saves $5 later in the costs of special education, public assistance, and crime."

Funds are taxable upon withdrawal. This translates into a possible $4,000 contribution for each of the company's 35,000 employees.

- The company will assist employees in procuring federal student loans, will pay a 3-percent loan guarantee fee, and will further subsidize the debt by paying 3.25 percent of the interest payments.

- Nabisco estimates that as many as 5,200 employees will take advantage of the program in the next few years on behalf of nearly 7,000 eligible

After the devastating riots in Los Angeles in 1992, Bank of America introduced a $25 million Small Business Investment Program to help entrepreneurs rebuild. Here, Bank of America vice-president Suse Nakata (right) and branch manager Ron Johnston (center), visit Cesar Palacios, whose iron products business reopened with help from Bank of America's program. Bank of America believes such programs are socially responsible and can also increase bank business when entrepreneurs grow in terms of operations and profits.

dependents—all at a cost to the company of nearly $7 million annually.

- All Nabisco employees are eligible with the exception of the 147 top ranking executives who, presumably, can afford to pay tuition and related fees for their children. *(Nabisco News Release,* March 6, 1992)

With $13 billion in annual gross sales, it can be argued that a $7 million allotment toward educational expenses is paltry. Yet Nabisco's initiative merits favorable attention in a book focusing on business ethics because it is the first significant corporate commitment of its kind—and because the company launched the program *even* in the midst of a global recession.

A Variety of Learning Environments Exist
Other organizations have responded with myriad programs aimed at meeting the needs of dependent education.

Stride-Rite Shoes houses an on-site intergenerational daycare facility at its Cambridge, Massachusetts, headquarters where young children and aging parents of workers can learn, play, and interact with each other. In just the past two years, teams of human resource personnel from corporations in such diverse nations as Great Britain, Yugoslavia, Hungary, and Chile have visited the facility as they seek to model their own programs after that of Stride-Rite.

Smaller companies that cannot afford to construct their own learning environment are finding that participating and sharing costs in an educational consortium works to their advantage. The Tyson's Corner Play and Learn Center in Virginia was launched after 20 area corporations donated $100,000; each may send a predesignated number of employee children to the center, and scholarships are available for employees whose salaries do not exceed preset limitations. Citibank recently expanded its Las Vegas, Nevada learning center for young children due to surging employee demands. The company believes that its low turnover rate among working mothers can be primarily attributed to the security of knowing that their children are in close proximity.

Providing tuition reimbursement and learning environments for employee dependents makes economic as well as social sense. Low-income parents pay an average of 23 percent of their entire family income for daycare expenses, compared to 10 percent for the rest of society (More than one-fourth of the 1,500 members of the International Ladies Garment Workers Union surveyed responded that child care consumes more than 35 percent of their entire income). By providing daycare and tuition support to low-income workers in particular, corporations are often assured that workers who fill necessary but often unfulfilling positions remain loyal.

Study Indicates Commitment to Social Responsibility Varies

The New York-based Families and Work Institute, a nonprofit think tank that examines employee benefits, recently surveyed 298 of the largest U.S. companies and ranked the 198 that responded. The results were less than impressive—the average company scored only 68 out of a possible 610 points. Of 298 companies, only four companies were considered exemplary—Johnson & Johnson, IBM, Aetna Insurance, and Corning Glass. Common threads among those who scored well included on-site daycare for children, significant numbers of scholarships to employee dependents, the presence of referral services and educational counseling for dependents, and a menu of other tax-sheltered, educational options.

How Acute Are Employee Needs?

In searching for an ethical program of employee benefits, many organizations begin the process of assessing needs. Corporate managers frequently argue that they lack the knowledge and expertise to determine whether their organization should consider offering expanded educational benefits to worker dependents. A logical solution is a fact-finding process accomplished with the use of a Delphi survey of employee attitudes. An initial survey is the genesis for further studies and inquiries that provide continuous feedback and responsiveness.

The results of data received from surveys can be used by a committee of workers and management to prioritize the programs that may be considered in the future. After that prioritization is complete, a comparative budgetary and fiscal analysis can help determine what is feasible and what deadlines should be established for the group.

The human resource department of a corporation is often best equipped to coordinate surveys of full-time employees. Among the most pertinent questions to be asked concern the employee's length of service with the company; the number and ages of dependents, including parents; what percentage of salary (independent of payroll deduction) if any, is currently dedicated toward educational expenses for dependents; and whether the worker anticipates assuming financial obligations for any new dependents in the foreseeable future (adoption, new birth, relocating and aging parents). Clearly the responses to these and other questions unique or of interest to the corporation will help company executives assess the scope of programs that they can reasonably accommodate within their existing corporate culture and budget. Eldercare and educational benefits are also emerging in importance. Many organizations tend to ignore the issue because it is a difficult one to quantify, but new data is emerging here as well. For example, Transamerica Life Companies (insurance) recently completed a companywide survey of 1899 employees. According to *Personnel Administrator*: "It was determined that 1600 missed work days per year could be attributed to 21.6 percent of employees providing care to one or more elderly people. The annual loss for Transamerica was approximately $250,000 in salaries and benefits."

Summary
The addition of educational benefits is an ethical yet expensive proposition for any employer. Nabisco is a case in point (although the vast majority of organizations

are obviously not of comparable size or asset base). The costs of launching an on-site daycare and learning center for approximately 50 children averages about $100,000 while annual maintenance, insurance and equipment costs, including salaries for personnel, will double this figure. These estimates are comparable for learning-care centers constructed for parents. Several surveys in recent years indicate that between 25 to 35 percent of employers reduce their operational budgets by charging modest fees to participants. (*Employee Benefit Plan Review*, 58)

Sources: Laurence, Barton, "A Cross-Cultural Comparison of Child Care as an Employer Provided Benefit," *International Journal of Sociology and Social Policy*, Volume 11, Number 5, 1991. Portions of this Ethics Brief are based on that article; Nabisco News Release, "Nabisco Announces Innovative Educational Benefit," dated March 6, 1992; Select Committee on Aging (U.S. House of Representatives), *Exploding the Myths: Caregiving*, 1987 U.S. Government Printing Office, Pub. 99-611; and "Shrinking, Changing Labor Force Prompts Johnson & Johnson Family Issues Policies," *Employee Benefit Plan Review*, September 1989, 58.

some pretty stupid things to women. Jack seemed to think that women liked his loud, friendly style—and in many cases, Calvin thought that they probably did. Jack was a paunchy, balding, middle-aged fast-talker. Who could take him seriously? And what was the harm in it?

For the first two months of the summer, Calvin was convinced that there was no harm in it. Sarah "had a feeling" that Jack was doing more than just leering at the women employees, but she was unable to offer any specifics. Jack never said anything to her at all. In fact, he often cut conversations short when she entered the room.

Then Debbie Boland, the billing clerk, quit with no notice, and Sarah agreed to fill in until a replacement could be found.

The typist and two of the reps (who worked in the same large room as the billing clerk) all pitched in to help Sarah learn the billing system. The third rep, Jack, was on the road for the week.

Three hours into her job as the substitute billing clerk, Sarah walked into her father's office and shut the door. Looking furious, she sat down and said nothing.

Calvin quickly finished his phone call. "Sarah, what happened?"

"Fire Jack Johnson!"

"Why? What happened?"

"I just talked with him on the phone. He didn't know that Debbie had quit, and he thought that I was Debbie. He said, 'How's my little bombshell today?' I said, 'Who is this?' He said, 'Don't play hard to get with me, blondie. We both know what the score is. You can say whatever you want about me, but we both know who Cal my pal will replace if there's any trouble. Your job is to keep me happy, get it? And I don't appreciate your threats to tell anyone about our little fun in the parking lot last week.'"

"Oh my God," Calvin said, as he watched his daughter cry angrily. "I'm sorry you had to hear this."

"I couldn't stomach any more so I said, 'This is Sarah Yorsborough, not Debbie.' and he hung up."

Calvin got up and went toward his daughter. "Honey, I'm sorry. I don't know what to say." He gave her a tissue and put his hand on her shoulder. "Why don't I have your mother come and pick you up? You should take the rest of the week off. Maybe you two can go shopping."

"Is that what you tell the other girls who have had to take whatever Jack Johnson dishes out? You don't get this, do you, Daddy? It's not just disgusting, it's against the law! You have no choice but to fire him."

"Sarah, you have every right to be upset—"

"Upset? This was the ugliest, creepiest conversation I've ever had, and you think I might be upset?" Sarah stood up. "Is this the way the world is? Men can dish out whatever they want because women like Debbie are disposable? And you put up with it! How many other times have you put up with whatever it was that he did to her in the parking lot?"

"Sarah, you have to believe me. This was the first time anyone has ever told me—"

"And why do you think that is?"

Calvin didn't leave the office when his wife came to pick Sarah up, but he might just as well have. He couldn't concentrate. He didn't take any calls, he kept his door shut, and he didn't even touch the financial report that was in front of him.

Calvin didn't for a second doubt that Jack was capable of saying everything that Sarah had reported. He didn't doubt that Jack had said the same—and probably worse—to other employees before. And who knows what had gone on in the parking lot? Billing clerks never lasted long. Calvin recalled that Jack once said, "Dizzy girls don't know enough math to do the job. They get all flustered at the drop of a hat." Now, Calvin realized what a mistake it had been to let Jack be in charge of hiring the billing clerks. And no wonder they were flustered—if Jack propositioned and threatened them. Or worse. And now Sarah, who had always seemed to admire her dad, said she thought he was just as sleazy as Jack Johnson.

Calvin stood up and looked through his office door's window. No doubt about it. Jack was a jerk. But fire him? He brought in 50 percent of the company's sales. The other two reps each only brought in 25 percent—and they were two of the better reps he'd had over the years. If Jack left, the business would suffer. They had just purchased a new machine from Germany, and cash was tight. Jack would probably get a job from one of Yorsborough's competitors within an hour. Had they survived the recession, only to be ruined by this?

Calvin sat down on the side of his desk and rubbed his eyes. Jack was guilty of sexual harassment. No doubt about it. But if he left the company would lose a significant number of sales. Calvin would probably have to lay people off. And what would happen to them?

What if he would call Jack in and lay down the law? What if he said, "This is wrong. Leave the girls alone or you're out"? Calvin imagined two different possibilities. Either Jack would quit on the spot, or he would quit when he was caught a second time.

Could Jack change? Calvin doubted it. The very idea of an "enlightened" Jack Johnson was ridiculous.

The image of his angry daughter haunted him. How could he ever let something like that happen to her? He had spent the last 20 years protecting his little girl and letting her think he had all the answers. And now this.

Calvin reached over and picked up his suit coat. He slid it on as he went toward his door. He didn't know where he was going, but he knew that he could no longer remain in his closed office.

What should Calvin Yorsborough do?

REFERENCES FOR CHAPTER 4

Associated Press. "EECO Backs Sex-Bias Suit at Ortho." Undated article from *Las Vegas Review-Journal.*

Associated Press. "Worker's Bogey: Bosses on Links, Too." *Las Vegas Review-Journal*, October 8, 1993, 14.

"AT&T Ex-Employee Admits to Conspiring to Extort $1 Million." *The Wall Street Journal*, September 13, 1993.

"Banking by Paper Bag." *Newsweek*, February 25, 1985.

Barton, Laurence, and Hardigree, Donald. "You Are Not Alone. " *Small Business Forum*, vol. 10, no. 2, 1992.

Brown, Carl P. "Crimes of the Vault." *Security Management,* January 1990.

Bulkeley, William M. "Voice Mail May Let Competitors Dial E for Espionage." *The Wall Street Journal*, September 28, 1993.

Burrough, Bryan. "How American Express Orchestrated a Smear Campaign of Rival Edmond Safra." *The Wall Street Journal*, September 24, 1990.

Carley, William M. "Rigging Computers for Fraud or Malice Is Often an Inside Job. " *The Wall Street Journal*, August 27, 1992.

"Companies Pay For Fraud." *USA Today* Snapshots column, September 13, 1993.

Crino, Michael D., and Leap, Terry L. "What HR Managers Must Know about Employee Sabotage. " *Personnel,* May 1989.

German, Jeff. "Troubled Waters." *The Las Vegas Sun*, April 11, 1993.

Gibbs, Jack P. "Conceptions of Deviant Behavior: The Old and the New." *Deviant Behavior: A Text-Reader in the Sociology of Deviance.* Edited by Delos H. Kelly. New York: St. Martin's Press, 1989.

Jacobs, Deborah L. "Sexual Harassment: What You Don't Know Can Destroy Your Firm." *Your Company*, Spring 1993.

Knight-Ridder Newspapers. "Dishonest Workers Stealing Billions." *Las Vegas Review-Journal*, May 2, 1993.

Knight-Ridder Newspapers. "Employers Use Misdeeds to Fight Discrimination Suits." *Las Vegas Review-Journal*, May 14, 1993.

Littman, Jonathan. "The Last Hacker. " *The Los Angeles Times Magazine*, September 12, 1993.

Moore, James F. "Predators and Prey: A New Ecology of Competition." *Harvard Business Review*, May–June 1993.

ETHICS BRIEF

Employers Beware on Claims

According to *Business Insurance* (July 17, 1994, p. 1), the number of sexual harassment charges filed with the EEOC have risen dramatically in recent years in some states:

	Number of charges filed in 1993	% increase since 1989
Highest		
Illinois	616	433.4%
Wyoming	37	428.9
New Hampshire	59	385.9
North Dakota	17	316.7
Florida	830	261.2
Nationwide	**11,908**	**111.8**
Lowest		
Arizona	165	36.9
Vermont	21	27.3
Hawaii	51	13.6
Rhode Island	29	10.4
California	656	0.8

Source: Equal Employment Opportunity Commission; State University of New York at Albany.

Nickell, Daniel B. "Networked for Crime. " *Security Management*, December 1991.

Palmer, Thomas. "US Told Bank of Trouble in 1982." *The Boston Globe,* February 27, 1985.

"Speed Brake." *Forbes*, October 11, 1993.

Stein, Charles. "Bank of Boston Defends Currency Business." *The Boston Globe*, February 12, 1985.

Watson, Traci. "Computers: Bugging Out." *U.S. News and World Report,* November 15, 1993.

Winokur, L.A. "Harassment of Workers by Third Parties Can Lead into Maze of Legal, Moral Issues." *The Wall Street Journal*, October 26, 1992.

Wolfe, Craig. "An Inside Job." *Mortgage Banking*, May 1991.

Woo, Junda. "Edward Dunne Gets Probation in Trading Case." *The Wall Street Journal*, September 14, 1993.

Yoodin, Ted. "Internal Theft via Sick Days." Monograph in Management at the University of Nevada, Las Vegas, May 1993, 4.

CHAPTER 5

Who Audits the Auditors?

All in all, a picture emerges—from interviews, indictments and now a court-ordered report—of Phar Mor as a thicket of conflicts of interest, corporate negligence and outright corruption. For six years, some officials seemingly used the company as their personal plaything, falsifying financial ledgers and allegedly raiding company coffers. . . . Chairman Shapira, asked if he didn't have reason to suspect fraud well before it was revealed in mid-1992, says that "all along we got consistent audits and unqualified financial statements from extremely qualified accountants. There were numerous due diligences by some of the most sophisticated investors. Everyone came to the same conclusion that this was a sound company growing quickly."

The Wall Street Journal,
January 20, 1994, p. 1

Thus far we have explored the variabilities in ethics between employers and employees. In this chapter, we will look at one of the largest professions in the United States where the lines of distinction between employer and employee are remarkably vague. In recent years, accountants have come under siege from regulators, the news media, and even their own clients for a variety of abuses. Despite stiff ethical and legal principles that mandate candor, auditors claim that they are often pressured to make "adjustments" to their formal audits, in which they report about the financial health of a client, or they risk losing that customer.

The litany of embarrassing cases in recent years suggests that a serious re-examination of ethical standards in accounting is necessary. Accounting is an integral aspect of business and finance, and in this chapter we will first examine why independent accounting is important and then look at one case in greater detail.

THE IMPORTANCE OF INDEPENDENCE

Accounting does not just happen. Literally reams upon reams of rules, regulations, and recommendations describe in detail what should and should not be done when auditors examine the books of a corporation. Because federal tax regulations are so complex and consistently changing, the profession must agree on a certain set of established rules about how such items as inventory, depreciation, payroll, and taxes are reported. The two most commonly accepted principles in North America are the Generally Accepted Accounting Principles (GAAP) and the Generally Accepted Audit Standards (GAAS).

Organizations typically have internal auditors, who ensure that company rules and regulations about expenses and income are being followed, as well as independent auditors. The independent auditors play an especially important role because they are required to be unbiased and to comment honestly and freely about any improprieties they detect. Their responsibilities are governed by a series of professional associations (for example, the American Institute of Certified Public Accountants [AICPA] and state CPA societies), as well as government interests such as state laws and the Securities and Exchange Commission (SEC). (Elliott and Jacobson, 37)

Trying to explain the technical aspects of an audit would be too voluminous for this chapter. Rather we will focus on the relationships surrounding an audit. Who is in control? Who is making the decisions? Do the people working with auditors risk monetary losses if a discrepancy is uncovered? More specifically, are internal controls in place that can recognize fraud before it turns into a crisis?

Although many organizations have input into the independence requirement, the bulk of responsibility lies on the shoulders of the individual public accounting firm. For example, employees must be informed of newly retained clients so that discrepancies or conflicts of interest in security investments can be avoided early. Also, family relationships must be reviewed to avoid improprieties. The bottom line is that an auditor's independence is requisite to establishing and maintaining a good reputation. Therefore, an auditor's independence is not only a requirement, but a necessity. If questions arise concerning principles of independence, they can be directed to either the SEC or the AICPA.

Independence is not only an issue with an outside auditor, but it also applies to individual committees inside the corporation. The SEC mandates that any corporate audit committees also be independent. Because of a series of recent scandals involving some of the "Big 6" accountant firms, the late 1990s will see a trend toward "pure" independence of both the compensation and nomination committees in a company.

The National Commission on Fraudulent Financial Reporting (also called the Treadway Commission) has articulated duties for a principal audit committee. Such committees should recommend independent auditors, approve the overall audit scope, review the adequacy of internal control systems (including internal audit activities), and review the annual financial statements and auditor's report. (Deloitte and Touche, "Current Issues for Audit Committees," 23)

The audit committee does more than oversee quarterly reports. The audit committee must make sure that the internal controls associated with an audit work together to perpetuate competent reporting. The committee should work assiduously to provide a comfort zone for the internal audit staff to function properly. This will ensure that internal audit personnel can proceed with the audit task unchallenged by management. The purpose of the audit—to inform management, employees, and owners the company's level of operations—can be subverted if the audit report sends incorrect financial signals.

In September 1992, the Committee of Sponsoring Organizations of the Treadway Commission (COSO) released a report titled "Internal Control—Integrated Framework." The report outlined practical standards for internal control that allow entities to assess the

ETHICS BRIEF

Ethical Investing Can Be Profitable in More Ways Than One

In the mid 1970s, college students raised the consciousness of the nation by arguing that institutional endowments should not be invested in South Africa (to protest the policy of apartheid) or in companies that primarily produced tobacco products or alcohol. These were but two of several social concerns that led students to publicly protest and threaten to walk out of classes. As a result, many boards of trustees eventually altered their college investment policies.

Twenty years later, millions of Americans engage in "ethical investing," a practice that has dramatically changed the economic landscape of Wall Street. By refusing to invest in companies that make weapons, test products on animals, or make philanthropic contributions to anti-environmental candidates, these investors have led to the creation of new investment vehicles that cater to such concerns.

In January 1994, *Money* magazine identified seven of the nation's best socially conscious funds. Their annualized returns on investments were remarkably robust:

Fund	Three-Year Return
Fidelity Select Telecommunication	31.9%
Fidelity Advisor Strategic	21.9
Flag Investors Telephone	20.3
IAI Regional	18.7
20th Century Balanced	17.8
Fidelity Select Software	45.7
Evergreen	22.4

Source: "Investment Trends," *Money Magazine*, January 1994, p. 89.

control system currently in place. The committee suggests typical questions that companies should ask about an internal audit: Is our internal control system effective? Do we spend too much, or too little, on our systems of internal control? How do we compare with our competition in terms of audit control? (Deloitte and Touche, 11) Before the "Internal Control—Integrated Framework" report was issued, the problem facing the audit committee was that internal control had different meanings to different managers. This report provided *all* stakeholders with a common understanding of what internal control is all about, giving companies a uniform standard on how to write an audit.

The audit committee of any corporation has many important relationships, one of which is with the independent auditor. This professional must communicate certain matters to the board of directors, preferably through the audit committee. The independent auditor has an ethical obligation to communicate with a client on a number of matters, including those listed here. (Deloitte and Touche, "Current Issues for Audit Committees" 19, 29)

- Errors, irregularities, and illegal acts found during the audit—unless they are clearly inconsequential, for example, overstatement of profits by senior management.

- Auditors' responsibilities—to be sure that the committee understands the *limitations* of an audit. For example, committee members need to be educated as to the difference between the expected level of assurance the independent auditor provides and the actual level of assurance that the independent auditor provides under GAAS.

- Significant accounting policies, both initial selections and changes—to be sure that the audit committee understands their implications, especially in controversial or emerging areas. Also to be addressed are significant unusual transactions.

- Management judgments and accounting estimates used in preparing the financial statements—especially those involving large amounts, long future periods, or several possible outcomes, for example, varying methods used to calculate depreciation.

- Significant audit adjustments, whether or not recorded by the entity—to focus on possible systemic problems in recording, processing, summarizing, and reporting financial information. An example would be changes in accounting standards that produce nonrecurring charges.

- Disagreements with management about significant accounting principles, estimates, and judgments—even if subsequently resolved, such as, differences between firm specific accounting methods and those recognized under GAAP.

The audit committee must also be able to communicate freely with their independent auditor: Each must be cognizant of the other's needs. When all groups—independent auditor, internal auditor, board of directors, and management—recognize their legal and ethical obligation to honest financial reporting, they can avoid a hemorrhage of capital and a loss of public trust. In severe cases, they can also avoid prosecution for financial impropriety.

One stakeholder concerned with the competence and process of the audit committee is the board of directors. Ideally, a board of directors boasts a healthy percentage of nonemployees who, like the auditors, project no bias toward projects or departments. Executive search consultant Jack Lohnes defines an independent director as a person who "has no current commercial or personal family relationship with the corporation served, is not a retired executive or employee of the corporation, and beneficially owns [votes] less than 5% of the voting shares of the company." Though the ratio of outside to inside directors is changing toward more outside directors, most experts agree that a good ratio is 4:1 between outside and inside directors. (Johnes, 13)

As legal owners of a company, the board must direct the CEO to effectively manage the company. The board of directors is increasingly expected to review the CEO's performance. To be successful, the CEO must keep the board informed of good *and* bad news. In his article, "The Changing Relationship between Outside Directors and the CEO," Thomas Neff makes this argument: When companies are hit by a sudden wave of bad news, the excuse most commonly offered by their directors is, "we had no idea it was coming" or "we were never told." Such professions of ignorance may be self-serving, but more often than not there is a basis in fact. The point is some CEOs fail to advise their fellow Directors of impending difficulties. (Neff, 7)

Having a clear and candid relationship allows for a feeling of open and ethical communication between the CEO and the board of directors. This relationship can help ensure that the owners' (and stockholders') best interests are kept at the forefront.

Effective internal control starts at the top. According to Richard F. Vancil, writing in *Harvard Business Review*, the most common form of dynamic management is the *duo-mode*. The duo-mode consists of two top executives, a chairperson and a president, with one serving as CEO. Vancil warns that the *solo-mode*, with only one executive at the top, most common in smaller companies, presents control problems. "With nobody else sharing major decision making, there are few structural constraints on the CEO's power. The danger is that the CEO may come down with a serious virus I call CEOitus." (Vancil, 109) It does not matter what title the executive in charge holds: One person wielding all the power, calling all the shots, left unchecked, can be devastating to a firm. The case that follows is ample evidence.

ETHICS BRIEF

It's a New Board Game

In the past three years, a number of publicly owned corporations have encouraged their board of directors to be more aggressive in evaluating the performance of senior managers. At least two dozen CEOs of such major corporations as American Express, Westinghouse Electric, Carl's Jr. Restaurants, and Apple Computer were terminated by activist boards.

As the president of the National Association of Corporate Directors, John Nash, told *The Wall Street Journal,* "In the past, CEOs treated boards like mushrooms. They kept them in the dark and fed them manure." Now, board members at some companies realize that they could be held legally liable as officers and directors if they are negligent in protecting the financial and reputational needs of the company they

serve. At Home Depot, a large home improvement chain, directors are required to make unannounced visits to at least eight stores a year to listen to employee and customer complaints.

Professor of management Ed Goodin, who teaches at the University of Nevada at Las Vegas, notes that "The era of a board member that received $5,000 a year in stipends for rubber stamping the decisions of day-to-day managers has ended. The courts, the public, and the media now expect board members to be ethical—to earn that stipend by actively asking questions and demanding accountability."

Source: *The Wall Street Journal*, October 15, 1993, p. 17.

PHAR-MOR'S TOP MANAGERS EMBEZZLE MILLIONS

In early 1992, the Phar-Mor Corporation of Youngstown, Ohio, was a shining star among retail drug chains with annual sales in excess of $3 *billion*. Phar-Mor's deep discounting strategy seemed to be paying off for its investors. Sam Walton, founder of Wal-Mart, was once quoted as saying that the chain he feared most was not Kmart or Sears, but Phar-Mor. (*Wall Street Journal*, January 20, 1994, 1).

Privately held Phar-Mor had some powerful backers, including Pittsburgh-based Giant Eagle, Inc., which owned 35 percent of the stock. Giant Eagle is a 50-store supermarket chain owned by five families, including Phar-Mor CEO David Shapira. With an estimated $1.5 billion in sales, Phar-Mor's other investors included Lazard Freres & Company's Corporate Partners investment fund,

Youngstown shopping-mall magnate Edward J. DeBartolo, PNC Financial Corp., Westinghouse Credit Corp., and National Westminster Bank. This was a very impressive portfolio of backers that most creditors would be delighted to be associated with.

In 1988, Phar-Mor retained Coopers & Lybrand as its independent auditors. Given rapid growth and wide customer acceptance, Phar-Mor's investors, along with its many secured and unsecured creditors, could not have been more pleased with a company that seemed to do everything right.

Phar-Mor was founded in 1982 by David Shapira and Michael "Mickey" Monus. The two met when Giant Eagle bought the Monus family grocery business in 1981. It was shortly thereafter that Shapira and Monus developed plans for a deep-discount chain of drugstores; Giant Eagle provided 50 percent of initial funding. The synopsis that follows lists the events that led to the massive ethical and financial crisis that took Phar-Mor, its creditors, its customers, and its prosecutors by surprise in mid-1992. As you read this chronology, consider the checks and balances and think about which questions you may have asked along the way, assuming you were a senior executive at Phar-Mor, a member of the company's board of directors, or an independent auditor assigned to monitor the company's finances.

1982   First Phar-Mor store opens in Niles, Ohio, outside Youngstown. Michael Monus is named president; David Shapira is named CEO.

1984   The chain grows to 20 locations by year-end.

1987   Phar-Mor opens 32 additional stores.

- Seemingly independent of his role as Phar-Mor president, Michael Monus establishes the World Basketball Association for players 6' 7" and under.

1988   Phar-Mor opens its 100th store in Boardman, Ohio.

1989   Annual sales for the company top $1 billion.

1990   Sales top $2 billion and Phar-Mor opens store number 200 in Hermitage, Pennsylvania.

- Concurrently, Monus becomes a partner in the Colorado Rockies professional baseball organization, another event seemingly unrelated to Phar-Mor.

1991   In June, Lazard Freres & Company's Corporate Partners investment fund invests $200 million for a 17 percent interest in Phar-Mor.

- In October, Phar-Mor sells $112 million more of stock in private placement. The chain has grown to 305 stores.

1992   In March, Phar-Mor increases its credit line to $600 million with PNC Financial Corp.'s Pittsburgh National Bank and 17 other banks. An additional $155 million is financed by eleven insurance companies.

- In June, Phar-Mor's fiscal year ends with sales reaching $3.1 billion.

- On July 28, Michael Monus is demoted to vice-chairman from president and chief operating officer of Phar-Mor. The FBI and U.S. attorney's office is asked by unspecified company officials to investigate possible fraud and embezzled funds.

- On July 31, Monus and Phar-Mor's chief financial officer Patrick Finn are fired by the company's board of directors. Financial manager Jeffrey Walley is also fired.

- Within days, Coopers & Lybrand is dismissed as Phar-Mor's outside auditor and replaced by Deloitte & Touche. Phar-Mor charges that Coopers & Lybrand contributed to the company's financial mess.

- On August 4, Phar-Mor announces it will take a $350 million charge, related to alleged embezzling and fraud by officers of the college, to reflect events that were not properly reported on previous financial statements.

- On August 5, Coopers & Lybrand's general counsel states that Phar-Mor has shown "no remorse for the hiring, retaining and promoting of this senior management the board now claims are 'crooks.' Responsible boards have oversight of their management and knowledge of their company's operations." (Stern, September 11, 1992, A3)

- On August 17, Phar-Mor files for Chapter 11 bankruptcy protection in Ohio and sues Coopers & Lybrand in a Pennsylvania state court for "grossly negligent, intentional or reckless failure to uncover a massive fraud perpetrated on Phar-Mor by two of its senior level managers over several years." (Stern, August 20, 1992, A3) Some stores refuse to ship goods to Phar-Mor stores out of concern that they may not be paid.

- On August 18, Phar-Mor lays off more than 1,000 employees from corporate headquarters and its distribution unit

E T H I C S   B R I E F

A Nation of Laws and Not of Men?

The pristine image of the Federal Bureau of Investigation (FBI) has been tarnished in recent years. First, several biographies of the late director J. Edgar Hoover emerged in the early 1990s that characterized the crime-fighter as a conniving autocrat who retained his position by spying on his enemies, including several U.S. presidents, only to then use that information as a lever to retain his job.

Anyone interested in Hoover would be well-advised to read several of the recent works on the content of his private versus public character. In an exhaustive analysis, Anthony Summers concluded that Hoover, like others with a penchant for power, actually lacked self-esteem, which propelled him to become a neurotic, self-serving narcissist:

> They come to think of life in terms of the Good, represented by themselves, and the Bad, represented by everyone and everything that seems to run counter to their way of thinking. Such people often gravitate to groups or organizations that reflect their own limited view of the world. They surround themselves with acolytes who will reinforce the notion that they are always right about everything. . . .
>
> A sociopath is a person who, because of mental illness, lacks a sense of social or moral responsibility. Edgar ran his course as head of the FBI, for half a century, by representing himself as the precise opposite.

Ethics ran amok in Hoover's personal life as well. He reportedly enriched his home and bank accounts at the expense of taxpayers with a variety of schemes; his largesse included gambling at several race tracks with sums that were astronomical by any standard. If that were not bad enough, Summers concluded:

> Edgar lived virtually free at taxpayers' expense. . . . His house in Rock Creek Park, the Justice Department report revealed, was completely painted and major maintenance performed inside and out every year while he vacationed in California. . . . Home appliances, air conditioners, stereo equipment, tape recorders, television sets and electronic wiring were serviced and repaired by Radio Engineering Section Employees. . . . Employees were on call night and day for complete repair and maintenance of the entire home and grounds.

More recently, the FBI continues to have its share of negative publicity over ethical abuse within its ranks. For example, agents have been charged with internal theft, a problem virtually unheard of a decade ago. In June 1994, a former Philadelphia agent, Kenneth R. Withers, confessed that he stole almost 100 pounds of heroin from the agency's storage facility and sold part of it to drug dealers. Withers reportedly sent mailings to drug dealers and offered them "unlimited quantities" of high-grade heroin with no down payment at half of the price being charged on the streets. He allegedly even included sample one-ounce packets in his promotional package.

Source: For more information see Anthony Summers, *Official and Confidential: The Secret Life of J. Edgar Hoover*. (New York: G.P. Putnam's Sons, 1993). Also, Joseph A. Slobodzian, "FBI Agent Admitted Drug Theft," *The Philadelphia Inquirer*, June 6, 1994, p. 6.

and eliminates its office furniture and team sportswear product lines. News reports indicate that the company's reported profits of $50 million in 1991 should actually have been reported as a *loss* of $150 million.

- On August 19, Coopers & Lybrand announces plans to countersue Phar-Mor. Coopers assistant general counsel says of Phar-Mor executive David Shapira, "As CEO and chairman of the board, he had an obligation to manage the company, to be familiar with Phar-Mor's affairs and to supervise Monus. It's *his* desk where the buck stops." (Stern, August 20, 1992, A3)

- On September 10, Coopers & Lybrand files a countersuit against Phar-Mor for unspecified damages. Coopers contends that Shapira and Monus established corporations to develop and lease real estate and lease office equipment and fixtures to Phar-Mor for private gain. An example, according to Coopers, is PMI Associates, at the time owned by Shapira and Monus, which in 1991 collected $4.1 million in rent from Phar-Mor and was in a position to collect $97.9 million in future rent. (Stern, September 17, 1992, A4)

- In the days that follow, Phar-Mor responds that these companies enriched all shareholders. Also, Phar-Mor says that before Coopers & Lybrand was fired as its outside auditor, Coopers knew of the companies in question and approved the relationship between the companies.

- As early as 1988, Coopers contends it reported irregularities concerning Phar-Mor's inventory. This prompted Phar-Mor to seek outside assistance with annual inventory counts. Coopers maintains in the countersuit that Phar-Mor's top officials got around the outside inventory counts by keeping two sets of inventory books and by overstating official books, "except those which they knew Coopers & Lybrand was independently testing." (Stern, August 20, 1992, A4)

- By September 16, Phar-Mor fires senior vice-president Joel Arnold. The company contends that Arnold knew that Michael Monus and then CFO Patrick Finn were altering financial statements by overstating inventories. Joel Arnold acknowledged he knew of the fraud and agreed to resign. News reports indicate that executives kept quiet in an effort to receive lucrative salaries and bonuses.

Charges of financial improprietary at Phar-Mor, a discount drug chain, originally placed the amount of missing cash at $35 million. By the time auditors and investigators ended their investigations in 1994, the amount of financial damage to the company had grown to an estimated one *billion* dollars.

- Phar-Mor closes 55 stores in an effort to maintain cash flow after Chapter 11 filings.

1993   In February, after a six-month investigation by the FBI, Michael Monus is indicted by a Cleveland federal grand jury on charges of fraud and embezzlement. The 129-count indictment against Monus includes counts of bank, mail and wire fraud, filing false income tax returns, conspiracy, and 118 counts of money laundering.

- The indictment continues, allegedly Monus falsified Phar-Mor books from June 1989 to July 1992 by overstating inventory and accounts receivable by a whopping $499 million. By concealing Phar-Mor's poor performance, Monus was reportedly able to receive substantial bonuses and stock options. The indictment alleges Monus received $1.3 million in 1991 from a stock redemption and $400,000 in bonuses in 1991 and 1992. The indictment further accuses Mickey Monus of embezzling $10.5 million from Phar-Mor by placing the money in the bank account of his now defunct World Basketball League.

■ Monus is also charged with embezzling $568,000 for his own personal use. The tax charges consist of filing false federal income tax returns by omitting an excess of $2.4 million in income in 1990 and $4.3 million in 1991. Monus is also charged with defrauding creditors and investors by falsifying financial statements.

■ Allegedly defrauded institutions include PNC Financial Corp.'s Pittsburgh National Bank and 17 other banks that provided Phar-Mor a $600 million line of credit; Lazard Freres & Company's Corporate Partners investment fund for $200 million; Sears Roebuck & Co., 11 insurance companies that purchased $155 million of senior secured notes in 1992; Westinghouse Electric Corp.'s credit unit , which loaned $50 million; and National Westminster Bank, which participated in a $112 million private stock placement in 1991. Seventeen insurance companies filed suit on April 25 in Pittsburgh against Phar-Mor's officers and directors, Coopers & Lybrand, and Giant Eagle, alleging they misled insurers into investing $155 million into the drug chain. (Stern, August 28, 1992, A8)

■ On May 6, Jeffrey Walley is sentenced to six months of home detention for his role in the reported fraud and embezzlement scheme; he pleaded guilty to aiding and abetting bank fraud.

■ Federal officials concede that David Shapira had no knowledge of the crimes committed, and as of this writing he remains chief executive of Giant Eagle.

■ On November 9, 1993, Patrick Finn was sentenced in a Cleveland court to 33 months in prison; by agreeing to testify against Monus, he avoided as much as 266 years in prison and an $8.75 million fine.

1994   In a major investigative report, *The Wall Street Journal* concludes that losses from mismanagement at Phar-Mor now exceed everyone's estimates and will top *$1 billion*, making the case one of the most expensive in U.S. history. *The Journal* reports that members of the finance team at Phar-Mor wrote memos to their supervisors advising that something was seriously amiss, only to be told to destroy the memos (which they did not). Former chief financial officer Patrick Finn and Jeffrey Walley cooperated with authorities and pled guilty to federal charges. The company closed 151 stores but is trying to rebuild its financial base with its remaining 150 units. (Stern, January 20, 1994, 2)

THE IMPLICATIONS OF PHAR-MOR

How could such an ethical and financial atrocity happen?

Phar-Mor apparently was not prepared for such a crisis. A spokesperson for David Shapira told *The Wall Street Journal;* "You don't look for fraud, and if there is one, you count on your outside auditors to be the ones to check on it." (Stern, August 20, 1992, A3) This statement is analogous to a parent assuming no responsibility for his or her child, expecting any deficiencies in behavior to be found and assessed by the child's schoolteacher.

So who is right? According to a 1992 report by the Committee of Sponsoring Organizations of the Treadway Commission concerning internal control:

> External parties, such as independent auditors, legislators, regulators, customers, and others transacting business with the company, contribute to the achievement of the entity's objectives, but they are neither responsible for nor part of the entity's internal control system. . . . Management has the ultimate responsibility and should assume "ownership" of the system; the board of directors should provide governance, guidance, and oversight; and other personnel should communicate upward any non-compliance with the code of conduct, any other policy violations, any illegal actions, and any problems in operations or related matters." (Deloitte and Touche, "Current Issues for Audit Committees," 12)

These statements are not meant to alleviate Coopers & Lybrand from blame, as their complicity, if any, will be decided by the courts. It is, however, meant to point out the fact that companies *are* responsible for their internal controls. At the heart of the Phar-Mor case is the issue of accountability. Is it possible for one or two executives to divert tens or hundreds of millions of dollars to their personal interests or sports teams without scrutiny? Where were the internal auditors at Phar-Mor? If any questions were raised, were they silenced by senior management? How can a well-respected firm such as Coopers

E T H I C S   B R I E F

An Enemy Who Cleaned Up

Sometimes the enemy in the workplace is neither accountant, scientist, nor aggrieved ex-employee–it's the chief executive officer.

In the late 1980s, Wall Street was dazzled when Donald D. Sheelan assumed the position of CEO at Regina Company at the age of 38. Armed with an MBA from Syracuse University and a marketing background cultivated at Johnson & Johnson, Sheelan was an ambitious, tireless worker who masterminded several product successes, including the Homespa, a $100 whirlpool that fit into a standard bathtub, and the Regina Housekeeper, a nifty, lightweight vacuum.

Sheelan's personality was reportedly anything but cordial, however. Welcoming visitors to his office door was a Hoover doormat so people could "walk over" his rival. Employees complained that he repeatedly intimidated customers as well as coworkers.

But as signals of trouble mounted, such as when 40,000 Housekeepers were returned in just one quarter, Wall Street continued to sing praises of Regina. *Business Week* documented that with companies such as Shearson Lehman Hutton praising Regina to clients, the company's stock value shot from the equivalent of $5.25 in 1985 to $27.50 in 1988. Yet behind the scenes, Sheelan was busy falsifying company financial records, understating expenses, and engaging in other questionable practices. He pleaded guilty in February, 1989 and was sentenced to a work-release program at a correctional facility in St. Petersburg.

Sheelan has since been released. Regina has closed its doors.

Source: For more information see "How Don Sheelan Made a Mess That Regina Couldn't Clean Up," *Business Week*, February 12, 1990, p. 46.

& Lybrand retain the confidence of other clients in the midst of this ethical and fiscal mess? What if the accused are innocent?

Some organizations require that all employees, including senior managers and external auditors, file an annual disclosure statement on all business transactions and investments external to the company. Although such a mandate smacks of an invasion of privacy on the one hand, it may be an unfortunate necessity in certain companies and industries given the volume of cases that have similar characteristics to the Phar-Mor debacle.

How did this mess unfold? According to Phar-Mor, an outside firm responsible for counting inventory would turn its figures over to Monus and other executives who would then increase the numbers. This practice, once realized, caused Phar-Mor to "write down" inventory from $900 million to $775 million. (Stern, A1) The company claims that Monus, with the help of Finn, shifted $10.5 million to his failing World Basketball League in an effort to bolster the organiza-

E T H I C S   B R I E F

An Enemy Who Sits in the Corner Office

Who are the most common perpetrators of crime in a company? The U.S. Sentencing Commission reported in 1992 that owners are, by far, the greatest thieves in the percentage of cases where serious crime has been reported:

Owners	51.6%
Unknown	22.3
Top Executives	16.1
Managers	7.0
Supervisors	1.8
Employees	1.1

Source: "To Catch a Thief," *CFO Magazine*, February 1992, p. 30.

tion. Also, Monus and Finn allegedly collected vendors' payments for exclusive supplier arrangements and reported them up front instead of deferring the payments over the period of the vendors' contracts, as is common in the industry.

How could Michael Monus operate with such little oversight? Phar-Mor's headquarters was contacted in an effort to gain some understanding into its corporate structure. Phar-Mor spokespersons, however, declined to give any information due to the pending lawsuits, despite repeated attempts. But Assistant U.S. Attorney John Sammon told the Associated Press (March 3, 1993) that "Monus was clearly the leader of this scheme. He was the one who devised it and directed it, and then Finn carried out his orders."

A *Business Week* investigation drew this conclusion:

Monus operated with amazingly little oversight. In the past 10 years, Monus took stakes in, or purchased outright, more than two dozen companies. He also founded a fledgling pro basketball league and sponsored women's pro golf tournaments. . . . One Phar-Mor backer says that he only started receiving actual financial statements this year [1992]. (Stern, A1) Shapira told *The Wall Street Journal* that he is "satisfied I acted as a reasonable, prudent businessman. Many people were fooled. I was only one of them. I'm not embarrassed by the fact that I didn't find this problem any sooner." (Stern, A4) *He's not embarrassed?*

Coopers & Lybrand is also not without its vulnerabilities. Independent auditors are concerned with the fair presentation of the financial statements in accordance with GAAP (although manage-

ETHICS BRIEF

A Profession Under Fire

Accounting and auditing firms typically appreciate publicity; one or two strategically placed mailings or profiles in the news media can land a new client. But accountants can also seek to veil their identities when it serves their purpose.

For example, when members of the U.S. Senate began receiving mail from constituents regarding a bill that would help the accounting profession, senators were surprised that so many people would be interested in such an obscure bill. They shouldn't have been surprised at all: The nation's third-largest accounting firm, Deloitte & Touche, had orchestrated a letter-writing campaign.

According to *The Wall Street Journal*, company accountants were urged to write their senators "specifically without identifying themselves as accountants." An internal memo to some of the company's 1,400 partners urged:

> You are being asked to write a letter now, using your home address, with no indication of your firm affiliation, to your senators. . . . Hand written letters are encouraged. . . . Our job is to overwhelm them with an outpouring of constituent requests.

The effort backfired when Capitol Hill staffers suspected a campaign orchestrated by partisan interests. "This seems ham-handed and . . . a little bit crude," noted James A. Thurber, director of the Center for Congressional and Presidential Studies at American University. "I think the deception is foolish and wrong." Hogwash, said the accountants. "Just because I am an accountant does not mean I am not a private citizen and have my own views about any number of pieces of legislation," responded William Ezzel, a partner with Deloitte & Touche.

Questions for Consideration

1. If you were managing a large accounting firm with an interest in a piece of legislation, how would you orchestrate a lobbying campaign aimed at influencing public officials?
2. Was the criticism leveled at Deloitte and Touche justified?
3. What kinds of burdens are placed on employees or partners of a firm who receive this kind of letter from their company?

Source: For more information, see Richard B. Schmitt and Amy Stevens, "Deloitte Pushed for Anonymity in Lobby Effort," *The Wall Street Journal*, April 21, 1994, p. B1.

ment is ultimately responsible for the company's financial statements and operating results). End users tend to believed auditors should be able to detect all fraud, when in fact they can only really set out to prove material fraud. (*Australian Accountant,* 15) Although there are many ways to dupe auditors, a physical check of inventory is supposed to be a clear method of cutting through any potential deception.

Why didn't Coopers discover discrepancies in inventory figures? Coopers contends Phar-Mor executives fooled the firms even during on-site inventory inspections. Says one attorney for Coopers & Lybrand, "They made bloody sure there was nothing wrong with the inventory in the stores we checked. The manipulation was in the other stores we didn't go to." (Stern, A3) Another concern for Coopers is the size of the payments by vendors for exclusive supplier contracts. (Stern, A3)

With several lawsuits still pending, it is clear that Michael Monus ran Phar-Mor, a company with revenues in excess of $3 billion in 1992, virtually unchecked. In this sense, the Phar-Mor case underscores the need for the duo-mode of top management. Phar-Mor appeared to have this type of leadership, but a closer look reveals that top management's "team" consisted of only one player—Michael Monus. Although a mistrial was declared in his trial in June 1994, charges of jury tampering may necessitate another trial.

WHAT CAN WE LEARN?

An effective management team should maintain communication with members of the Board of Directors between meetings and inform them of any important financial developments. Top management and its auditors should provide complete agendas with reports, allowing sufficient time for directors to review the material in advance. Directors should also be encouraged to meet with mid-level managers to ascertain which checks and balances are working and which are deficient.

A good starting point to prevent rampant fraud is the proper selection of board members. Board members should possess a variety of technical, financial, and human relations skills necessary for effective oversight. The free flow of information between top management and the board will help facilitate successful operations.

The audit committee is key to the audit process and the audit itself. If supported correctly the audit committee can greatly reduce chances of fraudulent employee practices, including the practices of senior management. The audit committee is the *direct link* between the board of directors and the independent auditor. It is paramount for the audit committee to ensure this process is free from encumbrances. As for the accounting profession, charges of inappropriate

---

ETHICS BRIEF

Reefer Madness: Blowing Away Potential Profits?

Selling cigarettes and cigars in the 1990s is an increasingly difficult challenge. Antismoking messages permeate our society, and many domestic tobacco producers have shifted their marketing focus away from North America to international markets where there are no bans on advertising and product give-a-ways.

Imagine the dilemma that struck Havatampa, Inc., in 1994, the Tampa-based manufacturer of Phillies Blunt cigars, a product that sells for about $1 for a five-pack. Company officials found that Latino music rap groups, such as Cypress Hill, were extolling the virtues of their product, not a bad vehicle for free publicity. But the intended message shocked company officials when they concurrently found out why sales of Phillies Blunt were skyrocketing: The marijuana smokers have been remov-

ing the tobacco and replacing it with marijuana, a trick that gives a potent high while masking the distinct smell of pot.

What can or should Havatampa executives do in a situation such as this? No one has suggested that they condone drug use, and they cannot be prevented from selling a product that is legal, though possibly inappropriately, misused. Does the company have any responsibility to the public? Should it accept increased sales and profits without taking any demonstrable action? If a manufacturer is aware of unintended use of a product that could cause harm, what is the responsibility, if any? What would you recommend?

Source: For more information, see *Business Week*, January 24, 1994, p. 42.

---

behavior continue to mount. In March 1994, Deloitte & Touche agreed to settle government negligence suits related to work it had performed for several savings and loans; the cost was a whopping $312 million. Ernst & Young agreed to pay $400 million. Arthur Anderson paid $82 million, and Coopers & Lybrand forked over $20 million for effort related to a single institution. (Schachner and Shapiro, 1)

We have, in all likelihood, not seen the last of the charges that threaten the credibility of what was once a noble profession.

This chapter was written with the research assistance of Gary Miller.

CASE STUDY:
WHEN EMPLOYEES ARE ACTIVISTS

Until about 1980, animal rights activism in the United States was not very well organized. With the emergence of the People for the Ethical Treatment of Animals in 1980, however, laboratory animal research facilities and other enterprises using animals in various endeavors found themselves faced with an uncompromising philosophy and the prospect of their animal facilities being infiltrated by activists posing as employees.

As you read the following case, consider your response to this question: If you were managing an animal laboratory in the midst of protests, what would you do?

History of the Animal Rights/ Animal Welfare Movement

The animal welfare movement in the United States was founded in 1867 with the American Society for the Prevention of Cruelty to Animals (ASPCA). Another group, the Humane Society of the United States (HSUS), was founded in 1954. Originally, the philosophies and activities of these organizations were primarily animal welfare oriented, specifically the *humane* use of animals, rather than the abolition of all activities utilizing animals. In 1883, the American Antivivisection Society was founded in Philadelphia when the founding member of the Pennsylvania SPCA opposed the use of animals in biomedical research.

The welfare and antivivisection movements remained separate until the origin of the modern animal rights movement, when antivivisectionists joined ranks with participants of the animal rights movement. Since then, animal rights activists have made a concerted effort to gain influential positions in the traditional animal welfare organizations in order to gain access to the resources and membership of these organizations. This has led to a dramatic change in the animal welfare movement in the past ten years from a traditional animal *welfare* to an animal *rights* philosophy. Many people recruited for membership are not even aware that the objectives of some organizations had changed (Lutherer and Simon 1992)

Source: This case was written by Frances R. Taylor who has been the supervisor of Laboratory Animal Care Services at the University of Nevada, Las Vegas, for 13 years.

Fueled by Peter Singer's book, *Animal Liberation*, published in England in 1975, the animal right's movement in the United States gained momentum throughout the 1980s until, by the mid-1980s, there were more than 400 groups with combined annual funding in excess of an estimated $150 million.

Animal rights groups have successfully targeted every industry and endeavor that utilizes animals, including but not limited to the fur coat industry, laboratory animal research, consumer product safety testing, rodeos, farming, use of animals in entertainment, horse and dog racing, hunting, and, most recently, zoos and public aquariums. In various forums, they raise a host of serious ethical questions.

Laws Governing the Use of Animals

Numerous laws and regulations govern the use of animals in most endeavors. Research facilities, zoos, and animals used in entertainment are regulated by the United States Department of Agriculture (USDA) Federal Animal Welfare Act, which was first enacted by Congress in 1966 to regulate dogs and cats purchased for research. The act was later expanded to cover all warm-blooded animals except rats, mice, and birds.

Research facilities that receive federal funding involving animals are also regulated by the Public Health Service (PHS) policy and that agency's *Guide for the Care and Use of Laboratory Animals*. The PHS policy covers all live vertebrate animals including fish, amphibians, reptiles, and birds.

Zoos are also regulated by peer-reviewed organizations such as the Association of Zoos and Aquariums (AZA). In addition to the Federal Animal Welfare Act, facilities using animals in consumer product safety testing are also regulated by the Food and Drug Administration (FDA). Hunting is regulated by state wildlife laws and regulations, and horse and dog racing are regulated by their respective commissions.

The fact that facilities are regulated does not pacify most animal rightists. The major complaints of activists are that the Federal Animal Welfare Act only covers warm-blooded animals, does not prohibit any procedures, and is poorly enforced because of budgetary constraints and lack of inspectors. Animal rights activists have openly stated in public protests they do not want cleaner cages, they want empty cages. They consider this stance to be both reasonable and ethical, and they often seem willing to participate in visible public acts to pursue their cause. In fact, one of the leading animal welfare groups is called People for the Ethical Treatment of Animals (PETA).

Animal Rights Activists as Employees

The primary animal rights movement in the United States began in 1981 with the infiltration a Silver Spring, Maryland, lab where monkeys were housed as part of a research project funded by the National Institutes of Health. The monkeys were liberated by Alex Pacheco after he obtained access to the lab by working as an animal caretaker. (McCabe 1990)

Then in 1988, a PETA representative employed as a laboratory worker of Biosearch, Inc., of Philadelphia (a small commercial research company) presented alleged documents at a press conference to support animal cruelty allegations. Multiple investigations by the Food and Drug Administration and U.S. Department of Agriculture found no basis for these charges. As a result of the charges and negative publicity, however, the company suffered harassment and the threat of contractors withdrawing their contracts (FDA 1988).

Mitroff (1990) describes a situation involving a major zoo (city unknown) charged with alleged animal abuse. Zoos, like many other community supported organizations, risk loss of community support and donations in addition to sanctions by the federal authorities if the allegations are justified. The organization believed it had a great scientific standing and credibility and that its own employees would not sabotage the organization. The zoo expected that sister institutions would come to its defense in time of need. In actuality, the great majority of the general public is not composed of scientists; the *employees* of the zoo first released the allegations to the press and the other organizations never emerged to defend the zoo.

In 1992 alone, there were two incidents of infiltration by animal rights activists. (Lee Group 1992) A PETA agent infiltrated Commonwealth Enterprises, a producer of foie gras (pâté) in Hudson Valley, New York, in May 1992. The "employee" videotaped the production facility, as well as what was purported to be inhumane processes in slaughtering the hybrid waterfowl. The videotape was determined to be inconclusive by a group of experts and animal cruelty charges were dropped.

A PETA staffer also infiltrated the Laboratory Animal Resources facility as a student employee at Wright State University in October 1992. She was later charged with tampering with facility records.

The University of Nevada, Las Vegas (UNLV), known throughout the country for a championship basketball program, thought it was exempt from target by animal rights organizations because of the species utilized in its research program. The institution was known for active support of endangered species and desert physiology research using primarily fish, amphibian, and reptiles. The use of "non-targeted" species lulled the administration, the faculty and staff, and the researchers into a false sense of complacency, however. The researchers and staff created an environment that was actually ripe for animal activism. The facility had no crisis plan, no security system, and fostered an environment of openness.

On August 13, 1987, the author of this case, working as a laboratory animal technologist and facility supervisor, found three of five newly acquired goats stolen from the kennel compound behind the research facility. The goats had been acquired less than a week before from a dairy goat farm to study how goats utilize water in arid environments.

The incident appeared to be a planned animal rights attack rather than a random act of vandalism. The local animal rights movement had recently gained momentum, and both membership rolls and publicity generated by the chapter were on the increase. The timing of the theft was curious: Access was made on Thursday, giving the perpetrators of the crime the entire weekend to begin their campaign.

With an acting police chief and a small force, the university lacked a tested response mechanism to a theft involving animals. The facility staff was advised by two officers who responded and initiated the investigation not to inform anyone of the theft. At the time it was not clear if the theft was an act of animal rights activists or a fraternity prank. A group claiming to be the Animal Liberation Front (ALF) called the university president's office and claimed responsibility for stealing the goats the day after the theft.

The results of the initial investigation revealed the animals had probably been collared with duct tape and hoisted over the six foot block wall that surrounded the compound. The goats were never recovered, nor were any of the principals apprehended.

The theft of the goats caused the institution to install a monitored alarm system and cyclone and barbed wire fencing around the kennel enclosure. The goat theft did not cause the university to cease research on animals, and in most cases, the animal rights activities *do not* cause the abolition of the use of animals. Instead they usually cause the facility to increase security at a significant cost to the taxpayer. Animal rights activists usually gain substantially through post-attack fund raising efforts and publicity given by the media to their activities.

The FBI has conducted ongoing investigations of animal rights groups based on Racketeering and Corrupt Enterprise (RICO) statutes. Federal grand juries in several states are investigating animal rights activists on similar statutes initially designed to target organized crime. (Burd 1993)

What Organizations Can Do to Protect Themselves

How, then, are institutions and organizations to deal effectively with perceptions regarding animal rights, some of which are legitimate when established research protocols are not followed, and the competent research of employees of facilities where essential scientific and medical research is conducted? Ethical questions abound in any discussion of the animal rights movement because of (1) changes in militarism in some animal rights groups (2) societal changes with the coming of the industrial revolution and corresponding increase in urbanization, and (3) information campaigns that feature hunting of whales and seals but are rarely counterbalanced with thousands of safe and responsible practices involving animals.

Through PETA publications such as "Becoming an Activist" and "Animal Rights 101 Workbook," members are trained and encouraged to infiltrate animal facilities. The ethical and moral questions raised by these activities are enormous.

In addition to activists infiltrating facilities, institutions may have employed dedicated animal rights activists who may provide information to the animal rights activists. The employee may become convinced that a procedure is cruel and may feel compelled to reveal her or his findings. Additionally, informants may not be dedicated to the cause or people associated with the movement, but, instead they may be paid informants. PETA has advertised in university newspapers offering $200 for photographs revealing cruelty in laboratories. Such is analogous to bounty hunting in the nineteenth century.

It is necessary for organizations to address the animal rights issues and include employee education and screening as part of the organizational crisis management plan. Any organization that utilizes animals is a potential target of criticism and potentially, theft and vandalism. This includes organizations in the fur industry, zoos and aquariums, research facilities (biomedical, university, and consumer product safety testing), farms, and companies in sports and entertainment sectors.

Likely sources of activism include disgruntled employees. Secretaries, custodial staff, and maintenance staff should be included in training programs to understand the benefits of animal use, as well as the mechanisms available to their concerns and grievances. These include arbitration panels and institutional whistle blowing policies discussed elsewhere in the book. Without question, animals have been abused in the past. Yet we must question whether the destruction of property, theft or "liberation" of animals, and the destruction of research papers does not undermine the significant benefits that have come from animal research.

The Federal Animal Welfare Act in the 1989 revision requires the inclusion of a whistle-blower protection clause. This act requires that personnel be trained and instructed in "methods whereby deficiencies in animal care and treatment are reported, including deficiencies in care and treatment reported by any employee of the facility. No facility employee, committee member, or laboratory personnel shall be discriminated against or be subject to any reprisal for reporting violations of any regulation or standard under the Act."

While this requirement is acceptable for legitimate violations of the Federal Animal Welfare Act, in fact the majority of animal rights activity is not due to legitimate violations, but instead to the philosophical position of activists that it is morally "wrong" to use animals for human needs.

Any person being seriously considered for employment, even voluntary service, should be thoroughly screened. Specific questions that relate to the use of animals should be asked and the responses noted. All references should be verified and police checks performed. Technicians who volunteer to work late hours, weekends, or holidays should be reviewed carefully. Animal rights activists can be well meaning and intentioned, but extremists have included police, security, janitors, students, physicians, and animal technicians—all implicated in animal rights activities at institutions around the world. The ethical implications are clearly immense for both sides of the issue.

Questions for Consideration

1. How can institutions balance their needs for research that benefits society with legitimate concerns of activists regarding animal welfare?

2. What do you think institutions can do to educate their employees and the public on animal welfare issues? What do you think is ethical and reasonable?

3. In as much as animal welfare / animal rights issues are a matter of "drawing the line," where do you draw the line relative to

animal use? Food? Some research? All research? Captive management (for example, zoos and public aquaria)? Pets?

4. What major changes in society have fueled the increase in the animal rights movement?

5. What part should the media play in the ethical assessment of institutions that use animals?

References for Case Study

American Association for the Advancement of Science. "Keeping Score on Animal Activism." *Science*, October 1, 1993, 34–35.

Burd, Stephen. "U.S. Probes Animal Rights Groups for Link to Raids on Laboratories." *The Chronicle of Higher Education*, June 23, 1993, 19–20.

Food and Drug Administration. "Investigative Report of Biosearch." Prepared by Ann L. deMarco and Richard P. Bradbury, Washington, D.C.: Government Printing Office, 1988.

Lee Group, Inc., 1992 Worldwide Animal Rights Incidents, Virginia, 1993.

Lutherer, L. O., and Simon, M. S. *Targeted: The Anatomy of an Animal Rights Attack.* University of Oklahoma Press, 1992.

McCabe, Katie. "Beyond Cruelty." *The Washingtonian*, February 1990, 73–77, 186–195.

Mitroff, I., and Pauchaunt, T. *We're So Big and Powerful Nothing Bad Can Happen to Us.* New York: Carol Publishing Group, 1990.

Singer, Peter. *Animal Liberation: A New Ethics for Our Treatment of Animals.* New York: Avon, 1975; 2nd ed., New York: Random House, 1990.

REFERENCES FOR CHAPTER 5

Carey, John. "A Scandal Waiting to Happen." *Business Week*, August 24, 1992.

"CEO's: Setting the Agendas." *Australian Accountant*, July 1992.

Deloitte and Touche. "Current Issues for Audit Committees, 1992."

Deloitte and Touche. "Current Issues for Audit Committees, 1993."

Elliott, Robert K., and Jacobsen, Peter D. "Audit Independence: Concept and Application." *The CPA Journal*, March 1992.

Johnes, Jack. "Identifying and Attracting Qualified Directors in the 90s." *Point of View,* Spring 1991.

Neff, Thomas J. "The Changing Relationship between Outside Directors and the CEO." *Point of View,* Fall 1989.

Schachner, Michael, and Shapiro, Stacy. "Bulk of Deloitte Settlement Insured." *Business Insurance,* March 21, 1994.

Stern, Gabriella. "A Founder Embezzled Millions for Basketball, Phar-Mor Chain Says." *The Wall Street Journal,* August 5, 1992.

Stern, Gabriella. "Chicanery at Phar-Mor Ran Deep, Close Look at Discounter Shows." *The Wall Street Journal,* January 20, 1994.

Stern, Gabriella. "Coopers & Lybrand Alleges Officers of Phar-Mor Pillaged the Company," *The Wall Street Journal,* September 11, 1992.

Stern, Gabriella. "Coopers and Lybrand Brings Countersuit against Phar-Mor over Firms Problem." *The Wall Street Journal,* August 20, 1992.

Stern, Gabriella. "Grand Jury Indicts Monus on Charges of Fraud, Embezzlement at Phar-Mor." *The Wall Street Journal,* February 1, 1993.

Stern, Gabriella. "Phar-Mor Dismisses Another Executive, Says He Didn't Disclose Alleged Fraud." *The Wall Street Journal,* September 17, 1992.

Stern, Gabriella. "Phar-Mor's Profit Growth Since 1989 May Have Been Inflated, Sources Say." *The Wall Street Journal,* August 28, 1992.

Stern, Gabriella. "Phar-Mor Seeks Chapter 11 Protection from Creditors." *The Wall Street Journal,* August 18, 1992.

Vancil, Richard F. "A Look at CEO Succession." *Harvard Business Review,* January 1987.

Exposing the Enemy Within: The Ethical Implications of Whistle-Blowing

To one who was in the White House and became somewhat familiar with its interworkings, the Watergate matter was an inevitable outgrowth of a climate of excessive concern over the political impact of demonstrators, excessive concern over leaks, an insatiable appetite for political intelligence, all coupled with a do-it-yourself White House staff, regardless of the law. . . . After I was told of the presidentially approved plan that called for bugging, burglarizing, mail covers and the like, I was instructed by Halderman (President Nixon's chief of staff) to see what I could do to get the plan implemented. I thought the plan was totally uncalled for and unjustified.

White House Counsel John Dean
quoted in Glazer and Glazer, 35

A good employee never questions anyone anyway.

Anthony Ramirez, a no-show employee of then Chairman of the House Committee on Ways and Means Dan Rostenkowski. Ramirez was on the Congressional payroll for nine years.

"Perspectives," *Newsweek*, June 13, 1994, 15

At the time he made the above statement, John Dean was the most influential attorney in the United States, ranking second only to the U.S. attorney general in status. Though he had pledged to uphold the law, he acknowledged under oath that he had direct knowledge of illegal activities in the White House that subverted the U.S. Constitution. When he was asked by one senator during the Watergate hearings; "What did you know, and when did you know it?," his response and that of others led to the first resignation by a president of the United States. John Dean was a whistle-blower who emerged *after* wrongdoing had already been exposed within his circle of influence. Most whistle-blowers do not wait for Congress or the press to expose wrongdoing before they speak out: Their concerns are often expressed long before such public forums are provided.

Few issues discussed in this book are as unsettling and provocative as that of whistle-blowing. This powerful social and business force is changing the very landscape of how we interact with others in the workplace.

The term *whistle-blower* is borrowed from sports where the referee, a third-party neutral observer, also serves as the source of a warning when he or she blows a whistle to report an infraction by one of the players. Today, we have whistle-blowers in government, academe, industry, and the not-for-profit sector. The consequences of their actions pose legal, ethical and human resource questions for which there are no easy answers. Indeed, *The National Law Journal* (September 20, 1993, 37) reports that this issue is likely to be the most dominant force in law for the next decade:

> And it also illustrates the potential for litigation in what many employment lawyers call the hottest niche of their practice today. Whistle-blower law has moved from a corner where only public employees could make claims into the center of the ring, where private-sector companies now stand vulnerable to the dreaded knock-out punch from within.

In this chapter you will read about how organizations currently grapple with whistle-blowers. While some are encouraging the practice (and even reward such behavior), others continue to believe that private resolution (or *no resolution*) is the preferable alternative to reporting indiscretions in the workplace. The chapter concludes with a case study that examines the ethical questions raised by a veteran employee of Dow Corning, whose revelations regarding unsafe breast implants led to one of the most controversial and costly product defect cases in this century. In addition, you will read the compelling story of an employee of Prudential Securities who blew the whistle and paid dearly for his honesty, only to be vindicated by his employer and emerge as a genuine hero.

WHO BLOWS THE WHISTLE, AND WHY?

When President George Bush signed into law the U.S. False Claims Act in 1992, he did so after Congress and agency policy makers recognized that many government contractors and employees had historically abused the public trust by accepting or paying bribes or other illegal activities. Although the first False Claims Act was passed by Congress in 1863 following reports of contractor fraud perpetrated on the Union Army, that piece of legislation was largely ignored because there were few incentives for anyone to complain. The 1992 act rectifies this deficiency by promising to pay any U.S. citizen up to 25 percent of the value of any loss, cost overrun, or fraud that is proven.

The U.S. False Claims Act has been viewed by many ethics experts as welcome relief after decades of trying to get the government to encourage whistle-blowing. Certainly it is true that something had to be done after dozens upon dozens of controversies surfaced in Congress and elsewhere about illegal activity by such companies as Lockheed and General Electric—all working on projects subsidized by the taxpayers.

For many years it was extremely difficult for employees of these companies and the federal government to report activities that they suspected or knew were illegal: A single comment or question about possible impropriety could jeopardize a project or contract, and any employee might fear he or she might be fired. One of the terms that whistle-blowers frequently use in their articles and books (written after they lost their jobs) was *incest*: They witnessed a pattern of closeness that was so evil, so unspeakable, that those on the periphery of the activity dared not even speak about what they saw.

Job security means far less than it did ten or twenty years ago; employees in a wide variety of organizations enjoyed stability and financial health throughout the 1970s and 1980s as military spending increased amid concerns that threats in the former Soviet Union and Middle East could erupt into widescale war. For military personnel as well as employees working in research and nuclear-related companies in particular, looking the other way was not uncommon, not only because employees feared possible backlash, but also because they were financially secure by doing so.

Political scandals, the rise of activism during the Vietnam War, notable public protests against companies such as Nestlé, Hooker Chemical, General Motors, and individuals such as New York police officer Frank Serpico—who exposed widespread corruption among his colleagues—all transformed our perceptions of the whistle-blower. (Barton, 153) Indeed, as President Bill Clinton and Hillary Rodham Clinton found in 1994, several former associates leaked considerable details of the First Family's questionable investments in Whitewater Development Co. to investigators and the press. The motivations of these whistle-blowers remain open to conjecture. Such individuals could be perceived as a disloyal, back-stabbing, and retribution-driven idealist, or conversely reasonable white knights who were pursuing justice amidst improper conduct.

In their major study of hundreds of whistle-blowers, Glazer and Glazer make this argument:

> Whistle-blowers, we discovered, are conservative people devoted to their work and their organizations. Those we studied built their careers—whether as professionals, managers or workers—by conforming to the requirements of bureaucratic life. Most had been successful until they were asked to violate their own standards of appropriate workplace behavior. Invariably, they believed that they were defending the true mission of their organization by resisting illegal practices and could not comprehend how their superiors could risk the good name of their company by producing defective products, the reputation of their hospital by abusing and neglecting patients or the integrity of their agency by allowing their safety reports to be tampered with or distorted. (Glazer and Glazer, 6)

Based on several studies (Miceli and Near, Glazer and Glazer, and others) in which cases of whistle-blowing were examined, the following profile emerges of the typical manager who cries foul. In general, whistle-blowers

- Have high self-esteem and often feel that their contributions can lead to a cleansing of organizational problems;

- Possess a higher-than-average need to control their environment and believe that the absence of controls could jeopardize progress in the organization;

- Have stronger religious convictions than coworkers; two experts conclude that "whether Catholic, Mormon, Protestant or Jewish, several of the resisters we interviewed felt that their

New York police officer Frank Serpico was a fore-runner to the scores of whisle-blowers who are today leveling charges against their employers regarding unethical or illegal behavior. Serpico's efforts at exposing payoffs and drug deals in his ranks was later portrayed in a successful motion picture starring Al Pacino.

religions provided meaning through which they could interpret the events around them and guide them to respond appropriately" (Glazer and Glazer, 117);

- Are married rather than single and middle-aged rather than younger; slightly more men blow the whistle than women;

- Tend to be better educated than those who fail to report indiscretions; one study suggests that "higher educational levels may be associated with higher status in the organization and hence more power to bring about change" (Miceli and Near, 119); and

- Are almost always found to be high achievers rather than low performers who "have an axe to grind."

A case in point: B. Scott Davidson began work at Temple University in Pennsylvania on January 3, 1994, as a radiation-safety officer. When he informed his bosses of multiple incidents of non-compliance with Federal Safety Standards, he was fired after four weeks on the job because of "philosophical differences." Not so, said a U.S. Labor Department investigation, which found in a preliminary report that "the weight of evidence to date" suggested that blowing the whistle led to retribution. Davidson's attorney agreed: "A university is supposed to be a repository of knowledge, and here they are trying to stifle a whistle-blower." (Goodman, 16)

EXHIBIT 6-1   Blowing the Whistle: Selected Categories of Reported Abuse

Financial
- Bribes
- Extortion
- Embezzlement
- Illegal political contributions
- Money laundering
- "Rigging" bids
- Price-fixing

Policy
- Illegal "bait and switch" sales tactics
- Sexual harassment
- Environmental abuse
- Spreading false rumors regarding competitors
- Nepotism
- Invasion of employee privacy

The U.S. False Claims Act encourages citizens to report wrongdoing that has financially harmed taxpayers. This exhibit demonstrates the wider spectrum of recent whistle-blower cases that have emerged nationwide. Many of these cases have more of an impact on human resources than the financial condition of the organizations.

ETHICS BRIEF

The Abraham Lincoln Who Feared Defections

The sixteenth president of the United States was a remarkable leader who worked diligently to free the slaves and unite a divided country, but Abraham Lincoln also practiced a management style that would raise eyebrows today.

Lincoln used government agents to spy on his enemies and unilaterally suspended habeus corpus in defiance of the Constitution. Yet one footnote in Civil War history offers insight into a somber president who feared that his own cabinet members would work to undermine his successor, should he lose the presidency in the election of 1860.

Just before the election of 1860, Lincoln summoned his cabinet members and told them that he feared that their loyalty was blind and that their duty was to country, not to him personally. Fearing defeat to his former general-in-chief, Democrat George McClennan, Lincoln asked each official to sign a loyalty oath. The oath was not directed to Lincoln, but rather, to the person whom he thought would unseat him in sev-

eral weeks. The oath read, in part: "it seems exceedingly probable that this administration will not be reelected. Then it will be my duty to so cooperate with the president-elect, as to save the Union between the election and the inauguration; as he will have secured his election on such round that he cannot possibly save it afterwards."

Loyalty oaths were widely continued into the twentieth century, and many institutions, such as the state of Pennsylvania, still require employees to sign them today. In the midst of World War II, employees of the CBS broadcasting network were required to sign an oath of loyalty to the American government that one 20-year employee said caused "widespread dismay and loss of morale."

Source: For more information on the Lincoln oath, see *200 Years*, (Washington, D.C.: U.S. News and World Report Books, 1976), 2:42. For information on the CBS debacle, see Alexander Kendrick, *Prime Time: The Life of Edward R. Murrow* (Boston: Little Brown and Company, 1969).

THE MOTIVATIONS TO ACT

Although most whistle-blowers believe that their actions and statements will ultimately cleanse an organization of wrongdoing, this is not always the case. Some act out of anger or spite, for example when they

- Fail to receive a promotion, or merit pay increase;

- Believe that their department has been "short changed" in recent budget or personnel allocations; or

- Hope that their accusations will lead to the transfer or termination of a supervisor or colleague whom they dislike.

It is clear that whenever these or related motivations are the genesis of whistle-blowing, the accuser's behavior is unacceptable; to falsify charges for the sake of retribution is morally abhorrent. Usually, however, we see other motivations for blowing the whistle. The accuser, for example, may believe that

- The good name and reputation of the employer is threatened by continued illegality or morally questionable acts;

- Various publics have already been damaged by ethical misconduct and others may be damaged in the future (for example, a defective product leads to illness, fraud leads to abuse of taxpayer dollars, and so on);

- A number of similar or related wrongdoings are taking place in the organization and publicity surrounding this incident may prevent future abuse;

- The actions of one colleague could lead to financial ruin (and the end of the careers) of many innocent employees. This reasoning is in concert with the notion discussed earlier in the book of the greatest good for the greatest number;

- Someone is likely to learn about this wrongdoing eventually, thus the whistle-blower believes that by speaking out first, he or she may avoid prosecution or embarassment later;

- His or her disclosures will lead to a financial reward or bounty; or

- Society as a whole benefits if the wrongdoing is exposed, so the whistle-blower seeks to provide an example that will motivate others to act in a similar fashion.

Of course any one of these statements may not stand alone; a whistle-blower may have multiple reasons for seeking redress of grievances. Regardless of the source of the motivation, the ultimate impact of a whistle-blower's actions can cause both positive and negative ramifications for colleagues.

THE BENEFITS OF SPEAKING OUT

Whistle-blowing constitutes more than someone "snitching" on a boss or coworker: The process of speaking out about a perceived injustice can help an organization if charges can be proven, if they underscore an organizational or departmental deficiency, and if they lead to one or more positive changes in the workplace.

The benefits of whistle-blowing include identifying workers and managers who act illegally or immorally, sending a message throughout the organization that unethical behavior will not be tolerated, and alerting coworkers that their valid complaints about other abuses will also be heard and adjudicated.

The Public Good

Although each of these signals are encouraging, it is interesting to note that whistle-blower's are rarely seen in a positive light except when their revelations are so enormous in their impact (such as promoting public safety, or revealing a product defect) that the depth of their convictions and the power of their evidence generate public appreciation.

Such accolades were accorded to Daniel Ellsberg, who released classified documents known as *The Pentagon Papers* in 1971, and Karen Silkwood, a technician at Kerr-McGee Company in Oklahoma, who blew the whistle regarding worker contamination from allegedly defective fuel rods at a nuclear power plant. Ellsberg's actions led to a Supreme Court ruling upholding the public's right to know about complicity and falsification of data regarding U.S. commitment to the Vietnam War. Silkwood died in a mysterious car crash en route to meet with a *New York Times* reporter where she was about to produce evidence supporting her allegations; Silkwood's campaign was later immortalized in a film bearing her name. These are two of several hundred whistle-blowers whose acts of courage helped to change the way society thought and acted upon questionable public and corporate policies.

A Charge of Disloyalty

The decision to blow the whistle carries with it several special burdens, including potential retaliation. A number of whistle-blowers are also victims of stalled access to financial or promotional rewards, which are fairly easy to document and discern. Less obvious are questions about whether the whistle-blower is a loyal employee; coworkers may feel that the very person whose charges are meant to enhance honesty at the workplace is actually undermining the spirit of the team. Hence, the whistle-blower is often perceived as being disloyal, another kind of enemy within. Robert A. Larmer of the

University of New Brunswick disagrees that whistle-blowers are disloyal, however:

> Loyalty does not imply that we have a duty to refrain from reporting the immoral actions of those to whom we are loyal. An employer who is acting immorally is not acting in her own best interests and an employee is not acting disloyally in blowing the whistle. Indeed, the argument can be made that the employee who blows the whistle may be demonstrating greater loyalty than the employee who simply ignores the immoral conduct, inasmuch as she is attempting to prevent her employer from engaging in self-destructive behavior. (Larmer, 127)

Indeed, the courts have increasingly agreed with the argument that whistle-blowing is hardly an act of disloyalty, but can often serve as the progenitor for change in public policy. For example, the Supreme Court ruled 9-0 in 1990 that employees who are fired or punished after they complain about safety violations may sue their employer for emotional distress. In that case, *English* v. *G.E.*, 110 S. Ct. 862 (1990), an employee intentionally left a small amount of radioactive matter exposed to prove her point about the absence of safeguards. She won an important moral victory that sent shock waves throughout the nuclear industry.

For the worker in the nuclear plant, local bank, United Way office, or accounting firm, the decision of whether to "go public" is often driven by a sense of fulfilling a mission. Indeed, Professor J. Vernon Jensen of the University of Minnesota argues that whistle-blowers believe that while loyalty to one's coworkers is important, such sentiments are "superceded by other values, such as the dignity of life and equality and efficiency. . . . Whistleblowers challenge the assumption that what is good for the organization is good for the larger public." (Jensen, 324)

Financial Incentives

While research indicates that the vast majority of whistle-blowers do so out of ethical or moral concern and not out of spite or the desire for financial gain, there is no question that the 1992 U.S. False Claims Act and other incentives can and do play a role in spawning complaints.

For example, in one of the largest awards ever given to a whistle-blower, an employee sued General Electric after alleging that the company had overcharged the federal government for aircraft parts being sent to Israel. The company was fined $59.5 million for its actions, and Chester L. Walsh was awarded $11.4 million under the

ETHICS BRIEF

A $124 Million "Personnel Error"

On the morning of August 15, 1989, 46-year-old Jimmy Janacek was earning $93,000 per year as controller for Triton Energy Company of Dallas, Texas. That afternoon he was fired for whistle-blowing.

Following accounting principles, Janacek insisted that Triton's 10K filing with the Securities and Exchange Commission indicated that company chairman William Lee owned a company that Triton had purchased. His insistence on that public disclosure cost him his job.

But, according to *The National Law Journal*, revenge is sweet. "Last year, Mr.

Janacek drank deeply from the well of vengeance when he sat in a Dallas courtroom and listened to a jury award him $124 million from his former employer—an amount that equalled nearly half of Triton's revenues for the preceeding fiscal year." According to Janacek's attorney, Fritz Barnett of Houston; "The Janacek case shows . . . jurors don't like abusive and corrupt organizations."

Source: *The National Law Journal*, September 20, 1993, p. 37.

False Claims Act. (Associated Press, 6F) More recently, Douglas Keith, a former finance officer with United Technologies in Connecticut, was awarded $22.5 million in 1994 for alerting government auditors to fraudulent billing practices at Sikorsky Aircraft, a United Subsidiary (Worthington, F1) Thus, one of the benefits of whistle-blowing is that the punitive damages for wrongdoing can be stunning, forcing employers to listen to employee and activist concerns in the future or risk paying enormous sums in judgments and defense fees (in this one case, payments totalled well in excess of $70 million for a single case).

Today some 35 states have passed whistle-blower statutes, and 11 of these states prohibit any employer, private or public, from firing a worker who discloses information that falls under the umbrella of "public interest" disclosures.

THE DRAWBACKS

Not all whistle-blowers walk away from their cases wealthy or vindicated. Indeed, the ethical quagmire they face as to whether to blow the whistle or remain silent is laced with issues including invasion of privacy, isolation, intimidation, and even violence.

From the perspective of the employer, whistle-blowing can be equally damaging: The company may have invested enormous sums of capital and talent to develop proprietary designs and systems, only to find that one embarrassing case could open its trade secrets to predatory competitors here or abroad. In addition, after building a work force that embodies teamwork, one case of whistle-blowing could rupture group spirit and lead to anxiety, suspicion, and ultimate disharmony. Third, there is always the possibility that in the aftermath of one legitimate case where an employee makes a valid complaint about an organizational defect opportunists will try to duplicate the incident and seek financial gain based on greed and false charges.

In recent years, as whistle-blowing has become a well-understood concept in the workplace, a variety of new aspects of this issue have emerged. For example, a worker at the Resolution Trust Corporation (RTC), the federal agency responsible for cleaning up the costly savings and loan debacle of the 1980s, complained that agency supervisors searched his desktop computer after he testified to Congress in the summer of 1992 about agency mismanagement. Indeed, an Associated Press investigation (May 11, 1993, 4A) identified an E-mail directive from RTC assistant general counsel Barbara Shangraw to a computer technician that reportedly read:

> I have been requested by DC to get into Bruce Pederson's Word Perfect. Please copy into a directory for me what Bruce has in his Word Perfect.

State and federal statutes generally prohibit unauthorized wiretapping, including unauthorized entry into computer systems and electronic mail. Yet such intrusions are commonplace whenever a whistle-blower case emerges: The documents, work products, and personnel file of the complaining party often provide the employer with insight into the person making the charges. Concurrently, organization attorneys and psychologists have been engaged in some cases to help the employer determine if the nonconformist is likely to follow through on his or her charges or might be willing to settle the manner out of court and away from public scrutiny.

Another drawback to whistle-blowing is the gamut of questions about how charges are to be adjudicated. Should an organization designate an internal task force of employees who will investigate all complaints? Is it preferable to engage the services of a neutral third party such as the American Arbitration Association?

One fact about whistle-blowing is clear: This social and business trend is not going away. The incentive is obvious: One government prosecutor was able to secure judgments and fines totaling $110 million from National Health Laboratories of La Jolla, California, after charges of Medicare and Medicaid billing fraud were reported. Indeed, *The National Law Journal* reports that attorneys throughout the United States are flocking to represent whistle-blowers because of the enormous financial sums open to plaintiffs as a result of the U.S. False Claims Act and similar state laws:

> Given the number of cases in the pipeline– and not all are public because they are filed under seal to give (the Department of) Justice time to decide if it will join the suit—the expectation is that recoveries will reach the $1 billion mark in the next two years the . . . False Claims Act now has shown enormous potential as a new area for legal practice for those firms that have both the taste and the capacity for handling longer-term, complex civil litigation. (June 21, 1993, 16)

PREVENTING EMBARRASSMENT: WHISTLE-BLOWING POLICIES AT WORK

Cases of whistle-blowing can be prevented when organizations design and enforce policies aimed at encouraging employees to speak up when a troubling issue emerges and traditional channels seem inadequate.

After reviewing dozens of policies in existence at the corporate and public levels, the following recommendations seem appropriate for companies that seriously want to encourage disclosures of inappropriate behavior in their ranks and who concurrently wish to protect anyone in the organization who may be innocent of charges being brought against them:

1. Policies should be written and implemented that are customized to the specific industry of a company. For instance, a policy in effect at a biotechnology company should mention several examples of the types of behavior that would be the source of management concern; policies at a petroleum company would be different. While commonality exists among most organizations (for instance, suspected embezzlement or sexual harassment would be unacceptable in most cases), the policy should clearly indicate that a wide variety of possible scenarios could jeopardize the future viability of the organization.

2. Policies should be provided to employees upon hire, and a signed acknowledgment form should be placed in each employee's personnel file.

3. At least once a year, each employee should participate in a training program on whistle-blowing and grievance-related matters. At these sessions, trainers can explain and clarify the rules in force at the organization, and how the employer is equipped to respond to concerns, and should distribute copies of pertinent articles from trade magazines and academic journals about this issue to generate discussion.

4. Fairness and equity should be emphasized both in written and verbally delivered materials. Senior management must convincingly assert that if charges are made against any employee, the whistle-blower must be able to document and prove his or her charges and that no action will be taken to jeopardize either party until the fact-finding process is completed. To assist in an objective assessment, management should indicate that depending upon the nature of the charge, a third-party investigator or someone outside the whistle-blower's chain of command may be called in to oversee the process.

5. Cases of wrongdoing that are substantiated should be aggressively communicated throughout the company to visibly demonstrate that the organization will not tolerate unethical or illegal behavior. Prosecutions, including those that would seemingly damage the reputation of the employer, actually help employer if the company manages the case with thought and care. The prosecution of criminal acts sends a powerful message to the rest of the work force that honest, prudent management will be rewarded and that dishonesty will be punished.

TELEDYNE'S MODEL POLICY

In 1989, after a series of legal problems associated with U.S. government contracts at Teledyne, a major defense contractor and product manufacturer, the company responded with a model program of business ethics. The program is continually monitored and upgraded to ensure that it responds to the needs of the company's employees and business activities.

Each employee must receive formal business ethics training on an annual basis, using an impressive package of printed materials, overheads, videotapes and other material supplied by the company's full-time corporate ethics compliance officer Richard Harshman, who is based at Teledyne's corporate headquarters in Los Angeles. The package is updated annually.

Employees are shown a nine-minute video that introduces the subject of ethics at Teledyne. In the video, company chairman William P. Rutledge explains the company's commitment to ethical business practices and director of ethical compliance Richard Harshman explains how the system for reporting concerns works. After showing the video, the divisional ethics officer explains a series of transparencies that illustrate "the fundamental difference between right and wrong" at the workplace. The company's program emphasizes that even when an employee is not sure that her or his concern is valid, calling the ethics officer is a prudent first step. The company has a toll-free, confidential Corporate Help Line where concerns, which can be anonymous, are received and investigated.

The best part of the Teledyne response is situational training. Employees are taken through a series of brief mini-cases that typify actual or contrived misdeeds and asked, in effect, "What would you do?" A variety of examples are utilized. For example, the 1993 training program asked employees whether substitution of a component on a U.S. Navy contract—even a component of *better* quality than specified in the original contract—is allowable. The company provides at least three alternative responses to examples, each of which may have some merit, but only one is clearly the best approach for the organization.

Yet another example asked employees what they should do when a supervisor wants to charge the labor fee for an employee to one client's account when yet another client is already paying for the original labor. Other cases in the Teledyne package address issues such as conflict of interest, insider trading, accepting and giving gifts, the proper use of technology, and procurement practices.

What makes the Teledyne program so impressive is not that it is exhaustive, which it is, but rather that it teaches by illustration: It does not confuse the employees with paradigms and theories that they may not understand. The language is specific and easy to appreciate, the cases are relevant to Teledyne's corporate mission, and the mandate is clear: We will not tolerate infractions of this ethics code. The theme of Teledyne's program is "Do It Right." The company did.

CASE STUDY:
HE TOLD, HE SUFFERED, NOW HE'S A HERO

Mark Jorgensen thought he was just being an honest guy, exposing fraud in the real estate funds he managed for the Prudential Insurance Company of America.

Then his world fell apart. The boss who had once been his friend abandoned him. His circle of colleagues at work shunned him. Company lawyers accused him of breaking the law. The once powerful and respected executive soon found himself hiding in the local public library, embarrassed that he had been forbidden to return to the office and hoping not to be seen by his neighbors. His long and successful career seemed to be dwindling to a pathetic end. Finally, in February, the bitterest moment came: A middle manager at Prudential phoned to tell him he had been dismissed.

How could it have happened? Jorgensen and his wife, Billie, prayed and consulted the Bible. That night, they lay in bed, unable to sleep. They talked about their finances and worried what would happen when their health benefits were cut off. They decided the only way to survive financially would be to sell their home. Overwhelmed, Billie Jorgensen held her husband and cried. It seemed they had been defeated.

"That was the low point," Mark Jorgensen said in a recent interview. "It was very, very sad. All of our dreams and aspirations had just fallen apart."

Then, last month, salvation arrived in the form of another phone call. But this time the caller was the most powerful man at the financial-services giant, chairman Robert Winters. He wanted a meeting with Jorgensen to convey some stunning news: Prudential now believed him. Moreover, the company wanted to reinstate him and force out the boss he had accused of falsely inflating the value of properties in the real estate funds.

Mark Jorgensen had blown the whistle on company misdeeds. The turnabout resulted from the persistence of the man, who, even when he felt the most powerless, impressed some of Prudential's largest institutional investors with his willingness to fight for his convictions. Faced with continuing questions from those investors, Prudential shelved the results of an internal inquiry that found no

Source: By Kurt Eichenwald. Copyright © 1994 *The New York Times.* Used with permission.

wrongdoing and commissioned a second inquiry, filling hundreds of pages which could be summed up in four words: Mark Jorgensen was right.

That realization put Prudential in an unusual position in corporate America—siding with a whistle-blower it had battled for months against one of its own top executives. The decision, which will cost the company as much as $50 million to compensate investors harmed by overvaluations, has transformed Jorgensen from a soft-spoken man battling for survival to an industry hero.

Perhaps the most distressing lesson in Jorgensen's story is that even when a company's top management encourages its employees to speak up about misdeeds, as Prudential's did, whistle-blowers can be cut down by middle managers who may play down the problem and even accuse the employee of improprieties in an attempt at intimidation. Indeed, had Prudential not reversed itself, Jorgensen's life could well have been destroyed.

At age 53, Jorgensen's future looks bright. He rejected Prudential's job offer, electing instead to move from New Jersey, where he worked, closer to his sons in the West. The company paid him a sizable amount to settle his lawsuit, and he is now considering his next career step. As part of the settlement, the company stipulated that Jorgensen not discuss his accusations or details of what happened to him at Prudential. But during his ordeal, Jorgensen, on his lawyers advice, kept detailed records, including memos, diaries, and other documents, describing everything that happened. Many of those records were obtained by the *New York Times* before last month's settlement and are used here, along with interviews with people involved in the case, to reconstruct this whistle-blower's story.

The Path to Prudential

Mark Jorgensen had made a decision—the hurly-burly world of finance was not rewarding enough. In 1964, he walked away from his first job out of Lehigh University, an analyst's position at Manufacturers Hanover Trust, to return to his true love: clam-digging. He dipped into his savings to buy a dredge boat—already showing the kind of independence and ability to risk his career that later played a role in his journey into whistle-blowing.

His clam-digging business was a success. But in 1965 he became engaged to Billie Danjczek and decided to return to Wall Street, for an easier life. "I was working about 100 hours a week in the clamming business," he said. "You can't raise a family like that."

Jorgensen worked in mergers and acquisitions at Donaldson, Lufkin & Jenrette, then moved to real estate investments. Looking for new opportunities, the Jorgensens packed up their two young sons for the cross-country car trip to San Diego. On the way they took a fancy to Phoenix, stopped the car and moved in. Jorgensen took a job with a local developer.

A few years later when the developer closed its doors, Jorgensen called Prudential, one of the biggest companies in the real estate business. The call paid off. In June 1973 he joined Prudential's Phoenix office as a senior appraiser. Soon, he was promoted to San Diego, then Los Angeles, and finally Houston, where he ran Prudential's southern developments.

While in Houston, he grew close with an aggressive general manager who reported to him, Charles Lightner. The two became fast friends and occasional hunting partners. Jorgensen laughs when recalling the night in Monterrey, Mexico, when he and Lightner hitchhiked in search of a nearby boxing match, only to decide once they were picked up that they were being kidnapped. Instead, their Spanish had not been very good, and their ride was taking them many miles to a wrestling match.

Jorgensen moved back to the West in 1984, leaving Prudential to run his own consulting business. It was a big success: In 1987, he won the contract to manage the real estate portfolio of the California State Teachers Retirement System. By the early 1990s, with the children off to college, his life seemed settled.

Then, in 1992, Lightner called with a tempting offer: return to Prudential to manage the prestigious funds that are part of the Prudential Property Investment Separate Account, or Prisa. The funds had been managed for years by Lightner, who had been promoted to be the next managers boss. Lightner lobbied the Jorgensens with frequent phone calls. He sent flowers to Billie Jorgensen, along with a note begging her to let her husband take the job. The efforts paid off. In May 1992 Jorgensen decided to return to Prudential. Unlike his many earlier job changes, this would be a career move that would change his life.

The Discovery: Inflated Appraisals Stun a Newcomer

Touring about 160 Prisa properties, Jorgensen realized a shocking fact: The appraisal values of some properties were wildly inflated. Because those appraisals are used to determine the value of the funds holding the properties, such inflation would raise the cost of investing in the funds beyond their actual worth. And because Prudential's fees for managing the funds were based on their value, the amount the company was paid would be improperly increased.

In November 1992, Jorgensen told Lightner what he had learned: Outside appraisers hired by Prudential appeared to have improperly pushed property values too high, which would prevent the funds from performing well as the real estate values actually did climb. The values, he said, should be lowered.

Lightner did not seem surprised by the news. Don't blame the appraisers, Lightner said, because he was the person responsible for the value inflation. As described in Jorgensen's lawsuit and his other legal papers, Lightner said that when he took over managing the funds in 1987, they were lagging other funds badly and investors were pulling out their money. So, the filings quote him as saying, he had appraisers inflate values so the funds would look as if they were performing better and attract more investors. Moreover, the filings say, Lightner indicated he was proud of what he was doing to help the funds.

Through a Prudential spokesman, Lightner has denied making those statements. In the second report on Jorgensen's accusations, Lightner is quoted as saying that he never engaged in any effort to pressure the appraisers. The report concluded that while some properties were being carried at improperly high values, potentially in violation of Prudential's fiduciary duties, there had been no scheme to defraud.

The meeting with Lightner shocked Jorgensen. He thought that carrying the properties at improper values violated his fiduciary duties to investors. In addition, it virtually guaranteed that his unknowing investors would see poor performance in the years to come unless values were inflated even further.

So Jorgensen began a quiet campaign to lower the values of certain properties, among them the New York Hilton. His persistence began to fray his relationships at Prudential. Soon Lightner was threatening to remove him from the Prisa funds.

Last June, Jorgensen attended a meeting with Robert Winters, Prudential's chairman. At the meeting, Winters was asked whether he worried that division might cut corners to bolster profits. Jorgensen later told Lightner the chairman's answer: Those responsible would be dismissed. Within a day, documents filed in Jorgensen's lawsuit say, Lightner said he would lower the New York Hilton's value, although not by as much as Jorgensen thought necessary.

Jorgensen then decided to contact the legal department about the overvaluations. On July 3 a company lawyer, Ray Giordano, interviewed Jorgensen and picked up a report he prepared about the accusations. Now, Jorgensen thought, everything would be fixed. Still, when a friend advised Jorgensen to get a lawyer for his own safety, he listened. He turned to Nancy Erika Smith, a New Jersey employment lawyer who in 1991 won an age discrimination suit against IBM.

While Jorgensen protested that Prudential would do the right thing, Ms. Smith thought he was in a bad position. She told him to keep detailed records of everything that happened.

Within days, Jorgensen's confidence in the company began eroding. On July 20, Tom Biolsi, Prudential's chief compliance officer, called him in to discuss the accusations. But the meeting quickly focused on Jorgensen's behavior. If Jorgensen thought property values were inflated, how could he have signed the funds' 1992 annual report, Biolsi asked, according to Jorgensen's lawsuit. By doing that, he said, Jorgensen was just as guilty of overvaluation as anybody. In a statement, Biolsi said he had realized Jorgensen's accusations raised "serious questions about Prisa," and he recommended hiring independent lawyers to investigate. Afterward, he had no contact with Jorgensen.

The Reaction: A Counterattack by Colleagues

Jorgensen grew afraid to make a move that might raise suspicion. Days later, when the funds' second-quarter report landed on his desk for his signature, he agonized over what to do. He called Prudential's legal department, which, he said later, declined to give him advice. Lightner insisted he sign, telling him that otherwise he was not doing his job, according to the lawsuit. Jorgensen refused, and the report went out unsigned.

On July 29, Jorgensen spoke with Norman Cardinali, the valuation manager for Prudential, who was soon to retire. Any doubts he had about whether something improper had happened in the appraisals vanished during that conversation.

After hearing Jorgensen tell what Lightner had said about inflating values, Cardinali spoke up. "It wasn't Chuck's fault solely, it wasn't my fault solely," he is quoted as saying in Jorgensen's documents. "It wasn't the appraiser. We just worked in sync and we perceived an opportunity and we went ahead and we did it."

In an interview, Cardinali said he had never worked in such a way with Lightner simply because the two men were distant and rarely spoke, and because he was not part of the department's inner circle. "I refuse to believe that I implied to Jorgensen that there was some devious planning on our part," he said.

According to the documents, Cardinali described pressure being applied to appraisers to increase valuations, saying how executives "harassed" the New York Hilton's appraiser when she was valuing the hotel. "We only had to do it in a handful of properties and with a handful of appraisers," the documents quote Cardinali as saying. In an interview, Cardinali said, "Nobody ever used leverage on anybody. I would not tolerate any kind of intimidation and harassment." He added of the appraiser for the Hilton, "if I used the word harassment, it was certainly inappropriate."

In the report from the second investigation into Jorgensen's accusations, the appraiser for the Hilton stated that the values she assigned to the hotel reflected her own views and were not the result of presentation from Prudential.

The afternoon after his meeting with Cardinali, Jorgensen met with lawyers from Howery & Simon, a Washington law firm that had represented a Pentagon whistle-blower in the 1980s and that Prudential had hired to investigate his accusations. But the fund manager quickly came to believe that the lawyers might play down his concerns. One lawyer, William Wallace III, said he saw nothing wrong with overvaluing properties and had done that himself when applying for a mortgage, Jorgensen's lawsuit says.

In an interview, Wallace said that Jorgensen misinterpreted his comments and that he had not condoned the overvaluing of properties. Rather, he said, he asked Jorgensen whether it would be improper for the lawyer to accompany an appraiser examining his home to ensure that everything was accounted for. He said Jorgensen replied yes. "We fundamentally disagreed with that," Wallace said.

As the meeting drew to a close, the lawyers did express concern about one thing—what Jorgensen was doing. Late in the meeting, he alleged, they said he had violated federal disclosure laws in a meeting with a client the previous day by telling of his concerns about overvaluation—an accusation he denied. Jorgensen stood up and said that if the company was going to investigate him, he wanted his lawyer there. Soon Prudential was aggressively pursuing accusations of wrongdoing against Jorgensen. Lawyers began interviewing his subordinates, trying to find out whether he had told clients about the overvaluations.

At 10:30 p.m. on July 29, the telephone rang at the Jorgensen house. On the line was Al Toennis, a Prudential lawyer. He had a harsh message for Jorgensen: Prudential knew he had violated disclosure rules, and now it was deciding whether to turn him in to the Securities and Exchange Commission.

Jorgensen denied wrongdoing. The SEC was not called. But the signs were clear that his career was falling apart. On July 30, Giordano, the Prudential lawyer investigating Jorgensen's accusations against his boss, slipped into the fund managers office. The lawyers message was unmistakable: start looking for a new job.

"You unleashed forces that couldn't be controlled," Giordano was quoted as saying in Jorgensen's documents about the meeting. Even if the investigation proved the accusations against Lightner, "all that means is that Chuck's got a big problem. Doesn't mean you do too." Jorgensen again said he had done nothing wrong. If only, he said, he could talk to the chairman, the company would see he was right.

Giordano scoffed. Did Jorgensen think that the head of such a huge company would throw open his doors, thank him for his honesty and, on Jorgensen's word, dismiss Lightner? "Do you really think companies work like that?" Giordano is quoted in the documents as saying. At the least, the lawyer said, Jorgensen would have to take a paid leave during the investigation. Giordano declined to comment.

Within days, Jorgensen received a memo. "Prudential Realty Group and human resources are in agreement with you to place you on a paid leave of absence," it read. Jorgensen was crestfallen. He had never agreed to any such thing.

The Shame: As World Collapses, A Couple Prays

Without his work, Jorgensen was lost. He felt useless hanging around the house in Madison, New Jersey. His wife suggested they go on a trip, but he refused, saying that he was sure Prudential would want to talk to him and that he would soon return to the office. But few colleagues from Prudential wanted anything to do with him. "Company friends just disappeared," he said in an interview.

Restless at his house, Jorgensen spent days at the Madison public library. Even there, he felt compelled to hide from his neighbors, embarrassed that he was not at work. "If I saw someone I knew, I would sneak around the books so I wouldn't have to confront them," he said. "I didn't want people seeing me and saying, 'How come you're not at work like everybody else?'" Weeks passed, and Jorgensen's worries grew. The stress was straining his marriage, and the couple, devout Catholics, turned to prayer. The events perplexed his father, a long-time executive, who, while never doubting his son, thought there had to be a misunderstanding.

In August, Jorgensen received a telephone call from William Therrien, a vice-president of human resources at Prudential. The investigation was over, and no evidence of wrongdoing had been found. Jorgensen could return to Prudential, but no longer as the manager of the Prisa funds. The change, he was told, was part of a division reorganization.

In late September, Jorgensen returned to Prudential. His new office was on the fourth floor, far from the managing directors of his division. No one reported to him anymore. His former secretary told him that she had been advised to take another job at the company because Jorgensen would not be returning. He was assigned to a feasibility study on some real estate projects, with one caveat: He was not permitted to contact anyone outside Prudential to gather information. Inside the company, he was ostracized. Few talked to him, or went near him. In one large meeting, executives stood against the wall of a conference room rather than sit in the chairs on either side of him.

The Jorgensens decided to sue. But in that decision, they realized Jorgensen's income could well disappear. Billie Jorgensen began planning to return to work as a dietician. They tried to cut expenses. They abandoned plans for their annual Christmas trip. Accepted to the local country club, they passed on the opportunity. They went so far as to stop buying paper napkins because it was cheaper to wash the cloth ones. Billie Jorgensen said then that she would know when their ordeal was over when she saw paper napkins on the table again.

Jorgensen's lawsuit, filed in November, contended Prudential had retaliated against him for his whistle-blowing. In comments to reporters at the time, Prudential executives said that Jorgensen's accusations had been investigated and no supporting evidence found. This, the executives said, was simply the case of a bitter employee upset about a reorganization.

The Court Fight: A Judge's Advice—Fire the Man

Judge Dickison R. Debevoise of federal district court in Newark was livid. He did not like to see confidential company records filed publicly in his court. So when Jorgensen's lawyer filed the report Jorgensen had prepared in July to back his accusations, Judge Debevoise had a suggestion for Prudential: Fire him.

"For him to go out and spread this in the world is highly offensive," Judge Debevoise said at a hearing this past February. "I think this is grounds for firing him on the spot." Within hours, Prudential agreed. The phone call from Prudential to Jorgensen's home came that afternoon. As the couple listened on a speakerphone, a human resources executive told him that he had been dismissed for unethical conduct in filing the confidential records.

The Jorgensens were enraged. How could Prudential dismiss her husband for simply trying to do the right thing, Billie Jorgensen shouted at the phone. The call soon ended and the Jorgensens felt defeated. But unknown to them, pressure had been building for months at Prudential because of Jorgensen's accusations. After he had filed his lawsuit, angry investors demanded to know how a respected manager could make such serious accusations. Prudential assured them that an investigation had found no basis for the charges. When the pressure continued, another investigation, to be conducted by outside lawyers and accountants, was commissioned.

Then the stakes grew. In February, the month Jorgensen was dismissed, federal prosecutors subpoenaed Prudential for information about the funds. Jorgensen was subpoenaed as well, and testified before prosecutors. Commenting on that investigation, Prudential said it had no knowledge of a continuing criminal inquiry involving the funds.

The Apology: For Rare Courage, Prudential's Praise

The first sign to the Jorgensens that something good was finally happening came at 2 o'clock in the afternoon on April 27 when the telephone rang. Billie Jorgensen answered and heard an unfamiliar voice say; "Hello Billie. Is Mark there?" She asked who it was, and the caller replied, "Bob Winters." The chairman of Prudential Insurance asked Jorgensen to come to his office the next day. He agreed on the condition that his lawyer be present.

The following morning Jorgensen and his lawyer arrived at Winters's office in Prudential's headquarters in Newark. Over the next few minutes, Jorgensen could not believe what he was hearing. Winters said a second investigation had been completed, and it had found that a large percentage of Prisa properties had been overvalued. Investors were being told at that moment, he said, and would be compensated. And Prudential had asked for the resignation of Lightner and one of Jorgensen's subordinates. Then Winters praised

Jorgensen for his courage, saying the company would never have found the overvaluations had he not been so persistent. The company was proud of him, and wanted him to return.

Jorgensen sat almost in shock, unable to respond. Finally, Winters asked him how he was feeling. With that, the emotions built over the last year poured out of Jorgensen, as he recounted his trials: when no one believed him, when he was threatened, when he was avoided, when his wife cried.

For a moment the room was silent. Then, softly, Winters apologized. "Even when you win a jury case, they don't come over and apologize," Smith, the lawyer, said later. "It was really something."

Prudential settled Jorgensen's lawsuit that afternoon. From the company offices, Jorgensen called his wife, his father, and his two sons. It was over, he told them. Prudential realized he was right.

The next morning, Prudential's turnabout was front-page news across the country. Hundreds of phone calls flooded Jorgensen's home. Industry executives, aware that he had declined the offer to return to Prudential, approached him about job opportunities. The time had come, the Jorgensens decided, to celebrate. So the next day, they drove to the grocery store. And there they bought a brand new package of paper napkins.

CASE STUDY: CRISES IN COLLEGE PARK—THE LEN BIAS CRISIS AT THE UNIVERSITY OF MARYLAND

In this next case study, crisis management and ethical management collide.

Twenty-two-year-old Len Bias, a senior at the University of Maryland, was one of the finest college basketball players in the country. On Tuesday, June 17, 1986, Bias was the second person chosen in the National Basketball Association's annual draft of college basketball players. His selection by the popular Boston Celtics virtually guaranteed Bias fame and fortune. Bias' early selection in the draft ensured him a multimillion dollar contract.

Less than 48 hours later, however, Len Bias was pronounced dead by a physician in a College Park, Maryland, emergency room. The cause of death was cocaine intoxication. Bias and several of his

Source: The author of this case, Francis J. Marra, is Assistant Professor of Communication at the Roy H. Park School of Communications at Ithaca College in New York.

friends were winding down an all-night party when the cocaine that Bias used triggered a fatal heart attack.

Bias's death, by itself, was a tragic but relatively small part of the turmoil the University of Maryland faced for the next six months. Bias's popularity and drug-related death prompted questions from reporters that quickly uncovered item after item of bad news about the University of Maryland's men's basketball team, the school's athletic department, and the university.

Within a week of Bias's death, it became clear the student-athletes at the University of Maryland were not recruited for their potential to become outstanding scholars. The student-athletes on the men's basketball team alone, for example, generated almost *25 percent* of the athletic department's $7.3 million budget in 1985.

Reporters learned that the University of Maryland regularly admitted many basketball players with poor high school academic records and bent the rules on a number of occasions to ensure players remained eligible. Molly Dunham, a reporter for the *Baltimore Sun* said: " 71 percent of the basketball players and 55 percent of the football players enrolled from 1980 to 1884 did not meet the school's regular admissions requirements." Fraser Smith, another reporter for the *Sun*, said, "less than half of the school's black basketball players had graduated during the years 1977 to 1986." *Baltimore Sun* columnist (and University of Maryland alumnus) Michael Olesker also criticized the campus for exploiting its basketball players.

> In his final semester, he [Bias] took five courses and passed all but five. And it didn't matter. While this was going on, five of the 14 Maryland basketball players were flunking out of school last winter—only to be reinstated—and the news has now emerged that, in the past five years, only one Maryland player managed to maintain a B average. And the people who run this school are suddenly wringing their hands and saying for public consumption, "My goodness, we had no idea." This is known as lying.

The drug-related death of a popular student, the mismanagement of the university's athletic department, and the exploitation of student-athletes, were not, unfortunately, the only crises the campus faced that summer. State and local officials clamored for (and obtained) two grand jury investigations. And, just because Bias died from a drug overdose, university administrators had to face numerous allegations that the campus was a haven for drug use.

Media coverage of these crises was very intense—and embarrassing—to the university. The *Washington Post*, for example, published

96 stories and columns about the University of Maryland crises over 42 straight days. Almost two-thirds of these stories and columns were on page one or the front page of the metro or sports sections of the newspaper. During the first six weeks of this crisis, the number of negative or embarrassing stories outnumbered the positive stories in the *Washington Post* by a margin of five to one.

What Went Wrong?

In-depth interviews with many administrators at the University of Maryland, including the chancellor and all of the vice-chancellors, indicated everyone cared deeply for the well-being of the students enrolled on the College Park campus. But if this was the case, why did these administrators handle these incidents so poorly? As you read the following analysis, consider the ethical aspects of key decisions that were required by University employees.

Communication Wasn't a Management Function

The senior public relations practitioner at the University of Maryland was a vice-chancellor who reported directly to the chancellor. Although he was a member of the chancellor's cabinet, several factors prevented him from providing important communication counsel and advice during the crisis.

Interviews with the PR specialist, his colleagues, and other administrators indicated the senior public relations practitioner had very limited experience in public relations and even less in crisis management. His expertise, instead, was in development and raising money for the campus. His inexperience prevented him from establishing and implementing the communication policies for the campus during the crisis. He was also unable to provide much-needed guidance and counsel to the chancellor.

The chancellor and other vice-chancellors were, therefore, forced to set the university's crisis communication strategy on their own. Although these people are competent managers, their rather substantial ignorance about communicating with reporters, employees, and other important publics helped make a bad situation worse.

The chancellor and his vice-chancellors should have realized they lacked crucial communications skills and immediately hired outside public relations counsel. Instead, they believed they could deal with reporters, employees, and other important audiences themselves. Many of these senior administrators felt providing information about these crisis was an after-the-fact and secondary responsibility to managing each event. The senior attorney for the University of Maryland, for example, said, in no uncertain terms, that communication should *not* shape an organization's response to a crisis. "Communication advice," he said, "has to do with timing and style and *not with substance.*" The senior public relations practitioner, unfortunately, didn't have the experience or power to refute this naive understanding about the importance of communication during crisis.

A Defensive Communication Philosophy

Prior to Len Bias's death, the University of Maryland did not do a good job of providing honest, complete information to its important audiences. The school's communication philosophy, many administrators agreed, was, at best, defensive and closed. Communication, for the most part, was not given a high priority. It is not surprising, then, that the university's crisis communication plan was equally defensive as well as being an incomplete and superficial document. The resulting problems, such as the death of Bias, simply magnified the university's inability and unwillingness to communicate.

The executive assistant to the chancellor, for example, acknowledged that the campus ignored many of its important publics. He said the University of Maryland practiced public relations poorly:

> It really . . . was a terribly isolated institution in terms of its relations with virtually all of its external publics. I mean, there may be exceptions to that rule, but by and large, it was an institution that had the view that the public was a kind of nuisance. "What we do basically is right. Questions from the public will be tolerated, if they have some power. But don't bother us." And don't think it's a particularly subtle thing, but the notion of "we've got external publics or customers that we've really got to attend to, we've got to worry about their concerns" just wasn't even a part of it.

Other senior administrators agreed that the campus had a closed communication culture in place when Len Bias died. How can universities teach ethics to students when their own administrators may fail even the most basic litmus of candor? One vice-chancellor said the campus "has not had a long tradition of sharing information." Other senior administrators described the communication philosophy at the University of Maryland as "difficult" and "not very good."

The communication philosophy, not surprisingly, shaped the communication policies the University of Maryland used during the crisis caused by the death of Len Bias. One assistant dean said the campus "would not release information" and that the administrators "closed up ranks." Several vice-chancellors argued strongly that the chancellor should *not* answer questions from reporters. Many reporters who covered the crisis said the university didn't cooperate, volunteered very little information, and became overly protective.

This closed, "no comment" communication strategy was very ineffective. Almost one-half of the stories published in the *Washington Post* during the first six weeks of the crisis did not include a response or comment from a University of Maryland administrator or spokesperson, because there was none. In addition, almost two-thirds of the stories published during this period did not include a comment from a campus official in the first ten paragraphs or until the story was continued to an inside page of the newspaper from the front page or the front page of a section.

This defensive communication policy not only prevented the university from refuting untrue or inaccurate allegations, but it projected an image of an institution that had something to hide. Statements that damned the campus went unanswered. A more open and two-way crisis communication strategy could have, at the very least, provided some balance and rebuttal to exaggerated and inaccurate allegations made against the university. On radio talk shows and letters to the editor, alumni, students, and members of the general public repeatedly asked, "When will we learn the *truth* about Len Bias?"

A Lack of PR Power

A third organizational characteristic that contributed to the University of Maryland's weak response to the ethical and communication crises it faced in 1986 was the inability of its public relations staff to quickly provide information to important publics. Most crises create an immediate need for information from many audiences, such as reporters, employees, and their families, local and federal governmental agencies, community residents, and customers. Many of these same publics wanted and needed information about problems at the University of Maryland. But, in a crucial mistake, the campus simply prevented its public relations staff from releasing information.

The chancellor and his staff quickly decided to funnel all requests for information through one person, the director of public information. This person, in turn, told her staff that she, *and she alone*, would answer inquiries about Len Bias. The magnitude of the crisis, however, quickly overwhelmed this person's ability to provide information. She was unable to provide information and arrange interviews as quickly as was required.

Reporters from the *Washington Post* and *Baltimore Sun* said they rarely received information on a timely basis. One reporter said he often would not get a response to a question for several hours or until the next day, which was not acceptable for his deadlines. An assignment editor from ABC-TV also criticized the University of Maryland's decision to channel all requests for information through one person on campus:

> There was nobody from the PR department at the hospital [when Bias died] from the University of Maryland. Nobody at all. There was nobody out at the courthouse [during the grand jury investigations] for the entire month of August from the University of Maryland that I saw. There is no method to deal with the University of Maryland's point of view on any of the things or any of the players that we dealt with. We had to go back to the University of Maryland every time, on each question, on each thing, and it was like we're almost telling them what we're doing, which is very sad.
>
> There were 15 crews at the high point of that grand jury. Six live trucks. And they didn't have somebody there who is monitoring the case and able to speak to it on any given occasion, speaking to the people outside, knowing the press people who are covering the story, knowing what angle they are going for. I mean, even if he doesn't make any statements, there should have been somebody there monitoring us as a press organization.

The resulting delays in providing information could have been alleviated if the director of public information had allowed her staff to do what they were trained to do—provide honest, complete information. But another, more serious, roadblock further prevented the University of Maryland's public relations department from providing information on a timely basis.

Neither the director of public information, or any member of her staff, had the *authority* to release information about the crisis without approval from senior administrators. This lack of authority—a lack of power—explains, in part, why the campus could not and did not provide information as quickly as it needed to.

The director of public relations said she "automatically would show everything to be legal that I did in the Bias thing, . . . *even if it has nothing to do with any legality.*" Information was further delayed because the chancellors and vice-chancellors also reportedly demanded that they see all material before release. One dean summarized the lengthy approval process by saying it took "three cabinet meetings to decide by that afternoon whether you could have an answer for a reporter" about a relatively basic piece of information. For a variety of reasons—some psychological, some historical—we often question the honesty of individuals in the midst of a newsworthy story who refuse to release information. Indeed, that very *suspicion* of "a cover up" can assume a life of its own in various public forums.

There, but for the Grace of God, Go I

Many people recognize that the crises at the University of Maryland that were triggered by the death of Len Bias could have occurred at many other colleges and universities with large athletic programs. But while that is true, it does not rationalize the University of Maryland's poor response to its crises.

All managers must recognize that crises are no longer unlikely events. They should expect and prepare for crises, and not assume that crises will never happen to them or their organization. The people who managed the University of Maryland in 1986 never expected to face such a traumatic set of incidents. These managers chose not to anticipate what might happen and gave crisis management and the conveyance of ethical, follow-up data a very low priority. The campus, therefore, like many other organizations, was unprepared to manage a crisis that escalated from a tragic, isolated incident to a six-month series of events that became national news.

Being "prepared" for a crisis, however, goes beyond preparing a crisis communication plan and sounding ethical. The University of Maryland case study clearly showed that several *organizational characteristics* contributed to its weak response. The case suggests that, in addition to being caught without a comprehensive crisis communications plan, the university mismanaged its crises because:

- The campus administrator did not understand or value public relations,

- The university did not have an experienced senior public relations practitioner to design ethical, effective crisis communication strategy and to provide candid counsel and insights to the chancellor,

- The communication philosophy used by the institution was inappropriate for an institution that should be a societal model for candor, and

- The university's public relations staff did not have the power to release information quickly.

Questions for Consideration

1. What would you have done differently if you were a university administrator in this case?

2. What are the ethical implications of this case? How can student confidentiality be balanced with the public's right to know?

3. Legal counsel often advises a client to release little or no information during a crisis. What are the ethical ramifications of such advice?

4. Speculation can be just as unethical as "clamming up" when the public demands answers to sensitive questions. Did the University of Maryland serve its mission well by avoiding any comment or speculation?

References for Case Study

All information in this case study comes from Marra, F.J., *Crisis Public Relations: A Theoretical Model*, unpublished dissertation, University of Maryland, College Park, 1993.

REFERENCES FOR CHAPTER 6

Associated Press. "11.4 Million Awarded to Whistle Blower." *Las Vegas Review-Journal*, April 23, 1993.

Associated Press. "Search of Whistle Blower's Computer Probed." *Las Vegas Review-Journal*, May 11, 1993.

Barton, Laurence. *Crisis in Organizations: Managing and Communicating in the Heat of Chaos.* Cincinnati: South-Western Publishing, 1993.

"Blowing the Whistle," *National Law Journal*, September 20, 1993.

Glazer, Myron, and Glazer, Penina. *The Whistle Blowers.* New York: Basic Books, 1989.

Goodman, Howard. "Government Blows the Whistle on Temple." *The Philadelphia Inquirer*, June 7, 1994, 16.

Jensen, J. Vernon. "Ethical Tension Points in Whistle Blowing." *Journal of Business Ethics* 6, 1987.

Larmer, Robert A. "Whistle-blowing and Employee Loyalty." *Journal of Business Ethics* 11, 1992.

Miceli, Marcia, and Near, Janet. *Blowing the Whistle.* New York: Lexington Books, 1992.

"Whistle Blowers on Fraud Bring New—and Paying—Business to Lawyers." *National Law Journal*, June 21, 1993, 16.

Worthington, rogers. "Revealing Fraud Can Be Very Lucrative." *The Philadelphia Inquirer*, June 7, 1994, F1.

Managing across Borders: When Do You Cross the Line?

The truth is that the great factors in human history are so complex, and so intertwined that any single-track doctrine which tries to set up one among them as the principal one, "ever moving and never moved," necessarily leads to erroneous conclusions and false applications, especially when it undertakes to explain the whole past and present of humanity by following one method and looking at them from a single point of view.

Gaetano Mosca,
The Ruling Class, 1896

The world, it seems, is getting smaller. With the collapse of Communism as an economic and political theory in Eastern Europe, and with a new model of a market economy slowly emerging in such formerly socialist societies as Vietnam and Cuba, there is ample evidence of a global move toward a "customer-driven" marketplace spanning the continents. While not every society embraces the U.S. notion of free enterprise and capitalism, many are unquestionably following this trend toward "freer markets," where fewer barriers to trade should theoretically expose consumers of different societies to more reasonably priced products and services offered by foreign competitors.

Bringing these products and services into the global marketplace does not happen by chance, but rather by careful design. As the level of global trade reaches new heights each year, it is clear that increased sensitivity to the variables that make the United States different from other cultures—language, ethnicity, religion, and certainly ethical and cultural values—certainly must be explored in greater depth and with more conviction than ever before. In this chapter, you will read about how business ethics vary from culture to culture and how different societies reward appropriate behavior and punish violators of the public trust.

NO COUNTRY SEEMS IMMUNE TO CASES OF ABUSE

The Romans and Greeks fought corruption among government and commerce leaders; centuries later, civilization still seeks to define what is right and wrong. In the early nineteenth century, one company, The English East India Company, controlled an astonishing one-half of all world trade. (Labich, 174) Today, the stakes seem even higher. Well-publicized embarrassments about bribes, corruption, or other scandals can cost an organization dearly when it later seeks to build a reputation abroad. Let's begin by briefly examining a series of recent ethics cases:

- The chairman of Italy's IRI SpA, the country's largest state-owned conglomerate, was arrested on corruption charges in 1993 amid allegations that he paid kickbacks to the country's Democratic and Socialist parties on public works projects. Italy has the largest Communist party in the West, and for many years, a massive patronage and kickback system has operated in government and industry. *U.S. News and World Report* writer Alexander Stille estimates that Italy's political parties "may have siphoned off as much as $100 billion over the past decade—about a tenth of Italy's national debt." He adds:

> The Italian system resembles a sweetheart relationship between business and Japan's scandal-plagued politicians. But while Japan is in effect a one-party state, Italy has been governed by a coalition of four or five parties. The competition among the parties . . . helps explain how the bribe-taking frenzy got out of control. (Stille, 44)

The enormity of Italian corruption is almost mind boggling to Americans who do not follow the international press. Nearly 3,000 corporate executives and government officials have been arrested for corruption in Italy since February 1992 and many CEOs have acknowledged that their company was involved. One example is auto giant Fiat, where a number of executives resigned or were fired in 1993 for their alleged role in corrupt activities. The company's finance director was arrested in February of that year for "alleged illegal payments made as part of contracts won by Cogefar-Impresit, Fiat's construction arm." (*The Economist,* "Fingering Fiat," 76) The chairman of Fiat, Gianni Agnelli, urged the government to prosecute those "who founded their fortunes almost exclusively on systematic collusion with the political system." (Cowell, D8)

The good news? Italy's reputation has been so badly tarnished on a global scale that the citizenry is finally demanding change. Argues *The Wall Street Journal*:

> For decades, Italy has offered a textbook example of how not to run a country. It was dominated by corruption. It could never keep the Mafia in check. Its fractious political system virtually invented legislative gridlock. But now, Italy has a historic opportunity to clean up its act. (Forman, 1)

- A branch manager for the Commercial Bank of Korea, Lee Hi-do, committed suicide in November 1992 when it was revealed that he had diverted 85.7 billion won into his personal accounts. More than half of the theft was from certificates of deposit which were in the bank's custody on behalf of a client. (Cho, 16)

- In Hong Kong, school headmaster Mong Kam-hong was found guilty by a district court in November 1992 of having accepted two bribes worth $150,000 from Longman Group Publishing in return for his guaranteeing that Longman books would be used in his school. *The South China Morning Post*, in a major analysis, concluded that "the amounts of money involved and the intricacies of those who choose textbooks for the territory's children suggest it could be an established and widespread problem." (Chan, 23) Mong Kam-hong was forced to pay a series of fines and is currently serving a two year jail sentence.

■ In March 1994, eight former executives of Japanese-owned Honda pleaded guilty to bribery, mail fraud, and conspiracy charges. According to a U.S. investigation, individuals seeking a new Honda or Acura dealership in the United States paid between $100,000 to $750,000 in cars, jewelry, and other luxuries to Honda executives. Honda promised to implement a financial disclosure policy and a whistle-blower hotline, even though the practice had been widespread for nearly 20 years. (Miller, A4)

■ In January 1991, Argentine President Carlos Saul Menem pardoned several military leaders who were partly responsible for the executions of between 10,000 and 30,000 people during the 1970s "dirty war" between government and civilian factions. Prominent Nazi-hunter Simon Wiesenthal, who analyzed the brutality of the murders in Argentina, said, "The Argentine generals committed the same kinds of crimes against humanity as the Nazis. That is why I can't understand their release." (Kowalski, 43)

■ French Minister of Urban Affairs Bernard Tapie resigned in May 1992 when he was charged with fraud after he reportedly received a $2 million payment from Japan-based Toshiba Corporation. (Cohen, C4) Tapie came from a modest family and emerged in the 1990s as one of France's most flamboyant business executives who owned 54 percent of sportswear giant Adidas A.G. In another matter, France was also embroiled in a major ethics case when three senior national health officials were charged with criminal neglect in 1991 for their knowledge in distributing AIDS-contaminated blood to hemophiliacs who later contracted the virus. Canadian health officials faced similar charges of ethical misconduct over tainted blood in 1994.

■ In Japan, several major ethical embarrassments have caused tremors both in government and industry in recent years: Prime ministers resigned in 1993 and 1994 amid corruption charges, Nintendo was charged by the U.S. government for price fixing in its computer game products, and officials of Hitachi were indicted by a U.S. grand jury for systematically stealing trade secrets from IBM in 1988. There are other more recent examples involving Japan:

Case 1: The Japanese, who spend more on prescription drugs than anyone else in the world ($228 per capita versus $169 paid out by the second largest spenders, the Germans) are establishing national price controls to be tied to wholesale prices by 1996. The reason: Japanese doctors both prescribe and sell drugs, with markups that often exceed several hundred percent.

Case 2: The FBI has charged that some operatives of the *yakuza*, Japan's organized-crime network, have channeled as much as $1 billion in laundered Japanese money throughout the United States in recent years. The agency says that Japanese "executives" have purchased properties in Hawaii, Nevada, and California with funds that were either stolen or generated by drug and prostitution operations, which are more widespread in Japan than most westerners realize.

Case 3: U.S. academics have charged that their Japanese counterparts are unethical in terms of allowing U.S. students access to Japanese universities. According to the *Los Angeles Times,* the United States granted 34,657 five-year student visas to Japanese students wishing to attend U.S. universities in 1992, yet only 1,428 U.S. students were granted similar visas to study in Japan. "We feel there are real inequities and are beginning to view this as a trade issue," said William Sharp, dean of Temple University's Tokyo campus. "We are at a tremendous competitive disadvantage because few of our students can come here to Japan to study." (Watanabe, A6)

IS A GLOBAL ETHICAL STANDARD POSSIBLE?

For decades, management theorists and sociologists have tried to define a common set of ethical principles that would be acceptable across national borders. In these draft principles, theorists argued that every society would benefit if all agreed on what constitutes fair pricing of products, appropriate behavior in the workplace, and related issues. Unfortunately, the various drafts that have been shared at international academic and business conferences are so divergent that the search for a common ground seems to have stalled. The closest example of a global compact on acceptable behavior is the United Nations Declaration on Human Rights, yet this document addresses only a few limited items involving commerce, such as condemning child labor.

For instance, NBC's "Dateline" rattled Wal-Mart executives in December 1993, when their reporters went undercover in Bangladesh and found children, some as young as 10 years old, working in "sweatshops" where Wal-Mart brand clothes were reportedly made.

The company's president stumbled so badly during his interview with reporter Brian Ross—even after being shown graphic video-taped evidence of child labor—that a Wal-Mart senior executive interrupted his boss and suggested that it was best to stop talking. Images of children in sweatshops may not startle those living in Bangladesh, but they would likely cause an outcry in Spokane. Indeed, that's exactly what happened: Wal-Mart was caught on camera with racks of clothes under a sign that read "Made in the U.S.A.," only to have NBC trace the clothes to a sinister practice condemned by most consumers. Wal-Mart promised to investigate and take remedial action, but its good name was seriously tarnished by one overriding factor: It should have known. When confronted, it should have expressed outrage and a promise to clean up its act.

AN AMALGAM OF INFLUENCES

As discussed earlier, our concept of business ethics is influenced by our family and personal values as well as factors such as religion, workplace standards, legal norms, and several others. Some argue that *all* corporations, large and small, must begin to think about their ethical conduct in terms of the multinational environment because global trade is increasing at such a frantic pace and no economy can survive by being self-sufficient: Virtually every economy derives a part of its natural resources, food, energy or military hardware from another member of the international community. This trend is likely to proliferate in the future as governments impose fewer import and export quotas.

Although a common set of ethical principles has yet to emerge, we are inching closer to a global culture in which certain values and beliefs generate wide acceptance. That is true in terms of the notion of individual freedom (Chinese students in Tiananmen Square clutched pictures of the Statue of Liberty when they were murdered by government troops in 1989), international corporate and activist "greening" programs that encourage environmental responsibility, and the increasing number of multinational corporations who are adopting and enforcing codes of ethical behavior (see the Appendix).

Just as individuals differ on their opinions as to what constitutes right and wrong, so too do different cultures. In fact many times even the ethical values maintained within in a singular culture will shift, sometimes with remarkable speed. For instance, the corruption in Italy that has been so prevalent since the Fascist regime of Benito Mussolini assumed power in 1921 only began to crumble 70 years later; but within three years, society embraced rapid reform and prosecuted those who had previously committed widely accepted acts of bribery. Similarly, South Korea's ongoing crackdown on bribes began in 1993 but had been so widespread prior to this time that officials in government, academe, and industry considered the practice to be acceptable, even though it was legally (and under Korean norms, certainly morally) wrong.

Let's look at the various influences on business that have applicability for anyone thinking about expanding their business into another society.

The model in Exhibit 7-1 suggests that in order to be an effective global thinker, one must engage in a comparative thought process: What does my government say about paying or accepting bribes versus the practice in another country? What if our company is prevented from paying bribes in the United States, but we have offices in Mexico (where the practice is encouraged) and in Peru (where signals are mixed)? The questions raised by this model usually keep corporate attorneys, ethics officers, business development managers, and prosecutors all very busy.

THE PRESSURE ON NATIONAL GOVERNMENTS

There are many reasons why managers get into hot water when working abroad or seeking to expand their business in another country. Sometimes the absence of research can lead to a snafu in terms of business etiquette (for example, never take the business card from a Japanese executive and shove it in your pocket as is common in the

EXHIBIT 7-1   Influences on Business Across National Borders

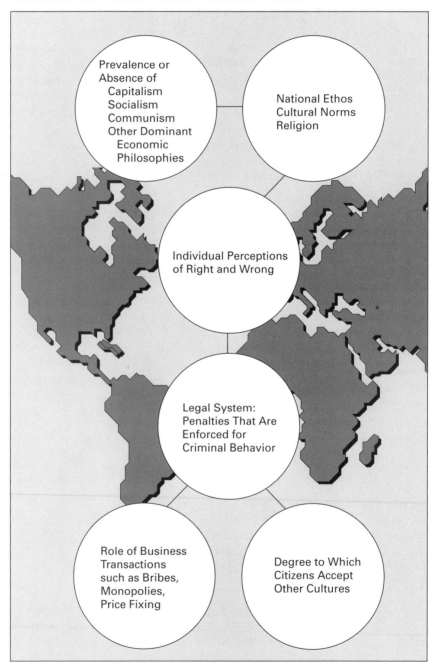

United States; rather, learn the custom for accepting, reading, and then putting away the card), but in this chapter we are much more interested in issues that involve ethical and moral quagmires in global business.

Earlier in the book we discussed the question of whether managers are generally prone to be ethical or unethical, or whether their employers also sway the pendulum from one side to another by a variety of programs, policies, and strategic tactics. In the global environment, the pressure to outperform the competition is intense. But some profound changes are underway in international business. For instance, Harvard Professor Raymond Vernon argued in his 1977 book, *Storm over the Multinationals*, that

> the multinational enterprise has come to be seen as the embodiment of almost anything disconcerting about modern industrial society.

Less than two decades later, however, the concentration of wealth had shifted, at least partly, with the proliferation of thousands of joint ventures, and now everyone wants a piece of the action. Speaking of multinational corporations, and pondering Professor Vernon's theories, *The Economist* recently presented this argument:

> Yet now it is only a slight exaggeration to say that it is seen in the reverse, as the embodiment of modernity and the prospect of wealth: full of technology, rich in capital, replete with skilled jobs. Governments all around the world, especially in the developing countries, are queuing up to attract multinationals. The United Nations, which spent decades tut-tutting about these firms and drawing up codes of conduct to control them, now spends much of its time advising countries on how to best seduce them. ("Multinationals: Back in Fashion," *The Economist*, 5)

Let's try to place international business in a general context before we discuss the ethical challenges that face managers who may be traveling and negotiating in a global context. For a moment, let's assume the following statements about the international business environment are true:

1. With a marked production shift to the Pacific Rim where production and labor costs tend to be far more competitive than in the West, and with huge income gains for residents in Japan, South Korea, Hong Kong, Singapore, and other countries in recent years, there is extraordinary pressure on these and other Asian countries to maintain competitive momentum well into the next century.

2. Concurrent with Pacific Rim economic growth are other markets, notably Latin America and Europe, which have attempted to get back into the arena of international competitiveness via economic and judicial reforms. The European Community (EC) is a regional economic force that is likely to boast more than 20 members by the year 2000. Residents in EC countries will have one currency, one passport, and one set of import/export standards to follow. The EC is also insisting on uniform manufacturing standards such as ISO 9000, detailed requirements on how products shall be designed and manufactured if they are to be sold in EC-member countries. ISO 9000 has required the costly retrofitting of many plants and the redesign of products around the world.

3. Having experienced economic turbulence requiring massive layoffs and restructurings in the early 1990s, yet boasting the most ingenious engineers and scientists in the world, the United States will not sit idly by and allow the Pacific Rim and the EC to re-align global wealth while it remains comatose. Thus, the unification of two mature economies (Canada and the United States) with an emerging one with low labor and production infrastructure (Mexico) was achieved with the North American Free Trade Agreement (NAFTA).

4. Despite massive infusions of developmental aid in the 1970s and 1980s, both by direct foreign aid from the industrialized nations as well as from the United Nations, the World Bank, and regional development banks, any of the poor remain noncompetitive due to lack of modern transportation and warehousing infrastructure, the absence of natural resources that can attract foreign investment, and serious gaps in technological training. As a result, the notion that the rich are getting richer and the poor are getting poorer has changed only modestly in the past 50 years. Notable gains have occurred in just two regions, primarily in the Pacific Rim and Organization of Petroleum Exporting Countries (OPEC) member nations where caps on production levels transformed entire economies in a matter of just a few years. Yet Africa, much of Latin America, and Eastern Europe remains fragmented economically.

The concentration of wealth in the industrialized nations is nothing to be ashamed of: Citizens of these countries have expended unprecedented ingenuity and innovation to reach these plateaus. The geniuses of modern commerce—Henry Ford, Andrew Carnegie, and

---

ETHICS BRIEF

In China, Survival of the Certified Fittest?

In the past decade, China has made considerable progress in reducing a birth rate that threatened to compromise food supplies: The country has 22 percent of the world's population but only 7 percent of its arable land. As a result, the government mandated in 1979 that families be restricted to only one child per family.

But in late 1993, the international community raised concerns over a government proclamation that China would now use abortions, sterilization, and marriage bans "to avoid new births of inferior quality and heighten the standards of the whole population." The New China News Agency reported that if government officials believe that a couple is likely to pass on congenital illnesses or defects (such as mental retardation) the government would *mandate* one of these options to end the pregnancy.

In China, mentally retarded citizens are mandatorily sterilized in the northwestern province of Ganzu, where some 260,000 mentally retarded persons live. But never has China sanctioned a national policy of this nature where a potentially "inferior" birth is ended to increase the quality of the population.

Are such policies ethical? What if a family objects to this policy? What of the government's opinion that China cannot move ahead economically when such births are considered a drain? Didn't Nazi Germany also seek to purify its population by eliminating sectors that it, too, considered "inferior"?

The United Nations Population Fund in New York protested the China policy, but the U.N. admitted that its ability to influence policy in China was minimal. Spokesperson Alex Marshall told the *Washington Post National Weekly*, "In principle we are against any form of compulsion with respect to family planning. Family planning must be voluntary, and that has no qualifying clauses to it."

What are the ethical ramifications of family planning? What are the obligations of government officials as well as those of parents?

Source: *Washington Post National Weekly*, January 2, 1994, p. 17.

Bill Gates among them—simply understood that their respective efforts in selling cars, steel, and software could not be sustained by domestic sales alone: Expansion abroad made economic sense and concurrently satisfied a consumer need.

Of course, volumes have also been written about the other side of enterprise in which to expand abroad, industry pursues exploitive practices and policies. Issues range from the practice of slave labor used both in the United States and Europe in the nineteenth century to price-fixing by the seven largest western oil producers in the twentieth century to charges that child labor is still actively subsidized by major Pacific Rim and Western manufacturers.

The pressure on national governments to ensure that their industries remain competitive in the century ahead will dictate many ethical and moral challenges, and most of the challenges in international business will be placed squarely on the backs of managers in the United States and Europe. Why? In 1993, the United Nations completed a major study in which it sought to identify the largest 25 nonfinancial institutions ranked by foreign assets. Interestingly enough, while the Japanese own 24 of the 25 largest banks in the world, not a single nonfinancial megaorganization is Japanese:

Ranks		Indsutry	Country (in billions)	Foreign Assets
1.	Royal Dutch Shell	Oil	Britain	Not available
2.	Ford Motor	Cars	U.S.	55.2
3.	General Motors	Cars	U.S.	52.6
4.	Exxon	Oil	U.S.	51.6
5.	IBM	Computers	U.S.	45.7
6.	British Petroleum	Oil	Britain	39.7
7.	Nestlé	Food	Switzerland	Not available
8.	Unilever	Food	Britain/Holland	Not available
9.	Asea Brown Boveri	Electronics	Switzerland	Not available
10.	Philips	Electronics	Holland	Not available

Source: United Nations, 1993.

The flow of capital and management across borders is reaching new heights and is certain to increase pressures on all organizations with a vested interest in trade issues.

The United Nations reports that about 35,000 multinational corporations are operating (with 170,000 foreign affiliates), accounting for $3.1 trillion in worldwide assets. Seemingly, the wealth is concentrated. Professor Howard Perlmutter of the Wharton School in Philadelphia estimates that 80 percent of the noncommunist world's productive assets will be controlled by fewer than 300 companies by 1995. ("Multinationals Back in Fashion," *The Economist,* 6) Yet a marked shift is underway in which the small, embryonic affiliates of the multinationals are gaining autonomy from the parent company, often via joint ventures with a healthy percentage of local ownership and control. Motorola, Inc., for example, has successfully practiced this model for 20 years. It is in both arenas—the multinational corporations whose ethical mistakes are well publicized and in small enterprises where they can be far more costly (sometimes putting the enterprise out of business)—that we should raise awareness about the implications of appropriate behavior. For instance, it was a complaint by the European Community and an antitrust investigation that led to Microsoft Corporation's signing a July 1994 consent degree on the way the company offers volume discounts. Domestic competitors charged that Microsoft's pricing strategy unfairly prevented competition; Europeans feared that bundling software with their machines would prevent their software companies from gaining market share.

Although a discussion of international business ethics could fill an entire volume, let's focus on several issues of paramount importance before turning to a roundtable discussion of experts and several cases that will challenge you. There are four cornerstones to any meaningful discussion of international business ethics: 1. Sociocultural Environment, 2. Stereotypes, 3. National Policies, 4. Technology

Sociocultural Environment

In a classical study of 116,000 IBM employees, Geert Hofstede identified four dimensions of national value systems that impact both employees and employers. His findings are important because they indicate that both our society and that of others must be analyzed in depth if we are to succeed in working effectively with organizations abroad.

Hofstede's four social values are as follows:

Power Distance. People in high power distance countries such as the Philippines and Panama accept inequality among institutions and people as a way of life; people in low power distance countries such as Israel and Denmark expect equality in power regardless of a person's social or economic rank.

Uncertainty Avoidance. People in certain high-avoidance nations such as Greece and Uruguay seek a uniform set of principles about fair play to avoid being in conflict. People in low-avoidance nations such as Malaysia tend to flourish, even when there are no standards about what is right or desired in the workplace or when those standards conflict.

Individualism and Collectivism. People in highly individualistic countries such as the United States and Britain strongly believe that individuals should chart their own destinies and not be reliant on others. People in collectivist societies such as Ecuador and Cuba embrace systems where individuals are encouraged to protect the interests of all others.

Masculinity and Femininity. Those working in societies with strong masculine values such as Japan and South Korea pursue material success and assertiveness by encouraging competition and devotion to work, even at the expense of personal relationships. Feminine societies such as Denmark and Sweden place more value on relationships and caring for the less fortunate.

These findings urge us to recognize reality: Managers operating in different environments bring to the table a variety of values and beliefs, ranging from their perception of a work ethic and social responsibility to philanthropy and bribery. To a certain degree, the developed countries share a common trait because they are ethnocentric, often believing that their culture is superior to others. Sometimes workers and managers practice ethnocentricity abroad and can offend international colleagues by being abrupt, rude, or even callous to local tastes and beliefs. Corporations can also practice ethnocentricity: Disney received widespread, negative publicity in Europe in 1992 when EuroDisney opened its doors because its heavily U.S. corporate culture and business practices offended many Europeans. In a different matter, although price-fixing is common in Japan, Nintendo of America found itself fined by the U.S. government for reportedly forcing U.S. retailers to accept a benchmark price for its computer games under threat of losing complete access to future shipments.

Understanding the significance of the four factors cited above, as well as ethnocentricty, can contribute to more effectiveness for businesses operating in the global environment. Certainly to be seen as fair, rational decision makers who can motivate local workers as well as potential customers, business leaders must tailor their management style to the various cultures in which they operate.

Stereotypes and Misunderstanding

At the heart of understanding international business ethics is the notion of stereotypes, those false assumptions we make about people who are, at least in our perception, different from us. Common and completely outrageous stereotypes include those that assert that all Italians are corrupt, all Americans are rich, all British are snobs, all Japanese are shrewd, and all Africans are inferior.

Today, large corporations such as IBM, Nabisco, and Intel try to shatter stereotypes about other cultures by conducting extensive training programs in international business and ethics practices before sending their employees abroad. In these programs, expatriates who have recently returned home from abroad often share with their colleagues detailed experiences about the nuances of negotiating business deals while they lived in Quatar Thailand, Peru, or Nepal. In most programs, expatriates speak in detail about their successes and mistakes in preparing their families for foreign assignments that might last from one to five years. Often such programs also focus on stereotyping—both how those in other countries inaccurately stereotype Americans (lazy, rich) and how Americans inappropriately stereotype others.

Although most corporations work diligently to educate their workers about being good global citizens before venturing abroad, an occasional slip occurs. For example, for a male business executive to bring his wife to a business dinner in certain Middle Eastern countries would be well-intentioned but disastrous. In most Muslim countries, women are considered subservient to men and are never included in business meetings; in fact, including a woman is likely to ruin a business deal. In some parts of Mexico, Italy, and France, businesses are closed on Sundays as Roman Catholics adhere to church tradition and avoid business transactions; similarly, proposing a meeting in Israel on the Jewish Sabbath of Saturday could undermine a pending deal.

The lessons offered by those who have studied history, civilization, and cultural stereotyping helps to explain why ethics is assuming more and more importance in the conduct of international business. If we are prone to stereotype others, we are undermining the core of ethics: to be fair and pursue transactions based on equity and fairness. Yet despite the best efforts of public service campaigns (such as "Stop the Hate"), and educational systems, bias remains part of our collective conscious, undermining the ethical practice of business.

For example, ponder the words of Nigerian writer Chinua Achebe, whose first novel, *Things Fall Apart*, sold three million copies and was translated into 30 languages. The author's message about how we perceive other cultures could have emanated from anyone living in a developing country:

> If you accept Africans as people, then you listen to them. They have their preferences. If you took Africa seriously as a continent of people, you would listen. You would not be able to sit back here and suggest that

you know, for instance, what should be done in South Africa. When the majority of the people in South Africa are saying "'This is what we think will bring apartheid to an end," somebody sits here and says "No, no, that will not do it. We know what will work."

Margaret Thatcher sits in Britain and says "Although the whole of Africa may think that this works, I know that what will work is something else." That's what I want to see changed. The traditional attitude of Europe or the West is that Africa is a continent of children. A man as powerful and enlightened as Albert Schweitzer was still able to say "The black people are my brothers—but my junior brothers." We're not anybody's junior brothers. (Moyers, 335)

In recent years, increased levels of international trade, fewer barriers to global travel and the phenomenal increase in international television programming sent by satellite have all reduced our anxieties and fears, and subsequently our stereotypes, about those living and working in other cultures. But serious lapses still occur.

In September 1993, for instance, AT&T apologized to U.S. civil rights groups after an employee magazine used monkeys to depict Africans. In a graphic that accompanied an article about international phone service on each continent, humans were used to depict individuals conversing on a telephone, except for the African graphic, which featured the monkey. "Our people should have caught it, but they didn't, so that's left us with a great embarrassment," said Walter Murphy, AT&T's director of corporate information, to the Associated Press. (McTillmon, 13) McDonald's didn't fare much better in June 1994, when, in promotion for the World Cup of Soccer, two million food bags featured an Arabic passage: "There is no God but Allah, and Mohammed is his Prophet." Muslims protested that such sacred words should not be thrown in the trash, and the company acknowledged its error.

National Policies

Every country is interested in having its citizens achieve a better standard of life; to be self-sufficient in achieving this goal is almost impossible unless a country is willing to sell, buy, and engage in joint ventures with foreign entities so as to achieve better housing, transportation, and access to food and energy. National governments, therefore, play an unusually important role in shaping policies that govern the behavior of corporations seeking to expand their contacts and operations abroad. Whether these contacts are ethical and moral in character in large measure depends upon the degree to which a government insists, on a routine and determined basis, that a series of standards are equitably applied to all players.

Three principal factors influence workplace ethics in other cultures and sometimes in U.S. culture as well: **economic policies** (such as exchange rates and resource development), **legal and political policies** (such as legal restrictions and quotas), and **informal organizational policies** (such as lifetime employment).

Economic Policies. The free enterprise system encourages maximum return on stockholder investment by ensuring that the marketplace shapes the price of goods or services. Theoretically, demand for products or services encourages healthy competition and thus impacts price attractiveness. With very few exceptions (such as goods that it directly purchases or regulates, for example, airfare prices), the U.S. government does not directly influence the price of goods, but this policy is misleading. Indeed, subsidies to key industries such as farming and tax credits and incentives provided to thousands of others, are enormously influential in allowing U.S. companies to be competitive around the world.

Other nations have similar economic policies. In Japan, the government subsidizes the *keiretsu*, a series of conglomerates who compete very effectively both at home and abroad because of generous government assistance in terms of tax credits, leniency in allowing joint ventures and monopolies, and extraordinarily high tariffs on imported products—thus protecting domestic producers. *Business Week* explains how the *keiretsu* system works:

> Think of it this way: imagine that Citicorp owned 10% of all shares in General Motors, Westinghouse Electric, Boeing, IBM, Travelers and 25 other major companies. Imagine, further, that each held shares in other members of the Citicorp group. Consequently, all these companies would be takeover proof. But the arrangement would go beyond cross-shareholding or overlapping boards of directors. The companies would be linked in a . . . "multiplexity" of relations, doing business together and maintaining other formal and informal ties. (Holstein, 10)

Jon Woronoff, who has authored ten successful books about Japan's economic policies, asserts that members of the *keiretsu* have assumed power that sometimes rivals that of the government, which seems incapable of being able to control corporate incest:

> This means that, for example, the "core" company can keep its prices lower by forcing suppliers to reduce their prices, a measure which has

President Kim Young Sam of South Korea has removed more than four dozen senior government officials since assuming power in February 1993. He argues that corruption, ethical misconduct, and bribes stalled South Korea's economic recovery. As a result of his actions, his public opinion ratings have soared and Korea's economic growth ranks as the fourth fastest in the world.

been taken time and again. Subcontractors can be forced to adjust their activities to the parent company's every need. Distributors can be made to sell at the producer's fixed price and usually pressured into meeting a sales quota. Practices like this are unethical and some are even illegal. But the laws are not effectively enforced by the authorities and the underlings are in no position to resist. (Woronoff, 54)

Legal and Political Policies. Each of us tends to understand the basic tenets of what our government prescribes to be legal and illegal behavior: Theft, bribery, insider trading, and collusion on price-fixing are commonly prohibited crimes in the United States and other western countries. Yet because formally imposed penalties for these crimes are seemingly nonexistent at home, it is completely understandable why managers may be tempted to engage in such practices when operating abroad.

The notion of ethnocentricity is one factor affecting the international conduct of U.S. businesspeople ("If we're so ethical and allow Michael Milken to serve a modest jail sentence for *his* crimes, my crimes are so small by comparison. I'll *never* be convicted"). But other issues also play a role, such as sales quotas (in a high-stakes environment, cutting corners and bending the rules is seen as necessary to move ahead) and the desire for upward mobility ("If my boss understands that I know how to play the game, I'm more likely to be seen as a team player and thus promoted at the first opportunity"). Legal and political policies are supposed to curb these temptations, but they have generally failed to curb abuse both domestically and internationally.

Domestically, the courts are filled with cases involving violent crime and civil disputes. The Securities and Exchange Commission (SEC) and Federal Trade Commission (FTC) achieve comparatively few prosecutions because of their limited staff and budget horizons; the greatest effectiveness of these organizations results from fining those who break a particular federal statute or from ceasing their licenses to operate. The courts, however, seem unwilling to mix violent criminals with "white collar" offenders. Michael Milken, Leona Helmsley, and Charles Keating, three business moguls who were in the minority in that they were jailed for business crimes, all were assigned to minimum security locales.

Internationally, the horizon is even more bleak. Although any member of the international community can ask the United Nations for a hearing regarding a grievance, the U.N. is far better equipped to adjudicate cases involving territorial disputes than complaints against a multinational. These cases are usually filed in the courts of either the host country (where a foreign company was operating) or in an international forum, such as the International Court of Justice (ICJ). Yet prosecutions are extremely difficult, and participation at the ICJ is entirely voluntarily; thus, unless a member country agrees to be bound by the decision of the international court, there is no guarantee that any country or manager found to be guilty of an impropriety will actually be brought to justice.

The international burden of raising awareness about the necessity for a high moral and ethical ground when business venture abroad rests, then, in the educational arena. The business community needs to effectively educate managers about what is considered legal and moral before they cultivate agreements abroad. Trade associations, the news media, and universities all play a role in fulfilling this mandate.

Informal Organizational Policies. In analyzing ethical practices in other countries, it is important to examine not only what appears on paper, but also those myriad informal practices that differ slightly from employer to employer but that nevertheless constitute something tangible to be said about how people behave in other settings. A case in point is the notion of lifetime employment.

During the first three decades of the 1900s, lifetime employment was virtually guaranteed to most Americans who worked in the railroad, petroleum, and banking industries. During the formative period of growth for these sectors, workers were accustomed to spending their entire careers working for one employer; as long as the quality of their work was high and they did not violate company policies, continuous improvement was guaranteed.

In the aftermath of World War II, returning veterans who benefited from formal training programs in the emerging aerospace, engineering, and computer industries dynamically altered the nature of the U.S. economy. The mature industries slowly faded (as did the notion of lifetime employment), and in the far more competitive workplace, workers who did not hesitate in leaving one employer to seek better pay and benefits elsewhere. Employee loyalty was no longer guaranteed, and, as we have seen throughout the 1990s, employer guarantees that "there will always be a job for you here" have been shattered at Hewlett-Packard, Scott Paper, IBM, Kodak, and elsewhere. No one ever asserted that lifetime employment was guaranteed (because legally that would be an implicit warranty that could be enforced by the courts), but the ethical assertion of continuous loyalty from both employer and employee was a hallmark of U.S. enterprise.

Today, lifetime employment has been shattered in almost every society except Japan, and even that country shows emerging signs that the practice is fading. Yet the Japanese feel a strong, moral obligation to retain a worker once they have welcomed him (rarely her) into their management ranks. In Japan, a worker who fails to maintain the trust of the employer is rarely fired; rather, the worker becomes a "window sitter," usually assigned to a basement office where he is stripped of title, seniority, and any duties. *The Wall Street Journal* recently profiled ethics in Japan with the story of Yasuhiko Ushiba, an employee of Mitsubishi Corporation who has spent the last ten years killing time:

> Posted in a "planning promotion group," he was given no assignments by the giant trading company. When he tried proposing projects, the plans were thrown back in his face. So Mr. Ushiba hung out at the zoo

and took in triple features at adult movie theaters. All the while his pay-checks—about $85,000 a year—keep sailing in. "The message from management was, you can stay here if you want to, but we're not giving you any work to do," says the 55-year-old Mr. Ushiba. (Ono, 1)

Although westerners may find the concept of "window sitting" strange, it is perceived in Japan to be highly ethical and necessary in rewarding loyal employees who could have joined a competitor years ago. Ethics and morality are not only proscribed in policy manuals internationally; sometimes unwritten but enforced practices such as lifetime employment speak volumes about another culture and how it values and rewards appropriate workplace behavior.

Technology

Technology has been a blessing in terms of maximizing efficient productivity in the twentieth century with the advent of computers, videos, and satellite telecommunications. Yet it has also opened the avenue for widespread abuse and theft. The extraordinary ethical and moral challenges raised by technology are simply overwhelming.

Although we have largely focused so far on the burden of U.S. managers to be educated about international business ethics, let's shift the discussion for a moment and examine how U.S. companies have been victimized by the practices of others in recent years:

- According to *World Trade*, U.S. manufacturers lose $60 billion each year because foreign companies steal U.S. products and technology via the theft of intellectual properties such as copyrights and patents. The thefts are most common in terms of software, book publishing, musical recordings, and apparel designs. (Strugatch, 101)

- Three countries in particular—China, India and Thailand—have been singled out by the U.S. government in the past three years as the largest perpetrators of organized theft where government complicity is apparent. Since cross-border thefts generate greater income at home, and a higher standard of living is desired by developing economies, governments tend to look the other way in terms of cooperating with investigations and prosecutions.

- Industrialized countries are not immune to unethical practices in this area. The Japanese are notorious for waiting for a U.S.

ETHICS BRIEF

If You Think the United States Has a Lock on Ethical Misdeeds

Although much of the research and analysis in this book focuses on U.S. corporations, the United States has no monopoly on embarrassing misdeeds. Consider the fact that these are just a few cases reported in one of Japan's leading newspapers, *The Mainichi Daily News,* in just one week in November 1993:

- Business tycoon Ryoei Saito admitted to government prosecutors that he gave a 100 million yen bribe to the governor of the Miyagi Prefecture in return for permission to build houses and a golf course. The governor, Shuntaro Homma, was indicted for taking another bribe from Taisei Corporation after a wide-scale government investigation into corruption involving construction firms and politicians.
- Three members of a right-wing political group called Nihon Doto-Kai were arrested for extorting 50 million yen from a former high school principal who allegedly sold passing grades to students who were failing. The principal, Yokoo Gakuen Kamogawa, reportedly sold the grades for prices ranging from thousands to hundreds of thousands of yen.

- The Daishowa Paper Manufacturing Company gave 127 million yen to the Natori municipal government to upgrade a public sewer system just before the company requested permission to build 2,000 houses in the area. *The Mainichi Daily News* reported that the company president "offered the bribe in hopes of raising the value of land in Medeshima to help save the company from financial crisis." (November 17, 1993, 12)
- Japanese maritime officials reported that operators of Asahi Glass Company, the largest glass manufacturer in the country, allowed highly alkaline liquid waste into Tokyo Bay for over a year. The company expressed "regret" over its actions and promised to develop a "safe counter plan."
- In an act increasingly common in Japan, a 14-year-old junior high school student hung himself in Tochigi Prefecture Park after leaving a note stating that he could no longer tolerate corporal punishment from his language teacher. The student alleged that the teacher used beatings to ensure student compliance with homework and classroom duties.

company to file a patent application for a new design or technological advance, only to rush to a U.S. or Japanese patent office and "surround" the application with hundreds of variations, effectively crippling the original manufacturer from a redesign, modification, or future improvement.

According to William K. Krist, vice-president of international affairs for the American Electronic Association, "A company like Mitsubishi will pull stuff out of physics textbooks and file two or three hundred patents around yours. You've got to refute each one of those, and that takes forever." (Strugatch, 102) Some U.S. companies, notably Hewlett-Packard, have successfully embarrassed Japanese companies for such bully tactics in recent years with both prosecutions and out-of-court settlements.

■ Foreign espionage against U.S. firms has reached extraordinary heights in the 1990s. The American Society for Industrial Security reported in 1992 that 37 percent of the 165 firms that it surveyed said that they have been spied on by foreign competitors in the past few years. IBM alone lost $1 billion due to economic espionage by French and Japanese operatives. *Newsweek* writer Douglas Waller reports that while the Japanese are the most incentive intelligence spies, the French and Egyptians are gaining in their sophistication. Common tactics include entering hotel rooms of U.S. engineers and scientists when they are traveling abroad and photocopying documents and computer disks left in the room and the systematic bugging of phone conversations of professors, corporate executives and software developers both in the U.S. and abroad. In its major analysis, *Newsweek* noted, "Welcome to a world order where profits have replaced missiles as the currency as power. Industrial spying isn't new, and it isn't always legal, but as firms develop global reach, they are acquiring new vulnerability to economic espionage." (Waller, 58)

A U.S. RESPONSE:
THE FOREIGN CORRUPT PRACTICES ACT

In an attempt to ensure that Americans do not violate U.S. laws while operating abroad, Congress passed the Foreign Corrupt Practices Act (FCPA) in 1977. The law provides fines of up to $1 million for each corporate violation and other financial penalties and jail terms for individual violators.

The law applies only to U.S. corporations operating abroad, not to foreign entities operating in the United States. Although the law leaves much to be desired (it provides no penalties for individuals who commit illegal acts abroad), it constitutes the first legislative attempt to encourage U.S.-based multinationals to avoid bribery of officials abroad, even in jurisdictions such as Mexico or Peru where bribery is a way of life. According to *The National Law Journal:*

> The FCPA is the first and only statute prohibiting bribery and other corrupt practices by U.S. citizens and companies conducting business overseas. The anti-bribery provisions of the act forbid an individual or entity that satisfies the definition of an issuer or a domestic concern from paying or attempting to influence the actions of a foreign government. . . . Congress carefully considered the extent to which the FCPA would regulate the conduct of foreign corporations. It defined issuers to include only corporations with a registered class of securities or those required to report to the Securities and Exchange Commission. It defined domestic concerns to include only corporations in or having their principal place of business in the United States. And it extended the FCPA only to individual agents of domestic concerns and issuers, not to corporations. (Dugan and Jorden, 20)

Some executives like the FCPA because it provides them with a legitimate excuse in not having to pay bribes to solicit business abroad. In other countries, despite the FCPA, officials still try to extract payments, even when the U.S. company could be exposed to negative publicity and prosecution if it engages in complicity.

The FCPA does not preclude payments to lower level figures whose assistance may be necessary to provide the necessary "juice" to land a contract or buy a piece of commercial property. All the law requires is that the companies maintain reasonably detailed records of transactions with these officials. Naturally, the demands tend to be for sizable "donations" if the project or sales contract has a high dollar value, and it is here that Americans continue to be stumped about how to follow the spirit and intent of the FCPA without breaking U.S. law. For instance, the implications of the FCPA go far beyond the one or two individuals who may be asked to "grease the palms" of a local official in Kenya, Nepal, or South Korea; the law provides penalties not just for those who are involved in a bribe, but "also those who know or have reason to know that a bribe is being given." (Shaw, 792)

In 1986, the *Harvard Business Review* assisted its readers by suggesting methods to avoid prosecution by encouraging "well publicized, carefully tailored 'donations'—an approach that offers both idealistic and practical appeal." For instance, it was noted that IBM guaranteed Mexican officials that it would employ a certain percentage of Mexican nationals in return for the ability to build a plant; Coca Cola chose to plant trees in one developing country rather than pay bribes. All seems well and good until you begin to ponder certain questions: Who judges what is reasonable? Who judges how many Mexican workers should be employed as opposed to, let's say, a $100,000 bribe? Who can estimate how many trees will satisfy the value for a $25,000 "donation"?

You be the judge. Was Harvard acting to encourage the high ground of ethical standards or was it actually publicizing strategies aimed at circumventing Congressional intent?

> At the national level, for instance, the most appropriate and satisfying corporate response to ministerial requests for "contributions" toward the construction of a hospital, such as occurred in Kenya, might actually be to provide one, down to the final door and stethoscope, while simultaneously insisting that monetary payments of any kind are proscribed by U.S. law.
>
> Businesspeople can also resolve the ethical dilemma. Turning private payoffs into public services should meet both U.S. and corporate moral standards. While one measure of corporate responsibility is to generate the highest possible returns for investors, this can usually be best achieved within a climate of goodwill. In contemporary Third World cultures, this climate can more often be created by public service than by private payoffs. (Fadiman, 136)

In 1988, Congress slightly modified the FCPA to provide companies a bit more flexibility, precisely because of the various, imaginative "strategies" such as that mentioned above that were being tailored to thousands of attempts by U.S. companies to build bridges, secure visas for their employees, or even open offices. While many complain that the act unfairly compromises the competitiveness of U.S. companies at a time when the U.S. trade deficit is too high, most multinationals have learned to adapt to the law. The good news from the FCPA is the mere fact that it was passed in the first place. Seeking an international standard on business morality may be next to impossible given differences in cultures. But the world's most prestigious business journal seems to have gotten it right:

The success of the Foreign Corrupt Practices Act ought to have encouraged other governments to copy America's virtuous example. None has: nearly all countries have laws against the bribing of their own officials, but only America forbids the bribing of other people's. ("On the Take," *The Economist*, 22)

In the sections that follow, you will read about how several international analysts view international business ethics, and you will be challenged by several cases aimed at increasing your sensitivity to these issues.

CASE STUDY: WHEN SCIENCE AND ETHICS BOTH FAIL— A DECADE OF LOSSES IN BHOPAL, INDIA

Although industrial accidents happen every day, even engineers and scientists were astonished at the massive loss of life in Bhopal, India, a decade ago at the Union Carbide plant. Today, much of the legal, medical, and technical relief that was promised to survivors has yet to arrive, leaving us to wonder who bears the ethical as well as moral burden for those unfortunate enough to have lived their lives in that city. In this Washington Post *article by Molly Moore, you will read about the serious questions of ethical and moral responsibility that continue to linger for both Americans and Indians.*

In Bhopal, a Relentless Cloud of Despair

Nine years after a Union Carbide chemical plant spewed a deadly cloud of gas over this city, the victims of the worst industrial disaster in history have received miniscule financial compensation, and the overburdened government relief programs created to help survivors are mired in corruption and mismanagement. Special courts established to parcel compensation to gas victims have paid out only $3.1 million of the $470 million damage settlement the American chemical giant negotiated with the Indian government in 1989, according to court documents.

"These people are still suffering while the vultures—doctors, lawyers, bureaucrats—become rich off the carcass of Bhopal," says Heeresh Chandra, who was the city's chief medical examiner the night of Dec. 2, 1984, when a cloak of poison gas dropped over Bhopal, killing an estimated 2,500 in the first week and injuring as many as 500,000 more.

A combination of corruption, incompetence and the overwhelming logistics of tracking more than a half-million mostly illiterate victims has created major failures in every system created to assist the gas victims of this central Indian city, whose name has become synonymous with industrial disaster.

The legal, medical and economic relief programs in Bhopal have suffered numerous failures and delays.

Claims courts that will determine final compensation for victims from the Union Carbide settlement were not established until last year—eight years after the gas leak. Of an estimated 615,000 death and personal injury claims, only 5,700 have been decided. Lawyers and officials say it could take another 10 years to hear all the claims, even though the Indian government says it agreed to the controversial settlement with Union Carbide to ensure speedy compensation to victims.

Hospitals built to serve the hundreds of thousands of people who still suffer from gas-related illnesses are hopelessly overcrowded. Doctors say they see as many as 150 patients on a four-hour shift, and patients lie on the floors of hospital corridors for up to three days waiting for beds to become available. Medicines that are supposed to be given free to victims are often unavailable because hospital staffers sell them out the back door to local shopkeepers.

The Indian government has poured $75 million into relief programs ranging from construction of 11 hospitals to building 1,000 apartments for widows of gas victims. But much of the money has been funneled into bloated gas relief bureaucracies and mismanaged projects.

Virtually every level of the relief bureaucracy is rife with corruption. Government officials demand bribes from illiterate victims trying to obtain documents required for relief money; doctors take bribes from victims to testify in their court cases; and unscrupulous agents fish for bribes by claiming they can get victims' cases moved to the front of the crowded dockets.

Inefficient Indian government agencies have been overwhelmed by the mammoth task of identifying more than 600,000 gas-affected people, the majority of whom live in slums where mail delivery and other basic services are virtually nonexistent. As a result, thousands of people reportedly have filed fake claims using forged medical documents and other bogus evidence, clogging the courts, hospitals and government programs struggling to serve legitimate victims.

"It's a horrible situation," says Gurudatta Tieari, an internist at one of the government medical centers established to treat gas victims who testifies a least once a day in the claims courts.

"Whatever we have done, we feel has been done properly," says a senior official of the government's relief program who agreed to be interviewed on the condition that his name not be used. "Whether it is sufficient is a valid question."

Though many of the problems of corruption, mismanagement and overtaxed facilities are widespread in the Indian government, doctors, lawyers and government officials say the amount of money involved in the relief programs and the suffering endured by more than half the residents of this city for almost a decade make this an exceptional case, even by Indian standards.

To drive through the streets of Old Bhopal, where the poison gas cloud was the most lethal, is to see a city reliving a nine-year-old tragedy every day. Hundreds of people line up each morning at dozens of government "identification centers" to apply for interim relief payments of $6.45 month. The payments, which began three years ago, are supposed to tide them over until the overbooked courts can hear their claim cases.

Although people continue to die everyday from gas related complications—authorities estimate the death toll at anywhere from 4,000 to 14,000—no cure and no definitive treatments have been found for victims. A second generation of victims—children born since the accident whose parents were gas victims—is believed to be suffering, and in many cases dying, as a result of the 1984 disaster, according to medical studies.

"The government is blind to us," says Jehana Bi, 60, a widow who was joining in one of the victims' rights rallies that are held almost daily in Bhopal. "God knows how many more rallies we have to go to. I have fought many of these fights and all I have to show for it is 200 rupees" a month in government aid.

The Union Carbide pesticide plant has long been shut down. One of the main gates of the compound has been painted with a large skull and the epitaph "Killer Carbide." A 12-foot-high statue of a woman, her face twisted in anguish and her arms clutching a dead baby, was erected across the street as a reminder of the tragedy, which provoked international debate over the ethics of Western nations exporting some of their most dangerous industries to Third World countries.

Union Carbide extricated itself from relief efforts in 1989 by agreeing to pay the Indian government $470 million to be divided among victims and their families, a sum that outraged many Indians who charged that the American chemical company got away with paying only a fraction of what its liabilities would have been in an industrialized country.

"We feel we fulfilled our obligations in 1989," says Union Carbide spokesman Bob Berzok.

Though Union Carbide and the Indian government defended the controversial settlement by arguing that it would speed the process of getting compensation to victims, claims courts were set up only last year to begin awarding the money. Today those courts are mired in inefficiency, deluged by the volume of cases and riddled with abuses. As of the end of August, the courts had paid out $3.1 million in claims. Though government officials would not provide details of the interest earned on the settlement money, which has been kept in a bank account under the protection of the Indian Supreme Court, published reports estimate the fund is worth about $650 million.

Union Carbide still has not begun construction of a 500-bed hospital the Indian Supreme Court ordered it to build for gas victims. The company says the Indian government's freeze on its Indian assets is to blame; Indian officials argue that is merely an excuse to delay building the hospital and say the company could easily use funds from its vast holdings outside India.

Efforts to distribute the settlement money moved so slowly that in 1990 the Supreme Court ordered the government to finance interim payments—$6.45 a month—to gas victims who lived in areas affected by the gas. After numerous court battles, the court determined that about 600,000 people deserved to get those payments. The Indian government plans to reimburse itself for the approximately $115 million it has paid out in interim relief from the $470 million Union Carbide settlement.

But government officials and victims' rights advocates say a huge number of victims may never see any more of the money. The Indian

Supreme Court ordered the government to set up 40 claims courts by February 1992 for sorting through the 14,129 death and more than 600,000 injury claims that are expected to be filed. To date, judges have acted on 5,763 death cases, rejecting 75 percent, documents show. None of the injury cases has been heard. Where awards were made, the average compensation was near the minimum amount allowed—about $3,500.

Most claims were refused because the applicants did not have the necessary paperwork, even though in many cases the government had certified the death claims as valid. Victims' rights advocates argue that it is unreasonable to base awards on paper proof when the government has not kept records.

When Gladys Amolik filed for her share of the $470 million settlement, the court judge rejected her claim, saying she did not have enough evidence to prove that her husband had died from the gas. The courts ignored evidence that the Indian government had categorized the death as gas-related and had granted Amolik a $322 one-time payment under one of its limited relief programs and, three years ago, had given her one of the apartments built for widows of gas victims. "They said, 'You don't have any papers,'" says Amolik, whose eye pupils have turned milky white from gas damage. "The doctor who testified against me was not even the doctor who had treated my husband—he had left town."

Many of the problems of distributing the funds were born on the night of the accident. In the first hours after the leak from an underground tank allowed 42 tons of poisonous gas to escape, tens of thousands of people flooded the hospitals, overwhelming a system ill-equipped to handle such an emergency. Frantic doctors did not bother to identify the dead. The next day, government workers burned hundreds of bodies on the municipal funeral pyre. Most of the bodies were cremated without medical examinations because of a religious culture that frowns on autopsies, and hospitals were too overrun to keep records, creating problems that still haunt victims and the government.

Today, even the 12 hospitals and dispensaries built for survivors of the gas leak are overcrowded, understaffed and frequently run short of critical medicines. On a recent day, more than 100 patients were jammed into an open-air waiting area outside one doctor's office at the Shakir Ali Khan Hospital in Old Bhopal. A few yards away, Roop Chand was lying on the dirty concrete floor of a busy corridor, a tube of fluids draining into his arm from an intravenous bottle tied to a window grate. His wife, who hunched on the floor beside him, said he had been waiting three days for a bed.

Though hospitals throughout India are usually overcrowded and often run short of medicine and equipment, authorities say the sheer volume of patients who need frequent care as a result of the gas-related ailments and the lack of effective treatments make the situation in Bhopal's hospitals far worse. Some doctors blame the overcrowding on patients who attribute all of their medical problems to the gas. Though the hospitals were built specifically for gas-affected victims, doctors say patients are not screened. "Officially the hospitals are for the gas victims," says Tiwari. "Unofficially, we welcome everybody."

Among the Indian government's other relief efforts, economic rehabilitation programs for gas victims have been among the most mismanaged, say government officials and victims' rights groups. The state government spent $2.5 million in relief money to build a vast training center and 152 work sheds for welding, carpentry and other industries. But not a single gas victim has received any training at the site and the buildings have been empty since their completion two years ago. The government is trying to sell the buildings to private businesses that they hope will hire gas victims to work in their facilities.

"The emphasis is on government construction projects, not getting jobs for the gas victims," says Abdul Jabbar Khan, a victims' rights leader in Bhopal.

Questions for Consideration

1. What are the ethical obligations of a company operating in a foreign environment? Is the employer always responsible for the actions of its employees who break local laws?

2. In the case of Union Carbide, the company claims that its obligations to the residents of Bhopal ended by paying a $470 million settlement. What is your opinion?

3. Accidents are inevitable. Given that fact, what would you recommend to other companies that face a similar catastrophe in the future? Where do their moral, medical, and ethical obligations begin and end?

A ROUNDTABLE DISCUSSION ON MAINTAINING ETHICS AND VALUES IN FOREIGN CULTURES

How can organizations ensure that their employees are managing in an ethical mode when representing their employer abroad? In the following discussion, several thoughtful executives with extensive experience in global business and ethics share their insights on this issue. Among them are:

- *William C. Norris, Founder and Former Chairman of Control Data Corp. of Minneapolis, Minnesota*

- *Shirley V. Paterson, Vice-President of Ethics and Business Conduct for Northrop Corporation in Los Angeles*

- *Peter Thigpen of Executive Reserves in Mill Valley, California; Former Senior Vice-President at Levi Strauss & Co.*

- *John J. Ursu, Vice-President of Legal Affairs and General Counsel at 3M Corporation in St. Paul, Minnesota*

- *James O'Toole, Chairman of the Management Department at the Graduate School of Business, University of Southern California*

- *Barbara Levy Toffler, Senior Principal at Resources for Responsible Management in Boston*

- *Graydon R. Wood, Vice-President of Quality and Ethics at NYNEX Corporation, White Plains, New York*

Question: Bribes and "facilitation fees" seem to be accepted business practice in many countries. Is the U.S. Foreign Corrupt Practices Act, which forbids many of these payments by U.S. companies, unrealistic and unfair? Is it ethical for an U.S. company to hire local companies and law firms to make such payments? Is it reasonable for the U.S. company to be ignorant of what its foreign agents do on its behalf?

Mr. Ursu: There is no question that it is often difficult for an American company to compete with foreign companies that do not have such laws, at least over the short term. I think over the long

Source: From "Maintaining Ethics and Values in Foreign Cultures," *Ethics: Easier Said Than Done*, 1993 issue 22, p. 41-48; published by The Josephson Institute of Ethics, Marina Del Ray, California. Used with permission.

term we're probably not at that great a disadvantage because bribery is not a reliable mode of competition, at least not for a company like 3M. 3M tries to develop unique products that deliver high value. If we were selling sugar or other commodities where there was very little difference in the product, very little difference in the service, I suppose bribery would be a different issue. But we try to out-compete our competitors not based on things like bribery or even price but based on quality and product performance and service. Companies like 3M cannot sustain competition over the long haul on an unethical plane, because there will always be people who are better crooks. We're better engineers, better scientists, and better salespeople.

Facilitating payments can be ethical . . . because I think it's a way of life that's well understood by all the affected parties including the governments themselves. So if you are required, for example, to help fund the prosecutor in a Third World country or the police department in investigating a crime against your company, that is just how the whole government system works there. Bribery, by contrast, has to do with separating out an employee of an organization from the organization itself. When we or any other American company pay a facilitating payment to an employee of a government, we're not putting that employee into a conflict with his government.

Mr. Norris: That's a difficult problem. If you're going to do business in Iran, for example, you're better off to have a local organization you go through. You can own part of it so you can control it. But let them deal with the local customs and don't get directly involved. Because there's just no way of handling that is acceptable, either from a moral standpoint or legal.

Mr. Ayers: That's a very difficult issue. Sometimes it's cultural, sometimes it's not. You can academically construct an argument that distinguishes between bribing a government official to betray a trust, and paying a facilitation fee which is to encourage somebody to do their job more quickly than they might otherwise do it. Our policy is that we don't pay facilitation fees. I might debate that. Is tipping a bribe?

We have to be very careful about ethical imperialism, [thinking] that we have an absolute lock on everything that's right, good, and pure in the world. We don't. I think there are core ethical values, and I think they are universal, but this is a difficult issue. I've worked in Egypt, where the customs official probably is paid $25 a month and everybody expects that he will supplement his income by getting tips. [The word] "tip" means "To Insure Promptness." We don't pay facilitation fees, even though the FCPA would permit that. In our mind, the corporate mind, it's the first step down a slippery slope.

It's absolutely essential to know and be accountable for what any agent representing us is doing. Ignorance is absolutely not an excuse. We make our agents and representatives sign statements in their contracts saying that they've gotten a copy of our standards of conduct and that they will comply. If we detect one that isn't complying, they're terminated.

Dr. Edwards: Many times in our work with companies, they are of the opinion that doing business overseas is much more difficult than doing business in the United States because people who are overseas do not have the same ethical standards that we have, often do not have the same legal requirements that we have, and are willing to engage in bribery. Sometimes they get confused when they compare bribery and gift-giving as being just merely different quantifications of the same practice. That is, if it's OK to give a cabby a tip or waiter to get better service, and it's OK to exchange very fine gifts between corporate heads, then it's OK to give larger gifts to buyers and contracting officials [which may] influence their decision to buy from you rather than someone else.

If there is a sliding scale from gift to bribery, business people do well to remember at the far end of the scale, governments fall. Every civilized country on the planet, to my knowledge, has a law forbidding the bribery of public officials. Nobody wants their government bought and paid for. You justify making payments to government officials in order to get into a market and do your business in that market or do business with that government. You are undermining the integrity and viability of that government. You do not have right to do that in order to increase your sales.

There may be some markets into which some companies simply should not go. We had, a few years ago, a consumer products firm that was growing very rapidly every year, and the strategic business plan called for them to double the size of their business in five years, largely by acquisition in the Pacific Rim and in Latin America. They did a risk assessment country by country, and they made a decision that [they would not enter] certain countries in the Pacific Rim [because of] the probability of being involved with companies that were already corrupt. It was not worth the risk to their reputation to try to enter those markets through acquisition. They just plain wrote them off.

The Foreign Corrupt Practices Act is neither unrealistic nor unfair. It does acknowledge the legal acceptability of facilitation payments and does require the facilitation payments be properly recorded in the books and records of the corporation. That seems to me to be very realistic and hardheaded, given the fact that standards do vary around the world.

Dr. Toffler: If you initiate a payment to wield influence to get something sooner or better or above somebody else, that's a bribe. If you're asked to do that to get either special favor or something you feel you're entitled to, you're responding to extortion. Facilitating payments say there are certain things you ought to be getting—like having your raw materials moved in a timely fashion through customs—but may not be. But if you give [custom officials] $50 and record it in your books, that's viewed as a facilitating payment and is allowed. Is it proper or is it not proper? You really can't make a statement like that. I'll tell you right now, almost every single company is doing one thing or another, through agents or whatever. That is the reality if you're going to do business around this world. Every [company] will tell you that it takes responsibility for what its foreign agents do, but foreign agents are doing a lot of stuff out there.

One of the big problems for American companies is that they send mid-level managers overseas and then [let them] hang out to dry. They say, "Don't make any illegal payments, but don't you dare lose the contract or don't you dare put us in a position where we can't do business there." And the manager doesn't know what to do. They are damned if they do and damned if they don't. [I know an executive who] was heading a company in another country. He was essentially asked by an export official to give a gift and if he did not give the gift he was not going to be able to export this product. He called his boss back home, very, very high level.

The answer he got from back home was don't do anything illegal or to embarrass this company but if you lose our contract back in the States, if you don't get that product out, you're dead meat. Direct quote, "you're dead meat." At responsible companies, the decision is not in the hands of the local manager; instead, the very highest leadership is involved in trying to sort through what the appropriate behavior is. Sometimes when the very highest level gets involved it turns out that things can get done without payments being made. It's a far too complicated problem to give a snappy little answer to.

A bank manager in Hong Kong [said to me] the next place you're going to see a lot of business opening up in is Vietnam. But, he said, you know why nothing's really been done yet? They don't have enough of a bureaucracy in place [yet] to know how to make the payoffs. As soon as they get that in place, it's going to open up like mad. Of course the U.S. will get there much too late. We'll make a lot of noise about how ethical we are. Eventually we'll get in and pay, but by then everybody else will have established themselves, and we'll be also-rans.

It's a very complicated thing. The question is how are you going to manage in that reality. I'm not saying you go along to get along. Expressions like that are foolish. It is a very complicated world. There's a hundred thousand ethics consultants running around the United States and everybody is saying all these lovely platitudes. Nobody seems to realize that it is incredibly hard to figure out how to manage responsibly. It's simply one blah, blah, blah thing after another. It is hard work. For all that everyone is running around screaming about how we need to return to traditional values and where have our morals and values gone, let me tell you in business we are a thousand percent more ethical, tighter in our standards, than we ever were.

I'm so tired of this thinking that there's somehow going to be simplistic statements or solutions to this stuff. It is hard, hard work. Ethics is in the process, not in standing up and saying I'm not going to do that because I think that's bad or I'm going to go, along to get along.

Dr. O'Toole: I think the U.S. Foreign Corrupt Practices Act is both fair and realistic, and I think we can live with it. I think it's been a much bigger problem in the past than it is now. This is a question that is sort of dated, I used to hear companies complaining about it, I don't hear them complaining about it anymore. I don't think you have to go beyond compliance with that. It's a pretty good law.

Mr. Hanson: Through the Foreign Corrupt Practices Act the United States made a decision that its companies ought to behave by a set of standards that we set within the U.S. and that as a nation we would pay the price if this limited some business opportunities abroad. It may not always be a level playing field, but we have determined that we all benefit from the encouragement of ethical behavior. Some companies clearly skirt the intent of the law by hiring local agents and deliberately avoiding knowledge about techniques used to get and keep business. The Foreign Corrupt Practices Act cannot be written tightly enough to avoid all such arrangements.

Companies make a decision in defining their fundamental values whether they will be characterized by minimum compliance or adherence to the spirit of the laws and of their own [stated] values. Many companies have a minimalist compliance approach to behavior at home and abroad. Others take more seriously the implications of their own avowed values and attempt to implement them consistently across the company. This drives them to go beyond the minimum requirements of the law and I believe they reap rewards in [terms of] respect from their various stakeholders and in increased employee morale and productivity from such an approach.

Dr. Hoffman: What can be considered a facilitating payment is a fairly gray area. A clear case is when you have some product on the dock of a foreign country and you need to get that product moved to some other location in the country. It may require [making] some kind of payment [just as] you would give a gratuity to a person who carries your bags or to a waitress who brings you your food. But if a corporation is [constructing a] building in another country and an inspector doesn't pass it because you have refused to give him money, I think most people would see that as a bribe.

But what is that manager to do when everything he does continues to be rejected because it's not "up to code" and his competitors are not receiving those kinds of rejections because they are paying money to make sure that they do pass? Do you pay, or do you continue to hold out and say that I won't pay and take the consequences? I've heard of a company that simply did not pay and finally had to pay much more in terms of redoing the buildings. It was an Indian company. They were operating in a Mid-East country. The manager on site begged the home office to pay because it was so much cheaper. But the home office wouldn't do it. It cost them millions of dollars.

A lot of people have the impression that it's just American companies that have this high sense of moral superiority or integrity. [But in general] I think Americans place a higher importance on doing business ethically. . . . In other countries, I think a lot of people see business as sort of a fundamentally amoral or unethical arena to start with, so they don't expect business to operate as ethically as Americans expect business to operate. I do think it has historical and religious roots in our country, whereas it doesn't so much in other countries. I do think that American corporations, as painful and difficult as it may be to compete, do have an ethical responsibility not to pay bribes to foreign officials to achieve contracts, even though our European and Japanese competitors do not have the same kind of ethical feelings of obligation.

Mr. Wood: U.S. companies can do business in very difficult markets. When you stick up for your own standards you earn respect. You establish a good bargaining position. If you're looking for the long term, you're always going to be held accountable in the last analysis to U.S. standards, not the standards of some foreign turf.

Question: Is there an ethical problem when a U.S. company runs a foreign operation that complies with local laws but is below the minimum health and safety standards mandated for U.S. employees? Are the ethical considerations different when the company simply contracts with local business people who make all employee-condition decisions?

Dr. O'Toole: One of the biggest ethical problems that American corporations face is in subcontracting abroad. They close an operation here where they are forced to provide safe and healthy working conditions, provide the minimum wage, and they open up a sweat shop in the Philippines where people are paid 40 cents a day. This is far and away, of all ethical questions, the most difficult one that the corporations face. Until recently, they have just turned their backs on this. I figure it's where most American businesses are most vulnerable. There are very, very few companies—I'm having difficulty thinking of one—that treat their employees in the Third World as well as they treat their employees here. And I'm not talking just about wages, but in terms of benefits, in terms of participation, in terms of respect.

The problem is far away; it's out of sight and out of mind. The corporate executives tend not to go through the factories [abroad]. They tend not to understand conditions of people who speak different language. They don't understand what their lives are like.

[There] is a failure to empathize, to see that a worker in the Philippines is as much a human being as a worker in the United States. [American companies] went to get the cheap labor. I think that it is possible to say that we are going to assure that all employees, everywhere around the world, have safe conditions and that they earn a living sufficient enough to support themselves and their families with some opportunities for savings.

If laws are woefully inadequate, if the company is poisoning water supplies and the local government doesn't care about it, I think that the corporation has a responsibility. These questions are very, very tough. Do we go to the standards of the U.S. or do we go to some other standard? Where do you draw the line? These questions really become true ethical dilemmas, because the managers have to make moral judgments without any kind of legal guidelines. The highest standard is unrealistic.

Standards that are set in the United States for environmental questions and occupational safety and health are arbitrary; they're not scientific. I don't think, from what I see, that many American corporations ask the tough ethical questions about operations overseas. When they go overseas the notion is that it is now somebody else's problem. I talk with CEOs all the time. They spend their time worrying about the EPA, about competitors, about their employees. How much time do they spend asking questions having to do with their operations in the Third World? I've never heard anybody ever [list] it on their agenda.

Mr. Hanson: I believe nothing is credible except [adhering to] a worldwide standard in health, safety and human rights that demonstrates a consistent concern for employees, customers and communities in which the firms operate. . . . I think the most enlightened and thoughtful companies define a worldwide standard which is applied consistently. This probably at least meets the minimum standards of United States compliance. It may go well beyond that. Most of the large and enlightened companies in the United States have looked at the risks of having different standards of health, safety and human rights in different parts of the world and have concluded that such practices would give mixed signals to their own managers and employees and would expose them to liability suits and public pressure when disasters strike.

Union Carbide was not held in the court of public opinion to the Indian standard; they were held to the American standard. . . . But standards must be implemented with a sensitivity to the level of development and the culture of the local economy. This does not mean that you value life less in other parts of the world; it merely means that you may need to adapt policies to confront the realities of family and social structure in certain parts of the world. There are many organizations which do operate according to lower environmental standards, but I think that is changing. I think public opinion will not tolerate that over the next five years.

I don't think one is required by a worldwide standard of ethics to pay the same wages, [but] there clearly is an ethical issue. It's related to traditional religious concepts of a living wage or to how wages can improve the skills and lives of the people employed. . . . There is probably an obligation to make total compensation enable workers to provide for their families and improve their own skill level.

"Beyond compliance" is not the right way of describing [ethical duties], nor is that the way most companies think about it. They think about in terms of what should we provide for our employees that is economically viable but is still sensitive to their development. And, generally, the minimum requirements are far below that.

Dr. Edwards: The question suggests that the minimum health and safety standard mandated for U.S. employees is somehow itself, perforce, an ethical standard. The people of [a lesser developed] country, if they have a freely elected government that represents them, may be willing to accept costs that we in a more well-developed economy and society would not be willing to accept, including environmental damage [and] a lower degree of protection for people in the workplace. By avoiding those preventive costs, they may be able to develop their economies more rapidly, prevent starvation, malnutrition, disease. That's a reasonable cost-benefit analysis for people to make. The difficult problem is when U.S. companies acquire overseas subsidiaries or operate in countries whose governments are not freely elected or representative. Then it becomes a harder question, whether the government that exists has the right to make those decisions on behalf of its people.

Dr. Hoffman: It seems to me that corporations have a responsibility to demonstrate ethical or moral leadership in going beyond what the law says they have to do in the case of environmental protection. I don't think they should go it alone. Several years ago a paper company manufacturer got environmental religion and decided to put all sorts of expensive equipment on his paper company so that his effluence would not pollute this small New England stream. Well, none of the other manufacturers did that, so his company couldn't compete, went broke, and put 500 people out of work.

The bottom line is that the stream was no cleaner because all the other companies were still dumping their pollutants into the stream. There has to be moral leadership taken on the part of corporations to find ways to bring all of their competitors into line. That's why we have laws. Corporations need to take some moral leadership and work with government to help set appropriate standards.

When you're abroad, it seems to me that you have a responsibility to live up to the same kind of standards you are operating under in this country, especially when you're dealing with environmental standards, with the health and safety of employees and so forth. Now, I'm not saying you should pay employees the same amount in Nicaragua or in other foreign countries that you pay them in the United States. That might even have harmful effects in terms of disrupting the economy. But I do not think that a company is being ethically responsible in going into Mexico and practicing things that it would be forbidden to do in this country.

It has an ethical obligation to make sure that the same kind of health and safety standards that are in effect in this country are employed there and the same kind of environmental practices are employed there as are required here. You have to look at these things on a case-by-case basis. There may be products that we do not want used in this country but because of different circumstances in other countries may be appropriate there; for example, DDT. In a country that has a tremendous problem in terms of starvation, where crops are essential, then I might reassess whether that product should be used.

Mr. Ayers: I won't apply California's standards to my business in Minnesota. Why should I apply California's standards to my business in Tijuana? It's clear that the environmental health and safety standards and laws in some countries are not adequate to protect either the environment or the employee, in which cases I will apply a standard that does protect the environment and the employee. I won't sign up for applying California's standards or Sweden's standards, but I'll apply an appropriate standard which goes well beyond the local, legally required standard. I have to make a judgment call as a businessman.

Mr. Ursu: Do we have an affirmative duty to try to lobby a [foreign] government to raise standards? I doubt it. Right or wrong this is a commercial organization. Our employees on their own may choose to affiliate with the Sierra Club of Mexico or Peru or wherever and do things on their own because they have values that they want to serve. . . . As far as doing good, unrelated to [serving] stakeholders, 3M and many other companies have foundations that give grants, support starving children in Africa, things like that that really don't have a direct link to the stakeholders.

Mr. Norris: I think that you have to be governed primarily by the laws of the country you're operating in, not by U.S. laws. . . . We can't be responsible for the world. If you try to do that, where do you stop? We had a terrible situation in South Korea. We wanted to do the right thing. The government said that if you treat your employees better you're going to screw up the whole system. . . . We wanted to pay them a little bit more, provide them a little health care and give them a little more flexibility in their working hours, trying to do for them what we were doing for other employees. All we succeeded in doing was getting into a pissing contest with the government. . . .

There's the practicality you have to always keep in mind. If [for example] you can't afford to stop dumping in the Rio Grande, you keep dumping until you get the laws changed . . . then the others would have to comply, so you would not be at a competitive disadvantage. . . . You should [stop dumping] if you can afford to, even if it's not required by the law. Any company that conducts itself in an ethical manner would do that.

Mr. Dolan: I don't think this is an ethical problem. It assumes first of all that U.S. standards are the right standards. I'm a firm believer that the United States should not be imposing its standards on the rest of the world because we know better than everybody else. Shouldn't we leave it to Mexico to determine what is in the best interests of the Mexican people? It's possible that a certain set of standards imposed upon Mexico would cut back on jobs substantially and produce greater harm. There are limits to all of this. We all have a feeling for minimal health standards, minimal environmental standards—I mean in our own minds what we think is really right. That's the ethical line.

The ethical line is not necessarily drawn by the U.S. Congress when you're dealing outside of the country. If you're in Mexico, you comply with their legal requirements. If you think those requirements would still present a health hazard to your employees then you got an ethical issue. How you define that, I think that's something on which reasonable people can differ. Let's say you have a plant down in Mexico and all of the sudden, like Constantine [seeing] the Cross in the sky, you're a believer. You say what we're doing is wrong. But I don't think you can say we're going to shut that plant down tomorrow and throw 1,000 Mexicans out of work. To satisfy your own conscience, you're causing immediate harm to a whole lot of people.

Mr. Johnson: You have to recognize your limitations. One of the most ethical things would be to work in alliance with other like-minded companies in pressing governmental change. That's an affirmative duty. For example, the automakers don't have a legal obligation to go to the safety agency and say, "We have come up with a way to save many lives. No one of us can afford to do this voluntarily because it will put us at a competitive disadvantage." But that would be a highly ethical initiative.

Question: When companies derive large portions of their business from other countries, do they have an ethical obligation to see that persons from those countries are fairly represented in the employee

pool and management ranks? Should the board of directors reflect the international diversity of the revenue and production sources?

Dr. Hoffman: The employees of a particular plant should be appropriately represented by the kind of diversity that country represents. It's the same kind of consideration that we have in this country in which we try to hire people who appropriately represent the diversity in our country, and also, if we are going down to another country and using their natural resources, using their roads, their infrastructure, in order to profit, we have some obligation to hire local people to help run that operation. The consideration there is fairness. From a practical, perhaps less ethical point of view, it would also seem to be the best way of building good community relations. . . .

There seems to be some ethical issue as well as good management policy to have people on the board that appropriately represent the country or countries that you're doing business with. For one thing, they are going to provide perspectives that you're not going to have as an outsider. From an ethical point of view, the interests and concerns and problems that might arise [in a foreign] operation should be represented by someone who knows that country.

Mr. Ayers: There ought to be some representation in employee pool and management ranks. [But] the board of directors reflects ownership. If [foreigners] own stock and want to elect board members, they ought to do that. We have non-U.S. citizens and residents on our board. But I don't know that you can link board diversity to revenue and production sources.

Dr. O'Toole: I don't think that having, for example, a Filipino businessman on the board of Levi Strauss would make Levi Strauss any more ethical. The Filipino businessman's probably exploiting his own people. Merely getting ethnic representation doesn't ensure anything at all. The board of directors [should] include people with sensitivity toward these broader ethical questions, regardless of national origin.

Dr. Edwards: I don't think there is any moral or ethical obligation to do that. I certainly don't think there's any ethical obligation that the board of directors reflect the international diversity of the revenue and production sources. There may be prudential reasons to do it and may be good business reasons to do it, but I don't think ethics has a vote here.

Mr. Hanson: I don't think there's an obligation for quotas by country, but there is certainly the opportunity to create employment and promotion opportunities for nationals of every country in which a company [operates]. It is simply wise for the board of directors to reflect the international diversity of a company's operations, but I don't think there is any obligation to have a proportional representation based upon revenue or production.

Ms. Paterson: We're seeing great efforts made, [but] there needs to be more effort to seat women and minorities on boards of directors. I would think that same [logic applies] when it comes to multinational companies. They're going to benefit in the long haul by [having diverse boards] because it says that they recognize the input from these diverse stakeholders is going to [help them] stay profitable.

Mr. Thigpen: I'm not sure it's an ethical consideration. Companies that don't do that are stupid. They ought to have an international perspective. Globalization is yesterday's news. Unless you are globalizing across the board, and that includes in your board of directors, then you've got a problem.

Question: Are U.S. standards of conducting business appreciably different from the standards of Western Europeans, Eastern Europeans, or East Asians? How can U.S. companies maintain their values and ethical standards when doing business in countries that apparently permit standards considered lower from the U.S. point of view?

Dr. Hoffman: When people start talking about cultural differences in terms of ethical behavior, my suspicion is that the differences are quite often much more superficial in terms of action and mores rather than in terms of ethical standards and principles. It can be a matter of interpretation as to how to abide by an ethical standard. . . . The Eskimos used to commit patricide. They would literally put their parents on an ice floe because the older the parents got, the more difficult it was for them to live that kind of nomadic life.

Part of it was religious because they believed that they entered the afterlife in the same physical form that they departed this world. But the Eskimos certainly believed in the ethical principle of honoring their parents, and we also believe in the ethical principle of honoring our parents, even though we practice very different methods of doing that. We put them in old age homes. I'm not sure which is more humane. The point is, it's not true that the Eskimos were operating under a different ethical standard than we were.

Mr. Hanson: It is the excuse of ineffective global managers that they can't achieve their goals because they are not allowed to stoop as low as local business practices. Even when local business practices do reflect questionable behavior I think American companies have an obligation to align themselves with the reform elements in those countries to wipe out corruption and favoritism in business.

In any country there are reform elements that are trying to clean it up. And for the American companies to come in and simply say that's the way it is and therefore that's the way we'll behave means they become part of the problem rather than part of the solution. . . . I strongly believe have been involved in pressuring the South African government for apartheid reform should be involved in the development of ethical and social policies which reflect concern for human rights, for employee and community safety, and for environmental concerns.

The principle has been established in South Africa that the corporate obligation is, number one, to operate business according to ethical, human rights, safety and environmental practices. It is further established that it's the obligation of companies to protest and lobby when local policies do not provide adequate protection for human beings or the environment. What form that takes will depend upon the national setting that the company operates in.

In some countries visible protests will be counterproductive. . . . In societies where there are no avenues for promoting liberalization of policies, companies probably have no alternative but to withdraw. . . . It is clearly the obligation of the companies to operate by standards that are ethical and defensible, and, secondly, to contribute to the process of liberalization which makes the benefits of such policies available to all within the country.

Dr. O'Toole: I think that too much is made about the differences among cultures and not enough of the similarities. A lie is a lie the world around. And trust means the same thing pretty much the world around. I don't think that Americans are being undercut because we're forced into this higher standard. I don't believe that is happening, or to the extent that it's making a hell of a difference. Americans have trouble when they assume that the whole world thinks like Americans. There are handicaps in not understanding foreign languages [and] cultures that Americans suffer from, but I don't believe that is the same thing as saying that American ethical standards are higher. Across cultures and religions the questions of morality are all pretty similar.

Ms. Paterson: I think all of these cultures value integrity, responsibility, fairness, trust, and honesty, those kinds of virtues or traits. That's what we've got to focus on for the future, common character values. The standards of conducting business that come through law are much more rigid and higher in the United States. But I think we'll see that change, too. . . . I think [American companies] have to continue to adhere to the standards they have operated by in the United States and be a catalyst, a real advocate, in the world marketplace that will cause those kinds of standards to be adopted internationally.

Mr. Norris: The best way for most companies to operate [abroad], particularly smaller [companies], is to work through local organizations. You may own part of it so you have some control over it. But don't try to change their culture, their standards. It's awfully hard to do. It's a loser. They don't appreciate it.

Mr. Ayers: There's difference in local practices and how people view the world, but when you get right down to it, nobody likes to be lied to, nobody likes to be cheated. The president of Brazil was thrown out of office; the prime minister of Japan lost his job. I used to think that the Brazilians loved corruption. The people of Italy are standing up and saying we're not going to take this anymore. The world is becoming more mature, more sophisticated, and communications are better. I think you're beginning to see a convergence around some core ethical values and a growing unwillingness of people to tolerate [bad behavior]. My [company's] values are integrity, quality, performance, mutual respect, and diversity. If I'm in Russia, should I adopt their legal standards, is that my base line? Just because I happen to be an American does that mean my laws are the right ones? Maybe they don't go far enough.

Mr. Thigpen: I think they are different. You have to go for the high-water mark. You also have to make a very reasoned judgment as to what standards you consider absolute minimums and what standards you're willing to surrender. Senior [executives] have to make the decisions. What the senior guys have to do is say beyond this we will not go, we won't do business in a country unless [certain] conditions are extant.

Mr. Ursu: 3M's been in Italy a long time. As you read in the paper, virtually every quarter of Italy has been touched by scandal. We have not. We have in fact been told by customers who are now coming to us after they or their suppliers were implicated in these corruption problems, that they want to do business with us because they know that we don't do these kind of things. In the current environment these people want a measure of safety in dealing with a company that has a high reputation for integrity. That's been useful to us.

CASE STUDY:
WHEN CULTURES COLLIDE—ETHICS IN AN
INTERDEPENDENT BUSINESS ENVIRONMENT

As explained earlier in this chapter, the issue of business ethics cannot be solely examined within the context of an American or even a Western context. The discussion and case that follow will prompt you to consider the unique set of circumstances regarding ethics in both Japan and South Korea, two countries where U.S. business people are finding it increasingly necessary to be more sensitive to cross-border differences in ethical negotiation.

Background

For more than two decades, economists and international management experts have debated whether South Korea will eventually emerge as the next Japan. The foundation for this debate is the rapid transformation of South Korea's economic prowess. In helping their country become a major manufacturing and distribution center in Southeast Asia, managers from South Korea have found it necessary to adjust to international norms, business practices, and ethical beliefs quite different from their own and certainly different from their primary competitor, namely Japan. Some general observations on business trends in South Korea and Japan will help in understanding the ethics case that follows.

Japan is a thriving island nation with virtually *no* natural resources. It overcame incredible damage to its national infrastructure after World War II and was appropriately stripped by the global community of any meaningful military capacity. The Japanese seized this historical opportunity to divert intellectual and production capabilities into mass manufacturing and research and development. Using the ingenuity of the Japanese people and technical training from American quality experts such as W. Edwards Deming, Japan created an impressive series of design innovations and products that threw traditional business theories out the window.

This case is purely fictitious and any situation or names that resemble actual cases are unintentional and coincidental. It originally appeared in Laurence Barton's article "When Cultures Collide" in *Global Access*, published by Addison-Wesley, September 1993. Used with permission.

The economic concentration of power in Japan—the *keiritsu*—allowed the government to favor a group of key companies and primary industries that would take Japan from being a defeated nation militarily to being the economic victor. Japan's ascendancy to power came about precisely because of direct government intervention in the everyday lives of its major corporations. (In the United States, such a process would never gain public support. The concentration of wealth and power via direct government support largely ended in the early 1920s; public opinion turned against monopolies in most industries, including notably railroad, banking, and petroleum concerns. By the early 1930s, Congress and the Supreme Court had ushered in a new era of entrepreneurism and individualism and removed barriers to competition. In Japan, however, the government favored a limited number of companies.)

To achieve global economic success by the 1970s, South Korea found it necessary to pursue the Japanese economic model. Major Korean corporations, forming the *chaebol*, owe their very existence to the same kind of government subsidies and tax benefits that the Japanese provided to Sony, Mitsubishi, Matsushita, and other corporate giants. In Korea, however, it was Samsung, Lucky Gold Star, and Hyundai that were the beneficiaries.

The relationship between these two societies—the Japanese and Koreans—has been strained at best for decades; the historical impact of several events plays an especially important role. Korea was occupied by Japan from 1904 until the end of WWII. Writing in *The Chaebol*, three experts offered this argument:

> By all accounts, the period of occupation was a cruel one. Japan saw Korea as a colony that could be exploited in support of the Japanese industrial complex. . . . As part of the colonization process, efforts were made to eliminate all vestiges of a distinct Korean culture. Laws were passed forbidding all political activities. Books about Korean heroes and history were destroyed. . . . Finally, the Korean language was essential outlawed; all teaching, newspapers and commerce were to be in Japanese. . . . In short, Japan campaigned to make Korea "a little Japan" although clearly not an equal to Japan. (Steers, Keun and Ungson, (10)

As we approach the twenty-first century, Korea boasts a population of 42 million people, of which about 75 percent live in an urban setting. Although Korea prefers to be called the "Land of the Morning Calm" this poetic description can be misleading. It is a land of competition, of zeal, of managers who want to move ahead of the

Japanese in terms of volume and quality. A new generation of managers is composed of young people who struggle between identities that are traditionally Asian, but not Asian, modern, but sometimes antiquated.

South Korea now constitutes one of the greatest economic miracles in the world. There are more than 50 conglomerates that can be considered members of the chaebol, many controlled by families. Samsung, for example, has more than 60 divisions and 175,000 employees working in 40 countries.

The government of Korea has traditionally favored the chaebol members with tax credits, R&D initiatives, and other generous subsidies. Yet Korean business managers face a dilemma. Adding to an already complex geopolitical puzzle in international business is the realization that Korean companies such as Kimpo must pursue strategic alliances with new partners in the years ahead. The hypothetical company discussed below should be the genesis for thought-provoking analysis.

The Ethical Quagmire at Kimpo Electronics

Kimpo Electronics, created by Kim Bong Won in 1959, is a member of the Korean chaebol and employs about 80,000 persons. As a leading manufacturer and distributor of consumer electronics such as CD players, televisions, and stereo systems, the company has developed an international brand name and distribution system.

In recent years Kimpo has also successfully pursued research and development in semiconductors and emerged as a major player in the global marketplace for advanced computer system technologies. About 94 percent of the entire manufacturing output of Kimpo Electronics is sold abroad. Mr. Kim, now 74 years old, believes that to become one of the world's top ten sources for technology by the year 2,000 his firm must identify new strategic partners, even at the expense of traditionally held Korean norms.

Mr. Kim has periodically held discussions with Sun Semiconductors of Japan (SSJ), Japan's second largest exporter of semiconductors, for over two years. SSJ believes that a joint venture with Kimpo will lower its production and distribution costs because of favorable Korean labor rates. Kimpo seeks access to the advanced semiconductor technology offered by SSJ. Mr. Kim and his Japanese counterparts have discussed the possibility of a joint venture that would give SSJ a minority stake in Kimpo (about 15 percent equity ownership) in return for exclusive distribution rights to SSJ and Kimpo semiconductor products throughout the Pacific Rim for the next 20 years.

Mr. Kim must now determine how to best package this proposal to several audiences. The Korean government must approve any such joint venture, and animosity between Korean and Japanese interests is well documented. Members of the Kim family, his board of directors, and certainly Kimpo employees will all question the wisdom of a Korean company "bowing" to a Japanese concern when Koreans have worked diligently for years to establish technological autonomy. Similarly, many of the same players on the SSJ side of the fence will oppose a high-profile Japanese company finding it necessary to cooperate with a Korean firm when many Koreans, let alone their companies, have traditionally had been characterized in poor terms by the Japanese.

Ethics and Interpersonal Pressure

At their most recent meeting, Mr. Kim expressed his concern that the joint venture will be difficult to sell at home. His Japanese counterpart responded that one potential solution is for Mr. Kim to privately inform key audiences at home that Kimpo has just learned from a highly regarded consultant that SSJ has created new semiconductor designs that will soon make Kimpo products virtually obsolete.

"This will provide you with a sense of urgency, of immediacy," the Japanese executive advises. "Do not concentrate on the fact that your partner is Japanese. Focus on the message that your semiconductor unit could soon lose all value. Once your officials and colleagues are told that your competitiveness is about to be shattered, they will welcome a partnership with us. You will be seen as visionary. Each side will benefit." Mr. Kim responds that such a message could be demoralizing to Korean engineers and managers. On the other hand, he desperately seeks the SSJ distribution contract.

With that, the executives at SSJ advise Mr. Kim that they must have an answer within 30 days or they will conclude all discussions. They state that a firm from Singapore has approached them with a similar proposal, and they must move quickly. He believes them.

Analysis

If we are to better understand international business, we must recognize that the business choices of managers are influenced by a number of personal factors such as cultural norms and ethical beliefs as well as external factors such as government regulations and public opinion. In the case of Kimpo Electronics, we must set aside traditional American value systems and try to comprehend a set of circumstances between companies in two other societies. As you can see, the case has clear financial and marketplace considerations that seem overshadowed, at least for the moment, by questions of the historical rivalry of Japan and Korea as well as the concurrent need for cooperative synergy between two leading companies in these countries.

Questions for Consideration

1. What are the ethical beliefs of Japanese and Korean managers? Are they similar or different? How can you be assured that your response is accurate?

2. As you read this case, you may have integrated certain assumptions about the actors and cultures mentioned. Are these perceptions based on your own personal experiences with Japanese or Koreans, on news media or popular culture depictions, or on other sources?

3. Based on your own perception of business ethics and international business, what suggestions would you offer Mr. Kim regarding his desire to secure a deal with SSJ?

4. Does Mr. Kim have alternative strategies that could accomplish the same objectives? If he has alternatives, please identify three possibilities?

5. What is the role of business ethics in each of these three options from the perspective of both a Korean and a Japanese?

6. If Mr. Kim were to accept the recommended suggestion of the SSJ executive and claim that Kimpo will soon lose its competitive advantage, do you believe this strategy would be successful given economic and social conditions in Korea? Why or why not?

7. What if this case were different and Mr. Kim (now Mr. or Ms. Jackson) was an executive of a U.S. conglomerate based in Toledo, Ohio, trying to convince his contemporaries of a strategic alliance with SSJ? Would the ethical considerations be different if the American returned home with a message that the

Japanese would soon outdistance the products offered by the U.S. company ? Why or why not?

References for Case Study

Steers, Richard, Keun, Yoo Shin, and Ungson, Gerardo. *The Chaebol: Korea's New Industrial Might.* New York: Harper & Row, 1989.

REFERENCES FOR CHAPTER 7

Chan, Yuen. "The Lesson a Corrupt Teacher Had to Learn, " *South China Morning Post,* November 25, 1992.

Cho Jae-hyon. "Financial Scandal Spawns Sequels." *The Korea Times,* November 20, 1993.

Cohen, Roger. "French Ex-Cabinet Member Charged with Business Fraud." *The New York Times,* May 28, 1992.

Cowell, Alan. "Corruption at Fiat Is Admitted by Chairman." *The New York Times,* April 19, 1993.

Dugan, Christopher F., and Jorden, Stephen J. "Scope of Anti-Bribery Rules Still Unclear." *The National Law Journal,* September 13, 1993.

Fadiman, Jeffrey A. "A Traveler's Guide to Gifts and Bribes." *Harvard Business Review,* July–August 1986.

"Fingering Fiat." *The Economist,* February 27, 1993.

Forman, Craig, and Bannon, Lisa. "A Corruption Scandal Leaves Italy's Leaders Weakened and Scorned." *The Wall Street Journal,* March 1, 1993.

Hofstede, G. "Motivation, Leadership and Organization: Do American Theories Apply Abroad?" *Organizational Dynamics,* Summer 1980, Number 9.

Holstein, William J. "Japan's Ties That Bind" *Business Week,* May 10, 1993.

Kowalski, B. J. "Argentine Anger." *World Press Review,* February 1991.

Labich, Kenneth. "Risky Business." *Fortune,* July 11, 1994.

McTillmon, Joya. "AT&T Apologizes for Monkey Drawing." *The Boston Globe,* September 11, 1993.

Miller, Krystal. "Former Honda Executives Plead Guilty," *U.S. Journal,* March 15, 1994, A4.

Mosca, Gaetano. *The Ruling Class.* New York: McGraw-Hill, 1939.

Moyers, Bill. *A World of Ideas.* New York: Doubleday, 1989.

"Multinationals: Back in Fashion." *The Economist,* March 27, 1993.

"On the Take." *The Economist,* November 19, 1988, 21.

Ono, Yumiko. "Unneeded Workers in Japan Are Bored and Very Well Paid." *The Wall Street Journal,* April 20, 1993.

Shaw, Bill. "Foreign Corrupt Practices Act: A Legal and Moral Analysis." *Journal of Business Ethics* 7 (1988).

Stille, Alexander. "Italy's Woes," *U.S. News and World Report,* October 11, 1993.

Strugatch, Warren. "Rip-Off." *World Trade,* August–September 1991.

Waller, Douglas. "The Open Barn Door." *Newsweek,* May 4, 1992.

Watanabe, A. "A Fullbright Analysis of Japanese-American Student Visas." Japan-U.S. Friendship Commission, 1993.

Woronoff, Jon. *Japan as Anything But Number One.* New York: M.E. Sharpe and Co., 1990.

C H A P T E R   8

Ethics and Intellectual Property: When Thieves Steal Software and More

The development and distribution of information is the single most important issue that characterizes global business as we approach a new century. Indeed, wireless data transmission, 500 channels of cable television and satellite communication are the only part of this equation. Today, global sales of software alone exceed the value of the gross national product of 70 percent of the nation's economies. By 1997, you will be able to use your cellular telephone from any point on earth—from the depths of Africa to a cruise liner in the Pacific and send you fax or participate in a staff meeting across borders via a three-inch screen with built-in camera. Plato argued that knowledge is power. Today, power is defined by who *owns* that knowledge.

The author, in a speech to the Society of Competitive Intelligence Professionals, May 1, 1994

T hus far we have examined ethics in the context of organizations and individuals. We have also profiled several professions such as accounting where the personal and professional ethics of managers are increasingly under scrutiny. Yet virtually everyone working in today's managerial environment is impacted to some degree by the profound questions surrounding the appropriate use of software.

In a global economy that is increasingly information intensive, intellectual property is often the most valuable corporate asset and one that is particularly vulnerable to theft. (Dwyer, 78) Traditionally, ownership of intellectual property has been protected through the use of patents, copyrights, and trade secrets, but ethical and moral questions abound: To what extent have these tools been effective in preventing infringement by others? Should software manufacturers take other steps beyond those currently in place? To frame this discussion, this chapter pursues three themes: technological options, competitive responses, and legal and ethical issues regarding copyrights.

THEFT OF INTELLECTUAL PROPERTY

According to estimates provided by the U.S. Customs Service, average annual losses due to intellectual property rights infringements amounted to approximately $20 billion between 1989 and 1992. ("U.S. Software," 34) Counterfeit trade had risen to the point that the United States, the European Community, and Canada, sought a change in rules within the General Agreement on Tariffs and Trade (GATT) that would impose severe penalties against countries which permitted the manufacture and sale of pirated goods. ("U.S. Software," 34)

The theft of patents, copyrights, and other forms of intellectual property by international competitors is rising dramatically. (McDermott, 36) According to the U.S. International Trade Commission, lost U.S. sales contribute greatly to the $43 billion to $63 billion in annual worldwide revenues that foreign firms earn by infringing U.S. patents and copyrights. (Reynolds, 36) The U.S. software industry has annual domestic revenues of $4 billion and accounts for almost 80 percent of the software used in the world, yet

This chapter is adapted from an article by Laurence Barton and Yogesh Mahotra, "The International Violation of Intellectual Property," first published in *Industrial Management and Data Systems* 8, Number 2, 1993. Used with permission.

U.S. manufacturers lose an estimated $2.4 billion a year on average due to piracy of software *within* the borders of the United States. (SPA, 3)

Several questions emerge: Do those who copy software realizing that they are breaking the law? Do they care about the fact that the individuals who worked for years to develop a software program are not compensated for their innovation? Do they feel justified in their acts out of a false belief that the developers "are making money anyway, and copying won't injure anybody's finances"? How can manufacturers of software effectively remind those who copy and sell programs— appropriately called pirates—that their acts are illegal and immoral?

SOFTWARE PIRACY IN THE GLOBAL MARKET

The world market for software exceeds $43 billion annually. Europe, Asia, Latin America, and other international markets account for 58 percent of the total market for software produced by the U.S. companies. (IDC, 10) At the same time, worldwide losses due to software copyright infringements are estimated between $10 and $12 billion. The enormity of the software piracy problem is indeed disconcerting for the software companies. (See Exhibit 8-1.)

Until recently, many U.S. software companies failed to recognize that registration and legal ownership in the United States did not necessarily imply ownership in other countries. Their failure to adequately protect their intellectual property rights in foreign lands resulted in the loss of potentially profitable markets. Some of them later learned that their assets had been appropriated and profitably exploited, without license or reimbursement, by firms in other countries. They often learned that the *perpetrators* were also the *legal* owners of the pirated asset(s) in the countries in which they were operating. (World Press Review, 50) In some cases, the U.S. companies were forced to pursue litigation or had to pay enormous settlements to secure copyright of the very product that they had developed and that rightfully belonged to them.

Research by university and industry analysts indicates that patents, trademarks, and copyrights have not effectively controlled the widespread use of pirated software. Moreover, the degree of effectiveness of such measures is defined (read "restricted") by the copyright laws of the various countries and their trade agreements with the United States. Therefore, all software companies will need to

EXHIBIT 8-1   Estimated Software Piracy in the Global Marketplace (percentage figures for pirated software)

Country	Percentage
Uruguay	99%
Costa Rica	97%
Russia	95%
Greece	90%
Spain	90%
Portugal	90%
China	90%
Taiwan	90%
Switzerland	87%
Korea	85%
Italy	82%
Japan	81%
Chile	80%
Brazil	75%
Germany	73%
Colombia	70%
France	65%
Denmark	56%
United Kingdom	52%
United States	42%

Sources: Adapted from *Public Policy Initiatives to Prevent Software Piracy, June 1991–May 1992*, BSA & SPA (July 1991); and *Copyright Piracy in Latin America*, September 1992, International Intellectual Property Alliance.

E T H I C S   B R I E F

Your Chips or Your Life!

The world of microprocessing can be so valuable that ethicists and criminologists are grappling with one of the world's fastest-growing crimes: the theft of computer chips so small that they can be concealed inside a matchbook cover.

Time reports that principally Chinese and Vietnamese immigrants in California have successfully targeted several Silicon Valley high-tech firms. In 1993 alone, they stole over $40 million worth of chips such as the Intel 486 microchip. But the crime is hardly confined to the United States: Knife-wielding masked men tackled a security guard and stole nearly $4 million worth of chips in Scotland in May 1994. "Computer components are fast becoming the dope of the 90s because they're so easy to get rid of," notes Mark Kerby of the Santa Clara, California, police department.

One of the policy dilemmas regarding such trends is that there are few deterrents. As *Time* noted, most of those arrested for such crimes typically spend no more than six months to a year in jail. In some cases, the criminals befriended employees of the companies and, in return for information on security systems and the location of where chips were stored, received cash for their insider's knowledge.

Until the criminal justice system begins to view the theft of all kinds of intellectual property as a serious crime, the $86 billion a year global personal computer market will face an increasing menace from criminals who want a piece of the action.

Source: John Greenwald, "Your Chips or Your Life," *Time*, May 2, 1994, p. 43.

---

deploy more creative strategies to curb the rampant software piracy in the future until other nations adopt more stringent measures for the implementation and enforcement of copyright laws.

HOW SOFTWARE IS COPIED AND EXPLOITED

Software is routinely copied in the computer industry; copying may be done to follow standards, to write add-on products or to fine-tune a system. Software used for personal computers is more prone to copying than software in a mainframe or minicomputer environment where all software is stored on hardware that is locked inside a security-controlled room. Some copying is legal under the Fair Use Doctrine, but the fair use of software is difficult to define. Without an expansive and predictable definition, the threat of lawsuits arising from copyright infringements will continue to hamper innovation and ease of use. Generally, theft of computer software may occur in one of two ways:

1. Theft of the physical media (paper listings, disks, diskettes, tapes, and so forth) on which the software is stored,

2. Electronic theft, in which software is copied from one disk to another either on the same computer or to a remote computer over cable or phone lines.

WHO ARE SOFTWARE PIRATES?

Software pirates, who illegally copy software for retail sale or internal organizational use (Depke et al., 38), fall within the following categories:

- Dealers selling hardware preloaded with illegal software
- Retailers illegally reproducing and selling software copies
- User organizations making unauthorized copies of software for internal use
- Counterfeit software producers like those in pirate bazaars of Asia
- Competitors, ex-employees, or agents using unauthorized copies to develop competing derivative products
- Bulletin board operators offering illegal software to users
- Individual who makes a copy of someone else's program

The last group accounts for the largest number of software pirates and they are also the hardest to prosecute. In their efforts to curb piracy, software publishers generally target wholesale pirates. Bringing suit against an individual who made an illegal copy is inevitably more costly than effective because the ease of illegal copying has led to a proliferation of bootlegged products.

Various electronic bulletin boards have also been accused of distributing copyrighted codes without the copyright owner's permission. Upon being notified of this situation by the Software Publishers Association, the Federal Bureau of Investigation (FBI) closed down

ETHICS BRIEF

Job Seeker Beware: Electronic Hurdles to Employment

Ross Perot's eager campaign volunteers were stunned last year when they discovered that agents of the billionaire politician may have looked into some of their backgrounds. The news stimulated an FBI probe into allegations that the Perot campaign organization illegally obtained volunteers' confidential credit reports. The allegations made Perot seem paranoid and sleazy. Actually, he may just have been following the standard practice of many prudent managers, who have become some of the biggest users of electronic tools to investigate job seekers or recent hires.

These managers verify prior-employment claims carefully, of course. Nothing new there.

Then they check credit and criminal records online in a matter of minutes. If data is not available in electronic form—for example, college transcripts—they hire research services to get transcripts and deliver their contents to the client's online account in a day or so.

These efforts fit right into a corporate culture that leads a growing number of employers to require drug tests and, leaving nothing to chance, so-called personality profiles. Such profiles may contain hundreds of true-false questions, such as these typical examples: "I have read little or none of the Bible," "My sex life is satisfactory," and "I am very seldom troubled by constipation." They may be used to predict laziness, poor work habits, or psychological problems, or merely to verify whether the job seeker has mainstream values or an outlook consistent with company goals.

"Management is very pragmatic," says Alan F. Westin, a professor at Columbia University who is an expert on electronic privacy issues and an industry consultant. "Management will do whatever the social system and the legal system says, with a

the Davy Jones Locker service of Millbury, Massachusetts, in 1990 after the service had reportedly distributed over 200 illegally copied programs. In recent years the FBI has increased its antipiracy activities and conducted similar raids on other bulletin boards. (Daly, 12)

Yet the phenomenal success of the Internet, coupled with online services, such as America Online, Prodigy, and CompuServe, have all contributed to a condition in which downloading software without compensating the author and manufacturer can be accomplished with relative ease. The ethical and legal implications of such activities are enormous.

Flagrant theft of software produced by U.S. companies takes place in all parts of the world—developed and underdeveloped. Software piracy is institutionalized to such an extent that some companies have fully equipped software-copying centers, which even produce user manuals with the company logos on the covers. (Martin, 41) After the Montedison industrial group, which had 90 special emphasis on whether it helps get the work done to make a better product."

This pragmatic approach derives, in part, from skyrocketing health-insurance and legal bills. The cost of medical care has led many employers to screen out applicants who smoke or are overweight.

And until last summer, many employers searched online data banks to find out whether a job seeker had ever filed a workers' compensation claim—an insurance claim for an on-the-job injury. Some employers refused to offer a job to anyone who had ever filed a comp claim. The Americans with Disabilities Act, signed into law last year, limits the use of such data banks before a firm offer of employment has been made. But if an employer finds a history of compensation claims after making a job offer, the employer can shift the prospective employee to a job classification that reduces risk of reinjury. If in the employer's opinion no appropriately safe job is available, the offer can be rescinded.

And a rash of lawsuits in the 1980s accusing employers of "negligent hiring" has also pushed employer vigilance to a

new standard. You hire a man to do maintenance at your hotel, giving him a pass key to all the rooms, of course. That man rapes a guest. Because you failed to check his criminal history online, you didn't know that he served time for assault six years earlier. Welcome to court. Employers are caught in a dilemma, says Westin.

"Do they stay with the hands-off, respect-the-privacy, that's-not-our business view, or do they respond to their lawyers' warnings to protect themselves against liability, and their bean-counters' warnings that health-benefit costs are going to be out of sight?"

Employers have a responsibility to protect themselves from potential liability and their customers from undue danger. But privacy advocates ask whether society is well served by a business culture that can blacklist people with the cool efficiency of a 9600-bps modem.

Source: This article was reprinted from *Macworld Magazine*, July 1993, courtesy of Macworld Communications, 501 Second Street, San Francisco, CA 94107.

percent of its Lotus 1-2-3 and dBase software in unauthorized copies, was brought to court by the Business Software Alliance (BSA), Lotus's sales doubled in Italy. (Depke et al., 54)

DETRIMENTAL EFFECTS OF SOFTWARE PIRACY

Software piracy results in a loss of jobs, tax revenues, and high-tech investment and trade. (BSA, 3) Governments all over the world are realizing the need for stronger copyright laws and effective enforcement. In several countries, legal software usually constitutes a small fraction of the total software in use. The widespread use of counterfeit software poses one of the most significant threats to the growth of the worldwide software industry. The ethical implications of this activity, especially when management of an organization ignores or even condones such practices, is unprecedented in an era when copying is becoming more accessible to individuals and their employers. Indeed, many individuals try to justify their actions by arguing that the markup on software prices is so high that the activity is painless.

ETHICAL AND LEGAL CRUSADERS

A number of organizations have emerged in recent years to urge software users to practice ethical copying and distribution. The Washington-based Business Software Alliance, a trade group of U.S. software publishers such as Aldus, Ashton-Tate, and Microsoft, also known as BSA, has been crusading to reduce the scope and degree of international software piracy. Utilizing a combination of public policy, enforcement, and public awareness, BSA's initiatives have reportedly increased software users' understanding of and compliance with software copyright laws. (BSA Fact Sheet, 1)

BSA has sought to persuade governments around the world to enact and enforce software copyright laws. It has also been working with local software associations throughout Europe to implement the European Community (EC) software directive. On behalf of the software publishers, BSA organizes legal proceedings against software copyright infringers. Since its inception in 1988, it has brought more than 200 legal actions for software copyright infringements in countries throughout the world.

A second trade group, the Software Publishers Association (SPA), chases pirates via an antipiracy hotline (800-388-7478) on which it receives calls reporting software piracy—mostly from whistle-blowers who are temporary, former, or even disgruntled employees. (SPA, 3) Due to the intensified antipiracy efforts of the SPA, financial losses due to the piracy in the United States have been reduced dramatically in recent years. ("Software Group," B5)

COMBATING UNETHICAL AND ILLEGAL BEHAVIOR

Several management tools can help control software piracy. As some SPA members have learned, these efforts can

1. Reduce the financial incentive or motivation to copy

2. Make it difficult for users to issue unauthorized copies by improving the technology of copy protection

3. Lead to public education, publicized monitoring, and regulation (Helm, 63)

Technological Options

Technological solutions to prevent software piracy generally entail the use of an encryption process or other protective measures. Hackers, due to profit motive or otherwise, enjoy breaking the copy-protection code of any newly released "foolproof" software application. According to some software vendors, even the best-developed copy-protection code is susceptible to breaking within a period of a few weeks.

To battle the illegal sales of unauthorized software, many manufacturers are placing expensive and hard-to-copy holograms on their packages to distinguish them from black-market products. The practice of copying intellectual property denies royalties due authors and distributors.

E T H I C S   B R I E F

To Catch a Spy: Is Workplace E-Mail Private?

Most people believe that electronic-mail messages are secured by a personal password—as private as a letter in the U.S. mail. "They are finding out," says Marc Rotenberg, Washington, D.C., director of Computer Professionals for Social Responsibility, "that E-mail is more like a postcard than a sealed letter."

Test Case for Privacy
Employers have ready means to read E-mail messages, and many do just that, as computer executive Eugene Wang found out recently. His case, involving two Silicon Valley companies, could break new ground in electronic-privacy law. Wang, who was Borland International's vice-president for computer languages, defected to a direct competitor, Symantec Corporation, last September.

Court documents filed by Borland attorneys state that shortly after Wang announced his departure, Borland execs found E-mail addressed from Wang to Symantec CEO Gordon Eubanks. The messages allegedly revealed top-secret corporate data, including marketing plans, product-release dates, and detailed information on Borland's game plan against Symantec. The police and FBI were called in shortly thereafter, and seized other documents at Eubanks'and Wang's homes.

Because Wang used MCI Mail—a commercial E-mail service—allegedly to transfer data to Eubanks, electronic privacy has become a key issue in the case. Wang and Eubanks, who have been indicted on criminal felony charges involving theft of trade secrets, deny that they violated trade secrecy laws. They also argue that when Borland viewed Wang's MCI Mail messages,

the company may have violated federal law. If so, the confiscated E-mail messages might not be admissible in court.

The 1986 Electronic Communications Privacy Act (ECPA) protects messages sent on commercial E-mail, such as MCI Mail, from outside or unauthorized users. "Even if Borland had gathered evidence in a legitimate and legal way regarding privacy, [Eubanks and Wang] would still be innocent," says Symantec attorney James McManis. "But if after reviewing all the data, it appears to us that there has been a violation of the (ECPA) statute, we will raise that."

Borland counters that it paid for Wang's MCI Mail account, and therefore had every right to inspect the messages. "New employees at Borland are given an MCI [Mail] password that is on file with a Borland administrator," says Borland spokesperson Steve Grady. "You do not have a reasonable expectation of privacy in an E-mail system that is given to you for company business by your employer." If the privacy issue is litigated, it could set new standards on the privacy of commercial E-mail.

California Challenges
Federal rules regarding in-house electronic mail are less ambiguous than those governing commercial E-mail. ECPA treats internal company communications as company property. And a *Macworld* survey suggests that some 375,000 employers agree. About 9 percent of respondents—CEOs and MIS directors of U.S. companies of all sizes—indicate that they sometimes search employee E-mail files. This prerogative is being challenged in California, where the state constitution specifically protects privacy, unlike the U.S. Constitution. Court

documents indicate that Alana Shoars, formerly E-mail director of Epson America, claims she was fired in 1990 for questioning her boss's right to read hundreds of E-mail messages sent between other employees. Shoars filed wrongful-termination and class-action lawsuits against Epson. Her attorney, Noel Shipman, claims that by reading employee E-mail messages, Epson violated both the state constitution's privacy provision as well as a California eavesdropping statute.

Shipman also represents two employees of Nissan Motor Corporation embroiled in an E-mail controversy. Rhonda Hall and Bonita Bourke were allegedly fired from their jobs installing software and training other employees. A legal brief filed by Shipman claims that the two were fired or forced to resign after complaining about managers printing and reviewing printouts of personal messages from the company's E-mail system-messages they assumed were private. The two sued for invasion of privacy and wrongful termination.

Both the Nissan and Epson cases were dismissed by lower courts, but are now in appeal. If the plaintiffs prevail in either situation, the legal status of personal E-mail messages on internal company systems will be thrown open, perhaps resulting in greater privacy rights.

Souce: This article was reprinted from *Macworld Magazine*, July 1993, courtesy of Macworld Communications, 501 Second Street, San Francisco, CA 94107.

In addition to security locks and other measures, the newest weapon in the battle to combat illegal copying is the use of holographic images on software packaging. Because holograms cannot be created without using million-dollar laser equipment, several U.S. software companies started using holograms on their product packages in a bid to discourage piracy. Yet once again, some software pirates have successfully developed high-quality copies of the holograms. (Magnier, 1A)

Competitive Responses

A number of leading software publishers and developers have identified several strategies to reduce consumer thirst for pirated products. These strategies include multiple-copy discounts so that a large corporation, whose several dozen or several hundred employees, working on different computer networks, can benefit from significantly reduced pricing. (Eng, 122) Another solution is site licensing agreements, often used along with access keys or displays regarding licensing agreements that are replicated on any copies. Beside deterring the users from creating illegal copies, the licensing agreements also make the user aware of the illegitimacy of making unauthorized copies. (Bertolucci, 89) Other manufacturers offer financial rewards to software resellers who identify software copyright offenders. (Borzo, 91)

Will the Law Motivate Employees to Be Ethical?

In October 1992, the United States Congress enacted a law that makes the intentional copying of copyrighted software a felony, with penalties to violators of up to $100,000 in damages. (Meyer, 104) In a famous piracy case that involved MedPerfect (a software pirate) and Novell (a software supplier), a bankruptcy judge ruled that bankruptcy law does not permit debtors to set aside debts incurred for "willful and malicious actions," although bankrupt MedPerfect was directed to pay Novell, Inc., for use of the pirated copies of Novell's networking software NetWare. (Ubois, 46) In the future, software publishers are likely to continue prosecuting violators so as to discourage others from illegally copying their proprietary products.

INDIVIDUAL CONSUMERS ARE NOT IMMUNE FROM PROSECUTION

Some consumers may believe that they are justified in copying software because they cannot afford the price of legitimate copies. Some others may believe that they are justified in testing a program (preferably without incurring an expense, for example, by using a "free" copy) before buying it. Yet software manufacturers consider both activities to be unethical and illegal. (Markoff, A1) Despite the software industry's attack on piracy, most users are unsympathetic to an industry that has annual earnings of over $10 billion. This figure fails to underscore reality, however; earnings do not equate to profit, and with global competitive pressures mounting and the cost of research and development for new software increasing each day, the very survivability of some software manufacturers is challenged by the behavior of software pirates.

For example, students at the Massachusetts Institute of Technology and Brown University were charged with exchanging copyrighted software in April 1994. These arrests followed the earlier conviction of two Texas Tech University students on similar charges in 1993.

"We need to respond to the culture that no one is hurt by these thefts and that there is nothing wrong with pirating software," notes Donald Stern, U.S. Attorney for Massachusetts ("Crackdown on Theft," A32)

E T H I C S   B R I E F

Bosses with X-Ray Eyes

Each and every day, Gayle Grant and her colleagues were electronically monitored down to the second as they did their jobs.

Unplugging themselves from their job monitors could lead to dismissal. "We punch in and out of three units: the time clock, the VDT [computer terminal], and the telephone keypad known as Collins. We plug a phone jack into Collins that is attached to our headset and [we] receive telephone calls. The VDT and Collins track every second of our day, says Grant (a pseudonym), an airline reservations agent in California. She and her colleagues were allowed 11 seconds between calls and 12 minutes of personal breaks daily. Two episodes of unauthorized unplugged time in a week were cause for disciplinary action. She eventually cracked under the pressure. Grant suffered a nervous breakdown.

Grant's reaction may have been extreme, but her employer merely followed standard practice in many industries, and acted consistently with both the letter and intent of U.S. Federal law. The 1986 Electronic Communications Privacy Act (ECPA) prohibits phone and data-line taps with two exceptions: law-enforcement agencies *and* employers.

The police or FBI can tap lines—but only as a last resort under court order—to crack criminal conspirators, drug traffickers, and other serious-crime suspects. The courts permit fewer than 1000 such taps each year, nationwide.

Employers have no such limits. They may view employees on closed-circuit TV; tap their phones, E-mail, and network communications; and rummage through their computer files with or without employee knowledge or consent—24 hours a day.

The most pervasive use of monitoring takes place in occupations where tasks are highly repetitive, so productivity can be easily measured. The Communications Workers of America, the union that represents most telecommunications workers, estimates that employers eavesdrop on phone calls between workers and consumers 400 million times per year—more than 750 calls every minute. Mail sorters, word processors, data entry clerks, insurance adjusters, and even computer tech-support specialists, often working on terminals connected to a mainframe, may be monitored constantly or intermittently for speed, errors, and time spent working.

Working in Glass Offices
Most professional and technical employees assume that they have nothing to fear. Their privacy is protected by the nature of their jobs—too complex to evaluate by machine, right? To test that assumption, *Macworld Magazine* examined 25 popular network-management, integrated groupware, electronic-mail, and remote-access products to see if they could be used to invade employee privacy, and if so, how easily. The study used only Macintosh software, but similar tools are available on other platforms.

If your office network runs on a full-featured network operating system, like Novell NetWare or Microsoft LAN Manager, and is run by a technically astute manager, then your Macintosh and all data transferred from it is an open book. Working from an office across the room or across the country, a network manager—particularly in service-based local area networks—can eavesdrop on virtually every aspect of your

MACWORLD POLL

Electronic Eavesdropping at Work

Workers are routinely monitored in some industries, but how pervasive is the practice? To find out, *Macworld* conducted the first national survey designed to find out how and why businesses monitor employees. Top corporate managers from 301 businesses of all sizes and in a wide range of industries participated.

More than 21 percent of respondents—30 percent in large companies—have "engaged in searches of employee computer files, voice mail, electronic mail, or other networking communications." Nearly 16 percent report having

checked computerized employee work files, and 9 percent having searched employee E-mail.

These data suggest that some 20 million Americans are subject to electronic monitoring. Is your hard drive or office network searched? Better ask your boss directly. Only 18 percent of respondents' companies had a written policy regarding electronic privacy. And only 31 percent of companies that conduct electronic monitoring or searches of employee computers, voice mail, E-mail, or networking communications give employees advance warning.

Electronic Search Practices

Are employee files searched? **Yes 21.6%**

If yes:

Which files?

Electronic work files	73.8
E-mail	41.5
Network messages	27.7
Voice mail	15.4

On whose authority?

Executives	66.2
Middle managers	16.9
Personnel managers	10.8
MIS directors	44.6

Why?

Monitor work flow	29.2
Investigate thefts	29.2
Investigate espionage	21.5
Review performance	9.2
Prevent harassment	6.2
Seek missing data	3.1
Seek illegal software	3.1
Prevent personal use	3.1

How often? (last 2 years)

More than 100	3.1
50 to 100	3.1
25 to 49	0.0
10 to 24	7.7
6 to 9	6.2
1 to 5	70.8
None	4.6

Are employees warned?

Yes	30.8
No	66.2

Company Privacy Policies

Do you have a written policy on privacy? **Yes 35.9%**

Do you have a policy on electronic privacy? **Yes 18.3%**

Are privacy policies known to employees? **Yes 33.6%**

Company Personnel-Record Policies

Are personnel records kept electronically? **Yes 53.2%**

Do employees have access to records (in any medium)? **Yes 51.8%**

Who has unrestricted access?

Executives	51.8
Middle managers	14.0
Personnel managers	66.1
Payroll managers	2.0

Who has need-to-know access?

Executives	61.1
Middle managers	41.9
Personnel managers	53.2
Payroll managers	2.3

Management Philosophy on Electronic Monitoring

Never acceptable	34.6
Usually or always counterproductive	16.3
Good tool to verify evidence of wrongdoing	22.6
Good tool to routinely monitor performance	12.0
Good tool to enhance performance	7.3
Good tool to routinely verify honesty	4.0

Totals may not equal 100 percent, due to non-responses or multiple responses.
Margin of error for responses is ± 2.9 percent.

In 1993, Macworld magazine published a major report that concluded that there is widespread eavesdropping of employees by U.S. employers. The ethical, moral, and legal implications will be debated in the coming decade.

networked computing environment with or without your approval or even knowledge. The manager can view the contents of data files and electronic-mail messages, overwrite private passwords, and audit your time and activities on the network.

All the major electronic-mail and groupware products that combine messaging, file management, and scheduling (such as WordPerfect Office) allow the network administrator to change passwords at any time, then read, delete, or alter any messages on the server. With few exceptions, network-monitor programs, such as AG Group's LocalPeek, Farallon Computing's Traffic Watch II, and Neon Software's NetMinder, allow astute managers to read files transmitted over the net. In short, the tools are only slightly less invasive than others specifically designed for surveillance and used primarily on mainframe systems.

They Like to Watch

Network administration and communication tools were designed for valid reasons, not to invade employees' privacy. Like any technology, they are value-neutral. Some vendors even include strongly worded privacy warnings and a few offer options that allow a client Mac to shut out network managers.

The capacity to snoop is there, but is it used?

Old surveys and anecdotal accounts suggest that in some industries—telecommunications, insurance, and banking, for example—as many as 80 percent of employees are the subjects of telephone or computer-based monitoring. Such estimates may be inflated, but there is little dispute that many employers monitor routinely. And if the rapid sales and market growth of snooping tools is an indication, monitoring is on the rise. But virtually no rigorous research has been done about how much electronic eavesdropping takes place on the job.

Until now. *Macworld* conducted a survey of CEOs and MIS directors at 301 large, medium, and small businesses in a wide range of industries to find out how much they peek at their employees' work on their computers, and why. About 22 percent of our sample have engaged in searches of employee computer files, voice mail, electronic mail, or other networking communications. In companies with 1000 or more employees, the figure rises to 30 percent. Nearly 16 percent of respondents report that they have checked employees' computerized work files.

The average company in our study employs 3240 people, so the total sample represents the conditions experienced by nearly 1 million workers. This data suggests that some 20 million Americans may be subject to electronic monitoring through their computers (not including telephones) on the job. Meanwhile, only 18 percent of respondents' companies have a written policy regarding electronic privacy for employees.

Managers who endorse electronic surveillance argue that it helps them gauge productivity and chart the work flow of a group of employees. It can generate statistics on individual or departmental accomplishments and plot future work loads. Computer monitoring can even be used to give employees managerial feedback and reduce the need for personal attention from supervisors. In the *Macworld* survey, 12 percent of responding employers endorse monitoring for evaluating performance or productivity.

Monitoring can also increase safety or adherence to company rules, some employers contend. Some trucking companies, for example, set on-board monitors to record speed, engine-idling time, and length of stops. The system ostensibly tries to ensure that truckers drive safely and take adequate rest breaks.

Companies that deal in sensitive data may feel compelled to guard against disloyal or merely careless employees who might divulge it to competitors (see "To Catch a Spy: Is Workplace E-Mail Private?"). And 4 percent of survey respondents endorse electronic monitoring "for routinely verifying employee honesty." A much higher number—23 percent—feel electronic monitoring is a good tool where reasonable evidence of wrongdoing, such as theft or negligence, comes to light.

While nearly half of the managers in our survey endorse the concept of electronic monitoring, and nearly a fourth actually conduct electronic monitoring, most of those don't do it often. About 71 percent of those who conducted such searches did so only five or fewer times in the preceding two years. Only two companies had searched employees' work files, voice mail, electronic mail, or networking communications more than 100 times during that period.

From Watching to Intruding
The *Macworld* survey indicates that many employers may recognize that excessive monitoring has possible negative side effects. "Technology now allows employers to cross the line from monitoring the work to monitoring the worker," Cindia Cameron, a field organizer for 9 to 5, National Association of Working Women, told a Senate committee.

She cites the case of an express-mail company employee whose computer logs the length and frequency of her trips to the bathroom. The woman was reprimanded for using the bathroom four times in a single day.

Some employers use monitoring data in efforts to boost productivity through competition—by posting data publicly. One enterprising Florida company, Thomas Powell Associates, found a way to automate the process.

"I got the idea watching the [Miami] Dolphins [football team]," says a company founder. "Those athletes play their hearts out. Why? Certainly the money helps, but it's not the real reason. They play at 100 percent because everything they do is seen by hundreds of thousands of people instantly." The company produces and sells software that instantaneously puts every telephone operator or telemarketer's productivity statistics on a computer screen, visible to all employees.

Do such schemes pay off?

"Monitoring that creates feelings of surveillance and stress is antithetical to the new cultures of management that our society is moving toward," says Alan F. Westin, a professor at Columbia University and consultant to the data-gathering giant Equifax. Westin practically invented the idea of "electronic privacy" and has written on the subject for three decades. "[If management] doesn't motivate employees to be more participative, to be more committed to the workplace, then the chances of producing the kind of quality work that will compete with the Japanese and the Germans are very low."

And managers concerned with both productivity and containing health-insurance costs may find electronic monitoring to be self-defeating. Electronic monitoring increases employee "boredom, tension, anxiety, depression, anger, and fatigue," according to a recent study of 745 employees of telecommunications companies, jointly conducted by researchers from the University of Wisconsin and the Communications Workers of America. These findings confirm earlier studies that implicate electronic monitoring as a major workplace stress factor-linked, in part, to the sense of powerlessness that monitored employees feel.

Possible Legislative Relief

Such concerns have stimulated some members of Congress to ask what constitutes fair and appropriate monitoring. The proposed Privacy for Consumers and Workers Act failed in the last Congress, but Capitol insiders have high hopes for it in this session. The proposed law would limit how monitoring could take place in these ways:

- Employers would have to tell new hires how they might be monitored and how the collected data would be used.
- Employers would be required to give advance warning that monitoring will take place (except for employees on probation)—possibly including a signal light or beep tone during monitoring.
- The total time that an employee could be monitored would be capped at two hours per week.
- Secret, periodic, or random monitoring of long-term employees would be prohibited.

Macworld's survey shows that the law would force policy changes for many businesses. We found that only 31 percent of companies that conduct electronic monitoring or searches of employee computers, voice mail, electronic mail, or networking communications give employees advance warning.

Many companies recognize consumer demand for privacy protections, and they have stepped forward with pioneering consumer-privacy policies that go far beyond the limited legal requirements. But few companies have policies in place that go as far to protect employee privacy as the Privacy for Consumers and Workers Act would mandate.

Companies that have led the way on consumer-privacy concerns, such as American Express, Citibank, and Equifax, describe their electronic monitoring of employees as strictly limited. But they would not release internal policies on employee privacy, and they acknowledged surveillance practices beyond what would be allowed by some features of the congressional proposal.

One reason that employers may give less weight to employee privacy is that they feel countervailing pressure: legal requirements to monitor or audit employee activities, particularly in information-intensive industries. So most employers comply with employee-monitoring laws and regulations as they see fit, rather than breaking new ground by minimizing monitoring and using the least-invasive approach, says privacy expert Westin.

Industry groups also castigate the Privacy for Consumers and Workers Act. "An employer would be put in the absurd position of having to advise suspected thieves when they are being observed," Vincent Ruffolo, president of Security Companies Organized for Legislative Action, told a Senate hearing.

If the proposal is enacted, says Lawrence Fineran of the National Association of Manufacturers (NAM), customer service will erode, and manufacturers might have to abandon certain kinds of computer-aided manufacturing. "NAM opposes any legislation that will interfere with the ability of modern and future equipment that can assist domestic companies in their fight to remain competitive," Fineran says. "Otherwise the United States may as well let the information age pass it by." Yet Japan and most of Europe already impose much tighter restrictions on employee surveillance than the U.S. proposal would mandate.

Few privacy advocates argue that monitoring should be eliminated. But they say industry ignores a critical factor: most employees are hardworking and honest. "The problem with the business community," says Louis Maltbe, director of the American Civil Liberties Union's Workers Rights Project, "is that they are trying to make the rules with the assumption that every employee is a goldbrick."

Maltbe and other advocates see reasonable privacy protection going far beyond the provisions of the proposed law, to the point where employees have some control over monitoring practices and data collected.

"There has been kind of a reflex reaction, automatically resisting things that ultimately have been very helpful to industry," says Senator Paul Simon, D-IL., principal sponsor of the Senate version of the privacy bill. "The banking industry resisted hav-

ing—believe it or not—federal insurance for banks. Now no bank would want to do without it," he adds. "Some companies are [giving prior notice of monitoring] right now and having no difficulties. I think it improves employee relationships," Simon says. In any case, he argues, "employees should not be forced to give up their freedom, dignity, or sacrifice their health when they go to work."

Source: Charles Piller, "Bosses with X-Ray Eyes," *Macworld*, July 1993, p. 118–123. This article was reprinted courtesy of Macworld Communications, 501 Second Street, San Francisco, CA 94107.

CONCLUSION

The copying of software remains a relatively easy, low-risk activity for most consumers. Yet it will be increasingly difficult for current companies to protect their product amidst widespread abuses and comparatively few prosecutions. In November 1993, the first prison sentence enforced in the United States for software counterfeiting occurred in San Francisco. Benny S. Lee, a Hong Kong national, made and distributed at least 25,000 copies of Microsoft's MS-DOS operating software. He received a one-year prison sentence for his actions. ("Software Counterfeiter," B8)

The legal enforcement of the copyright laws and the prosecution of the offenders remains a primary obstacle to software manufacturers. To keep pace with the challenges discussed in this chapter, software companies must continue to adopt effective management strategies to control software piracy. These include incentives to users for purchasing legitimate software and disincentives for making or using pirated copies.

CASE STUDY:
THE MORALITY OF ENVIRONMENTALISM—
WHEN A MAGAZINE PUBLISHER IS
TARGETED BY HER OWN COLLEAGUES

What are the moral implications in the following case? Patricia Poore was a distinguished and well respected environmentalist—until she admitted something to her readers that changed just about everything. As you read this article, consider the moral, ethical and business considerations inherent in the case study.

Gloucester, Massachusetts—Patricia Poore was blessed with what appeared to be unassailable environmental credentials: Sierra Club at 18, walked to work every day, never even owned a car until two years ago, vegetarian, avid backpacker, and she founded a national environmental magazine called *Garbage*.

But then Patricia Poore committed a sin that would forever stain her environmental soul, a sin for which the true believers would provide no absolution: She confessed that in her home behind tightly shut doors, she had actually used disposable diapers.

This heresy brought the wrath of the greens crashing down upon her. Poore was cast out, a money changer in the enviro temple, a heretic of the worst sort.

Her penance was vilification and scorn, accusations from the readers of *Garbage* that she had sold out to the Moonies, to Coors Brewery, to General Electric, to a consortium of timber and petroleum interests.

Her further penance was plummeting circulation.

"At first my adrenaline was up," she says during an interview in her office here. "Then I get really depressed for a while. I was at war with my readers, and that's terrible. You should always identify with your readers."

Now the combative Poore talks of the "dark side" of the environmental movement, in which green "vigilantes" enforce unquestioned compliance with liberal environmental orthodoxy.

The experience has caused Poore to re-orient her own definition of environmentalism and to reposition her magazine dramatically.

Source: Charles Kenney, "Trashing Garbage," *The Boston Globe*, November 30, 1993, p. 61. Used with permission.

She says she has come "180 degrees" to the point where she actually places greater trust in industry—in major chemical companies—when seeking environmental information than she does in major environmental organizations.

This is all quite mad, in the view of some environmentalists.

"We are extremely disturbed by the recent change in editorial tone of the magazine," says Resa Dimino of Environmental Action, a Washington advocacy group. "It went from being a fairly useful, easy-to-understand explanation of environmental issues to being a voice for the anti-environmental movement. the change in direction of this magazine has really outraged a lot of us."

The rather remarkable transformation of *Garbage* coincided with a dramatic shift in Poore's personal views. "I was very much a liberal Democrat all my life, maybe even slightly left of that," she says. Now she characterizes herself as an independent who sometimes tends toward the left but who also sometimes votes "very right wing."

She talks fondly of officials at Dow Chemical and DuPont and notes that her father works for a pharmaceutical company.

"I know people in chemical companies who are responsible for compliance who say, 'I am an environmentalist. That's why I went into this,'" she says. "So many of the people who give $35 a year to Greenpeace think if you work for a chemical company you can't be an environmentalist."

Poore still lavishes praise on the early days of the environmental movement, back 15 to 20 years ago, when, she maintains, those calling themselves environmentalist were far better informed than their counterparts of today. She acknowledges that the movement successfully lobbied for clean air and water legislation while raising Americans' consciousness about the environment.

And she also asserts that environmental causes were clearer and more pressing a decade or two ago. "There were these obvious violations—for example, landfills built on wetlands," she says. "Groundwater and air pollution issues are concrete and specific, and things can be done about them."

But she contrasts those issues with more current concerns such as global warming, which she ridicules as a faddish issue that environmental groups raise with an apocalyptic tone.

Rather than retreating in the face of the widespread criticism from her readers, Poore fought back by writing a cover article for the magazine under the headline "Disposable Diapers: They're OK, You're OK." She wrote that "disposable diapers have been the quintessential symbol of the throwaway society, the garbage crisis, and the environmental legacy we're leaving our kids. But they deserve to be a symbol for vigilante environmentalism instead."

Poore despaired that the public has been badly miseducated on environmental matters, writing that surveys showed people think the most pressing garbage problems are "disposable diapers and aerosol containers."

"Almost any answer, " she continued, "from yard waste to construction debris, or even plastic packaging, would have been more accurate than the public's perception."

Her article on diapers maintains that "there is very little difference, if any, in the cradle-to-grave environmental impact of cloth vs. disposable diapers."

Both, she says, generate similar amounts of pollution in manufacturing, use of resources, cost of transportation and disposal.

She allowed that the diaper episode "has made me doubt other environmental symbols, other unscientific dogma, other questionable means used in service to righteous ends. Because it touched me personally, the bogus diaper debate has focused my attention on vigilante environmentalism: 'Ignore the facts! We've got a Good Cause here, and if you don't get in step, we'll make you pay.'"

One reader among the many criticizing her piece lashed Poore for becoming "an apologist for the disposable industry."

The diaper story was not the only piece that jarred some readers. before the diaper debacle, and her philosophical shift, Poore had run articles on the need for bottled water, on the toxicity of beauty products (the truth, she says now, is that "you can practically eat any cosmetic you buy") and articles about egregious examples of wasteful packaging.

These were articles that toed the leftist environmental line, she says, articles she now looks back on with embarrassment.

But they were stories she ran because her readers clamored for them. They were also stories writers wanted to do. "I would have these writers who came with good [resumes] and good clips, and they would write stories where I sort of smelled a rat and thought they were biased, but I thought maybe they know something I don't and I let them get away with things I don't anymore."

Out with the Old Garbage

The new *Garbage* has included stories defending nuclear power and questioning whether the ozone depletion is a scam or a crisis. A story on environmental education—is it "science, civics, or just plain propaganda?"—brought criticism from the National Audubon Society.

"It was very one-sided," says Christine Indoe, an Audubon spokeswoman. "It focused too much on the negative. It did not give a thorough assessment of some of the good programs that are out there."

But such comments don't deter Poore. When she shifted editorial direction late last year she wrote an article in *Garbage* in which she criticized both the environmental movement and the journalists who cover environmental issues.

"It's taken me a while to realize that many writers accept the platform of national environmental organizations as not only infallible but also sacred."

"I have pulled my punches, so to speak, to avoid alienating the well-meaning people who support environmentalist causes. . . . I have seen our sources, our writers, our editors, even our advertisers be affected by political correctness. The overwhelming pressure to be pro-environment has resulted in media bias, a distrust of business and scientists who won't talk because they refuse to be quoted out of context."

What punches had she pulled? When alarms sounded nationwide over the use of the pesticide Alar on apples, Poore had wanted to do a story "on the stupidity of the Alar scare," but she held back. She had a freelance writer who refused to get a comment from industry on a story, and Poore let her get away with it. "'I don't talk to industry,'" Poore says the reporter told her. "'I know what they'll say. They have a line.'" Pore wanted her reporters to quote "people associated with suspect industries such as timber and petroleum," but she "stopped short of insisting."

The pro-environmental group attitude among the press, she says, is so ingrained it's an epidemic. "It's about censorship. It's about sticking to a party line."

The letters she received in reaction to her magazine's new bent reflect that, she says.

"Tell the editor she's a traitor to the movement," one reader wrote.

Wrote another: "The sooner your magazine disappears into the dumpster, the better. You have obviously bought every single bit of propaganda the chemical and paper industries have doled out . . . with 'friends' like you, the environment doesn't need enemies."

Poore defenders also are heard on the pages of *Garbage*.

Jerry Howard of *New Age Journal* in Brighton wrote to *Garbage* that Poore was "right on, especially re: the tactics 'green' organizations use, and the generally repressive P.C. atmosphere among such folk."

Poore says that major environmental organizations such as Audubon, Greenpeace, and the Sierra Club harbor assumptions she believes are inaccurate. "The underlying assumptions are that Americans are wasteful, that our quality of life is going downhill, that we're fouling our own nest, that the environment has to come first no matter what."

Other assumptions, she wrote earlier this year, may be found in the standard environmental curriculum that "contains oversimplification and myth, has little historical perspective, is politically oriented, and is strongly weighted toward a traditional environmentalist viewpoint, i.e., emphasizing limits to growth, distrust of technology, misinformation concerning waste management, and gloomy (if not doomsday) scenarios."

In fact, says Poore, this country is the environmental envy of the world. "We don't have oozing sewers," she says. The country is generally clean, and "we can probably afford to fix the bad problems."

Poore was originally drawn to the environment as an issue as part of what she describes as her generation's concern about such matters. "This was when everybody wanted to go to school in Vermont, very back-to-the-land," she says.

She started *Garbage* in 1989 after spending the previous 11 years working on *Old House Journal*, a how-to magazine for homeowners and contractors fixing up old houses. Poore bought it when it was a typewritten neighborhood newsletter in Brooklyn and turned it into a lucrative national glossy magazine with a circulation of 160,000.

Old House Journal is so profitable that it not only supports itself but also covers *Garbage*'s substantial losses, says Poore. In 1991, Poore moved *Garbage* from New York to Gloucester, where she now lives. She has a 15-year-old stepson, a 3-year-old boy and is expecting another child in June.

Garbage got off to a hot start, selling phenomenal 120,000 copies of its first issue. But interest in environmental publications soon dwindled and Poore exacerbated her circulation problems with her shifting ideology. The result is that the *Garbage* circulation has plummeted to 50,000. But Poore thinks she's hit bottom and is pleased with the circulation she does have.

The magazine's readers are now largely people "hooked into the environment as a real world subject," she says, including chemists, officials in the packaging industries, municipal waste managers, corporate environmental planners and journalists.

Poore hopes to cling to these readers. Thus far, she says, she has lost $2 million on *Garbage*. "I'm not doing *Garbage* to make money," she says. "At this point, it's personal."

REFERENCES FOR CHAPTER 8

Bangsberg, P. T. "Hong Kong Software Pirates Face Crackdown." *Journal of Commerce and Commercial*, September 26, 1991, 1A; McCallister, C. F. "Hong Kong's Software Pirates May Finally Walk the Plank." *Business Week*, December 1, 1989, 114G; Depke, D. A., and Yang, D. J. "Casting a Worldwide Dragnet for Software Pirates." *Business Week*, December 25, 1989, 54H; Wheare, H. J. H. "Ideas as Assets: Hong Kong." *International Financial Law Review Special Supplement*, May 1991, 46-53; "Software Alliance files Piracy Suit in Singapore Court." *PC Week*, April 9, 1990, 133; Magnier, M. "Singapore Dealer Sued over Software and Copyrights," *Journal of Commerce and Commercial*, August 28, 1991, 1A–2A.

Brown, C. "Taiwan Agency Protests BSA's Tactics." *Computerworld*, July 1, 1991, 62.

Burke, S. "Software Group Pushes for Trade Sanctions." *PC Week*, March 2, 1992, 121.

Burke, S. "U.S. Agency Revamps Software Patent System." *PC Week*, May 27, 1991, 145–46.

Business Software Alliance. "Advancing Strong Intellectual Protection for Software." *BSA Worldwide Report 1990–1991*, September 1991; and MacKenzie, D. "Europe Lays Down the Law on Software." *New Scientist*, June 22, 1991, 20–21.

Business Software Alliance. *Fact Sheet.* 1992

Business Software Alliance. "The Software Industry and the Threat to its Success." *BSA Worldwide Report 1990–1991*, September 1991.

Business Software Alliance & Software Publishers Association. "Model Guidelines for the Legal Protection of Computer Programs." *Public Policy Initiatives to Prevent Software Piracy, June 1991–May 1992*, July 1991.

Business Software Alliance & Software Publishers Association. *Public Policy Initiatives to Prevent Software Piracy, June 1991–May 1992*, July 1991.

Charles, D. "Rights and Wrongs of Software." *New Scientist*, September 29, 1990, 44–47.

Clevenger, T. B., Ziegenfuss, D. E., Deck, A. B. and Clevenger, N.N. *Internal Auditor.* December 1988, 42–47.

"Computer Intellectual Property and Conceptual Severence." *Harvard Law Review*, March 1990, 1046–1065.

Cooper III, F. L. "Intellectual Property." *Law and the Software Marketer.* Englewood Cliffs, NJ: Prentice Hall, 1988, 6–9; Harris, III, T.D. "Defining

Intellectual Property and the Rights to It." *The Legal Guide to Computer Software Protection*. Englewood Cliffs, NJ: Prentice-Hall, 1985, 25–28.

Cooper III, F. L. "Software." *Law and the Software Marketer*. Englewood Cliffs, NJ: Prentice-Hall, 1988, 10–17.

Council Directive of 14 May 1991 on the Legal Protection of Computer Programs. *O.J. European Commission*, L122/44, May 17, 1991.

"A Crackdown on Theft," *Chronicle of Higher Education*, April 20, 1994, A32.

"A Crusade for Free Software . . . and a New Statute of Liberty." *New Scientist*, September 29, 1990, 48.

Depke, D. A., and Yang, D. J. "Casting a Worldwide Dragnet for Software Pirates." *Business Week*, December 25, 1989, 54H.

Dwyer, P. "The Battle Raging Over Intellectual Property." *Business Week*, May 22, 1989, 78–89.

Dwyer, P., Jereski, L., Schiller, Z., and Lee, D. "The Battle Raging Over Intellectual Property." *Business Week*, May 22, 1989, 89.

The Economist. August 22, 1992, 17.

Einhorn, B., and Yang, D. J. "Fake Windows, Ersatz DOS, Angry Uncle Sam." *Business Week*, May 18, 1992, 130.

Flannery, R. "Taiwan Fears U.S. Trade Retaliation." *Electronic News*, April 27, 1992, 10.

Gibbons, F. M. "Patent Throw Obstacles in the Way of Progress." *PC Week*, September 18, 1989, 77.

Gosch, J. "Coming in 1993: Europe's Community Patent." *Electronics*, December 1991, 48–50.

Groenewold, G. "As Simple as A-B-C?" *Unix Review*, October 1988, 42–46.

Husch, T., and Foust, L. "Protecting Your Ideas." *Nation's Business*, September 1991, 92.

International Data Corporation. *Worldwide Information Technology, Spending Patterns 1989–1994: An Analysis of Opportunities in Thirty Countries*, August 1990, 10.

Karnow, C.A. "Everyone Copies Software." *Computerworld*, August 19, 1991, 19.

Lowenstein, R., and Zachary, G. "Mysterious Group Is Pirating Apple's Super-Secret Code." *The Wall Street Journal*, June 8, 1989, B7.

MacKenzie, D. "Europe Lays Down the Law on Software." *New Scientist*, June 22, 1991, 20; "Soft in the Head." *The Economist*, March 10, 1990, 15; "Solomon Wanted." *The Economist*, September 22, 1990, 74–75.

Magnier, M. "Microsoft Says Taiwan Piracy Raid Just Scratched Surface of Operation." *The Journal of Commerce and Commercial*, February 3, 1992, 4A.

Magnier, M. "Pirated Software Seized in Taiwan Raid." *The Journal of Commerce and Commercial*, January 30, 1992, 1A.

Martin, J. "Pursuing Pirates." *Datamation*, August 1, 1989, 41–42.

McCauley, P. "The Pluses of Patents." *Computerworld*, September 16, 1991, 23.

McDermott, K. "Barriers to Marketing Services Overseas." *D & B Reports*, July–August 1990, 36–37.

McGregor, J. "China's New Software Protection Rules Are Called Inadequate by U.S. Official." *The Washington Post*, June 17, 1991, A7; Berg, H. "Software Firms Cite Concern over China's New Copyright Law." *Journal of Commerce and Commercial*, March 6, 1991, 4A; Berg, H. "New Software Rules in China Draw Fire." *Journal of Commerce and Commercial*, June 17, 1991, 5A; "China to Enact its Copyright Law." *Beijing Review*, April 15, 1991, 7.

Meads, L. "Copy-Protection Devices Provide Piracy Safeguard." *PC Week*, May 27, 1991.

Methvin, D., and Dunbar, A. "Security Keys: Pros and Cons." *PC Week*, May 27, 1991.

Millstein, J. S. *Institutional Investor*, December 1988, 16–17.

Millstein, J. S. "Wall Street Computers and the Law." *Financial Technology Forum*, December 1988, 17.

Owings, J. A. "Soft and Hard Tech Wars: Patents vs. Copyrights." *Business Credit*, January 1992, 10.

"A Plateau in Software Pirates' Pillage." *Security Management*, December 1991, 13.

Potts, M. "The Window on Copyright Law Remains Open." *The Washington Post*, April 15, 1992, B11.

Schwartz, E. J., Ed. "And Congress Gives Software Makers a Break." *Business Week*, November 19, 1990, 138C.

"Software Group Says Money Lost to Piracy Fell Slightly in '90." *The Wall Street Journal*, August 7, 1991, B5.

"Software Makers Sue Two in Canada." *The New York Times*, July 18, 1991, D5; Fisk, G. E., and Clark, J. E. "Hardware and Software Protection in Canada." *Computer-Law Journal*, December 1990, 483–516; and Clark, C. "Canadian Software Companies Aim to Sink Pirates." *Canadian Business*, March 1991, 13.

"Software Piracy Costs Firms Billions." *The Christian Science Monitor*, January 17, 1992, 8.

E T H I C S   B R I E F

Will the Real O. J. Simpson Please Stand Up?

The major news magazines have repeatedly expressed deep concern over the growing popularity of "newspapers" such as *The National Enquirer* and *The Star*, but when football legend O. J. Simpson was charged in the murder of his ex-wife and friend in June 1994, it was *Time Magazine* who was under scrutiny.

The cover of the June 27th issue showed Simpson's mug shot from police headquarters. The picture used would not have created much of a stir except that rival *Newsweek* ran the actual photograph, while *Time* had doctored the same picture with digital techniques, making the suspect appear notably more sinister, darker, and drawn. Although the inside credit line acknowledged artwork, the cover did not. In an editorial that ran nationwide, Scripps Howard newspapers said that the *Time* inci-

dent was a classic example for journalism ethics students to remember. "It undermines the consumer's trust in the vendor of news. It reveals the journalist as a manipulator of the audience, not an honest reporter of outside events." (*The San Juan Star*, June 23, 1994, p. 36)

A one-time lapse in ethics? Hardly. Just a year before, *Time* published a photograph of what it described as child prostitutes in Moscow. The shot was phony, and the magazine was forced to apologize to its readers.

Discussion Questions
1. What are the ethical obligations of reporters, if any?
2. How can consumers of news be more alert as to discerning the truth from manipulated or "doctored" information?

Southerland, D. "Piracy of the U.S. Software in China Is Big Problem, Commerce Officials Warn." *The Washington Post*, January 14, 1989, D10.

SPA White Paper on Software Piracy, Software Publishers Association.

"Spanish Court Rules for Novell in Copyright Case." *PC Week*, December 3, 1990, 153.

Wasch, K. A. "Before SPA Comes Knocking . . ." *Computerworld*, June 29, 1991, 80.

Wiley, J. S., Jr. "Copyright at the School of Patent." *University of Chicago Law Review*, Winter 1991, 119–185.

Wu, P. T. "Tougher Mexican Laws on Patents, Copyrights Win Wide Praise." *The Journal of Commerce and Commercial*, November 7, 1991, 1A.

Yamada, K. "Judge Rejects Most Remaining Claims by Apple against Microsoft, Hewlett." *The Wall Street Journal*, August 10, 1992, B4; and Burgess, J. "The Battle over Software Protection." *The Washington Post*, April 2, 1989, H1, 11.

Ethics, Profit, and Patients: When Pharmaceutical Companies Sponsor Medical Meetings

"They that be whole need not a physician, but they that are sick."

Matthew, 9:12

Health care consumes 16 percent of the U.S. gross national product (GNP), up from only 8 percent in 1980. Doctors have grappled with ethical quagmires for years, but increasingly their dilemma is focused not on patient care, but on questions of public trust. In this chapter, you will learn about a controversial practice of medical marketing. In the second part of the chapter, a breast implant patient will share her experience with medical ethics.

As a result of some of the issues discussed in this next section, you will learn more about an ethical dilemma that has lingered in the health care profession for decades: Should pharmaceutical companies sponsor meetings for physicians and other professionals, especially when those meetings may be held in resort locations at the expense of the sponsor? The implications of this question, in terms of ethics and public policy, are enormous.

BACKGROUND

For several years, the Food and Drug Administration (FDA) has expressed serious concern over the manner in which pharmaceutical companies promote new and existing products to the medical community. Traditionally, the most effective means of company-to-physician communication has been through the process of *detailing*, in which sales representatives visit physician offices to discuss the availability and suitability of products. The typical pharmaceutical salesperson visits an average of eight physicians a day, with meetings lasting from five to eight minutes each. (Soumerai, 555)

Today more than 28,000 such salespeople for U.S. pharmaceutical companies actively court America's physicians, and at least $5,000 is spent annually per physician for such outreach, exclusive of direct mail and journal advertising. (Soumerai, 550) The marketing impact of such efforts is unquestionably immense; physicians place credibility in the technical knowledge and expertise of these representatives, largely because salespeople have the ability to share new data and insight on the efficacy of products months before journals report detailed findings.

Product information is increasingly distributed through other channels as well. The use of medical television (such as the Lifetime

Source: The article by Laurence Barton on which this chapter was based originally appeared in the *Journal of Hospital Marketing*, vol. 8, no. 1, Winter 1993, Haworth Press, N.Y., William J. Winston, editor. Used with permission.

Cable Television Network) has led an incredible array of companies to sponsor programs—including many weekly series—on heart and liver problems, arthritis, OB/GYN issues, and a multitude of disorders. Other companies, such as Whittle Communications of Knoxville, Tennessee, have revolutionized the use of educational videotapes that are borrowed or purchased by physicians who hope to extend their education on a particular subject or to help patients understand treatment options. While medical journals and conferences remain the primary vehicles for the communication of knowledge, the variety of tools used is clearly expanding.

A DISTURBING TREND

All of this sounds encouraging. Education, after all, is the very centerpiece of effective patient care. It is hard to believe, however, that Hippocrates would find his mandate fulfilled by some of the disturbing trends of the last decade:

- In the 1980s, Ayerst, a New York pharmaceutical company, offered "frequent prescriber bonuses" to physicians who met a stated quota of prescriptions for the company's brand of beta blocker for heart patients; after filling out a short form on prescriptions issued, physicians could trade in the paperwork for free air travel to destinations in the United States and the Caribbean. (Soumerai, 553)

- Throughout the 1980s, it was common for a number of leading U.S. pharmaceutical manufacturers to offer educational symposia on a variety of medical issues. The symposia were later challenged by FDA officials as being a poor disguise to showcase that company's particular brand of therapies. (Banks, 410) Physicians were sometimes lured with free or heavily discounted airfare and hotel deals and extended golf or tennis programs that coincided with actual presentations, with the entire "program" sometimes offering educational credit. Programs for nurses, pharmacists, and other allied health professionals have also proliferated, although all companies have eliminated blatant physician "freebies" in the wake of negative publicity.

- In recent years most teaching hospitals, clinics, and research institutions have adopted explicit codes of conduct and ethics

ETHICS BRIEF

Universities Are Not Immune to Ethics Problems

Universities exist as an ethical repository for the creation and dissemination of information. In recent years, however, colleges and universities have found themselves under scrutiny for a wide spectrum of alleged abuses of the public trust.

From documented cheating on exams by some students at the U.S. Naval Academy to charges by female students that they were sexually harassed at over 150 universities, both scholars and campus administrators have struggled to define standards of ethical behavior that will enhance public confidence in public and private institutions.

One of the more troublesome cases involves Bernard Fisher, professor of surgery at The University of Pittsburgh. In 1994, the National Cancer Institute charged that he "submitted papers for publication that included data that he knew had been falsified." In addition, the government argued that "he covered up evidence that a drug being named in two breast-cancer studies had dangerous side effects and that it may have contributed to the deaths of at least six people. . . ." (Stephen Bird, "Research Powerhouse under the Microscope," *The Chronicle of Higher Education*, June 15, 1994, p. A25)

Although the professor denied wrongdoing, Leonard Minsky, president of the National Coalition for Universities in the Public Interest, decried a system that he says protects the very professors whom institutions should be working to remove whenever wrongdoing is uncovered. "They have covered up, stonewalled, refused to acknowledge misconduct, dragged their feet, except when they have gone after enemies of industrial interests. Obviously the university, which has publicly defended Fisher, should not be in charge of the investigation." (Bird, A27)

If that were not enough, The University of Pittsburgh must also contend with investigations that will last for several years regarding alleged spending by Fisher on several of his research grants. On June 15, 1994, Representative John Dingell of Michigan lashed out at the university and Fisher at a congressional hearing for a pattern of research and spending that he said was contrary to proper research. Dingell said money solicited from a pharmaceutical company for drug research was spent on "lavish parties and receptions" at academic meetings. Dingell said Fisher spent about $80,000 on a single reception at a 1991 meeting. (Kathy Sawyer, "Cancer Researcher Criticized," *The Philadelphia Inquirer*, June 16, 1994, p. 27)

A pioneer in the study of breast cancer, Fisher replied that he was so deeply involved in research that budget and administrative functions were managed by staffpersons. That didn't sit well with officials who began to reexamine both his budgets and the validity of his research findings. News reports suggest that The University of Pittsburgh (which has experienced several other major ethical controversies in recent years) has its work cut out: "Federal investigators subsequently discovered that Fisher and his staff had also been lax in dealing with reports of sloppy or possibly fraudulent data at several other sites." (Sawyer, 27) specifically aimed at curbing questionable business relationships between physicians and pharmaceutical companies. Some physicians privately argue that these norms reach too far, virtually curtailing any professional interaction between the R&D component of pharmaceutical entities and the prescribers. That is a legitimate concern, since the findings emanating from laboratories are of considerable importance to effective patient care. But these same physicians often fail to recall the bountiful feast that some colleagues enjoyed in the 1970s and 1980s as a result of such relationships: Lucrative stock options, cash bonuses, and deferred compensation were reportedly routine at a few manufacturers. The ultimate question for the consumer is paramount: If my doctor receives such enhancements from drug companies, could that significantly influence his or her choice of therapies? (In this sense, one is reminded of Cassius in *Julius Caesar*: "The fault dear Brutus, is not in our stars, but in ourselves.")

In recent hearings before the Labor and Human Resources Committee, Senator Edward Kennedy estimated that $165 million is spent each year on attempts to influence physician prescription decisions. (Halbrooks, 30) What is startling about that statistic and the questionable educational programs that constitute only a portion of that figure is that incestuous relationships between the medical community and pharmaceutical companies taint the reputation of the many other educational symposia that are absent any commercial sponsorship or promotion.

Many of the leading drug makers have repeatedly met stringent accreditation requirements of leading societies and associations such as the American Council for Continuing Medical Education (ACCME) or the American Medical Association (AMA) education requirements; these companies have historically banned any advertisement or reference to their products during symposia or conferences. Yet there is no question that past abuses were plentiful: Some companies would shop around until they found a Continuing Medical Education (CME) sponsor to accredit their activities; the amount of actual education versus external activities was comparatively modest; and companies treated physicians to a harvest of gifts, honoraria, spousal trips, and so on—all under the guise of medical education.

In essence, the FDA is proposing new guidelines that will govern the relationship between pharmaceutical companies and physicians because of concern that physicians may receive perks from pharmaceutical companies that the public ultimately subsidizes via higher priced drugs and services. Of equal concern to some policymakers is the degree of objectivity that is evident in monographs and conference presentations when an obvious commercial influence has contributed so heavily to the event.

CURTAILMENT OF PROMOTIONAL MEETINGS

Increasingly the FDA has expressed concern that the fine line between what constitutes education and what constitutes promotion has been blurred. The agency argues in its newest proposals that the participation of sales, marketing and public relations professionals in the design and presentation of medical educational materials will be the rationale for potential punitive action. It further defined that "sponsorship . . . includes any substantial support, financial or otherwise, provided directly or indirectly by the company. Such sponsorship may include, among other things, grants, payments, technical support, facilitation of the presentation or facilitation of press coverage." The agency is also concerned about "such publications as company-supported medical journals or supplements to medical journals . . . software and slide kits." To reduce the costs associated with promotion and (theoretically, at least) to protect public confidence in the credibility of medical education, the agency hopes to establish 20 separate criteria to determine if a program is educationally independent or promotional. (Kusserow, 6)

The FDA believes that these guidelines, which focus on business ethics that it feels it can regulate, may improve public policy:

- Sponsoring companies should not exert influence over the content of programs or the selection of speakers at presentations or authors in subsequent proceedings.

- Any financial relationship between a sponsoring company and experts participating in the meeting should be disclosed (stockholder, holder of options, member of board of directors, and so forth).

- Topics presented at a meeting should be on the wider aspects of a disease and not focus on a specific drug product's merits or applications or on the deficiencies of a competing product.

- Company personnel and its consultants should not be involved in ghostwriting for presenters or in the training of presenters at conferences.

E T H I C S   B R I E F

How Does 10 Percent Interest Sound?

Pretty good, especially in 1982 when the Dauphin Deposit Bank of Harrisburg, Pennsylvania advertised special individual retirement accounts (IRAs) that would pay *at least* 10 percent annually and "be renewed automatically every 18 months." (Stock, C1)

In 1982, interest rates were high and banks could afford such lofty assurances. By 1993, however, Dauphin Bank was paying 10 percent on about $150 million in IRAs when the marketplace was paying less than half that figure.

Grin and bear it? Hardly. The characters at this institution wrote to its customers and said it "would no longer pay 10 percent on accounts." When the depositors complained to state banking officials, the bank first dropped the idea. Then it imposed a "main-

tenance fee" on the accounts. Then it decided to sue its own customers—some 4,881 depositors—asking the local court to cancel the 10 percent deal.

"They enticed me with this good offer and I took them up on it," customer Jered Hock told *The Philadelphia Inquirer.* "Now they're trying to go back on the word they gave me." The bank is getting plenty of bad press for a promotion that was full of promise.

Craig Stock, financial editor for the paper, opened his story on Dauphin with a nifty line: "You may want to count your fingers next time you shake hands on a deal with Dauphin Deposit Bank."

Source: Craig Stock, "When's a Deal Not a Deal?" *The Philadelphia Inquirer,* June 14, 1994, p. C1.

■ Promotional exhibits, booths, and sales presentations should not be scheduled near an educational symposia; a company's support for a particular program can be acknowledged appropriately, but overt advertising and promotional displays would be banned.

These and the other criteria proposed by the FDA may be both reasonable and consistent with the goal of reducing promotional costs and protecting the consuming public from hidden agendas. In fact, a number of pharmaceutical manufacturers and other medical companies have respected these norms for years without federal intervention. Yet the reaction of some factions in the medical community has been hostile.

For example, Pharmaceutical Advertising Council (PAC) president James Dougherty sent 17,000 letters to a variety of medical schools and other institutions charging that the FDA was seeking to "create a new limitation on the free flow of scientific information by defining any communication that receives funding from a pharmaceutical company as 'promotion' and extending their regulatory controls to physicians and CME providers who accept company support . . ." (FDC, 10) Dougherty went on to argue that the Supreme Court has protected the First Amendment right to free speech that is truthful.

The Pharmaceutical Manufacturers Association (PMA) went further, asserting that the FDA proposals will "severely and unnecessarily limit the continued and timely dissemination of medical and scientific information to physicians." (PMA, 5) The PMA warned its members that the FDA would "impose an absolute prohibition on any pharmaceutical company involvement whatsoever—even a mere suggestion as to program topics or expert speakers—in programs it funds." It adds, "Strict new FDA rules governing CME activities are not needed, would be counterproductive to the cooperatively formulated voluntary guidelines, and undoubtedly would cause companies to withhold funding of CME programs." (FDC, 10)

The wrath of pharmaceutical interests is understandable, if not misguided. In the wake of widespread negative publicity, the industry *has* begun to clean up its act. Now it is asking Washington to forgo stringent regulations as a result of its initiatives. And physicians, who rarely write or speak on the subject of their personal business relationships, often privately concede that the entire profession is now being punished due to the questionable practices of a minority of their colleagues.

The physicians may have a valid argument, one which has also been articulated in a surge of recent articles questioning whether physicians are not being punished for merely taking advantage of various *legal* opportunities presented to them (whether the issue is attending a seminar, serving as a partner in a joint venture, or purchasing stock in a medical equipment company). Typical of this philosophy, one expert defends physician involvement in joint ventures with hospitals:

> Not acknowledged by the current critics of medical practice ethics is the fact that most hospitals and physicians have been sensitive to even the appearance of unethical behavior and have avoided involvement in a business relationship. They have valued their medical integrity more than their financial well-being. With existing and future payments for medical services decreasing, the ethical physician and hospital will incur the largest loss in revenues by their refusal to compromise their ethical values. (Johnson, 11)

PHYSICIANS TEND
TO SUPPORT ACTION

The author mailed surveys to 280 physicians in California, Nevada, and Washington state regarding the proposed FDA regulations. General practitioners were excluded; rather pulmonary and infertility specialists were targeted because such specialties are often prime candidates for educational symposia. Some 142 responses were received by the deadline constituting a 51 percent response rate, of which 140 were usable. Numbers were rounded where necessary. The goal of the survey was to ascertain whether a cross section of specialists were aware of the proposed guidelines and whether they felt that such actions would enhance or restrain their practice of medicine. The results, appearing in Exhibit 9-1 on the next page, indicate a surprising lack of knowledge on the FDA proposals but broad support for the concept of increased regulation.

Survey Analysis

Given physician responsibilities, the level of knowledge regarding the proposed regulations is not necessarily surprising (76 percent unaware). More encouraging is the recognition by the medical community that the pharmaceutical industry has taken diligent steps to reduce questionable practices with regard to educational symposia (81 percent of respondents).

In question 3, responses favor the underlying precepts of the FDA regulations by nearly two to one (62 percent versus 38 percent against). This indicates that even in the absence of specific knowledge about the regulations, physicians and specialists acknowledge the need for concerted action.

Of considerable importance are responses to question 4 regarding why supporters of the FDA proposals seek the adoption of such measures. Public opinion (33 percent) and the opinions of their colleagues or institutional peers (29 percent) overshadow the ethical questions raised by these practices (17 percent).

Physicians are somewhat divided in question 5 as to the ultimate impact of educational symposia sponsored by an external source. The majority (54 percent) do not believe they are influenced by such meetings, while the remainder (46 percent) believe that influence exists.

A surprising response emanates from question 6 as to past participation in programs of this nature. Nearly three quarters (72 percent)

EXHIBIT 9-1   Physician Response to FDA Proposals

1. The FDA has recently issued draft guidelines that would significantly alter the method in which pharmaceutical companies sponsor educational symposia. Among the prime reasons why the FDA is acting are reports of business relationships between some physicians and pharmaceutical companies that could taint the presentation of data and/or increase the cost of patient care. Are you aware of the proposed guidelines?
   Yes   24%
   No   76%

2. Are you aware that most pharmaceutical companies have ceased questionable business practices such as providing free or subsidized trips, offering stock options, or providing other financial incentives to physicians in recent years?
   Yes   81%
   No   19%

3. In your opinion, are such regulations warranted?
   Yes   62%
   No   38%

4. If yes, why do you support these regulations? (If no, skip to question 5.)
   Public opinion and increased public scrutiny of such practices   33%
   Hospital, group practice, or society scrutiny of such practices   29%
   Ethically and morally sound   17%
   Other reason   21%

5. In your opinion, are physicians unduly influenced by educational symposia and conferences that are sponsored by pharmaceutical companies?
   Yes   46%
   No   54%

6. Have you ever participated in an educational symposium sponsored by a pharmaceutical company in which the company paid for part or all of the trip expenses, or in which ancillary events such as golf, meals, spouse expenses, were underwritten or reimbursed by the company?
   Yes   23%
   No   72% (Responses did not equal 100 percent.)

7. The pharmaceutical industry has worked to reduce or eliminate these practices in recent years. How do you rank the value of such meetings in terms of their impact on the quality of care and information provided to your patients?
   Very high   11%
   High   45%
   Moderate   23%
   Poor   21%

8. Do educational symposia sponsored by pharmaceutical companies add measurably to the costs of patient care?
   Yes   24%
   No   76%

Survey conducted November–December 1991.

Physicians, like other professionals, benefit from academic and trade association meetings where new ideas, theories, and treatments are debated. Some argue, however, that the independent judgments of physicians are compromised when they are offered free trips and gifts by pharmaceutical companies, clinics, and other health care providers.

say they have never participated in such meetings, while the rest (23 percent) have participated.

Despite that response, physicians indicate in question 7 that they place a high (11 percent) or very high (45 percent) value on such meetings. These responses do not completely correlate with the sentiments expressed in question 6, possibly because respondents were hesitant to admit past affiliation with such programs.

The results of question 8 indicate that the underlying motivational factor of the FDA for acting—that such symposia costs ultimately increase the cost of health care delivered to patients—is rejected by physicians by an overwhelming majority (74 percent to 26 percent).

WHAT CONSTITUTES REASONABLE SUPPORT OF MEDICAL EDUCATION?

In 1984, the ACCME adopted guidelines stating that accredited sponsors—not medical companies—are responsible for the content, quality, and scientific integrity of educational symposia. If sponsors abuse

E T H I C S   B R I E F

Putting Executives behind Bars

For many years sociologists and others have argued that "white collar crime" is increasing because the fear of being jailed for any wrongdoing is simply invalid: Indeed, well an estimated 98 percent of managers and executives who commit a crime and are found guilty succeed in plea-bargaining to avoid time behind bars. (Barton, 3)

There is some encouraging evidence on efforts to incarcerate corporate criminals, however. *Business Crimes Bulletin* (May 1994, 11) reports that in 1993 the U.S. Department of Justice adjudicated cases in which criminals spent 3,673 days in prison and another 2,704 days in confinement at home or in a halfway house. In addition, the Sherman Antitrust Act was amended in 1990 and increased the maximum fine that a company can pay for a single case involving antitrust statutes to $10 million.

Stiffer penalties have led the Assistant U.S. Attorney General, Anne K. Bingaman, to offer guarded optimism about the future. In the past year, the Antitrust Division has "returned five indictments involving obstruction of justice charges. Currently no less than 14 of our grand juries (over 10 percent) are investigating possible obstructions." She adds that the government "will continue to vigorously prosecute every obstruction and perjury violation that appears in any of our grand jury or other matters and to seek maximum penalties in such cases." Bravo.

Source: "The Business Crimes Hotline," *Business Crimes Bulletin*, Volume 1, Number 4, New York Law Publishing Co., May 1994.

that trust, the ACCME indicated that accreditation could be withdrawn. Such punitive measures would be clearly embarrassing to a pharmaceutical manufacturer and thus may provide a means of self-auditing that is so necessary.

The actions of the ACCME can only assure patients to a certain degree. The vast majority of patients (according to repeated public opinion polls) are already suspicious about the caliber of health care they receive by U.S. providers. Without question, educational symposia provide an invaluable forum for discussions on therapy options. At these meetings, colleagues have the opportunity to present their findings and debate the value of various procedures and medicines. These meetings take place during an era of great contradictions—cost containment is now directly juxtaposed against a trend in which many exciting new biotechnological products are promising, yet costly.

Furthermore, the costs of sponsoring educational symposia are clearly far too expensive for nonprofit medical societies or research institutions to bear independently. One pharmaceutical company that has a long-standing policy of prohibiting any commercialization of its products during the nearly 125 meetings it annually sponsors estimates that a two-day symposium in a major U.S. city can cost upwards of $50,000 when meeting space, meals, advertising, publishing monographs, and speaker costs are totaled. (Barton, 1991, 6)

Pharmaceutical companies constitute a financially sound source for the underwriting of such meetings. Yet a number of leading pharmaceutical manufacturers that sponsor educational symposia have created a clear line of demarcation between their not-for-profit educational divisions and their marketing and sales divisions, and therein lies one of the most important and meaningful steps in the right direction—educational programs should not be sponsored, organized, or in any way managed by sales professionals.

Pharmaceutical companies that sincerely believe that their mission is enhanced by physician education can and should be allowed to organize educational symposia, but the organization and sponsorship of these events must be void of contact with sales and marketing which is the essence of the proposed FDA regulations. The senior regulatory review officer for the FDA makes this argument:

> I suspect that scientific quality, objectivity, and rigor are not the goals of some sponsoring firms, and balanced administration and meaningful review of these activities is therefore not provided for by management or these firms. The scientific, regulatory and legal players of the industry also appear less than eager in some cases to become involved in review and administration of scientific/educational activities, because this role necessitates their becoming in-house obstructionists rather than facilitators of the firms' commercial goals. (Banks, 413)

It should be emphasized that the FDA has repeatedly indicated that one of its primary motivating factors for action is the belief that such educational activities increase the cost of health care; the impact of such meetings on prescriptive habits has been largely avoided by the agency. The ultimate consideration for health care providers, of course, is what steps the profession should take, either voluntarily or via federal regulation, to acknowledge the important contribution of the sponsoring drug manufacturer. Is placing an acknowledgment sign with the company's logo at the back of the meeting room sufficient for both parties? What about introducing a high-ranking executive of the firm to speak a few words as a means of introduction, or allowing a brief videotaped message to be aired, or granting the company permission to reserve a separate room down the hall where product literature is available for perusal?

The response to these questions can no longer be delayed. Washington is becoming impatient with the hesitancy of the pharma-

ETHICS BRIEF

The Saga of One Woman's Breast Implants

Never in my wildest imagination would I have thought I'd be involved in this current health nightmare. After nursing four children, I still had firm, full breasts. There was no family history of cancer and I tried to always eat low-sugar, high-fiber, low-fat foods and take care of my health, which included regular exercise. Why then was I suddenly involved in this controversy?

My nightmare started in May 1989. I noticed a lump in my right breast that seemed different than the usual fibrocystic lumps that I normally felt. I had a mammogram and made an appointment with my OB-GYN. When I had the lump checked, he stated he thought it was fibrocystic, although it felt different to me. He said we should wait for the results of the mammogram. "No radiographic abnormalities," it stated. Whew! I could go on living a normal life. Until suddenly in January 1990 I raised my arm to put on deodorant and saw it! The right side of my breast flattened and the nipple was pulled downward. This is every woman's worst nightmare! It couldn't be happening. I couldn't even think about it for a week but it must have gnawed at my subconscious. I couldn't ignore it for long. I made an appointment with the same doctor and went in immediately. He sent me for another mammogram and this time the news was not good. He was shaking my hand and wishing me the best. His grin told me he knew he had blown it eight months earlier, but that wasn't going to help me now.

He referred me to a surgeon. "These are wonderful," he stated. "We don't have any problems with these. Maybe six percent capsular contracture rate. You'll love this." I tried to read the consent form as he kept telling me the wonders of these implants. I finally quit trying to read the form and just signed it. He showed me the implants and told me that I would be getting the Mentor Becker. I didn't know a thing about breast implants so one brand would have been the same as another to me. Surgery was scheduled for the next day. I was in shock. I was making decisions that would affect the rest of my life without time to even process them. My cancer was large and time was of the essence.

Surgery was uneventful, so they said. Everything went well. It was routine. Not to me! I was in the hospital for three days before the oncologist came by to tell me that they had found cancer in one lymph node. I would need chemotherapy.

I began chemotherapy one month later. I had heard all the horror stories so I was apprehensive, but I am a survivor so I knew I would make it through. I was determined to beat cancer and also not to get sick from the chemotherapy. I did quite well. I generally was only sick about one day and that was four days after each treatment. I felt icky at times, but not down-in-bed sick. I never lost a hair. I got blood clots in my arm where the IV was given and after the fifth treatment I also had a blood clot in one leg. I had to go to the hospital, suitcase packed,

ceutical industry to police its own members. The proposed FDA regulations are hardly a panacea, yet they constitute an important first step in assuring the independent presentation of ideas to the medical community.

to have a venogram. If the clot was in the deep veins, I would have been admitted to the hospital for a ten-to-fourteen day stay. It wasn't, and I cried in relief most of the way home. I never had the sixth and final treatment. I knew after three treatments that I no longer had cancer but I felt I should go on with treatment to be sure. After the blood clot I couldn't justify finishing chemotherapy. My oncologist tried to convince me of the error of my ways, but I wasn't buying it.

During this period of time, my husband had come back from California for a few days. He had abandoned me two days after I was released from the hospital after the mastectomy. There had been no emotional support for several years. He just came in the house and made himself at home. (He was having an affair.) I was furious. How dare he desert me when I was in the most serious situation in my life and then just walk back in as if nothing had happened. After he spent the entire evening working in the study as though nothing was wrong, I told him I didn't want him to stay. He looked surprised and asked me where he should go. I told him I didn't care. He left and went to a motel.

At this time I was not yet aware of any of the controversy surrounding the breast implant issue. I didn't know that one should never have chemotherapy (or radiation) after having a breast implant. I didn't know that my particular implant was one of the worst for bleeding silicone oil nor did I know that this could damage my immune system. By the time I finished chemotherapy I thought my health problems were over. Boy, was I wrong! They had just begun.

My white blood count refused to return to normal. It increased for a while, but, unbeknownst to me, my implant had ruptured. I know now that it happened three and one-half months after implantation, but at the time I thought I had just pulled a mus-

cle. I just reached up to get my electric wok from the top of the kitchen cabinet when I felt something pull and also felt a burning sensation in my chest. It lasted for over a day but I had no way of knowing what had caused the pain. I had capsular contracture and constant muscle spasms.

When I finally told him the pain was too much to stand [my doctor] suggested we remove this implant and replace it with a textured one, same brand and size. He also wanted to do a reduction on the other breast to make it "match" the implant. When I objected, he acted like he couldn't do anything for me if I wouldn't do it. I finally decided to allow it. I was in so much pain from the implant, I had to do something. What a mistake! First, the implant was ruptured and difficult to remove. The surgeon was not able to retrieve all the silicone. It took almost three hours and I lost a lot of blood. Then they wanted to give me a transfusion, which I declined. I thought I had enough problems already. No one told me that the implant had been ruptured. It wasn't even written in my chart. Then the mastopexy (breast lift or reduction) was very painful. It took three months before it was even bearable to wear a normal bra. The pain lasted much longer.

My health really began to decline after this surgery. I began to feel constant, debilitating fatigue. My head began to ache all the time. My scalp itched, the skin on my arms felt rough and dry, I felt warm all the time, my white blood count continued its downward spiral and my vision began to blur. After a few months I began to have joint pain, especially in my hands. Knots began to form beside my finger knuckles. My memory was not reliable, one day it seemed OK and the next day it wasn't. My vision blurred randomly. I forgot things at work and, as a social worker, remembering is crucial. My personality fluctuated from day to day. I had fairly severe mood swings.

My stomach started giving me problems and I alternated between diarrhea and constipation. I couldn't concentrate for very long periods of time and I began to have insomnia and panic attacks.

By now I had heard some of the publicity about the breast implants and had even talked to several women with problems. I knew I had some problems but I also had a lot of denial. As time went on, I noticed that my implant began to sag. I hadn't even had it a year. My white blood count dropped more and more. I lost my job because I wasn't able to do it and I wasn't the same person anymore.

Finally, after a friend with implants died, I asked my plastic surgeon to remove mine. He resisted for two months, but I persisted. Unfortunately, I didn't know that I couldn't just have the implant removed under a local. This is what my plastic surgeon recommended and I didn't know enough about implants to know the proper procedure, so I allowed him to just slip it out. After a month I felt much better. The knots on my finger joints decreased, my headaches were much better, my fatigue lessened as did many of my other symptoms. I felt I was on my way to recovery. Then the improvement stopped. The lymph nodes in my other breast swelled and were painful. The white blood count continued to go down. My big toe joints swelled and turned red and my knees began to give me more trouble. I started to become extremely fatigued again. I went to Florida to see a specialist who worked with breast implant patients. He told me I had all the symptoms of silicone related toxicity. He also recommended that I consider having the capsule (scar tissue) removed because it holds a lot of silicone from the gel bleed. I was extremely depressed and every time I thought about it for the next three weeks, I cried. Finally I decided to have the surgery and get it over with. After I called and made the appoint-

ment, I quit crying. The indecision was over and I was moving ahead. I didn't find it easy to follow through with it, but I received a lot of support from my implant group. This group had expanded from the twelve who originally met to over three hundred by this time, and I was spending all my time coordinating it. We now have over fifteen hundred members.

I am very angry about the problems caused by my breast implants. I'm very angry that the manufacturers seemed to have information about the disastrous effects implants could have on women's health and concealed this information. I'm very angry that many more women will become ill and die before silicone and saline implants are removed from the market. I'm angry that our society is so sick that women have to alter their bodies to feel good about the way they look. I'm angry that our government had the right to regulate these devices for many years and took so long to take action (which still seems insufficient to protect the public). I'm angry that women have no money for implant removal and many insurance companies are playing games with our health. Many women cannot even obtain insurance. I'm also angry that women with no money and no insurance cannot get their implants properly removed (implant and entire capsule). I use my anger to organize and to help women who have problems with breast implants. If we can keep one woman from making the mistakes we have made and we help educate women to remove their implants before they have serious health problems, then we are doing our job.

In my opinion, there are no safe breast implants. Some MDs still mistakenly advertise that saline implants are FDA approved. The FDA has now required pre-market approval for these as well. There has *never* been FDA approval for any breast implant. The manufacturers say there is no proof that implants are not safe. There is no proof that they are safe because they have never released any research studies that lasted long enough to determine safety. We were the guinea pigs (lab rats) and we are the research subjects. We should all be angry at this devaluation of over half of the population. Women everywhere should be outraged at this blatant disregard for our health and well-being.

Women all across this country and in other countries need to work together to end this senseless experimentation on our sisters. We need to organize in a unified group to fight this type of greed and deceit by some manufacturers and the questionable ethics of some MDs. Until we do, this unfair system will continue and we may again suffer from another human experiment.

Author's Note: In May 1994, the major manufacturers of silicone breast implants agreed to establish a $4.3 billion trust fund to resolve tens of thousands of filed and expected product liability claims.

Source: This ethics brief was written by Lynda Roth, MSW, who is founder and president of the Coalition of Silicone Survivors, Inc., an education and support group organized to help women to inform themselves about breast implants. It is headquartered in Colorado and has members nationwide. A monthly informative newsletter is available by writing C.O.S.S., P.O. Box 129, Broomfield, CO 80038-0129 or by calling (303) 469-8242, FAX (303) 466-4084.

CASE STUDY: FOOD LION

The grocery store industry is notoriously competitive. Even the best run companies struggle to make just 1 cent of profit on each dollar of food that is counted by their checkout scanners. Yet, in every kind of business, there is always a standout performer. Among national grocery chains, that exception has been Food Lion. Over the last ten years, Food Lion has grown faster and been more profitable than its competitors. Between 1983 and 1992, Food Lion opened more than 800 stores in 13 states across the South, growing to more than 1,000 stores nationwide. Based on this staggering rate of growth, the company adopted a goal of "2000 stores by the year 2000." Food Lion's expansion was accompanied by impressive gains in sales and earn-

Source: This case study was written by Chuck Williams who is assistant professor of management at Texas Christian University.

ings, which increased an average of 22.5 percent and 23.3 percent per year, respectively. What was the reason behind this phenomenal success? Food Lion's operating costs are 13 percent of sales, nearly a third less than the industry average of 20 percent. Thus, like Wal-Mart, Food Lion had grown profitable by passing those savings on to customers in the form of everyday low prices.

In November of 1992, ABC's news magazine, *Prime Time Live* aired a story accusing Food Lion of selling old, unfresh meat and deli items to consumers. Seventy former and current employees who had worked in more than 200 Food Lion stores told ABC that it was common for old meat, meat that had yet not been purchased by its "sell by" freshness date, to be repackaged and relabeled with new "sell by" freshness dates. Bonnie Simpson, who worked for five years as a Food Lion meat wrapper, told *Prime Time Live* anchor Diane Sawyer, "We soaked the fish in baking soda and then we'd squirt lemon juice on it and put it back in the case and sell it for three more days. . . . The fish would be so rotten it would crumble in your hand."

Employees who said that they were under extreme pressure from their store managers to meet profit goals also reported that they were encouraged to hide all telltale signs of food deterioration. Deli employees told *Prime Time Live* that they regularly mixed old leftovers from slower selling deli items, such as rice pudding into newly prepared deli trays. One employee said, "Sell the bad stuff first . . . put the bad stuff on the top." And, for those products that couldn't be rewrapped by Food Lion employees, Simpson and 35 other employees told Diane Sawyer that it was standard practice to use fingernail polish remover to remove the "sell by" freshness date printed by product manufacturers on packages of cheese, yogurt, eggs, and meats. Former employee Jean Bull, who spent 13 years with Food Lion, said, "I've been told in every market I have ever worked to take fingernail polish remover and take the dates off. That's so they can leave it out there until it either molds or gets discolored or the vacuum goes on it."

Because these serious allegations were made by so many employees, with experience in several hundred Food Lion stores, *Prime Time Live* decided to try to obtain first-hand evidence of these problems by having the show's producers pose as job applicants in more than 20 different Food Lion stores. Food Lion hired two of them to work in meat and deli departments in three different stores. Using undercover cameras that produced startling video, the *Prime Time Live* staffers saw meat market managers repackage old pork chops which had been trimmed to remove the edges that were starting to go bad. They saw out-of-date ground beef mixed in with new ground beef. They saw old chicken, repackaged and covered in barbecue sauce, sent to the gourmet section, at full price.

Near the end of the televised story, Diane Sawyer explained that *Prime Time Live* had tried to obtain an interview with Food Lion chief executive officer Tom Smith. She said, "The company's position was that they'd give an interview, but only if we would promise not to show the hidden camera video you saw tonight. We declined. They filed a suit, charging us with fraud." Indeed, on September 28, 1992, a little over a month before the story aired, Food Lion filed a $50,000 lawsuit against ABC's parent company, Capital Cities/ABC, Inc., to prevent ABC from televising its report and to force ABC to allow Food Lion to view all of ABC's videos, notes, and audiotapes. However, a U.S. magistrate ruled against Food Lion, stating that prior restraint of the broadcast would violate First Amendment protections.

When local TV news stations and newspapers picked up the story over night, the impact was instantaneous. On the day after *Prime Time Live* aired its story, shopping aisles and parking lots were deserted at many Food Lion stores, especially in Texas where Food Lion had just opened 42 new stores in Fort Worth and Dallas. Kim Baker, who had never had any problems with Food Lion meat, was one of only six people shopping in a Dallas Food Lion store the morning after the story aired. She told the *Dallas Morning News*, "Shoot. I buy a roast here that's really good. Now I think, 'Dadgum. Is it bleached?'" She also said that she, "probably wouldn't buy the barbecued chicken, but I've always though it smelled good." Unfortunately for Food Lion, the bad news then spread from the food market to the NASDAQ stock market, where Food Lion stock was the most actively traded stock that day. Food Lion's class A stock opened at $9.25 a share, dipped as low as $6.50, and closed at $8.25. Food Lion's class B stock closed at $8.62, down $1.37 a share. Thus, as measured by stock price, Food Lion's total value as a company had dropped by approximately 15 percent in fewer than 24 hours.

Food Lion immediately fought back to protect its image. In some regions, the company began running commercials even before the story aired. Those commercials, which were in response to the 30-second advertisements that ABC was using to promote the *Prime Time Live* story, featured Food Lion chief executive officer Tom Smith who claimed that "Food Lion stores are clean. If there is ever a problem in any of our stores, we fix it." The day before the story was broadcast, Food Lion vice-president Vince Watkins was quoted in an interview as saying, "This is quintessential tabloid reporting. It's clear they have no intention of doing a balanced, complete piece of reporting."

Several hours after the program's broadcast, CEO Tom Smith issued a statement wherein he said several times, "These lies have got to stop." The day after the broadcast, Food Lion released this statement: "Food Lion stands behind our stringent policies and procedures and believes ABC has created news, not reported news. But Food Lion takes each of these allegations seriously and is promptly and thoroughly reviewing each and every one."

Vince Watkins of Food Lion also claimed that the story was the result of a "corporate campaign being waged by the United Food and Commercial Workers Union (UFCW), which fed (ABC) names for interviews." In a press release, Food Lion said, "Unfortunately it appears that ABC was an inadvertent tool of the UFCW which stands to gain as much as $18 million in just one year of union dues from Food Lion employees. For example, a spokesperson for the UFCW was quoted as saying that they had provided 65 of the 70 informants used in the story—not exactly a balanced perspective." The union responded by saying, "Food Lion's tactic for dealing with bad new is to impugn the motives of the messenger."

Customers, though, were slow to respond to Food Lion's aggressive defense tactics. Many of them simply took their business elsewhere. North Carolina-based Harris-Teeter, a small chain of 133 stores which competes with Food Lion, saw "double-digit" sales gains the week following the story's broadcast. Larry Niven of Harris-Teeter said, "We saw a demand for bone cuts, which means we're getting the kind of price shopper who normally goes to Food Lion." Another small competitor, Zettler's Thrift Mart, had "one of the biggest weekends we've ever had" following the story. One week after the story, stock analysts were estimating that Food Lions sales were down by 20 percent. However, Carol Herndon, Food Lion's director of financial accounting, would only speculate that sales "could have dropped." Said Herndon, "We want to make sure if we lost one customer, that customer comes back. We're contemplating additional legal actions against them, and we're working to reassure our customers."

Unfortunately, for Food Lion, this initial drop in performance was just the beginning of the damage the company would suffer as a result of the negative publicity from *Prime Time Live*'s report:

■ *November 15, 1992.* David Longman of Norfolk, Virginia, filed a lawsuit accusing the company of artificially inflating Food Lion's stock price by fraudulently promoting an image of cleanliness and customer service. Longman paid $44,000 for

2,000 shares of Food Lion stock in February 1992. After *Prime Time Live*'s story, his stock had declined $28,000 in value to roughly $16,000.

- *December 4, 1992.* Food Lion announced that sales had declined by 9.5 percent in November. The company attributed all of the decline to *Prime Time Live*'s report, but said that "sales have begun to recover and management is encouraged by this."

- *December 25, 1992.* Food Lion announced that it would slow its rapid expansion because of poor earnings. Food Lion placed a "moratorium" on development of new stores, except for those presently under construction or lease.

- *January 8, 1993.* Food Lion announced that, compared to the year before, same-store sales were down 6.2 percent. The company claimed that these sales figures indicated that customers were responding to Food Lion's "assurances about quality and cleanliness."

- *February 3, 1993.* Food Lion announced that payments of its first quarter stock dividend for 1993 would be delayed. A company spokesman said, "We had an unusual fourth quarter, let's face it, and the board just needs more time to look at financial results." Company directors will meet February 11 to decide on a dividend payment. Normally, they would have met on January 2 and then announced the dividend on January 9.

- *February 12, 1993.* Food Lion reported that fourth quarter 1992 earnings fell by 55 percent compared to last year. A company spokesman said, "We don't expect 1993 earnings to be any better than 1992." Company directors also cut the stock dividend on class A stock from 2.8 cents to 2.2 cents and on class B stock from 2.76 cents to 2.15 cents. For the year, net income dropped by 13 percent.

- *February 23, 1993.* Food Lion filed a lawsuit against the United Food and Commercial Workers Union, claiming that the union orchestrated a campaign against the company. Court records indicated that the lawsuit claims "abuse of process" and seeks "actual and punitive damages."

- *March 3, 1993.* After falling by 6.2 percent in December 1992, same-store sales fell by 7.6 percent in January 1993. Company spokesman Mike Mozingo said, "As we get further away from that [*Prime Time Live*'s story], we're beginning to see improvements in same-store sales, although it is still down from last year." Mozingo also said that, "The Texas market has been very competitive, and we're still trying to establish our name in that market."

- *April 9, 1993.* Food Lion announced that first-quarter earnings were down by 55.8 percent compared to 1992. The company released the earnings report after the stock market closed on Thursday, and before the Good Friday holiday.

- *April 9, 1993.* Food Lion had changed its lawsuit against Capital Cities / ABC, Inc. It added the claim that ABC is guilty under RICO, which is the Racketeer Influenced and Corrupt Organizations Act. Specifically, the lawsuit accused two ABC producers of committing mail and wire fraud in order to obtain their story. Food Lion sought $90 million in damages and an injunction which would prevent ABC from conducting future undercover investigations.

- *April 27, 1993.* Food Lion announced that chief executive officer Tom Smith received a $282,955 bonus last year, up 23 percent from 1991. Smith was also paid a 1992 salary of $628,788, up from $528,575 in 1991. Food Lion spokesman Mike Mozingo stated that, "the attacks the company has been under . . . and the fact that we have survived, warranted Mr. Smith's wage hike and bonus."

- *May 2, 1993.* Food Lion disclosed that 54 new stores it opened in fall 1992 in the Dallas-Fort Worth area of Texas were not profitable. Food Lion stated that the *Prime Time Live* broadcast damaged sales in most of its new Texas, Louisiana, and Oklahoma stores where it had not yet established a solid reputation with consumers. A company spokesman said that it is reevaluating these markets, but denied rumors that it plans to sell out stores in these states.

- *May 3, 1993.* One of Food Lion's founders, Ralph Ketner, resigned from the company's board because of disagreements with company management. In an interview with the *Salisbury* (N.C.) *Post*, Ketner said that he did not agree with the company's handling of the negative reaction to *Prime Time Live*'s story. He also disagreed with the quick expansion the company had made into Texas. Ketner, his brother, Brown Ketner, and William Smith, founded the company in 1957.

- *May 7, 1993.* CEO Tom Smith discussed his leadership of Food Lion before more than 1,000 shareholders attending the company's annual meeting. Despite seeing their Food Lion stock shrink by two-thirds since November, most of the shareholders rose to give Smith a standing ovation at the end of the meeting. Food Lion's class A stock closed at $5.875, a 52 week low, while class B stock closed at $6.125.

- *June 12, 1993.* Food Lion cofounder Ralph Ketner tried to sell 1.04 million more shares of his Food Lion stock. This year, CEO Tom Smith sold 150,000 shares, while Vincent Watkins, vice-president of special projects and development sold 70,000 shares. Smith Barney analyst Richard Church said, "It's not a good sign that Mr. Ketner and other insiders are dumping stock. If these guys have no confidence, why should anyone else?" Food Lion shares have dropped some $5 billion in value since late 1991. Three billion of the loss came after *Prime Time Live*'s report.

- *August 13, 1993.* Food Lion settled a long-standing wage and child labor law dispute with the federal government by agreeing to pay $16.2 million.

- *August 13, 1993.* Vice-President of special projects and development, Vincent Watkins, who headed Food Lion's expansion into Texas, resigned from the company. Spokesman Mike Mozingo would not comment on whether the resignation was related to recent company problems.

- *November 1993.* Food Lion filed a disclosure statement with the Security Exchange Commission in which it stated that it was considering selling the 105 stores it had recently opened in Texas, Oklahoma, and Louisiana.

Long after *Prime Time Live*'s story, Food Lion is clearly still suffering from negative publicity regarding public health and ethic management.

Challenge

Assume that you are part of Food Lion's top management team, on the day after *Prime Time Live* has aired its story, and that you have arranged to hold a press conference at 11:30 a.m. eastern time.

1. Formulate a strategy for dealing with this public crisis that you can defend as being ethically responsible.

2. Prepare a written press statement to be released at the beginning of the press conference. How would you emphasize ethics?

3. In order to better prepare for the press conference, formulate five questions that you know reporters will ask. Then write prepared answers to those questions.

4. Assume you are a member of the Board of Directors at Food Lion. The news conference and negative publicity are behind you, but you also believe that a thorough debriefing on the source of this embarrassment is vital. What questions do you intend to ask senior management?

References for Case Study

Associated Press, Salisbury, NC. "ABC Seeks Dismissal of Food Lion's Racketeering Suit." *Dallas Morning News*, May 5, 1993, 2D.

Associated Press, Salisbury, NC. "Food Lion Postpones Dividend." *Dallas Morning News*, February 3, 1993, 3D.

Associated Press, Salisbury, NC. "Food Lion Projects Director Resigns Amid Criticism of Texas Expansion." *Fort Worth Star-Telegram*, August 13, 1993, B3.

Barker, Leslie. "Food Lion Denies Selling Spoiled Goods, Chain's Business Dips after TV News Report." *Dallas Morning News*, November 7, 1992, 1A.

Bloomsberg Business News, Salisbury, NC. "Co-Founder of Food Lion Plans to Sell Additional 1 Million Shares." *Dallas Morning News*, June 12, 1993, 3F.

Charlotte Observer, Charlotte, NC. "Food Lion Exec Given $282,955 Bonus." *Dallas Morning News*, April 27, 1993, 4d.

Deener, Bill. "Food Lion Says Report Took Bite out of Sales." *Dallas Morning News*, December 4, 1992, 1D.

de Lisser, Eleena. "Food Lion Hopes to Prove It's Not a Toothless Tiger: Grocery Chain, Still Licking Its Wounds, Seeks to Regain Momentum." *The Wall Street Journal*, May 6, 1993, B4.

"Disputes Prompt Ketner to Quit Food Lion Board." *Supermarket News*, May 3, 1993, 6.

Files, Jennifer. "Food Lion Earnings Plunge 55.8%." *Dallas Morning News*, April 9, 1993, 1D.

"Food Lion Sues Union, Alleges Abuse of Process." *Dallas Morning News*, February 23, 1993, 4d.

"Food Safety: Food Lion Fallout." *Progressive Grocer*, December 1992, 9–10.

Halkias, Maria. "Feeding Frenzy for Food Chains: Local Grocery Eat Each Other Up." *Dallas Morning News*, May 2, 1993, 1H.

Halkias, Maria. "Food Lion Profits Drop: Dividend Cut." *Dallas Morning News*, February 12, 1993, 1D.

Kunde, Diana. "Food Lion Roars Back at Critics with Ad Blitz: ABC Report to Allege Unsanitary Conditions." *Dallas Morning News*, November 5, 1992, 1D.

Kunde, Diana. "Food Lion Sales Decline 6.2%." *Dallas Morning News*, January 8, 1993, 12D.

Kunde, Diana. "Report Batters Food Lion Stock." *Dallas Morning News*, November 7, 1992, 1F.

Kunde, Diana. "TV Exposé Targets Food Lion: Grocer Says Story Fabricated." *Dallas Morning News*, November 6, 1992, 1D.

Menn, Joseph. "Food Lion CEO Says Stores in Texas Hit Hard by Exposé: Smith Vows to Make Outlets Here Profitable." *Dallas Morning News*, May 7, 1993, 1D.

Miller, Anetta, Smith, Vern, and Mabry, Marcus. "Shooting the Messenger? How Food Lion Handled a Damaging TV Exposé." *Newsweek*, November 23, 1992, 51.

Simnacher, Joe. "Food Lion Puts Halt to New Stores: Current Projects Won't Be Affected." *Dallas Morning News*, December 25, 1992, 1D.

CASE STUDY:
SPEAKING FOR THE DEVIL—SHOULD STUDENTS BE REQUIRED TO ADVOCATE REPUGNANT IDEAS?

John Nelson teaches business communication to juniors at a large state-supported university in the United States. The university attracts students from many different racial and religious groups; 52 percent of the students are women. Last summer, while planning his courses for this year, John wrote the following questions on a piece of paper:

Source: This case study was written by N. L. Reinsch, Jr., Georgetown School of Business, Georgetown University.

1. What can I do to prepare my students to function effectively in a diverse, multicultural, and international workplace?

2. What can I do to help my students learn to really listen to ideas that are different from their own, that is, to really try to understand convictions they do not share?

3. The current emphasis on "politically correct" inoffensiveness may stifle free speech. What can I do to encourage my students to exercise their own rights of free speech and to tolerate the free speech of others?

In an attempt to answer these questions, John identified several acquaintances who seemed particularly skillful at understanding and tolerating (without necessarily agreeing with) diverse viewpoints. He asked each acquaintance how she or he had come to possess this particular ability. One woman's account of her undergraduate experience in intercollegiate debate—an activity that required her to advocate ideas she did not believe—particularly impressed John. A man's account of what he learned while playing the role of a bigot in a student theatrical production also caught John's attention. After a considerable amount of thought John developed a new "Written and Oral Advocacy" assignment as follows:

1. Each student would be required to write a persuasive report arguing that a U.S. company with extensive international operations should be permitted to practice sexual and racial discrimination anywhere such practices are "part of the local culture."

2. Each student would be required to participate in a videotaped "press conference." The student would make a three-minute oral presentation of his or her persuasive report, and then answer questions from other students who would play the role of "reporters."

When John distributed his syllabus at the beginning of the semester, several students expressed concern about the "Written and Oral Advocacy" assignment. When John formally made the assignment almost every student complained. The students told John that he wanted them to defend an immoral and repugnant position. They added that they feared copies of the written reports or of the videotapes falling into the hands of other students or even the student newspaper. John told the students he would consider their comments and respond at the next class meeting.

John's faculty office adjoins yours and you have followed developments closely. Just now you looked up to find John standing at the door to your office. "Do you have time to talk?" he asks. "I really need to talk to someone."

Questions for Consideration

1. Would you recommend that John withdraw the assignment? Why or why not?

2. Is John asking his students to behave unethically by expressing ideas they don't believe? Is John behaving unethically by making such an assignment?

3. Does a teacher who uses assignments like the one described in the case have special responsibilities to the students? If so, what?

4. What special challenges confront a teacher who uses assignments like the one described in the case?

5. Is John correct in assuming that "political correctness" can stifle free speech? Should business communication professionals be concerned about free speech issues?

6. How can a teacher distinguish between topics that would be appropriate for classroom use and topics that would not be appropriate? Would it be appropriate to ask a student to:

   a. Advocate that "new age" witchcraft should be taught in the public elementary schools.

   b. Argue that space aliens regularly visit the earth and "walk among us."

   c. Propose a constitutional amendment requiring daily Christian prayer in all schools.

   d. Deny that the Holocaust occurred.

   e. Defend the use of children in sexually explicit photographs and films.

   f. Argue in favor of affirmative action programs on behalf of gays and lesbians.

   g. Argue that the U.S. government was responsible for the assassination of President John F. Kennedy.

REFERENCES FOR CHAPTER 9

Banks, David. "Issues and Strategies of Continuing Medical Education in the 1990s." *Continuing Medical Education Issues*, vol. 46, 1991, 409–415.

Barton, Laurence. "A Profile of Not-for-Profit Educational Symposia Divisions of Pharmaceutical Companies." Working paper, Department of Management, University of Nevada, Las Vegas, July 1991. The PMA estimates that there are over 750 manufacturers of ethical drugs in the United States.

"Companies Will Withdraw Medical Education Funding under FDA Rules: PMA," *PMA Newsletter*, November 18, 1991, 5–6.

"FDA Panel Seeks Industry Feedback on 'One Only' Limit to Industry-Sponsored Symposia Suggested in Its Draft Paper." *FDC Reports,* November 25, 1991, 9–10.

Halbrooks, John R. "Substance over Style: Do New AMA/PMA Guidelines Mean an End to Pampering at Corporate Medical Meetings?" *Medical Meetings,* July–August 1991, 28–33.

Johnson, Everett A. "Ethical Considerations for Business Relationships of Hospitals and Physicians." *Health Care Management Review*, Summer 1991, 16 (3), 7–13.

Kusserow, Richard P. "Promotion of Prescription Drugs through Payments and Gifts." *Report of Office of the Inspector General,* U.S. Department of Health and Human Services, 1991.

Soumerai, Stephen B., and Avorn, Jerry. "Principles of Educational Outreach to Improve Clinical Decision Making." *Clinical Decision Making,* vol. 263, no. 4, 1991, 549–556.

Epilogue

"The image we get of America is modernist, fast, technological. We're focused on jobs and moving around; we're willing to sacrifice our family ties. But there are a lot of people who are not doing this. They are trying to live with values of their hometown and region, trying to contribute there, not living a fast life. They read, practice certain arts. They give themselves over to values and activities that nurture their soul. That spirit is this country's hope."

Thomas Moore,
author of *Care of the Soul*
and *SoulMates*, in *American Way*,
June 15, 1994, p. 111

Juxtapose Moore's message with headlines of our era: Police officers are arrested for selling dope, ministers are found guilty of abusing the very young people they have pledged to inspire, executives plea bargain after they are arrested for price fixing, and athletes acknowledge that they "fixed" games for a price. The list of ethical abuses in society seems endless and disturbing.

It is true, of course, that the vast majority of Americans are diligent employees and honest individuals. Yet it is also true that we are in the midst of a period unprecedented in history when our expectations for ethical behavior in business have never been higher, precisely because of the sheer number of ethical abuses.

At the core of our collective sense of ethics is the issue of trust. In some cases, societal pillars seem to be crumbling: While it can be argued that we always suspected that a few tycoons of industry were dishonest, certain icons—notably clergy, athletes, and public servants—seemed to be found only occasionally, and then sensationally, jettisoned in the headlines for their misdeeds.

Trust and business ethics are inseparable. Whether we trust a co-worker or job applicant can be determined by their age, words, past successes, gender, and countless other variables. But increasingly, we seek to validate our subconscious assessment of trust with techniques far more verifiable than intuitive judgments. We increasingly rely on drug tests, background checks, and polygraph results to determine the trustworthiness of others.

According to Eugene Webb of Stanford University's Graduate School of Business, we tend to define people as trustworthy (and increase the chance of their selections as business partners) when they meet standards that we employ in so many other social choices, for example, people who have values and interests similar to our own—in short, people we feel *comfortable* with. He's right.

President John F. Kennedy didn't select his brother Robert because his sibling was the most effective litigator in the nation; he was chosen because he could be trusted. While it is conventional to deride nepotism, it's a practice employed by countless small businesses governed by family members who would rather see cash transactions handled by a daughter or son than a stranger. We reinforce the probability of success when we are surrounded by advisors whom we trust to support, not undermine, our agenda.

Trust is especially important in terms of business ethics, yet widespread abuses reported over the past twenty years and chronicled in this book have somehow dampened our sense of trust. When heroes are burned at the public stake (e.g., Pete Rose, Michael Jackson, O.J.

Simpson, John Sculley, Geraldine Ferraro), the questions raised about such individuals seem far meatier than their responses, even when they are valid. With each succeeding case of ethics abuse against a prominent person, it is easier to believe the next round of charges against the next person who has been accused, whether it is a character in the Whitewater affair or a colleague down the hall.

Professor Webb has argued that loyalty is directly related to trust. It is generated by a number of forces, prominent among them the influence of reciprocity norms and learned responsibility. The well-known political admonition "dance with the one that brung ya" nicely captures this idea.

In his book *Hardball*, Chris Matthews labels a chapter with that phrase and attributes it to President Ronald Reagan. "He prided himself on staying with his old crowd through victory as well as defeat. Unabashedly, he appeared at rallies of the most passionate conservative fringe. Speaking to a convention of ideologues in 1985, Reagan said: 'I always see this as an opportunity to dance with the one that brung ya.'" (Matthews, 77). One of Reagan's advisors, George Shultz, once added another dimension: "don't say yes unless you are prepared to work your heart out to get it or think you can deliver it."

That leads one to wonder: In a world in which ethical behavior is desirable but clearly not always achievable, can there ever be such a thing as *too much* loyalty? (Can blind loyalty lead to a myopic, almost zombie-like situation in which a group of coworkers, indeed, entire organizations, are led astray?)

And so we arrive at a fascinating time in the history of U.S. industry. Behind us is the era of the "public be damned" earlier in this century when the great industrialists monopolized and cannibalized until they were forced—often after a Supreme Court edict or threatened regulatory decision—to abandon their mission. We then entered a mid-century phase in which ethics was mostly discussed in seminaries and philosophy courses, shunned by an economy that saw no need for such obscure discussions in an era of prosperity.

As we approach a new century, public activism and intense media scrutiny have reawakened our consciousness as to the ideals of right and wrong. Indeed, now the media is abuzz with talk of virtue, and William Bennett, a hard-nosed conservative who seeks the presidency, dominates the coveted best-seller list with a crafty treatise on ethics. Books about saints and songs by Tibetan monks are best-sellers, and for the first time in a quarter century, there is a nationwide, organized movement to return prayer to schools. We are searching for meaning, for truth, for inspiration. Unfortunately for most people, the very last place we look for these attributes is in our corporations.

Were they alive, the entrepreneurs who built the U.S. railroads, steel factories and other industries would be crawling into basements in raw fear of late-night commentators on television and social activists operating "1-900" telephone lines. Indeed, it would be difficult for the Fords, Carnegies, and Rockefellers to cope with the television newsmagazines that now clamor each weeknight with undercover cameras to capture breaches of the public trust by executives, board members, and salespeople.

If we can learn from the illustrations and case studies in this book and apply those lessons in the development of both honorable as well as profitable careers and businesses, we will have begun a journey where we are at least asking the right questions.

REFERENCES

Infusino, Divina. "The Reluctant Guru." *American Way*, June 15, 1994.

Matthews, Chris. *Hardball.* New York: Summit Books, 1988.

Webb, Eugene. "Trust and Crisis." Paper presented at Third Annual New Avenues In Risk & Crisis Management Conference, August 1994.

The Best of the Best: Ethics Policies from Leading Organizations

Increasingly, corporations are demanding that their employees adhere to strict codes of conduct that cover issues ranging from protecting the confidentiality of corporate information to insider trading, from giving gifts to potential customers to reading the electronic mail of colleagues.

Several forces have driven this environment, including societal expectations of appropriate behavior by corporate managers, embarrassing news stories regarding corruption and fraud in both small and large corporations, and a broad acknowledgment that the employer itself may be susceptible to a lawsuit from employees if its policies are ambiguous, or if no policy is in place.

This appendix offers an unprecedented look inside some of America's leading corporations and institutions. You will read the policies that now govern the behavior and actions of employees at such organizations as AT&T, Union Carbide, Harvard University, and Mobil Corporation. This is believed to be the first time that the policies of such distinguished organizations have been published in one umbrella fashion.

As you can assume, each of the organizations in this chapter has invested considerable time and capital in drafting and completing its individual policies on ethics and business behavior. In the pages that follow, remember you are seeing selected portions of the ethics policies at these organizations, not the entire policy. By selecting the "best of the best" in corporate America, this method of presentation provides you with a composite picture of a model set of systems and procedures on business ethics.

EXHIBIT A - 1   Model Ethics Policies Featured in this Chapter

Organization	What to Look For
Union Carbide	Allows token "trips" to vendors abroad if lawful. The company's insider information statement is simple and effective.
Rockwell International	Clear definitions of what constitutes "proprietary information." Employees leaving the company are debriefed on the value of what they know.
Mobil	CEO cover letter emphasizes that Mobil does not want to "snoop" on its employees. All political contributions must be cleared by general counsel.
AT&T	Clear language explains how to protect company data. Direct discussion explains how to avoid any activity that would benefit competitors.
Columbia Gas System	Articulation of key federal statutes. Excellent discussion of how antitrust laws pertain to employees.
Hewlett-Packard	Agreements not to compete are addressed to avoid price-fixing charges. Employees are told to avoid making negative remarks about competitors.
Teledyne	Clear rules on the ethical marketing of products. Dozens of hypothetical questions and answers provide insight on potential resolutions to ethical problems before they reach the crisis stage. Detailed policies on gifts, gratuities, and insider trading are stated.
NYNEX	Relationships with customers and suppliers are addressed. Notice that NYNEX emphasizes what gifts can be accepted as opposed to what cannot be accepted. Outside employment is generally prohibited. Ex-employers may not peddle to the company.
Harvard University	A leading not-for-profit allows reasonable outside employment but limits it to 10 percent of one's professional effort.
Mercedes-Benz	Mission statement emphasizes efficient, cost effective management and continuous improvement.
Jacksonville Shipyards	A sweeping sexual harassment policy that includes discussion of retaliation and how complaints are to be adjudicated.

UNION CARBIDE CORPORATION

Business Integrity and Ethics

Governing Principle

The fundamental principle governing Corporate actions and the actions of officers and other employees is that ethics and business are inseparable at Union Carbide. No business objective can be achieved without following the highest ethical standards and complying with all the local and national laws and regulations that pertain to our operations.

Conflict of Interest

No officer or other employee of the Corporation may have a personal, financial, or family interest that could in any way keep the individual from acting in the best interest of the Corporation. Any actual or potential conflict of interest must be reported to Corporate management as soon as recognized.

Business Relationships

Use of the funds or assets of the Corporation for any unlawful purpose or to influence others through bribes is strictly prohibited, i.e., there will be no reward, gift, or favor bestowed or promised with a view to perverting the judgment or corrupting the conduct of a person in a position of trust.

- Offering or accepting properly recorded business meals, entertainment, or token gifts intended and understood as simple courtesies meant to foster understanding and communication with suppliers, customers, and public officials is allowed, unless unlawful.

- Token tips or minor payments to government, institutional, vendor, or customer service personnel that simply facilitate service, are traditional in the country or locality, are nominal in amount, do not involve a perversion of judgment or corruption of conduct, and are properly recorded are acceptable, unless unlawful. Minor payments meet this test only if, through the generation of goodwill, and not by any other means, they encourage timely performance of an act, which the recipient already has a duty to perform because of some legal requirement or job responsibility.

Memberships

Memberships should serve legitimate business needs. They are appropriate only in organizations whose objectives and activities are lawful and ethical, and fit within the framework of broadly accepted social values.

Financial Integrity

No unrecorded fund will be established for any purpose. All assets of the Corporation will be recorded on the books of the Corporation at all times unless specifically exempted by Corporate procedures, which are consistent with generally accepted accounting principles.

- No false entry or entry that obscures the purposes of the underlying transaction will be made in the books and records of the Corporation for any reason.

- No payment on behalf of the Corporation will be authorized or made with the intention or understanding that any part of such payment is for a purpose other than that described by the documents supporting the payment.

Insider Information

Confidential information that may be considered material and important by investors and others will be disclosed to the public only by an authorized representative of the Corporation. Until such disclosure, material information, often referred to as "insider information," will be held in strict confidence within the Corporation.

Directors, officers and other employees will not (i) disclose any insider information to any outside person or group until the information has been released to the public, (ii) disclose insider information to other employees except on a strict need-to-know basis, and (iii) take any economic or personal advantage of any insider information, such as by buying or selling stock or other securities of the Corporation or of any other company to which the insider information may pertain.

Reporting Irregularities

Any departure or suspected departure from this policy must be reported to the Corporate Director of Internal Audits.

Legal Affairs Compliance

The Corporation will comply with all laws and regulations that apply to its business. Business and functional units will seek to ensure that employees are familiar with the laws covering their responsibilities, that employees comply with the law, and that any lapse is reported promptly to the management level with authority to restore compliance.

Protection of Rights

The Corporation will take all appropriate action to protect its legal rights and will not surrender, waive, or transfer those rights unless it deems such action to be in the Corporation's best interest. Business units will endeavor to see that managers understand their role in protecting the Corporation's legal rights, and that anything that places the Corporation's legal rights in jeopardy is reported promptly to the management level with authority to implement safeguards.

Dispute Resolution

The Corporation will make every reasonable effort to settle disputes without litigation. No lawsuit may be filed without approval of the General Counsel of the Corporation. Corporate or business general counsel must be notified immediately of any lawsuit or government or administrative enforcement action taken or threatened against the Corporation.

Affiliates and Affiliate Relationships

Affiliate companies are separate legal entities with their own boards of directors, which are accountable for the management of the affiliates. Relations with affiliates should preserve their separate identities and recognize the rights and interests of local shareholders and host governments.

Investment Management

To protect and enhance its investments in affiliate companies, the Corporation will exert its lawful influence and authority as a shareholder to require, among other things, that affiliates:

- Operate effectively in pursuit of the purposes and objectives for which they were formed.

- Avoid commitments or activities that might jeopardize the Corporation's investment or inadvertently create liability for the Corporation.

- Design their facilities and conduct their operations to meet or exceed the Corporation's standards for the protection of health, safety, and the environment.

- Comply with the law and maintain high standards of business integrity and ethics.

ROCKWELL INTERNATIONAL

Policy Regarding Safeguarding Company Sensitive Information

I. Policy

Company Sensitive Information is a valuable asset of the Corporation and will be protected and used only to promote Corporation interests. The courts have generally provided protection for Company Sensitive Information, such as formulas, patterns, devices, or compilations of scientific, technical or commercial information (including computer programs and databases), provided the owner has taken reasonable precautions to maintain it as confidential and such information gives the owner a competitive advantage over others who do not know it.

II. Definitions

Company Sensitive Information means both Proprietary Information and Company Official Information.

Proprietary Information means information applicable to research, development, and production technology which is generated by, or on behalf of, the Corporation and which is useful to the Corporation and would adversely affect the Corporation's interest if not properly protected. It may or may not be in documentary form and includes computer software programs, program descriptions and supporting materials and databases. For purposes of this Policy, it does not include information the Corporation has under limited rights granted by a third party, or information developed in the performance of a Government contract to which the Government has been granted unlimited rights.

Company Official Information means information applicable to the business, personnel, financial and legal affairs of the Corporation which is generated by, or on behalf of, the Corporation and which is, by reason of its sensitivity, to have limited dissemination.

III. General

The identification, availability and dissemination of Company Sensitive Information shall be governed by the following principles:

    A. Proprietary Information shall be prominently marked with the legend "Rockwell International Proprietary Information." Company Official Information shall be prominently marked with the legend "Company Official (Not to be disclosed to unauthorized persons)." Exceptions to these requirements are specified in paragraph C., below.

B. The employee who originates Company Sensitive Information and the employee's supervisor are responsible for ensuring that such information is properly marked upon its origination and is safeguarded in accordance with this Policy.

C. Company Sensitive Information otherwise requiring markings in accordance with this Policy need not be so marked when the cognizant Corporate Officer (or a direct report to whom such authority has been expressly delegated) determines that it is not practicable or necessary to mark it, that it is for internal use only, and that all the following precautions are in effect and are reasonable to protect unmarked Company Sensitive Information:

1. access thereto is restricted to a limited number of employees having a "need to know" in order to carry out their duties;

2. those employees allowed access thereto are made aware of its sensitive nature; and

3. procedures have been established to prevent the release thereof outside the Corporation unless it is appropriately marked before release.

D. The release, either written or oral, of Company Sensitive Information to persons, firms or organizations outside the Corporation is authorized only:

1. if it is appropriately marked and a confidentiality agreement has been entered into between the recipient and the Corporation;

2. if required by a final order, no longer subject of stay or appeal, of a court of law of competent jurisdiction;

3. if furnished in connection with United States Government procurement and it is marked with appropriate legend authorized by the procurement regulations of the agency involved;

4. if furnished to the United States Government as material exempt from disclosure under the Freedom of Information Act in accordance with Policy B-02 and it is marked in accordance with that Policy; or

5. upon approval of the cognizant Corporate Officer (or a direct report to whom such authority has been expressly delegated).

E. Company Sensitive Information shall always be kept from "open view" by unauthorized persons and shall be handled, transmitted and stored in a manner consistent with its importance.

F. Employees having access to Company Sensitive Information who are terminating or transferring shall be interviewed as to their responsibilities with respect to Company Sensitive Information. Interview guidelines or procedures shall be established in business units, with the advice and assistance of the Office of the General Counsel.

   The terminating or transferring employee shall be alerted to the legal consequences of (1) using or disclosing Company Sensitive Information for any purpose not expressly authorized by the Company, with the advice and assistance of the Office of the General Counsel, and (2) retaining or using any correspondence, notes, depictions, models, data, experimental results or any other manifestation of Company Sensitive Information.

G. The supervisor of a terminating or transferring employee having access to Company Sensitive Information shall require the employee to deliver promptly to the supervisor all materials, including documents and software which may contain Company Sensitive Information, and to acknowledge in writing that all such materials so required to be delivered have been delivered.

IV. Unauthorized Release

Any employee having knowledge of any unauthorized disclosure or removal of Company Sensitive Information will promptly inform his or her immediate supervisor and the Office of the General Counsel.

V. Responsibility

Business Unit Presidents and Senior Corporate Staff Executives are responsible for implementation of and compliance with this Policy. The Office of the General Counsel shall provide advice and assistance.

MOBIL CORPORATION

Conflict of Interest Policy

(Introductory Letter)

<u>To All Mobil Employees:</u>

One of Mobil's most valued assets over the years has been our reputation for ethical and lawful conduct in all that we do. Each employee has an important personal stake in assuring that the Company's reputation and commitment to the highest standards of ethical values and business conduct continue as our highest priority. The Company's continued business success depends on it, and so does our sense of pride in saying we work at Mobil.

In this connection, we have a practice at Mobil of periodically circulating copies of our Conflicts of Interest Policy to be sure each employee is familiar with its requirements. The Policy's main purpose is to protect the interests of the Company and its stockholders without unreasonably inquiring into the outside activities of its employees.

A very important feature of the Policy is the provision that employees shall not misuse information or documents to which they have access through the Company, or engage in the unauthorized disclosure to third parties of confidential Company information. Another important provision prohibits employees from accepting gifts, trips, entertainment or other favors of more than nominal value from companies or people with whom Mobil does business.

Please read the attached Conflicts of Interest Statement of Policy very carefully, and if you have an actual or potential conflict of interest or any question with respect to the Policy, contact your supervisor immediately. I am requesting that you sign the related certification that reconfirms you are familiar with its provisions, are acting and will continue to act in compliance with the policy and understand the consequences of any failure to comply.

I am confident we can rely on your continued cooperation to assure compliance with the Policy and protection of the Company's interests.

—Allen E. Murray,
Chairman of the Board
President and Chief Executive Officer

Mobil Corporation
Policy on Political Contributions and Activities

Management believes that all employees should periodically be made aware of Mobil's policy on political contributions and activities. The policy applies both to the corporation and to individual employees.

At the federal level, corporations are prohibited by law from making contributions to either candidates for political office or to political parties. Mobil resources, finances, and facilities may not be used to support federal political candidates or parties.

At the state level and overseas, laws very widely. In some instances, corporations are allowed to contribute to political candidates and to financially support or oppose positions put forth on public issues in referenda, constitutional amendments, or other means. However, even where allowed, a contribution can be made only after the Office of General Counsel determines it is legal and the Mobil Corporation Executive Committee or Political Oversight Committee approves it. Under no circumstances will a contribution be approved if the purpose of the contribution is to purchase favorable treatment for a particular Mobil operation.

No employee may propose that Mobil make a political contribution or authorize use of company resources or facilities for political purposes without a prior determination that such a contribution or use is lawful, and no such proposal may be acted on without express approval of the Mobil Corporation Executive Committee or Political Oversight Committee.

Employees, of course, are free to make personal contributions to candidates of their choice. Employees may also contribute through the Mobil Oil Corporation Political Action Committee (Mobil PAC), which supports candidates who are proponents of the free enterprise system. Mobil cannot contribute to the Mobil PAC, though Mobil may pay costs associated with administering it.

As a good corporate citizen, Mobil encourages employees to take part in the political process at all levels. The decision to do so, of course, is strictly a personal one, as is the amount of time or money an employee elects to contribute to a political candidate or party. Mobil may not reimburse, or otherwise compensate employees for any personal expenditures in this regard.

AT&T

Policy on the Privacy of Communications

Over the years, privacy of communications has been basic to AT&T's business, not only because it is required by law, but because the public has placed its trust in the integrity of AT&T's people and its service. AT&T customers expect, for example, that their conversations will be kept private.

In recent years, with the ever-increasing volume of data transmission over the network, that trust has taken on a special significance. Today it is the responsibility of every AT&T employee to protect not only the privacy of conversations on the network, but also the flow of information in data form that in the wrong hands could have serious economic or legal consequences for the parties involved.

The basic rules for privacy have not changed. Violating any one of them could tarnish a reputation AT&T has earned over many years. The basic rules are:

- Don't tamper with or intrude upon any transmission, whether by voice, non-voice or data.

- Don't listen to or repeat anyone else's conversation or communication, or permit them to be monitored or recorded except as required in the proper management of the business.

- Don't allow an unauthorized person to have access to any communication transmitted over AT&T facilities. This includes divulging information about who was speaking or what was spoken about, except as authorized by the customer or required in the proper management of the business.

- Don't install or permit installation of any device that will enable someone to listen to, observe, or realize that a communication has occurred, except as authorized by an official service or installation order issued in accordance with Company practices.

- Don't use information from any communication, or even the fact that a communication has occurred, for your personal benefit or for the benefit of others.

- Don't disclose information about customer billing arrangements, or the location of equipment, circuits, trunks, and cables to any unauthorized person.

Contact the AT&T Corporate Security Organization if you believe that the privacy of any communication has been compromised, or if you receive a subpoena, court order, or any other type of request for information from anyone (including law enforcement and other government agencies) concerning any AT&T service.

Making personal calls or establishing connections for non-official business from switchboards, test positions or equivalent work stations is prohibited. In addition, employees may not make personal or non-official calls except from telephones for which an accounting record is created and then only when authorized by supervision. Third number charges to official numbers are prohibited. Credit card calls must be properly charged to the number under which the credit card is issued.

Establishing unauthorized voice or data communications services is prohibited. Establishing a circuit connection or using other means to enable anyone to get free service is prohibited by Company instructions and is a criminal offense under state and federal statutes.

The use of any device or technique that manipulates or avoids billing arrangements to defraud the Company is prohibited, and is a criminal offense in most states.

The fundamental rule is that employees in their business dealings must never be influenced—or even appear to be influenced—by personal interests.

Employees are expected, both on and off the job, to support the Company's efforts to succeed in the worldwide marketplace.

Employees are not permitted to compete with the Company; they may not assist others to compete with the Company, and they may not use their position with the Company, its proprietary information or its relationship with customers for personal gain or benefit.

AT&T's policy concerning suppliers is to award business solely on merit, at the lowest reasonable price, and, wherever practicable, on a competitive basis.

Basic points to keep in mind are:

- Have no relationship, financial or otherwise, with any supplier or competitor that might be construed as a conflict of interest, or that might even appear to impair your judgment on behalf of the Company.

- Never accept or solicit, even indirectly, gifts, loans, "kick-backs," special privileges, services, benefits or unusual hospitality. This does not apply to unsolicited promotional materials of nominal monetary value of a general advertising nature, such as imprinted pencils, memo pads and calendars. Determining when hospitality is "unusual" is a matter of degree.

- Acceptance of a meal or entertainment in the normal course of business relations is permitted as a matter of courtesy and should be, when practical, on a reciprocal basis. Generally, any extensive hospitality beyond this would be considered unusual. Exceptions to this rule may be appropriate for special events, such as sporting events, or trade shows, where Company business may be conducted. You should report invitations to any such events to your supervisor for concurrence in your acceptance of the invitation.

- Report gifts other than promotional materials of nominal value promptly to your supervisor and then return them to the donor, if possible, or dispose of them in another appropriate manner.

- Do not give inappropriate gifts or provide unusual hospitality to customers or potential customers or their employees that will unfairly influence their purchasing decision. For example, do not give expensive gifts that could be construed as a bribe or a reward for purchasing from AT&T.

- Comply with local, state and federal laws and regulations governing relations between government customers and suppliers. These laws and regulations may prohibit or modify marketing activities used with other customers. Special care must also be exercised with customers that are heavily regulated by the government, e.g., banks, because they may be subject to similar restraints.

- Do not in any way assist competitors. Specifically, do not assist anyone outside the business in the planning, design, manufacture, sale, purchase, installation, or maintenance of any competitors' equipment or services. Do not become involved in activities or businesses that compete with AT&T activities or business. This policy, of course, does not apply to AT&T's partners in joint ventures, or to our competitors when performed under approved Company programs.

- Avoid any outside activity that could adversely affect the independence and objectivity of your judgment, interfere with the timely and effective performance of your duties and responsibilities, or that could discredit the Company or conflict, or appear to conflict, with the Company's best interests. Since each employee's primary obligation is to the Company, any outside activity, such as a second job or self-employment, must be kept totally separate from employment with the Company.

- Unless expressly authorized by the Company—for example, Junior Achievement—no outside activity should involve the use of Company time, its name or its influence, assets, funds, materials, facilities, or the services of other employees.

- Don't undertake any activity that is aimed at, or that could reasonably have the effect of, retarding the success of the Company in the marketplace. Avoid any actions inconsistent with this commitment to help the Company succeed, such as suggesting that customers or potential customers refrain from dealing with the Company, or deal with a competitor instead of with the Company.

- If an actual—or even a potential—conflict of interest develops, it must be reported promptly to supervision. The Law Department and the AT&T Corporate Security Organization may also be consulted.

COLUMBIA GAS SYSTEM

Policy on Federal Antitrust Laws

Introduction

The principal federal antitrust laws are the Sherman Act, the Clayton Act, the Robinson-Patman Amendment and the Federal Trade Commission Act. Their purpose is to maintain the fundamental business conditions necessary for the proper functioning of a free enterprise system by prohibiting unreasonable restraints on competition and discriminatory business practices having an anticompetitive effect.

The applicability of these laws in certain situations is clear and unmistakable; in other situations their applicability may be uncertain, and may at times be contrary to a company's natural competitive instincts. Thus, the usual reaction of an honest businessman as to whether a course of action is "ethical," or "morally right," or "sound business" is not an adequate guideline for the businessman in the antitrust field. In every case, however, businessmen must observe these laws in the day to day conduct of their affairs. Ignorance of the law or lack of legal training is no defense and in the case of a large company, would not even be considered in mitigation.

Violations of the antitrust laws can have serious consequences both to the company itself and to employees. The punishment can be severe:

1. Violations of the Sherman Act are felonies punishable by fines up to $1 million for each offense in the case of a corporation and, in the case of an individual, fines up to $100,000 and a maximum jail sentence of three years for each offense.

2. Any person injured by a violation of certain of these laws may recover triple the amount of his actual damage plus the cost of bringing suit. Further, under the "Hart-Scott-Rodino Antitrust Improvements Act of 1976," State Attorneys General may bring action for triple damages for violation of the Sherman Act on behalf of all residents of the state.

3. Violations of various provisions may result in dismemberment of the company, seizure of its goods and a wide variety of decrees or orders regulating the future conduct of offending companies and individuals thus placing the company at a severe competitive disadvantage.

4. There are also heavy indirect penalties. Antitrust litigation is notoriously long and costly, requiring large investments in time and money. To the sum of these costs must be added the indirect costs

in reputation and good will (particularly important to a public utility) that may result from a well-publicized violation.

5. Possible damage to reputation alone compels the prudent businessman to consider the applicability of the antitrust laws to every phase of his operations.

It is not possible in this manual to give a complete catalogue of all forbidden acts nor is it possible to detail all of the intricacies involved in the interpretation and enforcement of antitrust laws. The purpose of this manual is merely to furnish a general guide to compliance with those provisions of the antitrust laws which are of basic day to day concern to Company personnel. Advice of counsel must be sought in any case where there is doubt as to the applicability of these laws.

The Antitrust Statutes

1. The Sherman Act

The Sherman Act, passed in 1890, was the first and most basic of the antitrust laws. It is enforced by the Antitrust Division of the Department of Justice through criminal or civil actions or both. The Act also provides for the bringing of civil suits for treble damages by private litigants.

Section 1. Section 1 of the Act prohibits "contracts," "combinations" or "conspiracies" in restraint of trade or commerce. This section prohibits joint and collective action or conduct by two or more persons by agreements or understandings of any kind which unreasonably restrain competition. The section prohibits any arrangement or understanding with a supplier, competitor, reseller or customer, or even in certain situations with affiliated companies, which restricts the freedom of either party or a third party to make and carry out its own business decisions. In the case of many such agreements—such as an agreement to control prices—there is no room to argue that the agreement does not restrain trade unreasonably, or to try to justify the restraint; it is illegal per se.

The agreement prohibited is not limited to a formal agreement. It includes any kind of mutual understanding, whether written or oral, formal or informal, which gives any party to the agreement or understanding a basis for the expectation that a business practice or decision adopted by one will be adopted or concurred in by another.

The following are merely some of the business practices which have been held to violate this section of the Act:

- *Agreements not to compete*

- *Agreements to allocate customers, markets or territories*

- *Arrangements to control price, terms or conditions of sale*
- *Agreements to boycott*
- *Agreements to control production*

Section 2. Section 2 of the Sherman Act prohibits monopolization "of any part of trade or commerce." Its main purpose is to prevent a single company from acquiring or holding sufficient power to control prices or to foreclose access to the market. This section further prohibits any "attempt" to monopolize by a single person, or any "conspiracy" with others to monopolize.

2. The Clayton Act

The Clayton Act was passed in 1914. Unlike the Sherman Act, which focuses principally on joint action, the Clayton Act primarily prohibits certain practices which when committed by a company acting alone adversely affect free competition, though in certain instances it applies to collusive conduct. In essence, the Act seeks to prevent the use of a company's market power as a lever to further domination of that market or domination of a different market. The relevant sections of this Act are:

Section 3. Section 3 is directed at two types of agreements:

Requirements Contracts. These are contracts by which a seller with a dominant market position requires a buyer to purchase from him all of the buyer's requirements of a particular product (or under certain circumstances less than all of his requirements), where the effect of such contract is to foreclose competitors from a substantial share of the product line.

Example: A major oil company, having a substantial percentage of the gasoline market in a designated area entering into exclusive dealing contracts with a large number of the retail stations in such area.

Tying Contracts. These are contracts by which a seller conditions the sale of one of its products (the tying product) to a buyer on the buyer's willingness to purchase another product (the tied product) where the seller has sufficient economic power with respect to the tying product to restrain free competition in the market for the tied product. This economic power may result from the fact that (i) there is only one or a small number of sellers of a particular product, (ii) the product is in short supply, or (iii) the seller has a patent on the product.

Example: A manufacturer of business machines (the tying product) who has a large share of the business machine market requiring its customers to purchase its business machine cards (the tied product) as a condition of supplying business machines.

Section 7. This section of the Clayton Act prohibits acquisitions or mergers, the effect of which may be substantially to lessen competition or tend to create a monopoly. It is not limited to acquisition of an entire company. It can apply to the acquisition of a product line or a joint venture. Any proposed acquisition or merger should be appraised, with antitrust implications of this section in mind.

3.   The Robinson-Patman Act

This Act was passed in 1936 as an amendment to Section 2 of the Clayton Act. It prohibits discrimination in price or services by a seller in connection with a sale of goods and merchandise in interstate commerce where such discrimination has anticompetitive effects. The relevant sections of this Act are:

Section 2(a). This section prohibits discriminatory pricing, i.e., the charging of different prices to different customers, the effect of which may be substantially to lessen competition or to injure, destroy or prevent competition among either competing sellers or competing buyers or their customers. This prohibition is subject to two major exceptions:

(i)   where the difference in price is justified by differences in cost of manufacture, sale or delivery (e.g., some quantity discounts) and

(ii) where a price is lowered in good faith to meet an equally low price of a competitor

Section 2(d) and Section 2(e). These sections prohibit the seller's payment for, or the furnishing of "services or facilities" (primarily concerned with advertising and promotion) to any of its customers unless such payments or services are "available" on "proportionately equal terms" to the customers' competitors.

Section 2(f). This section applies to buyers and prohibits the knowing receipt of illegal price discrimination.

Section 3. This section prohibits (i) price discrimination among customers or between geographic areas and (ii) sales at unreasonably low prices for the purpose of destroying competition or eliminating a competitor. Violations of this section are punishable by fine and/or imprisonment.

4. The Federal Trade Commission Act

The Federal Trade Commission Act was passed in 1914 and is enforced solely by the Federal Trade Commission through administrative proceedings designed to secure a "cease and desist order" (injunction) against the prohibited acts. However, Commission action may be initiated by complaints of private persons.

Section 5 (the main operative section) contains sweeping prohibitions against all "unfair methods of competition" and all "unfair or deceptive acts or practices." This section has been construed by the courts to encompass many of the practices unlawful under the Sherman Act and the Clayton Act and goes further to prohibit all forms of "unfair" business conduct. It is not possible to describe in detail the many business practices held to violate this section. However, the following list is indicative of the types of business practices prohibited:

Misrepresentation and false advertising with respect to a product including its origin, composition, quality or exclusiveness of features.

Misrepresentation and false advertising with respect to a competitor's business methods or product which may result in a disparagement of a competitor or its product.

Improper influence of customers including giving or offering to give a customer's employee, without the employer's knowledge, any gift as an inducement to purchase the seller's product or to influence the purchaser not to deal with a seller's competitor.

The Antitrust Laws and Columbia

Court decisions have indicated that a public utility subject to federal and state regulation is not exempt from the antitrust laws even with respect to certain regulated "public utility" activities. There are at least five broad areas of business activity in which the antitrust laws may be of importance to Columbia and may affect the conduct of its operations.

1. Regulated Activities

The antitrust laws affect Columbia and must be given due consideration even with respect to business activities directly regulated by the Federal Energy Regulatory Commission (FERC) or state public service commissions, including setting of rates and the allocation of territories or markets. It must not be presumed that regulation yields an exemption or immunity from the antitrust laws. For instance, the United States Supreme Court has found the following to be violations of the antitrust laws:

(a) a merger which had been approved by the FERC, and

(b) an electric company's light bulb exchange program which was included in a tariff approved by the state's public utility commission.

2. Non-Regulated Activity

Any business activity which is not regulated is clearly subject to the antitrust laws. There are many instances of business activity which, while connected with Columbia's public utility function, fall outside the scope of either federal or state utility regulation.

For instance:

- The involvement of distribution subsidiaries in gas appliance promotions and general motion efforts including customer solicitation, advertising and public relations.

- The involvement of distribution subsidiaries in gas conservation activities.

- The role of Columbia as a substantial purchaser of materials and supplies.

- Licensing of patents developed in connection with research efforts such as those to improve natural gas discovery, transmission or utility service or to improve pipeline safety.

- Furthermore, there are activities which are only partially regulated. For instance, the import and subsequent transmission of LNG are regulated but all aspects of the purchase of the LNG are not. If some aspects of a transaction are not subject to regulation, conduct with respect thereto must comply with the antitrust laws.

3. Trade Association Activity

Trade association participation is particularly vulnerable to violations of the antitrust laws. By definition it involves activities of mutual concern to members (many of whom are competitors or potential competitors).

If trade association members pursue parallel courses of conduct, the possibility of inferences of unlawful concerted activity is great. Any agreement, understanding or association policy which might deter competition is to be avoided. For instance, the endorsement of products by an association cannot be limited to members, for such could give members an unfair competitive advantage.

4. Activity of Subsidiary Companies

The fact that our subsidiary companies are part of a single holding company system does not of itself confer immunity from otherwise unlawful concerted action by these companies. Serious antitrust problems would be raised if two or more Columbia companies should agree to some form of concerted action.

5. Activity of Competitors

It is not only Columbia's activities which should be scrutinized from an antitrust viewpoint, Columbia personnel should also be alert to activities of competitors which may involve violations of the antitrust laws detrimental to Columbia.

The Antitrust Laws and You

The purpose of this manual is to establish a framework within which all Columbia personnel should consider their day to day business conduct as it may involve the prohibitions contained in the antitrust laws. In order to ensure that no employee shall at any time commit an act in contravention of these laws, all Columbia personnel must constantly evaluate their activities from an antitrust viewpoint.

While it is not practical to set forth in detail a list of "do's and don'ts," there are certain precautions which must be taken by all Columbia personnel to avoid any possibility of a violation of the antitrust laws.

   A. If an action might restrain competition, constitute an unfair or deceptive business practice, or otherwise raise a question concerning the antitrust laws, counsel should be advised, even when the action is subject to the approval of a regulatory agency.

   B. All intracompany and intragroup communications should be reviewed with an eye to the business practices prohibited by the antitrust laws and in particular should avoid any inference of a collusive understanding between affiliated companies and competitors. All written material should be scrutinized carefully in the light of the possibility that it may be required to be produced for inspection by antitrust enforcement personnel.

   C. Intracompany and intragroup meetings should at all times be conducted in a manner consistent with the requirements of the antitrust laws. To ensure that no violations are committed at such meetings, their agenda should be reviewed with counsel prior to the meeting and the minutes or other written records of such meetings should be similarly reviewed by counsel subsequent to the meeting.

   D. All documents involved in any aspect of Columbia's operations, particularly those involved in the financing, leasing, advertising and promotion of any program designed to expand Columbia's share of the market for natural gas or any other product, should be carefully reviewed to avoid any possibility of antitrust violations.

E.   All communications with customers, potential customers, competitors or potential competitors, whether written or oral, should be considered from the standpoint of avoiding antitrust violations.

F.   With respect to trade associations and other formal or informal industry gatherings, it is difficult to pinpoint all of the danger areas. However, participation in trade association activities should be constantly reviewed to avoid any inference of unlawful concerted action. As in the case of company and group meetings, the agenda for trade association meetings should be reviewed with counsel prior to the meeting.

In the event that any issue is raised at any meeting which you feel may have antitrust overtones (for example, discussions with respect to pricing, market allocations, or purchasing policies) it is important that this issue be reviewed with counsel immediately. It may, in fact, at times be necessary for the individual involved to leave a meeting where an issue under discussion is manifestly improper. Similar precautions should be exercised with respect to other formal or informal industry gatherings. If it is necessary for an individual to leave a meeting, he should request that his departure be noted in the minutes of the meeting.

HEWLETT-PACKARD COMPANY

Policy on Conduct Involving Competitors

Competitor Relations

General. The greatest exposure to serious trade regulation violations stems from contacts with competitors. An agreement or understanding with a competitor concerning prices, terms of sale, production volume, or allocation of product markets is illegal. HP will not enter into any such agreement or understanding, whether formal or informal, oral or written, express or implied. It makes no difference that the agreement may seem to have a reasonable business purpose such as preventing overproduction.

Price Fixing between Competitors. Any agreement or understanding with a competitor regarding prices is illegal. This includes any agreement or understanding that affects prices or any other conditions of sale (such as credit, discounts or trade-in allowances). Thus, HP will not seek to establish maximum or minimum prices, to stabilize prices or to exchange future price information.

Agreements Not to Compete. Allocations of customers, territories or product markets among competitors are illegal. It is also illegal for competitors to agree to limit or suppress the quality of goods by restricting the development or production of new products.

Boycotts. Any agreement or understanding with a competitor not to deal with a particular customer or supplier is illegal.

Contacts with Competitors. In all contacts with competitors, HP personnel should avoid discussing such matters as price or other terms of sale, costs, inventories, product plans, market surveys or any other confidential or proprietary information. Customers purchasing and reselling HP products in competition with HP are also competitors; therefore, contacts with these customers should be limited to those matters relating to purchases from HP.

Trade Associations. Trade associations and professional committees can perform useful and legitimate functions in facilitating the exchange of information on such industry matters as technological developments or government regulations. However, there is always the risk that the member companies will be charged with having used the association to reach unlawful agreements. If a competitor begins to discuss prices, terms of sale, markets or other prohibited topics, the HP representative must refuse to participate; if such discussion is not stopped, the HP representative must leave the meeting immediately.

Obtaining Competitive Information

Methods. HP must be well informed of competitive developments and is entitled to review all pertinent public information concerning competitive products (e.g., published specifications and prices and trade journal articles). However, HP may not attempt through improper means to acquire a competitor's trade secrets or other proprietary or confidential information, including information as to facilities, manufacturing capacity, technical developments or customers. Improper means include industrial espionage, inducing a competitor's present or former personnel to disclose confidential information, and any other means that are not open and aboveboard. HP must not use consultants to acquire information by improper methods.

Confidential Material. HP employees should not receive or examine any information about competitive proposals or products submitted on a closed bid basis or under other circumstances indicating the information should be kept confidential.

HP employees must be especially alert to the risk of receiving confidential information from customers who are competitors with other HP product lines. Confidential disclosure agreements with competitors may not be signed without first consulting with HP's Legal Department.

Commenting about Competitors

General Rule. It is HP's policy to emphasize the quality of its products and to abstain from making disparaging comments or casting doubt on competitors or their products. If statements (oral or written) are made concerning a competitor or its products, they must be fair, factual and complete.

Advertising. All HP advertising must comply with HP's Advertising and Sales Promotion Policies and Guidelines. Any comparisons with competitive products must be substantiated with current factual data before the comparison is published. In certain countries outside the U.S., comparative advertising may be unlawful.

Specific Practices. HP employees should comply with the following rules when communicating about a competitor or its products:

1. Do not comment about a competitor's character or business practices. For example, do not tell a customer a competitor's sales representative is immoral or untrustworthy.

2. Sell on the basis of HP's capabilities, know-how and benefits to the customer and not on the basis of a competitor's deficiencies.

3. Avoid references to a competitor's troubles or weak points. For example, do not mention financial difficulties, pending lawsuits or government investigations involving the competitor.

4. Do not make any statement about the specifications, quality, utility or value of a competitor's product unless the statement is based on the competitor's current published information or other factual data. Even statements based on factual data must be complete. In some countries, such statements also must relate the positive aspects of the competitive product.

5. Do not make unsubstantiated claims that HP originated a product or one of its features.

TELEDYNE CORPORATION

Teledyne Corporation Policy on Proper Marketing Practices

The Rule

Teledyne employees may use only methods consistent with the standards set forth in this Code to market Teledyne products and services.

Why Does Teledyne Have This Rule?

Ethical marketing practices emphasize the merits of Teledyne's products and services and help our customers make informed purchasing decisions. Teledyne's ability to make additional sales and develop new markets depends on maintaining a reputation of fairness and honesty.

Marketing practices must not induce employees or representatives of our customers to place their personal interest above those of the organizations they represent. Marketing activities that could cause embarrassment to Teledyne, its employees or its customers are also prohibited regardless of the justification for such activity. To this end, Teledyne employees may use only methods consistent with the standards set forth in this Code to maintain markets for Teledyne products and services and to secure additional business.

How Does This Rule Work?

The fundamentals of ethical marketing are:

- Realistic Proposals: Our proposals must be realistic with regard to performance, cost and schedule.

- Personal Interests: Marketing practices must not induce employees or representatives of our customers to place their personal interests above those of the organizations they represent.

- Disparagement: Teledyne products and services should be sold on their merits and not by disparaging the products and services of competitors. Comparisons can be made with competitors' products, but such comparisons must be supported by fact.

- Contingent Fees on Government Contracts: In most cases, an arrangement to pay a third party (other than a bona fide agent) any commission, percentage, brokerage or other fee contingent upon the success of that party securing a U.S. government contract is prohibited. A bona fide agent is an established commercial or selling agency that neither exerts or proposes to exert improper influence to solicit or obtain a government contract. You must seek direction from the Corporate Legal Department before you enter any agreement which provides for the payment of a fee contingent upon the award of a government prime contract or subcontract.

- Access to Government Information: In order to prevent bidders and offerors from obtaining an unfair competitive advantage, certain agencies of the U.S. government have established various limits on the release of government-held information to potential contractors. Teledyne employees involved in contracting with the U.S. government must understand and adhere to any such regulations. Further guidance can be found in the Teledyne Government Contracting Guidelines.

Questions to Ask Yourself

- In business dealings with our customers, am I treating them in the same manner that I would like them to treat me? You should be.

- Do I have objective data to support my claims about a competitor's product? You should have.

- Can we really do what we say we can do? If you can't, reevaluate your proposal.

Common Questions and Answers

Q: A competitor has been making false and misleading statements about Teledyne products. How should I respond?

A: You should correct the misinformation by emphasizing the positive features and competitive advantages of the Teledyne products. If you need to discuss the deficiencies of the competitor's product, you must make sure such deficiencies are factually supported.

Q: I'm an engineer in charge of putting together part of a contract proposal. Our marketing people say the engineers are being too conservative and are including contingencies which will never occur. We think the marketing people are promising that we can do whatever the customer wants, no matter what the technical difficulties. What's the correct approach?

A: You raise a difficult issue. Competitive advantage is often gained by successfully pushing to the very limit of technical and scheduling capabilities. The ability of the Company to succeed over the long-term depends on developing a reputation for quality and reliability. Therefore, it is critical that proposals ultimately be achievable. Engineering must contribute realistic estimates and marketing must make realistic proposals. Occasionally, it is simply not possible to meet the conditions imposed by the customer. If this happens, a bid should not be submitted, or if submitted it must contain proposals which are realistic. Teamwork, communication, and trust are essential.

Teledyne Corporation Policy on Entertainment, Gifts and Gratuities

The Rule

No Teledyne employee shall accept or offer entertainment, gifts or gratuities in the course of his/her employment which has the appearance or effect of influencing the judgment of the recipient in the performance of his/her duties. In addition, no entertainment, gifts or gratuities may be offered to government employees unless permitted by law.

Why Does Teledyne Have This Rule?

Business decisions must be made impartially and on the basis of such factors as price, quality, service, financial responsibility and the maintenance of reliable sources of supply. Employees must ensure that any business courtesy offered or received does not influence, or appear to influence, business decisions.

How Does the Rule Work?

A "business courtesy" is something offered or accepted for which the recipient does not pay fair market value. Examples are meals, beverages, entertainment, recreation, transportation, discounts, tickets, passes, promotional material, and the recipient's use of the donor's time, material or equipment. Although business courtesies are occasionally appropriate in the ordinary course of business, they must always be consistent with the ethical principles set forth in the Code.

When doing business with non-governmental commercial customers and suppliers, Teledyne employees may accept and offer meals, refreshments, promotional items and entertainment which are not excessive in value and which are consistent with the business custom and practice in the place offered or received. Regardless of the situation, a Teledyne employee should not offer or accept a gratuity if there is any risk that a later decision to sell or purchase goods or services could appear to have been influenced by the gratuity. For example:

- **Received by a Company:** No Teledyne Company shall solicit or accept from any supplier or subcontractor a business courtesy for a Company sponsored activity.

- **Received by an Employee:** No Teledyne employee may solicit or accept, personally or through family members, a business courtesy which might have the appearance or effect of influencing the employee's judgment in the performance of his/her duties. Teledyne employees may accept meals, refreshments, entertainment or promotional items which are modest in value.

- **Provided by an Employee—Nongovernment:** No Teledyne employee or representative may offer or provide a business courtesy to a commercial customer or a commercial customer's representative which may have the appearance or effect of obtaining a competitive advantage or influencing the customer's business judgment. If this test can be met, Teledyne employees may provide meals, refreshments, and entertainment which are modest in value.

- **Provided by an Employee—Government:** The U.S. government, as well as some state and local governments, have very strict statutes and regulations prohibiting solicitation and acceptance of business courtesies. There are few exceptions. Accordingly, no Teledyne employee shall offer or provide meals, refreshments, transportation, or other business courtesies to government civilian or military personnel (or to commercial customers acting as procurement officials for the U.S. government) unless it is clear that the intended recipient lawfully may accept the business courtesy offered or provided.

Further guidance in this area can be found in the Teledyne Government Contracting Guidelines.

Questions to Ask Yourself

- Is the item offered to me within the bounds of good taste, moderation and common sense? If it is, you may accept the item.

- Would Teledyne offer the same business courtesy? If not, don't accept it.

- Are you sure that offering or accepting a business gratuity does not violate the laws or the business policies applicable to the other persons involved? If it does or if you are in doubt, don't offer or accept the gratuity.

- Will accepting a gratuity affect or appear to affect your ability to make an impartial decision with respect to the products or services of the giver? It must not.

Common Questions and Answers

Q: A commercial vendor who wants to supply parts for one of our products recently offered me an expensive pen and pencil set as a gift. I thanked him but said it was against Teledyne policy to accept such a gift. A colleague told me that we can accept small promotional gifts like pens, caps and mugs. Did I do the right thing?

A: Yes you did, but you raise an interesting question which faces employees involved in sales or purchasing. The question is one of judgment. Promotional gifts are used as part of marketing—they keep the name of the supplier on the mind of the recipient. Pens, mugs, caps, and other similar items of modest value bearing the giver's company logo, are common examples. The key word is "modest." An expensive pen and pencil set or a fancy western hat undoubtedly fall well outside the bounds of acceptable promotional items. But where is the borderline between acceptable and unacceptable? Remember, it's not necessarily what you think is appropriate, it's what others might think. Often it helps to ask the question, "What would others think if they read in the newspaper that I accepted this gift?" If you think eyebrows might be raised, you should politely turn down the offered gratuity.

Q: On several occasions after work I have seen our Air Force contracting officer standing at the gate waiting for a cab to take him to the airport. The airport is on my way home and it seems like it would be common courtesy to offer him a ride. Someone told me not to. Is she right?

A: Yes, your colleague is correct. You cannot offer him a ride to the airport. Before offering anything of value to a government employee be certain you have reviewed the Teledyne Government Contracting Guidelines and are familiar with the appropriate rules.

Teledyne Corporation Policy on Insider Trading of Securities

The Rule

Teledyne employees may not purchase or sell securities of a company if they have inside information about that company, nor may Teledyne employees furnish inside information to others.

Why Does Teledyne Have This Rule?

Various state and federal securities laws and regulations prohibit trading on "inside information" or sharing it with others. Generally, "inside information" is any "material, nonpublic" information.

Information is "material" if it could affect the market price of the securities of a company or if a reasonable investor would attach importance in the information in deciding whether to buy, sell, or hold the stock of a company. Information is "public" only if it has been effectively disclosed to the investing public (by press release, for example) and enough time has elapsed to permit the market to absorb and evaluate the information. Examples of such information include the potential award of a major contract to a company, unannounced earnings, the prospective introduction of a new product, or the prospects of major litigation.

The stock of Teledyne, Inc., is publicly traded. In addition, the stock of many of the companies with which Teledyne does business is publicly traded. Teledyne employees must be sensitive to the fact that information they possess concerning both Teledyne and the companies with which Teledyne does business may be inside information.

How Does the Rule Work?

Trading on inside information can give rise to substantial civil and criminal penalties, including fines and imprisonment. These penalties may apply to the individual employee violating the law as well as to Teledyne. Generally, the rules are:

- No employee may trade in the stock or other securities of a firm at any time when the employee, as a result of Teledyne employment, has material, nonpublic information about that firm. This restriction on "insider trading" is not limited to trading in Teledyne securities. It includes trading in the securities of other firms, especially those that are current or prospective customers or suppliers of Teledyne.

- Employees may not communicate material, nonpublic information about Teledyne or any other firm to other persons (except for authorized business purposes) and may not recommend to anyone the purchase or sale of any securities on the basis of such information. This prohibition on trading extends to members of the employee's immediate family and to others who have received the material, nonpublic information from the employee.

- After information has been publicly disclosed through a press release or other official announcement, employees should not trade in the affected securities until 14 hours following the announcement to allow the market to absorb the information (assuming the employees do not possess other undisclosed material, nonpublic information).

Questions to Ask Yourself

- If I am planning to buy or sell Teledyne stock, do I have any material, nonpublic information which other investors might want to know about in deciding whether to buy or sell Teledyne stock? If so, you should not trade. If you are uncertain, contact the Teledyne Corporate Legal Department for advice.

- Am I placing Teledyne, myself, or my friends and relatives at risk if I disclose to them material, nonpublic information about Teledyne? Yes, if they trade on that information.

- In addition, you should not disclose this information to anyone not in a need-to-know position. (See "Use of Property and Technology.")

- Am I looking to benefit from a "hot tip" about Teledyne or one of Teledyne's customers or competitors? If you are, you should not trade.

Common Questions and Answers

Q: I want to sell some Teledyne stock but I don't know if I have material, nonpublic information. How can I know whether I may sell stock?

A: If you are unsure whether you have material, nonpublic information, you should not trade in Teledyne stock or you can ask the Teledyne Corporate Legal Department if the information you have prohibits you from buying or selling your Teledyne stock.

Q: In the course of discussions with a customer I found out that the customer is going to announce some very positive news. I want to buy some of the customer's stock. Can I?

A: No. You must not buy or sell stock of another entity if you have material, nonpublic information. In addition, you may have an obligation to respect the confidentiality of the information because of Teledyne's obligations to the customer.

NYNEX CORPORATION

Policy on Conflicts of Interest

A conflict of interest can arise when the personal interests of an employee influence, or reasonably appear to influence, that employee's judgment or ability to act in the best interests of NYNEX.

All of us are required to avoid conflicts of interest. We must not put our own interests ahead of that of the Corporation when performing our jobs, nor should we use our position in NYNEX, or any information acquired through that position, for any non-Corporate purpose or gain. When a potential conflict of interest, or the reasonable appearance of one, cannot be avoided, we can best protect ourselves, and NYNEX, by disclosing the circumstances to our supervisor without delay. The reference section of this booklet contains a series of representative questions and answers regarding possible conflicts of interest and how they may be addressed within the context of the provisions of the Code of Business Conduct.

Relations with Customers and Suppliers

NYNEX conducts its business by buying and selling products and services solely on the basis of their value and merit. Those who make purchasing and contracting decisions for NYNEX, and for its customers, have a responsibility to their companies for independence and objectivity of judgment that must not be compromised, nor reasonably appear to be compromised. In our industry, customers can also be our suppliers and competitors. In our business dealings, we must understand these various relationships.

When we buy, we are responsible to our share owners and to our customers to seek the most technically efficient and cost-effective products and services and to evaluate them using consistent and unbiased standards. If purchasing or contracting decisions are, or appear to be, influenced by the receipt of personal gifts or favors, our share owners and customers may suffer. In addition, special personal, financial or other business relationships with suppliers and potential suppliers can bring into question our independence and objectivity in the selection process and, therefore, should be avoided.

When we sell, we recognize that our customers have a similar responsibility to their owners. We must not undermine their independence or objectivity with personal gifts or favors. Moreover, we must acquaint ourselves with their corporate standards of conduct so that we do not put our customers in compromising or questionable situations.

NYNEX has had its share of scandals, but the company is trying to increase the sensitivity of managers to ethical problems.
Grayton Wood (pointing finger), vice-president of ethics and
business conduct, is shown here playing the board game
Scruples at lunch with managers at the company's corporate
headquarters. Many other companies are testing a variety of
games and learning tools to encourage managers to simulate
their responses to ethical problems.

We want customers to buy NYNEX products and services because
those products and services meet their requirements and provide the
best quality at a fair price. Business gained by personal favors will be lost
in the long term by failing to serve the real needs of customers.
Furthermore, we will recommend to customers only those products and
services that are appropriate and suitable to their needs.

The exchange of business courtesies, such as reasonable entertainment and gifts of nominal value, is generally permissible. However, it is
essential to use good judgment and always act with moderation. All
employees engaged in external relationships on behalf of NYNEX are
required to observe the following general guidelines and to know and
abide by any additional NYNEX business unit or departmental rules
concerning relations with customers and suppliers.

- Occasionally, employees may offer or accept entertainment, but
  only if the entertainment is reasonable, occurs infrequently and

does not involve lavish expenditures. Entertaining customers and suppliers at cultural and sporting events that are sponsored by a NYNEX company is acceptable within this policy. Offering or accepting entertainment which is not a reasonable adjunct to a business relationship, but is primarily intended to gain favor or influence, is to be strictly avoided.

- Accepting or providing an occasional meal or refreshment in the normal course of business is permitted if circumstances dictate that a business meal is necessary. Whenever appropriate, these meals should be paid for on a reciprocal basis.

- We may give or accept gifts of nominal value. An item has "nominal" value when it is promotional in nature, imprinted with corporate advertising and typically distributed widely as a promotional item to others. Any other gift, to be considered "nominal" when it does not fit this definition, must have a retail value of $10 or less.

- We may not give or accept, even indirectly, bribes, "kickbacks," gifts of other than nominal value, loans, money, special privileges, personal favors, services, benefits or unusual hospitality. If we are given or offered any gift of value from a supplier, we must report it promptly to our supervisor and either return it to the donor, if possible, or dispose of it according to the procedures outlined in the reference section.

- Overseas, it may be lawful and customary in some countries for executives of companies that do business with each other to give or exchange gifts of considerable value. In situations where it is necessary to engage in such an activity, we may give or accept such gifts, but only in accordance with the Code of Business Conduct and the U.S. Foreign Corrupt Practices Act. Any gifts received will become Company property and must be properly documented, as outlined in the reference section.

Relations with Government Officials and Employees

The laws and regulations that apply to relations with government officials may differ from those that apply to relations with non-government customers and suppliers. Employees are responsible for establishing and maintaining relations with government officials and employees are responsible for knowing and complying with the laws and regulations that apply to those activities.

The acceptance of entertainment, meals and gifts by government employees who are responsible for purchasing and procurement may be strictly limited by law and regulation. Employees who sell NYNEX products and services to government departments and agencies are responsible for knowing and complying with the applicable laws and regulations.

Gratuities

Whether we are engaged in purchasing, selling or servicing on behalf of the Corporation, the acceptance of gratuities is not permitted. We should also carefully avoid giving any customer or supplier the impression that we expect or would accept gratuities. Still, a customer may occasionally offer a tip, either in appreciation of a job well done or to secure good service in the future. If we find ourselves in this position, we should politely refuse the gratuity, explaining that it is against Corporate policy for us to accept it.

Outside Employment and Other Activities

As NYNEX employees, our primary obligation is to the Corporation and any outside activity, such as a second job or self-employment, must be kept totally separate from employment with the Corporation.

We must avoid any activity or personal financial interest that could adversely affect the independence or objectivity of our judgment, interfere with the timely and effective performance of our duties and responsibilities, or that could discredit, embarrass or conflict, or appear to conflict, with the Corporation's best interests. Each year, all management employees are required to sign the Conflict of Interest Questionnaire, disclosing any personal or financial interests which may conflict with the interests of NYNEX.

Unless expressly authorized or sponsored by the Corporation—such as certain forms of volunteer work—no outside activity should involve the use of Company time, its name or its influence, assets, funds, materials, facilities or the services of other employees. We should not use our position, training or experience with the Corporation to promote off-the-job activities.

If we have an affiliation or interest in any outside organization or governmental body, we should disqualify ourselves from making any decision on behalf of the organization or governmental body that specifically involved the Corporation—such as a petition for zoning relief or a procurement decision—to avoid any conflict of interest and damage to the Corporation's reputation.

Competitive Activities

We should not engage in any activity that aids a competitor of NYNEX. We must not work for or assist anyone, including ourselves if we are self-employed, outside of NYNEX in the planning, design, manufacture, sales, purchase, installation or maintenance of any equipment or service that any NYNEX company currently provides, has known plans to provide, or is in competition with any service a NYNEX company currently provides or has known plans to provide. However, when authorized under Corporate programs, such as joint-venture activities, and in accordance with applicable laws or regulations, we may provide assistance to others who may be competitors.

Consultants, Representatives and Agents

When it is necessary to engage the services of an individual or a firm to consult for or otherwise represent NYNEX, special attention must be given to avoiding conflicts of interest between NYNEX and the person or firm employed. Consultants, representatives and agents of NYNEX must not act on our behalf in any manner that is inconsistent with our policies or any applicable laws or regulations.

Former Employees

Former employees are precluded from marketing and selling to NYNEX the products and services of other companies, or their own products and services if self-employed for a period of one year following separation from the Corporation. Due to special business conditions, there may be unusual cases that necessitate an exception to this policy. All such cases should be reviewed by the business unit Office of Business Conduct and approved at officer level.

The Corporation will not engage, or establish an external business relationship with, a former NYNEX employee whose employment has been terminated at the Corporation's initiative for reasons such as the employee's performance or conduct. All questions regarding this provision should be referred to the NYNEX Office of Ethics and Business Conduct.

Family and Personal Relationships

All our personnel decisions must be based on sound management practices and not be influenced by personal concerns. We are required to avoid family or personal considerations when making decisions related to personnel matters. We are expected to ensure that those with whom we have a close relationship are reasonably separated from our scope of supervision and from our influence in the areas of job assignment, appraisals, promotion and compensation decisions.

HARVARD UNIVERSITY

Policies Relating to Research and Other Professional Activities within and Outside the University

1. With the acceptance of a full-time appointment in the Faculty of Arts and Sciences, an individual makes a commitment to the University that is understood to be full time in the most inclusive sense. Every member is expected to accord the University his or her primary professional loyalty, and to arrange outside obligations, financial interests, and activities so as not to conflict or interfere with this overriding commitment to the University.

2. At the same time, no one benefits from undue interference with the legitimate external activities of officers of instruction who fulfill their primary full-time duties—teaching at the University, conducting scholarly research under its sponsorship, and meeting the other obligations to students and colleagues that faculty must share. Indeed, the involvement of faculty members in outside professional activities, both public and private, often serves not only the participants but the University as a whole.

   Instead of detailed rules or elaborate codes of ethics, the University has therefore provided its members with guidelines in conflicts of interest and commitment that leave as much as possible to individual discretion. It has been, and continues to be, assumed that all faculty members will be alert to the possible effects of outside activities on the objectivity of their decisions, their obligation to the University, and the University's responsibilities to others.

3. The areas of potential conflict may be divided into two broad categories. The first relates to conventional conflicts of interest—situations in which members may have the opportunity to influence the University's business decisions in ways that could lead to personal gain or give improper advantage to their associates.

   The second is concerned with conflicts of commitment—situations in which members' external activities, often valuable in themselves, interfere or appear to interfere with their paramount obligations to students, colleagues, and the University. Teachers and scholars are given great freedom in scheduling their activities with the understanding that their external activities will enhance the quality of their direct contributions to the University.

4. A Standing Committee on Professional Conduct, with broad representation from the different disciplines, shall advise the Dean

and individual faculty members on problems involving conflicts of interest and commitment.

5. It is assumed that minor conflicts will still be resolved primarily through individual discretion or informal administrative adjustment. It is also recognized that adequate protection for the University will frequently be derived through the traditional academic practices of scholarly publication and public disclosure of author and sponsor. However, if a member is engaged in an outside activity that could lead to serious conflict, it is mandatory that he or she inform the University of this possibility by consulting with the Dean of the Faculty or with the Chairman of the Committee on Professional Conduct.

   Whenever members have any doubts about whether an activity may involve a conflict of interest or commitment they are expected to seek such consultation. Guidance on what constitutes serious conflict is offered in the Appendix to this statement.

6. This statement will be distributed annually to all faculty members and published in the Gazette for the information of other officers.

APPENDIX

In the absence of specific rules (beyond the requirement of consultation), and in light of the difficulty of applying general statements of principle to specific cases, there follows a sampling of activities and situations that may present conflicts of interest or commitment.

They are divided into three categories:

A. Activities that are ordinarily permissible and usually do not require consultation;

B. Activities that should be discussed with the Dean of the Faculty or with the Committee Chairman even though the problems they present can probably be resolved, often simply by ensuring that the appropriate authorities know all pertinent facts;

C. Activities that should be brought to the attention of the Dean of the Faculty or the Committee Chairman and that appear to present such serious problems that the burden of demonstrating their compatibility with University policy rests with the faculty member.

Obviously, this list of examples does not include all potential problems and the separation into categories is somewhat arbitrary.

A. Activities That Are Clearly Permissible and That May Be Pursued without Consultation:

1. Acceptance of royalties for published scholarly works and other writings, or of honoraria for commissioned papers and occasional lectures.

2. Service as a consultant to outside organizations, provided that the time and energy devoted to the task is not excessive and the arrangement in no way inhibits publication of research results obtained within the University.

3. Service on boards and committees of organizations, public or private, that does not distract unduly from University obligations.

B.   Activities That Should Be Discussed with the Dean of the Faculty or with the Chairman of the Committee Even Though No Irreconcilable Conflict of Interest or Commitment Is Likely to Be Involved:

1. Relationships that might enable a member to influence Harvard's dealings with an outside organization in ways leading to personal gain or to improper advantage for anyone. For example, a member could have a financial interest in an enterprise with which the University does business and be in a position to influence relevant business decisions. Ordinarily, such problems can be resolved by full disclosure and by making arrangements that clearly exclude that member from participating in the decisions.

2. Situations in which the time or creative energy a member devotes to extramural activities appears large enough to compromise the amount or quality of his or her participation in the instructional, scholarly, and administrative work of the University itself. The guideline applicable to faculty members, as defined in the Fifth Statute, is that during the academic year (which extends through the summer for those who receive extra summer salary) no more than 10% of one's total professional effort may be directed to outside work.

   Activities (research projects, conferences, teaching programs, consulting agreements, etc.) that faculty members wish to undertake on an individual basis: (a) that involve or might reasonably be perceived to involve the institution, however slightly, and (b) that violate or might reasonably be perceived to violate any of the principles governing research supported by funds administered through the University (see Principles Governing Research Conducted within the Faculty of Arts and Science and Guidelines for Research Projects Undertaken in Cooperation with Industry) insofar as these principles are relevant to individual behavior.

Situations in which a member directs students into a research area from which the member hopes to realize financial gain. The difficulty, in such circumstances, of making an objective, independent judgment about the student's scholarly best interest, is obvious.

Activities That Seem Likely to Present an Unacceptable Conflict of Interest or Commitment and That Must Be Discussed with the Dean of the Faculty or with the Chairman of the Committee:

1. Situations in which the individual assumes executive responsibilities for an outside organization that might seriously divert his or her attention from University duties, or create other conflicts of loyalty. (Individuals should consult the Dean of the Faculty or the Chairman of the Committee before accepting any outside management position.)

2. Use for personal profit of unpublished information emanating from University research or other confidential University sources, or assisting an outside organization by giving it exclusive access to such information; or consulting under arrangements that impose obligations that conflict with University patent policy or with the institution's obligations to research sponsors.

3. Circumstances in which a substantial body of research that could and ordinarily would be carried on within the University is conducted elsewhere to the disadvantage of the University and its legitimate interests.

Any activity (research project, conference, teaching program, consulting agreement, etc.) that a faculty member may wish to undertake on an individual basis: (a) that involves or appears to involve the institution significantly (for example, through the use of its resources or facilities, or the participation of colleagues, students, and staff, etc.); and (b) that violates any of the principles governing research supported by funds administered through the University insofar as these principles are relevant to individual behavior. (In particular, members may not give other organizations the right to censor research any part of which is performed under Harvard auspices.)

MERCEDES-BENZ OF NORTH AMERICA

Mission Statement

We dedicate ourselves to customer satisfaction and quality in everything we do in order to sustain our leadership in the U.S. luxury car market.

Guiding Principles

In order to fulfill our mission, we will:

- Ensure that all activity is driven by a dedication to our customers: the owners and potential owners of our products, our dealers, and our fellow employees.

- Actively search out the needs of the market, our dealers and employees, and respond to these needs quickly and effectively—both through our own actions and by responsibly affecting and participating in the actions of MBAG.

- Continually develop the aspiration to own a Mercedes-Benz by providing the highest level of quality in products, services, communication, and overall representation in the marketplace.

- Create an open working environment which encourages everyone at MBNA to develop and work together in a true spirit of teamwork and fairness.

- Provide support to one another and motivate every individual toward taking those initiatives necessary to fulfill the mission.

- Foster a spirit of integrity, responsibility and accountability throughout the organization, and build our own knowledge of and identification with our products and company.

- Continually examine and refocus our efforts and resources and initiate changes necessary to fulfill our mission and maintain our competitiveness in a changing environment.

- Conduct all activities in an efficient and cost-effective manner.

JACKSONVILLE SHIPYARDS

Court Ordered Sexual Harassment Policy

The following sexual harassment policy is considered one of the strongest ever written: it was developed under court order against Jacksonville Shipyards, Inc. (JSI), after a major trial determined that company managers had systematically discriminated against female employees for over a decade. The company went out of business in 1993. The Court was so concerned that the company might not meet its obligations that the National Organization for Women was asked to assist in the development of the model policy.

Introduction

Title VII of the Civil Rights Act of 1964 prohibits employment discrimination on the basis of race, color, sex, age or national origin. Sexual harassment is included among the prohibitions.

Sexual harassment, according to the federal Equal Employment Opportunity Commission (EEOC), consists of unwelcome sexual advances, requests for sexual favors or other verbal or physical acts of a sexual or sex-based nature where (1) submission to such conduct is made either explicitly or implicitly a term or a condition of an individual's employment;

(2) an employment decision is based on an individual's acceptance or rejection of such conduct; or

(3) such conduct interferes with an individual's work performance or creates an intimidating, hostile or offensive working environment.

It is also unlawful to retaliate or take reprisal in any way against anyone who has articulated any concern about sexual harassment or discrimination against the individual raising the concern or against another individual.

Examples of conduct that would be considered sexual harassment or rated retaliation are set forth in the Statement of Prohibited Conduct which follows. These examples are provided to illustrate the kind of conduct proscribed by this Policy; the list is not exhaustive.

Jacksonville Shipyards, Inc., and its agents are under a duty to investigate or eradicate any form of sexual harassment or sexual discrimination or complaints about conduct in violation of this Policy and a schedule for violation of this Policy.

Sexual harassment is unlawful, and such prohibited conduct exposes not only JSI, but individuals involved in such conduct, to significant liability under the law. Employees at all times should treat other employees respectfully and with dignity in a manner so as not to offend the sensibilities of a coworker.

Accordingly, JSI's management is committed to vigorously enforcing its Sexual Harassment Policy at all levels within the Company.

Statement of Prohibited Conduct

The management of Jacksonville Shipyards, Inc., considers the following conduct to represent some of the types of acts which violate JSI's Sexual Harassment Policy:

A. Physical assaults of a sexual nature, such as:

1. rape, sexual battery, molestation or attempts to commit these assaults; and

2. intentional physical conduct which is sexual in nature, such as touching, pinching, patting, grabbing, brushing against another employee's body, or poking another employee's body.

B. Unwanted sexual advances, propositions or other sexual comments, such as:

1. sexually-oriented gestures, noises, remarks, jokes, or comment about a person's sexuality or sexual experience directed at or made in the presence of any employee who indicates or has indicated in any way that such conduct in his or her presence is unwelcome;

2. preferential treatment or promises of preferential treatment to an employee for submitting to sexual conduct, including soliciting or attempting to solicit any employee to engage in sexual activity for compensation or reward; and

3. subjecting, or threats of subjecting, an employee to unwelcome sexual attention or conduct or intentionally making performance of the employee's job more difficult because of that employee's sex.

C. Sexual or discriminatory displays or publications anywhere in JSI's workplace by JSI employees, such as:

1. displaying pictures, posters, calendars, graffiti, objects, promotional materials, reading materials, or other materials that are sexually suggestive, sexually demeaning, or pornographic, or bringing into the JSI work environment or possessing any such material to read, display or view at work.

    A picture will be presumed to be sexually suggestive if it depicts a person of either sex who is not fully clothed or in clothes that are not suited to or ordinarily accepted for the accomplishment of routine work in and around the shipyard and who is posed for the obvious purpose of displaying or drawing attention to private portions of his or her body.

2. reading or otherwise publicizing in the work environment materials that are in any way sexually revealing, sexually suggestive, sexually demeaning or pornographic; and

3. displaying signs or other materials purporting to segregate an employee by sex in any area of the workplace (other than restrooms and similar semi-private lockers/changing rooms).

D. Retaliation for sexual harassment complaints, such as:

1. disciplining, changing work assignments of, providing inaccurate work information to, or refusing to cooperate or discuss work-related matters with any employee because that employee has complained about or resisted harassment, discrimination or retaliation; and

2. intentionally pressuring, falsely denying, lying about or otherwise covering up or attempting to cover up conduct such as that described in any item above.

E. Other acts:

1. The above is not to be construed as an all inclusive list of prohibited acts under this policy.

2. Sexual harassment is unlawful and hurts other employees. Any of the prohibited conduct described here is sexual harassment of anyone at whom it is directed or who is otherwise subjected to it.

Each incident of harassment, moreover, contributes to a general atmosphere in which all persons who share the victim's sex suffer the consequences. Sexually oriented acts or sex-based conduct have no legitimate business purposes; accordingly, the employee who engages in such conduct should be and will be made to bear the full responsibility for such unlawful conduct.

Schedule of Penalties for Misconduct

The following schedule of penalties applies to all violations of the JSI Sexual Harassment Policy, as explained in more detail in the Statement of Prohibited Conduct. Where progressive discipline is provided for, each instance of conduct violating the Policy moves the offending employee through the steps of disciplinary action. In other words, it is not necessary for an employee to repeat the same precise conduct in order to move up the scale of discipline.

A written record of each action taken pursuant to the Policy will be placed in the offending employee's personnel file. The record will reflect the conduct, or alleged conduct, and the warning given, or other discipline imposed.

A. Assault

Any employee's first proven offense of assault or threat of assault, including assault of a sexual nature, will result in dismissal.

B. Other acts of harassment by coworkers

An employee's commission of acts of sexual harassment other than assault will result in non-disciplinary oral counseling upon alleged first offense, written warning, suspension or discharge upon the first proven offense, depending upon the nature or severity of the misconduct, and suspension or discharge upon the second proven offense, depending on the nature or severity of the misconduct.

C. Retaliation

Alleged retaliation against a sexual harassment complainant will result in non-disciplinary oral counseling. Any form of proven retaliation will result in suspension or discharge upon the first proven offense, depending upon the nature and severity of the retaliatory acts, and discharge upon the second proven offense.

D. Supervisors

A supervisor's commission of acts of sexual harassment (other than assault) with respect to any other employee under that person's supervision will result in non-disciplinary oral counseling upon alleged first offense, final warning or dismissal for the first offense, depending upon the nature and severity of the misconduct, and discharge for any subsequent offense.

Procedures for Making, Investigating and Resolving Sexual Harassment and Retaliation Complaints

A. Complaints

JSI will provide its employees with convenient, confidential and reliable mechanisms for reporting incidents of sexual harassment and retaliation. Accordingly, JSI designates at least two employees in supervisory or managerial positions at each of the Commercial and Mayport Yards to serve as Investigative Officers for sexual harassment issues.

The names, responsibilities, work locations, and phone numbers of each officer will be routinely and continuously posted so that an employee seeking such name can enjoy anonymity and remain inconspicuous to all of the employees in the yard in which he or she works.

The Investigative Officers may appoint "designees" to assist them in handling sexual harassment complaints. Persons appointed as designees shall not conduct [an] investigation until they have received training equivalent to that received by the Investigative Officers. The purpose of having several persons to whom complaints may be made is to avoid a situation where an employee is faced with complaining to the person, or a close associate of the person, who would be the subject of the complaint.

Complaints of acts of sexual harassment or retaliation that are in violation of the sexual harassment policy will be accepted in writing or orally, and anonymous complaints will be taken seriously and investigated. Anyone who has observed sexual harassment or retaliation should report it to a designated Investigative Officer. A complaint need not be limited to someone who was the target of harassment or retaliation.

Only those who have an immediate need to know, including the Investigative Officers and/or his/her designee, the alleged target of harassment or retaliation, the alleged harassers or retaliators and any witnesses will or may find out the identity of the complainant.

All parties contacted in the course of an investigation will be advised that all parties involved in a charge are entitled to respect and that any retaliation or reprisal against an individual who is an alleged target of harassment or retaliation, who has made a complaint or who has provided evidence in connection with a complaint is a separate actionable offense as provided in the schedule of penalties. This complaint process will be administered consistent with federal labor law when bargaining unit members are affected.

B. Investigations

Each Investigative Officer will receive thorough training about sexual harassment and the procedures herein and will have the responsibility for investigating complaints or having an appropriately trained and designated JSI investigator do so.

All complaints will be investigated expeditiously by a trained JSI Investigative Officer or his/her designee. The Investigative Officer will produce a written report, which, together with the investigation file, will be shown to the complainant upon request within a reasonable time.

The Investigative Officer is empowered to recommend remedial measures based upon the results of the investigation, and JSI management will promptly consider and act upon such recommendation. When a complaint is made the Investigative Officer will have the duty of immediately bringing all sexual harassment and retaliation complaints to the confidential attention of the office of the President of JSI, and JSI's EEO Officer.

The Investigative and EEO Officers will each maintain a file on the original charge and follow up investigation. Such file will be available to investigators, to federal, state and local agencies charged with equal employment or affirmative action enforcement, to other complainants who have filed a formal charge of discrimination against JSI, or any agent thereof whether that formal charge is filed at a federal, state, or local law level. The names of complainants, however, will be kept under separate file.

C. Cooperation

An effective sexual harassment policy requires the support and example of company personnel in position of authority. JSI agents or employees who engage in sexual harassment or retaliation or who fail to cooperate with company-sponsored investigations of sexual harassment or retaliation may be severely sanctioned by suspension or dismissal.

By the same token, officials who refuse to implement remedial measures, obstruct the remedial efforts of other JSI employees, and/or retaliate against sexual harassment complainants or witnesses may be immediately sanctioned by suspension or dismissal.

D. Monitoring

Because JSI is under legal obligations imposed by Court order, the NOW Legal Defense and Education Fund, its designated representative, and, if one is appointed upon motion and a showing of need, a representative of the U.S. District Court for the Middle District of Florida are authorized to monitor the JSI workplace, even in the absence of specific complaints, to ensure that the company's policy against sexual harassment is being enforced.

Such persons are not ordinarily to be used in lieu of the JSI Investigative Officers on investigation of individual matters, but instead are to be available to assess the adequacy of investigations. Any individual dissatisfied with JSI's investigation of a complaint may contact such persons in writing or by telephone and request an independent investigation. Such persons' telephone numbers will be posted and circulated with those of the Investigative Officers. Such persons will be given reasonable access by JSI to inspect for compliance.

Procedures and Rules for Education and Training

Education and training for employees at each level of the work force are critical to the success of JSI's policy against sexual harassment. The following documents address such issues: the letter to be sent to all employees from JSI's Chief Executive Officer/President, the Sexual Harassment Policy, Statement of Prohibited Conduct, the Schedule of Penalties for Misconduct, and Procedures for Making, Investigating and Resolving Sexual Harassment and Retaliation Complaints.

These documents will be conspicuously posted throughout the workplace at each division of JSI, on each company bulletin board, in all central gathering areas, and in every locker room. The statements must be clearly legible and displayed continuously. The sexual harassment policy under a cover letter from JSI's president will be sent to all employees. The letter will indicate that copies are available at no cost and how they can be obtained.

JSI's sexual harassment policy statement will also be included in the Safety Instructions and General Company Rules, which are issued in booklet form to each JSI employee. Educational posters using concise messages conveying JSI's opposition to workplace sexual harassment will reinforce the company's policy statement; these posters should be simple, eye-catching and graffiti resistant.

Education and training include the following components:

1. For all JSI employees: As part of general orientation, each recently hired employee will be given a copy of the letter from JSI's Chief Executive Officer/President and requested to read and sign a receipt for the company's policy statement on sexual harassment so that they are on notice of the standards of behavior expected.

   In addition, supervisory employees who have attended a management training seminar on sexual harassment will explain orally at least once every six months at safety meetings attended by all employees the kinds of acts that constitute sexual harassment, the company's serious commitment to eliminating sexual harassment in the workplace, the penalties for engaging in harassment and the procedures for reporting incidents of sexual harassment.

2. For all female employees: All women employed at JSI will participate on company time in annual seminars that teach strategies for resisting and preventing sexual harassment. At least a half-day in length, these seminars will be conducted by one or more experienced sexual harassment educators, including one instructor with work experience in the trades.

3. For all employees with supervisory authority over other employees, including leadermen, quartermen, superintendents, and all employees working in a managerial capacity: All supervisory personnel will participate in an annual, half-day-long training session on sex discrimination.

At least one-third of each session (of no less than one and one-half hours) will be devoted to education about workplace sexual harassment, including training (with demonstrative evidence) as to exactly what types of remarks, behavior and pictures will not be tolerated in the JSI workplace. The president of JSI will attend the training sessions in one central location with all company supervisory employees.

The president will introduce the seminar with remarks stressing the potential liability of JSI and individual supervisors for sexual harassment and the need to eliminate harassment. Each participant will be informed that they are responsible for knowing the contents of JSI's sexual harassment policy and for giving similar presentations of safety meetings to employees.

4. For all Investigative Officers: The Investigative Officers and their designees, if any, will attend annual full-day training seminars conducted by experienced sexual harassment educators and/or investigators to educate them about the problems of sexual harassment in the workplace and techniques for investigating and stopping it.

The training sessions for components 2-4 will be conducted by an experienced sexual harassment educator chosen jointly by JSI and the NOW Legal Defense and Education Fund after receiving bids. In the event of a disagreement between the parties, the parties will refer the matter to an arbitrator chosen by the parties.

Author's note: Jacksonville Shipyards ceased operations. The company experienced a down turn in business related to reduced defense spending and concurrently incurred numerous legal problems associated with documented sexual harassment.

ACKNOWLEDGMENTS

Special thanks are extended to the individual organizations who agreed to share their employment documents with the readers of this book.

AT&T policies on Privacy of Communications and Safeguarding Communications used by permission of AT&T.

Columbia Gas System Corporate Code of Ethics used by permission of Columbia Gas System.

Harvard "Policies Relating to Research and Other Professional Activities within and Outside the University" used by permission of the Faculty of Arts and Sciences, Harvard University.

Hewlett-Packard Company policies from "Standards of Business Conduct" permission to reproduce granted by Hewlett-Packard Company.

Macworld Communications for Privacy in Communication article reprints.

Mercedes-Benz Mission Statement used by permission of Mercedes-Benz of North America, Inc.

Mobil letter and policy on Political Contributions and Activities reprinted with permission of Mobil Corporation.

NYNEX policy used by permission of NYNEX Corporation.

Rockwell policies selected from "Ethics IS Good Business" used by permission of Rockwell International.

Teledyne Ethics Code of Business Conduct, Fourth Edition, used by permission of Teledyne, Inc.

Union Carbide policies from "Our Policies" used by permission of Union Carbide Corporation.

A P P E N D I X   B

For More Information

The following list of journals about business and ethics will be of interest to readers. The list was compiled by Dr. Peter Dean of Penn State, Great Valley.

Business Ethics
1107 Hazeltine Boulevard, Suite 530
Chaska, MN 55318

Business Ethics Quarterly
Bowling Green State University
Bowling Green, OH 43403

Business and Professional Ethics Journal
Center for Applied Psychology
240 Arts and Science Building
University of Florida
Gainesville, FL 32611

Business and Society Review
Management Reports Inc.
25-13 Old Kings Highway, Suite 17
Darien, CT 06820

Ethics: Easier Said Than Done
Josephson Institute
310 Washington Boulevard, Suite 104
Marina Del Ray, CA 90292

Ethikos
Ethikos Inc.
799 Broadway, Suite 541
New York, NY 10003

Journal of Business Ethics
PO Box 358
Accord Station
Hingham, MA 02018

Business Ethics: A European Review
Business Ethics Centre
King's College
Strand, London WC2R 2LS England

Business Ethics Videos

Program Title	Purchase Price	Rental Available	Length	Leaders's Guide	Workbook
"Business Ethics: What Are Friends For?"	$99	N	15:00	12 pp.	12pp.
"Business Ethics: We Were Just Following Orders"	$99	N	15:00	12 pp.	12 pp.
"Business Ethics: A Guide to Identifying and Resolving Ethical Dilemmas in Business"	$149	N	34:00	12 pp.	20 pp.
"The Parable of the Sadhu"	$149	N	30:00	4 pp.	—
"Business Ethics"	$189	N	58:00	—	24 pp.
"Marketplace Ethics: Issues in Sales and Marketing"	$500	Y	30:00	116 pp.	—
"Buying Trouble: Ethics Issues in Purchasing"	$500	Y	30:00	71 pp.	—
"It's Up to You: A Management Accountant's Decisions"	$500	Y	30:00	74 pp.	—
"A Matter of Judgment: Conflicts of Interest in the Workplace"	$500	Y	30:00	55 pp.	—
"Today's Life Choices: Business Ethics"	Nominal	N	28:30	—	—
"Good Ethics/Good Business" (two tapes)	$975	Y	30:00 30:00	59 pp.	63 pp.
"Business Ethics: The Roundtable"	$795	Y	56:20	4 pp.	—
"Ethics in American Business: Insider Trading"	$295	Y	20:16	—	—
"Ethics in American Business: Computer Monitoring"	$295	Y	22:45	—	—
"Management Ethics: A View from the Top"	Free Rental		14:30	—	—
"Business Ethics, 1987"	Free Rental		59:30	—	—

This chart identifies several of the best videos available to managers and future managers on issues discussed in this book.

Comments

Hosted by Barbara Tuffler, formerly of Harvard Business School.
Contact: MTI Film + Video, Deerfield, IL, (708) 940-1260

Cost-cutting orders challenge a manager's resolve to be human.
Also contact MTI.

Bribery and whistle-blowing are highlighted in three mini-cases.
Also contact MTI.

Based on a popular *Harvard Business Review* article. Hosted by Arthur Miller.
Also contact MTI.

Gifts, bribes, drug abuse, and more. Hosted by two Wharton School professors.
Contact Kantola Productions, Mill Valley, CA, (415) 381-9363.

Five dramatized cases.
Contact Ethics Resource Center, Washington, DC, (202) 333-3419.

Collusion, favoritism, vendors—what is appropriate? Five case studies.
Also contact Ethics Resource Center.

Five case studies devoted to ethics in accounting.
Also contact Ethics Resource Center.

Five dramatized cases expose a variety of ethical quagmires.
Also contact Ethics Resource Center.

Developed by University of Notre Dame. Five cases ranging from insider information to
the savings & loan scandal.
Contact Golden Dome, Notre Dame, IN, (219) 239-1616.

Two-tape set includes interviews with corporate executives.
Contact Videolearning, Haverford, PA, (800) 622-3610.

Students, executives, and scholars debate ethical problems and their response.
Also contact Videolearning.

Walter Cronkite narrates a profile of S&L rules.
Contact Video Publishing, (708) 517-8744.

Did Frederick Taylor's time-motion studies lead to systematized invasion of privacy?
Also contact Video Publishing.

The CEOs of Allied Corp., Standard Oil, and Johnson & Johnson discuss integrity.
Contact Ethics Resource Center.

John Phelan, CEO of New York Stock Exchange, speaks on financial ethics at Notre Dame.
Contact Notre Dame Alumni Continuing Education, (219) 631-6186.

Source: James O'Rourke, IV, *Video Resources in Business Ethics*. Notre Dame Center for Business Communication, 1993. Sponsored by The Boehnen Foundation, St. Paul, MN.

An Ethics Audit For Organizational Managers

Throughout this book you have read myriad cases of abuses by both employees and managers; certainly a significant number of these embarrassing incidents could have been avoided or significantly reduced in scope if senior levels of the organization had been more vigilant about potential abuses.

This ethics audit has been developed by the author to assist the reader in developing a strategic protocol for future management action and review. This section can be easily adapted to serve as the focal point for discussions at staff meetings, management retreats, and in classrooms and training environments.

A scoring formula has been designed to assist the reader in determining if their employer meets broadly accepted principles for an ethics awareness program. The scoring formula appears at the end of the audit.

Score 1 point for each Yes answer and 0 for each No answer

Topic
Policies And Procedures

Yes/No
1. Have we established a formal statement of ethics that explains how we expect all levels of employees to perform their duties and represent our organization? Have we provided credible examples that amplify upon our standards of integrity and clarify "cloudy" topics?

Yes/No
2. Do we schedule a discussion of management ethics at least once a quarter during meetings and/or retreats? Do we invite representatives of government agencies, local prosecutors, or academic experts to discuss actual cases in our industry and serve as an independent third-party for roundtable discussions?

Yes/No
3. Are our policies and procedures flexible or too rigid? Are they written in clear language so that there is no ambiguity? Are they legal and enforceable?

Yes/No

4. If infractions occur, is our organization ready to spend the time and resources necessary to arbitrate cases, adjudicate them, or prosecute wrongdoing, depending upon the severity of the incident?

Yes/No

5. What kind of fact-finding procedures do we have or should be established to ensure that fairness is paramount in our efforts?

Finance

Yes/No

6. Do we have sufficient safeguards in place to reduce or eliminate our exposure to embezzlement and related impropriety?

Yes/No

7. Have we ever attempted to test our financial system to ensure that it is "fool proof" to attempts to manipulate corporate funds, bonds, or stocks? Have we periodically engaged a third-party who specializes in financial security to benchmark our systems against those of comparable firms?

Yes/No

8. Do we periodically send various financial officers to training programs offered by credible banks, brokerage houses, and other financial institutions on issues such as money laundering, pilferage, the changing standards of accounting, and related matters?

Public Relations

Yes/No

9. Are we prepared for any kind of credibility crisis that could occur because of the activities of any of our employees? Have we considered the full gamut of possible management crises, ranging from environmental abuse to a felony that an employee may commit off-site?

Yes/No

10. Who will speak for our organization if an embarrassing incident occurred? Have we trained this manager in adversarial media relations, "ambush" interviews, the legal dimensions of libel and slander, and other pertinent topics?

Yes/No

11. Have we scheduled periodic "mock" interviews and news conferences to test our ability to speak to various media, including employees, neighbors, regulators, and our shareholders during a difficult and embarrassing incident?

Yes/No

12. If we truly believe that integrity is the hallmark of any successful organization, what measures can we take to ensure that we speak honestly, communicate all pertinent facts with clarity, and represent all interests of the organization with a view towards complete candor?

Yes/No

13. Does our public relations/public affairs department periodically circulate a series of clippings of news stories from the business and trade press that indicate new and disturbing trends, inci-

dents, and prosecutions from comparable organizations? Are these stories then reviewed and discussed during management briefings?

Human Resources

Yes/No

14. Have we developed a training protocol that communicates a message early in the tenure of each new employee that clearly explains our shared expectations regarding ethical behavior? Do we or will we ask each new and current hire to sign an acknowledgment form that they have received and read our ethics policies?

Yes/No

15. Have we clearly defined a role for human resources in terms of adjudicating any complaints or cases of whistle-blowing that may emerge? If so, have we provided the necessary books, videos, and other training tools necessary so that human resource managers can succeed in this task? If not, what is our timetable and budget to meet these goals?

Yes/No

16. Do we practice progressive discipline as is recommended by various legal and business experts? Have we clearly identified what infractions will not be tolerated by our organization? Do we selectively enforce these rules or are we willing to commit to across-the-board implementation?

Operations

Yes/No

17. Have we discussed current ethical and legal issues in a systematic manner with all levels of the organization? This opportunity includes issues such as sexual harassment, workplace diversity, employee privacy, and related issues that often are the genesis for misunderstanding in the workplace.

Yes/No

18. Do we recognize and honor ethical and moral achievements in our organization? Whenever a case of overcharging or a related incident occurs, do we generate positive attention for the responsible employee?

Yes/No

19. Does our organization periodically communicate our commitment to integrity and ethics to our vendors and other business partners? If we do not currently possess such a system, a timetable and strategic plan is required.

Yes/No

20. Have we taken quality time and examined areas of vulnerability in our organization where a seemingly small incident could escalate into a major ethical embarrassment? Would role-playing or a management simulation game help our personnel understand the dynamics at work whenever such an "embryonic" case arises?

Legal

Yes/No   21. If our organization were required to outline our ethics policies and procedures in a courtroom tomorrow, could we articulate a system that has been written, designed, tested, and implemented to meet current standards of comparable organizations in the same industry?

Yes/No   22. Does our legal counsel distribute periodic advisories on new challenges, threats, and cases related to our endeavors from which we can learn?

Yes/No   23. Has our employee newsletter/magazine featured at least one article in the past year that profiles the changing legal landscape in terms of various legislative requirements of our company?

Yes/No   24. In some cases, various departments and sectors may distribute policies and procedures that contradict or are not complimentary to organization-wide standards. Has legal counsel benchmarked any such policies to ensure comparability?

Implementation

Yes/No   25. If one or several of our senior managers is well versed and experienced in communicating the ethical standards in place at our company, have we made arrangements for these individuals to visit various locations and offer presentations to colleagues?

Scoring:

21 or more
Company has met or exceeded generally accepted ethics practices and scores exceptionally high in terms of preparedness.

16–20
Company meets many accepted practices necessary to achieve an "ethically clean" environment, but additional work is necessary to avoid potential problems.

10–15
Company does not currently offer a diversified and integrated approach towards ethics; there may be considerable ambiguity or gaps in existing policies and procedures that could be the genesis for future lawsuits.

0–9
Serious defects are probably evident in the company's ethics program; various control functions necessary to achieve an ethical environment are probably absent, which may actually encourage legal and ethical impropriety. A comprehensive program should be designed as soon as possible to reduce exposure by the organization to myriad ethical and legal threats.

Bibliography

Readers interested in more detailed information on the subjects in this work may wish to consult the following articles, monographs, and books that span the subject of ethical conduct. Many of these works were helpful in researching this book.

Ethics and Human Resources

Associated Press. "New York Sues Wal-Mart over Dating Policy." *Las Vegas Review-Journal,* July 15, 1993, p. 10D.

Barton, Laurence. "Corporate Sponsored Child Care: A Benefit with High Satisfaction, Questionable Future." *International Journal of Manpower,* vol. 13, no. 1 (1992), pp. 12–24.

Barton, Laurence. *Crisis in Organizations: Managing and Communications in The Heat of Chaos.* Cincinnati: Southwestern Publishing, 1993.

Barton, Laurence. "A Cross-Cultural Comparison of Child Care as an Employer-Provided Benefit." *International Journal of Sociology and Social Policy,* vol. 11, no. 5 (1991), pp. 34–47.

Brelis, Matthew. "Lawyer Says Post Offices Hide Sexual Harassment." *The Boston Globe,* June 10, 1993, p. 6.

Cronin, Michael P. "This Is a Test." *Inc.,* August 1993, pp. 64–68.

Hawkins, Chuck. "Denny's: The Stain That Isn't Coming Out." *Business Week,* June 28, 1993, pp. 98–99.

Jackson, Derrick Z. "A Healthy Package." *The Boston Globe,* September 22, 1993, p. 15.

Kennedy, John H. "Brooks Brothers Settles Bias Claim." *The Boston Globe,* April 21, 1993, p. B1.

Kever, Jeannie. "A Thousand Lives." *The San Antonio Light,* November 11, 1990, pp. 1, 4, 18.

Knight-Ridder Newspapers. "Employers Use Misdeeds to Fight Discrimination Suits." *Las Vegas Review-Journal,* May 14, 1993, p. 27.

Mello, John P. "Beware Broken Hiring Promises." *CFO Magazine,* September 1993, p. 17.

Moses, Jonathan. "Employers Face New Liability: Truth in Hiring." *The Wall Street Journal,* July 9, 1993, p. B1.

Stern, Gabriella. "Companies Discover That Some Firings Backfire into Costly Defamation Suits." *The Wall Street Journal,* May 5, 1993, pp. B1–B7.

Welles, Edward O. "Bad News." *Inc.,* April 1991, pp. 45–49.

Sexual Harassment and Bias

Barton, Laurence, and Hardigree, Donald. "Sexual Harassment: A Different Kind of Business Crisis." *Small Business Forum,* vol. 10, no. 2 (June 1992), pp. 17–19.

Frum, David. "Speed Brake." *Forbes,* October 11, 1993, p. 162.

German, Jeff. "Troubled Waters." *Las Vegas Sun,* April 11, 1993, pp. 1D–5D.

Jacobs, Deborah L. "Sexual Harassment: What You Don't Know Can Destroy Your Firm." *Your Company,* Spring 1993, pp. 34–39.

Mangan, Katherine. "Four Baylor Professors Asked to Leave Following Sex-Bias Complaints." *The Chronicle of Higher Education,* April 23, 1993, p. A17.

Wiley, Carolyn. "Perspectives on Sexual Harassment in the Workplace: Cases and Recommendations for Management Practice." *Journal of Business and Economic Perspectives,* vol. XVII, no. 2 (1992), pp. 46–51.

Winokur, L. A. "Harassment of Workers by Third Parties Can Lead into Maze of Legal, Moral Issues." *The Wall Street Journal,* October 26, 1992, pp. B1–B8.

Insider Trading

diNorcia, Vincent. "Mergers, Takeovers and a Property Ethic." *Journal of Business Ethics,* vol. 7 (1988), pp. 109–116.

Hyatt, James C. "Big Board Cites Two Concerns, 15 Individuals." *The Wall Street Journal,* April 30, 1993, p. A5A.

Truell, Peter. "Two Indicted in Trading Scam Involving Debt." *The Wall Street Journal,* May 18, 1993, p. A3.

Crime in the Workplace

Associated Press. "Disneyland Faces INS Fine for Record-Keeping Violations." *Las Vegas Review-Journal,* May 7, 1993, p. 10C.

Bulkeley, William M. "Police Turn to Databases to Link Crimes." *The Wall Street Journal,* March 8, 1993, p. B6.

Burrough, Bryan. "How American Express Orchestrated a Smear of Rival Edmond Safra." *The Wall Street Journal,* September 24, 1990, pp. 1–B9.

Chan, Sau. "Credit Card Fraud Takes Many Forms." *Las Vegas Review-Journal,* October 11, 1993, p. B1.

Henriques, Diana R. "Falsifying Corporate Data Becomes Fraud of the 90s." *The New York Times,* September 21, 1992, pp. 1–C2.

Mieher, Stuart. "Westinghouse Lawyer Urged in '88 Note That Toxic-Safety Records Be Destroyed." *The Wall Street Journal,* February 26, 1993, p. A4.

Quinn, Jane Bryant. "Too Good to Be True." *Newsweek,* May 17, 1993, pp. 44–45.

Roberts, Johnnie L. "Bribery Claims at Fingerhut Are Investigated." *The Wall Street Journal,* May 20, 1993, pp. B1–B10.

Corporate Espionage

Barton, Laurence. "Terrorism as an International Business Crisis: The Need for Managers to Assess Vulnerability." *Management Decision,* vol. 31, no. 1 (1993), pp. 22–25.

Barton, Laurence. "Why Business Must Prepare a Strategic Response to Corporate Sabotage." *Industrial Management,* vol. 35, no. 2 (March–April 1993), pp. 16–19.

Bulkeley, William M. "Voice Mail May Let Companies Dial 'E' for Espionage." *The Wall Street Journal,* September 28, 1993, p. B1.

Driscoll, Lisa McGurrin. "A Corporate Spy Story." *New England Business,* May 1989, pp. 28–78.

Strugatch, Warren. "Dangerous Liaisons." *World Trade,* April 1992, pp. 48–54.

Waller, Douglas. "The Open Barn Door." *Newsweek,* May 4, 1992, pp. 58–59.

Global Ethics

Baruch, Hurd. "The Foreign Corrupt Practices Act." *Harvard Business Review,* January–February 1979, pp. 32–50.

Buller, Paul F., Kohls, John J., and Anderson, Kenneth S. "The Challenge of Global Ethics." *Journal of Business Ethics* (1991), pp. 767–775.

Dobson, John. "Role of Ethics in Global Business Culture." *Journal of Business Ethics,* vol. 9 (1990), pp. 481–488.

Longenecker, Justin G., McKinney, Joseph A., and Moore, Carlos W. "The Ethical Issue of International Bribery: A Study of Attitudes among U.S. Business Professionals." *Journal of Business Ethics*, vol. 7 (1988), pp. 341–346.

Ono, Yukimo. "Unneeded Workers in Japan Are Bored and Very Well Paid." *The Wall Street Journal*, April 20, 1993, pp. 1–A4.

Perdomo, Rogelio Perez. "Corruption and Business in Present Day Venezuela." *Journal of Business Ethics*, vol. 9 (1990), pp. 555–566.

The Theories of Business Ethics

Barton, Laurence. "Coping with Crisis: Teaching Students Managerial and Ethical Constraints." *The Bulletin of the Association for Business Communications*, vol. LIII, no. 3 (1990), pp. 27–32.

Brooks, Leonard J. "Corporate Codes of Conduct." *Journal of Business Ethics*, vol. 8 (1989), pp. 117–129.

Brooks, Leonard J. "Corporate Ethical Performance: Trends, Forecasts and Outlooks." *Journal of Business Ethics*, vol. 8 (1989), pp. 31–38.

Harrington, Susan J. "What Corporate America Is Teaching about Corporate Ethics." *Academy of Management Executive*, vol. 5, no. 1 (1991), pp. 21–30.

Jones, Thomas M. "Ethical Decision Making by Individuals in Organizations: An Issue-Contingent Model." *Academy of Management Review*, vol. 16, no. 2 (1991), pp. 366–395.

Mayo, Michael A. "Ethical Problems Encountered by U.S. Small Businesses in International Marketing," *Journal of Small Business Management*, vol. 29, no. 2 (April 1991), pp. 51–59.

Oliverio, Mary Ellen. "The Implementation of a Code of Ethics: The Early Efforts of One Entrepreneur." *Journal of Business Ethics*, vol. 7 (1989), pp. 367–374.

Stark, Andrew. "What's the Matter with Business Ethics?" *Harvard Business Review*, May–June 1993, pp. 38–48.

Trevino, Linda Klebe. "The Social Effects of Punishment in Organizations: A Justice Perspective." *Academy of Management Review*, vol. 17, no. 4 (1992), pp. 647–676.

Intellectual Property and Ethics

Barton, Laurence, and Malhorta, Yogesh. "International Infringement of Software as Intellectual Property." *Industrial Management and Data Systems*, no. 8 (1993), pp. 20–28.

Caffey, Andrew A. "Licensing of Products Poses New Challenges." *The National Law Journal*, May 17, 1993, pp. S11–13.

Strugatch, Warren. "Rip-Off." *World Trade*, August–September 1991, pp. 101–110.

Wittenberg, Malcolm B., and Knudsen, Kit L. "RICO Increasingly Used in Infringement Cases." *The National Law Journal*, May 17, 1993, pp. 56–57.

Corporate Philanthrophy

Barton, Laurence. "The Corporation and Community: The Emergence of a New Communication Priority." *The Bulletin of Organizational Communication*, Association of Management, vol. 3, no. 2 (Summer 1991), pp 4–6.

Grant, Linda. "Acts of Charity." *Los Angeles Times Magazine*, September 13, 1992, pp. 39–43.

Hise, Phaedra. "Charity Begins at Home." *Inc.*, April 1993, p. 50.

Kirp, David L. "Uncommon Decency: Pacific Bell Responds to AIDS." *Harvard Business Review*, May–June 1989, pp. 140–151.

Kohl, John, Miller, Alan, and Barton, Laurence. "The AIDS Crisis in the United States: A Report on One Company's Policies and Programs." *Long Range Planning*, December 1990, pp. 31–34.

Nichlin, Julie L. "Corporate Giving to Education Rose by 1% in 1992, but Inflation Wipes Out Gain." *The Chronicle of Higher Education*, September 22, 1993, p. A31.

Spragins, Ellyn E. "Making Good." *Inc.*, May 1993, pp. 114–122.

Charges of Price Gauging, Questionable Acts

Associated Press. "Borden Accused of Rigging Bids in Milk Sales." *Las Vegas Review-Journal*, February 12, 1993, p. 6A.

Barrett, Amy. "Something Shady at Sunkist?" *Business Week*, May 17, 1993, p. 40.

Burton, Thomas M. "Methods of Marketing Infant Formula Land Abbott in Hot Water." *The Wall Street Journal*, May 25, 1993, pp. 1–A6.

Graham, Ellen. "Sprawling Bureaucracy Eats Up Most Profits of Girl Scout Cookies." *The Wall Street Journal*, May 13, 1993, pp. 1–A9.

Roberts, Johnnie L., and Robichaux, Mark. "Home Shopping Saga: From Dazzle of Success to Glare of Scrutiny." *The Wall Street Journal*, May 14, 1993, pp. 1–A6.

Public Relations and Marketing

Abratt, Russell, and Sacks, Diane. "The Marketing Challenge: Toward Being Profitable and Socially Responsible." *Journal of Business Ethics*, vol. 7 (1988), pp. 497–507.

Barton, Laurence. "Ethics, Profit and Patients: When Pharmaceutical Companies Sponsor Medical Meetings." *The Journal of Hospital Marketing*, vol. 8, no. 1 (1993), pp. 16–22.

Bivins, Thomas H. "Applying Ethical Theory to Public Relations." *Journal of Business Ethics*, no. 6 (1987), pp. 195–200.

Bivins, Thomas H. "Professional Advocacy in Public Relations." *Business and Professional Journal*, vol. 6, no. 1 (Spring 1987), pp. 82–93.

Jurgensen, John H., and Likasweski, James E. "Ethics: Content before Conduct." *Public Relations Journal*, March 1988, pp. 48–49.

Moses, Jonathan M. "BCCI Depositors Say Hill & Knowlton Misled Them and Charge PR Fraud." *The Wall Street Journal*, January 8, 1992, p. B2.

Wright, Donald K. "Examining Ethical and Moral Values of Public Relations People." *Public Relations Review*, vol. 15, no. 2 (Summer 1989), pp. 19–33.

Whistle-Blowing

Driscoll, Lisa. "A Better Way to Handle Whistle Blowers: Let Them Speak." *Business Week*, July 27, 1992, p. 36.

Jensen, J. Vernon. "Ethical Tension Points in Whistle Blowing." *Journal of Business Ethics*, vol. 6 (1987), pp. 321–328.

Kowitt, Arthur J., and Panich, Donna. "Whistle Blower Litigation: A Potential Explosion in the Nuclear Industry." *Public Utilities Fortnightly*, July 5, 1990, pp. 15–16.

Larmer, Robert A. "Whistle Blowing and Employee Loyalty." *Journal of Business Ethics*, vol. 11 (1992), pp. 125–128.

Miceli, Marcia P., Near, Janet P., and Schwenk, Charles R. "Who Blows the Whistle and Why?" *Industrial and Labor Relations Review*, vol. 45, no. 1 (1991), pp. 113–130.

Taylor, Gary. "Blowing Whistles." *The National Law Journal*, September 20, 1993, pp. 1–37.

Name Index

Subject Index